CANADIAN FAMILY LAW

9th Edition

CANADIAN FAMILY LAW

9th Edition

MALCOLM C. KRONBY

WILEY

John Wiley & Sons Canada, Ltd.

Library and Archives Canada Cataloguing in Publication Data

Kronby, Malcolm C., 1934-
    Canadian family law / Malcolm C. Kronby. — 9th ed.

ISBN-13 978-0-470-83849-5
ISBN-10 0-470-83849-3

1. Domestic relations—Canada—Popular works. I. Title.

KE539.2.K76 2006   346.7101'5   C2006-901398-5
KF505.K763 2006

Production Credits:
Cover design: Pat Loi
Interior text design: Tegan Wallace
Printer: Tri-Graphic Printing Limited

John Wiley & Sons Canada, Ltd.
6045 Freemont Blvd.
Mississauga, Ontario
L5R 4J3

Printed in Canada

1 2 3 4 5 TRI 10 09 08 07 06

To M. again and always

CONTENTS

PREFACE

What's a legal separation?

Doesn't the mother always get custody of the children?

Will I lose my property rights (whatever they are) if I break up the marriage?

In my practice, I've been asked these questions and others like them hundreds of times.

Most laypeople who attempt to achieve some understanding of family law are burdened by myth and confused by misconception. They hear third-hand and usually exaggerated stories of the complexity and cost of divorce proceedings. They are intimidated by the prospect of having to appear in court and put off by technical legal language.

That's why this book was written—to explain the rights, obligations, and remedies of family law.

What *is* family law?

It's the entire range of statutes, regulations, and precedents that govern the relations between spouses and among parents and children. This includes (but is not limited to) the body of law on marriage, divorce, annulment, on custody of children, separation, spousal support, child support, and property rights within the family. This vast and complex field of law touches the lives of all of us.

The law relating to formation and solemnization of marriage is contained in provincial statutes, which are roughly the same across the country. The *Divorce Act* is a federal statute, so that there is, thankfully, only one divorce law for the whole of Canada. However, the regulations governing the procedure of getting a divorce properly before the court vary somewhat from province to province.

The law concerning the custody of children is partly contained in provincial statutes and regulations, which are pretty similar from Newfoundland to British Columbia. The *Divorce Act* also has sections dealing with custody of children, but these apply only in connection with divorce proceedings. As we'll see, the *Divorce Act* states that orders for "corollary relief"—the things that may go along with a divorce, such as custody, support payments, and visiting rights—should be nationwide in scope and effect, but there is also a large body of provincial law in these areas that is not linked to divorce. Property rights are under provincial law.

When the *Divorce Act* of 1968 came into force, it created grounds for divorce that had never previously existed in Canada. For practical purposes, prior to June 1968, the only ground for divorce was adultery. If you lived in Quebec or Newfoundland there was no way to get a divorce under provincial procedures; a petition had to be presented to the federal Senate to pass a private Bill dissolving the marriage. These restricted grounds created many cases of hardship. For example, a husband and wife might have been separated for ten years, during which time the husband might be living with another woman by whom he had children, but there couldn't be a divorce unless his estranged wife saw fit to sue him on the grounds of his obvious adultery. Frequently she wouldn't do it, simply out of spite. In other cases, a wife might be the victim of sadistic cruelty, but she couldn't get a divorce unless her husband committed adultery. Even in marriages destroyed by incurable insanity of one of the parties, the other had no hope of divorce in the absence of adultery.

The *Divorce Act* of 1968 created grounds of cruelty and marriage breakdown (meaning, at a minimum, separation for a period not less than three years) along with adultery. Other grounds were established as well, but these rarely arose in actual practice; the grounds of adultery, cruelty, and separation probably covered 99 percent of the cases that came to court.

The current *Divorce Act*, in force as of June 1, 1986, establishes only one ground for divorce: marriage breakdown, which arises as a result of adultery, cruelty, or separation for a period of one year. The procedure has also been considerably simplified. But divorce is still a complex business (which is not to say it should be that way), despite the claims of those who sell do-it-yourself divorce kits or offer so-called divorce-aid services with supposedly guaranteed results.

I've tried to make the information in this book as accurate as my knowledge and the state of the law will permit, but laws change. Statutes are amended, appeal courts overturn long-standing precedents, and, especially, circumstances alter results. Often a fine factual distinction between two cases produces two markedly different judgments. There are, of course, limitations to the scope and content of this book. Some subject areas are not treated at all: paternity suits, child welfare legislation, and family aspects of criminal law are three such areas. Adoption is only touched on.

Not a week goes by without an interesting new decision being reported. That's one reason why family law is so interesting and challenging.

A second reason is the emotional load carried by so many cases. Two businesspeople can sue each other for $1 million, but have lunch together during a break in the trial. On the other hand, a parent fighting for custody of a child may feel (wrongly) that the only way to succeed is to destroy the other parent.

There's a third reason why this field of law is fascinating. Many cases in family law are what I would call "hinge points" in the lives of the parties. The course of a lifetime can be determined by the judgment in a divorce case; it's even more obviously so in a child-custody case.

A word of caution: If you have a family law problem, go to a lawyer. This book is no substitute for the working relationship between lawyer and client, nor can it possibly give you legal advice. In presenting a general survey of family law in Canada, it's quite impossible to deal with every aspect, or to deal with the narrow factual distinctions that may distinguish one judgment from another. At the end of the text you will find Appendix A: "What Your Lawyer Will Probably Want to Know," which is intended to save you and your lawyer time and effort in the first interview.

This book has been written for the most part from the point of view of a lawyer practising in Ontario. The principles in the text derive from cases from all across Canada, but I don't pretend to be intimately familiar with the statutes of each province. Although the broad principles of family law are similar in every province and territory, differences are often hidden in the interstices of statute law in each province.

INTRODUCTION TO THE NINTH EDITION

Since the publication of the eighth edition in 2001, statutory amendments and many court decisions necessitate this extensive revision.

The legal battle over same-sex rights and marriage is finished. The *Child Support Guidelines* have been clarified, and revised support figures will come into force in May 2006. The binding effect of separation agreements and marriage contracts has been the subject of a number of appellate decisions. The difficult question of determining child support in shared custody has been addressed by the Supreme Court of Canada. But the principles for awarding retroactive child support are the subject of an appeal in a group of cases pending in the S.C.C. A decision of the Ontario Court of Appeal in which the S.C.C. refused leave to appeal will leave open and controversial the circumstances in which spousal support can be varied after an agreement or judgment.

The growth and demand for mediation and arbitration (alternate dispute resolution) and possible faith-based arbitrations resulted in the controversial Boyd Report in Ontario. Although many recommendations in the Report were rejected, a Bill has been introduced that, if passed, will change aspects of family arbitration.

In January 2005, the Department of Justice released draft *Spousal Support Advisory Guidelines* (SSAG) intended to bring national consistency to spousal support awards. The SSAG are not law, and never will be; they are advisory only, unlike the *Federal Child Support Guidelines*, which are law. We expect a revised and final version of the SSAG to be issued in late 2006 or early 2007.

All of these (and more) will be discussed in the text.

Some of the material on same-sex rights and obligations and on the same-sex marriage litigation derives from memoranda written by my colleagues Martha A. McCarthy and Joanna Radbord, and is used with their permission and my gratitude. Even if there is now little legal controversy, I think the historical and constitutional context is worth preserving. Following the decision where the Supreme Court of Canada decided that exclusion of same-sex partners from spousal support rights under the *Ontario Family Law Act* is unconstitutional, eight Ontario statutes were amended to reflect and implement the decision, and soon after similar amendments were passed in all other provinces and territories except P.E.I. and Nunavut. This text reflects these changes and those that followed the ratification of same-sex marriage by the Supreme Court of Canada and Parliament. The text has been reorganized to place same-sex issues in the chapters on marriage and spousal support.

There is still no significant body of law on torts (civil wrongs) in connection with family law or domestic disputes. These claims might arise, for example, from spousal abuse or transmission of sexual diseases.

As in previous editions, there are some topics that this book does not cover. Derivative claims for personal injury or death, although included in Part V of the *Family Law Act* (Ontario), are properly left to other texts. Paternity suits are usually resolved by blood testing, now so accurate through DNA matching as to establish virtual certainty. Child welfare proceedings, such as protection and child wardship, are comprehensively treated elsewhere. Adoption is only touched on. Criminal matters are left to specialized texts and annotations to the *Criminal Code*.

And as in previous editions, my greatest problem is deciding what to put in and what to leave out. The book must be as accurate, comprehensive, and lucid as possible, but not overwhelming in bulk and scope. I am responsible for the inclusions and omissions, and for the accuracy of the text.

M.C.K.
January 2006

1

MARRIAGE

A "valid and subsisting marriage" carries with it legal rights and obligations that may not exist between unmarried partners.

A valid and subsisting marriage depends on having the capacity to marry and usually (but not always) observing the formal requirements for solemnization of marriage according to the laws of the province in which the marriage is performed, such as obtaining a licence or publishing banns (the announcement within a church of intention to wed), and going through some form of ceremony with a person licensed to solemnize marriages. Marriage may be solemnized between two persons of the opposite or the same sex.

Age of Consent
You have to be old enough to get married. The laws of each province establish an "age of consent," meaning that persons below this age are supposed to obtain permission to marry from one of their parents. By province, the age of consent is as follows: Nova Scotia and Prince Edward Island, sixteen; Alberta, Manitoba, New Brunswick, Ontario, and Quebec, eighteen; British Columbia, Newfoundland, and Saskatchewan, nineteen.

If nobody has status to give consent, the licence may be issued without it. Nobody under age fourteen has capacity to marry unless it is to prevent illegitimacy of an expected child. Where parental consent is unreasonably or arbitrarily withheld, or if it isn't clear who should be giving consent, an application may be made to a judge for an order dispensing with consent.

Mental Capacity to Marry

You must have the mental capacity to understand the nature of the marriage contract, and the duties and responsibilities that it creates. A person who is demonstrably insane at the time of the solemnization has not formed a valid marriage.

Consent of the Parties

You must truly consent to the marriage as a free agent. This means that there must be no duress or force inducing the marriage, or any misunderstanding as to the effect of the marriage ceremony.

Consanguinity

Your spouse must not be too closely related to you. Each province has established "prohibited degrees of consanguinity"—blood relationships that prevent valid marriage. You already know that brother and sister can't marry, but did you know, for example, that a man can't marry his ex-wife's aunt? Information about the prohibited degrees of consanguinity is available wherever marriage licences are issued.

Prior Marriages

You mustn't still be married to someone else. If you were previously married and your spouse is still alive, that prior marriage must have been effectively dissolved by divorce or annulment before you can marry again.[1]

This is no problem if, say, the prior marriage was solemnized in Saskatchewan, the spouses always lived there together, and later got divorced there. But the situation can become greatly complicated where the prior marriage or marriages were solemnized in one place and dissolved in another. Suppose, for instance, that the woman was first married in California, moved with her husband to New York, got a Mexican divorce, remarried in Florida, and got a second divorce in Massachusetts after several years of separation. Now she wants to marry again in Ontario. Before she can remarry, she'll have to satisfy the authorities that the divorces validly dissolved the prior

---

1. There is another way. If your spouse has disappeared and been absent for at least seven years without any information whatsoever about the spouse in that time, you can apply for a court order permitting remarriage. If the spouse turns up later, your first marriage is still valid and your second marriage is void. However, you haven't committed bigamy. The *Divorce Act* now permits a divorce after one year of separation, so applications merely to allow remarriage are unlikely.

marriages. In order to apply for a marriage licence, the woman in question must obtain an opinion from a lawyer that she's validly divorced, and file an affidavit—a sworn statement—that says, in effect, that she and her proposed new husband accept sole responsibility in the event that she isn't properly divorced. If it's absolutely necessary to clarify the effect of previous divorces, an interested party can apply to court for a declaratory judgment stating that this is so, but that may be an expensive and lengthy process.

Sometimes people can't be bothered to straighten these matters out, so they say nothing about prior marriage when applying for a licence. They run the risk of committing bigamy, which is still subject to criminal prosecution.

Annulment

In Chapter 9 we'll consider the distinction between marriage that is void *ab initio* (from the beginning) because of lack of capacity, and a marriage that is merely voidable. The latter arises most frequently in a situation where the parties had the capacity to marry, but the marriage couldn't be consummated by at least the minimal sexual relationship (penetration of the vagina and emission of semen) that the law requires in order to complete and validate the marriage. Nobody yet knows how this principle would apply to a same-sex marriage.

An Exception to the Rule

At the beginning of this chapter, it was stated that parties usually have to observe the formal requirements of a licence or banns and the prescribed ceremony, but there are exceptions. A valid marriage may exist where the parties had the capacity to marry, neither obtained a licence nor published banns, but went through some form of ceremony followed by cohabitation and particularly by birth of children. In one case, this validated a marriage where the husband specifically and intentionally avoided the formal requirements of solemnization, in the hope that his wife would not gain rights to any of his property.

Rights and Obligations of Marriage

Although a full survey of the legal effects of marriage is beyond the scope of this book, some should be noted.

A valid and subsisting marriage confers the right, and perhaps the duty, to cohabit—to live together in a conjugal relationship—although, as we'll see, this may be ended without misconduct and by agreement.

During cohabitation, the spouses have a mutual obligation of financial support, and an individual obligation of self-support. One aspect of cohabitation is the expectation of a sexual relationship. A persistent and unjustified refusal of sexual relations by one spouse may constitute "cruelty" as a basis for divorce.

In Ontario, the concept of desertion has been made virtually obsolete by the *Family Law Act*. The right or obligation of support is virtually independent of conduct.[2] The only area in which desertion may still be significant is in possession of a home; for instance, if a husband moves out without cause, he may find it difficult to force the wife out of the home.

No proprietary rights are created by marriage, in the sense that no spouse becomes the owner of the other's property in whole or part just because of marriage. Marriage does create a statutory right on breakdown of marriage to share in the value of property acquired during the marriage, and a right of possession (not ownership) of the matrimonial home (see also Chapter 7, "Property Rights"). These rights differ from province to province. In Ontario, they are codified in the *Family Law Act*.

Husbands and wives have rights to share in the estate after the death of the other, whether or not the deceased left a will. Under the *Succession Law Reform Act* and under similar legislation in every province, a spouse and dependent children can apply for a court order awarding them support from an estate even though the will of the deceased cut them out.

Common-Law Marriage

Through a long period of English history, competent individuals could marry without the intervention of any civil or religious authority. If there was at the time a statute governing marriage, this was not the only way a marriage could be formed. Parties could be married at "common law" quite apart from "legal" marriage or compliance with the formal requirements of a marriage statute, such as issuance of a licence and a ceremony of solemnization conducted by some person officially empowered to do so.

To create a common-law marriage, there had to be an agreement between the parties, as in some exchange of promises; legal capacity to make a contract, for example, sufficient age, sound mind, and

---

2. Conduct does not affect the obligation to provide support, but it may (in rare cases) affect the *amount* of support "having regard to a course of conduct that is so unconscionable as to constitute an obvious and gross repudiation of the relationship" as provided in section 33(10) of the *Family Law Act* (Ontario).

free will; cohabitation; consummation by sexual intercourse; and public and continued recognition of the relationship.

After a lengthy controversy, a statute was passed in England in 1753 aimed at the abolition of common-law marriages and secret marriages, and that contained strict requirements for a valid marriage. By 1844, as a result of judicial decisions, it was clear that no valid marriage could be formed at common law in England, and that this was the state of the law at least back to the 1753 statute. The effect of the English statute in Canada is not as clear as it should be after all these years. Probably the statute was not imported into Canada, so that in every province except Quebec it is possible to have a valid marriage in very special circumstances without strict compliance with the provincial marriage statutes. For instance, parties may not absolutely need a marriage licence if they go through a ceremony of some sort with the intent to be validly married and then live together, particularly if there are children of the union. This body of law is extremely technical. Our courts have a long-standing tendency to narrow the possibility of a valid marriage of this sort.

Also, the courts will interpret formal validity of marriage in accordance with the law of the place where the marriage was solemnized. Many places do not have procedures as strict as our provinces, or adverse conditions such as war make these procedures impractical.

So, although it is possible to create a common-law marriage recognized in Canada in the sense that common-law marriage hasn't been specifically abolished, no one who wants the legal state of marriage should fail to comply with all of the statutory rules of the place where the marriage is performed.

We generally use the term "common-law marriage" to describe the voluntary union of a man and a woman in a lasting relationship resembling marriage. The parties may indeed behave as if married, refer to each other as if married, and be recognized or assumed to be married in their community. In fact they are not married, no matter how long they have lived together, no matter how many children they have.

They may have specific rights as conferred by statutes. For instance, they may treat each other as dependants for tax purposes, and take the same deductions as if they were married. They have mutual obligations to their children, with all rights of custody and access, as if married. They receive Child Tax Benefits. They can insure each other's lives and qualify for pension benefits.

In Ontario, they have a mutual support obligation at law because of the *Family Law Act*. This arises because the Act states: "Every spouse has an obligation to provide support for himself or herself and for the other spouse, in accordance with need, to the extent that he or she is capable of doing so," and defines "spouse" to include two persons who have cohabited continuously for a period of not less than three years; or in a relationship of some permanence, if they are the natural or adoptive parents of a child.

Almost exactly the same words are used in the *Ontario Succession Law Reform Act* to permit an unmarried dependent "spouse" to claim against an estate (see Chapter 4).

Some years ago a remarkable case dealt with the effect of an incomplete sex change. The parties, both born female, had in the course of their lives married and had children. After that, they formed a relationship together that endured for twenty years. One of them, taking the male role, had extensive psychotherapy, hormonal injections, a double mastectomy, and a panhysterectomy, but no genital surgery. He (she) had changed the gender designation on his (her) birth certificate. They separated, and the male partner claimed support from the female. The court held that they were not a man and woman who had cohabited, since the sex change was incomplete and reversible if hormone injections were stopped. The mastectomy and hysterectomy were inconclusive, since many women have this surgery without any question of their gender. The result might well have been different if there had been genital surgery, and today each of the "two persons" would have spousal support rights and obligations

Parties who live together as if married have no statutory entitlement to sharing of assets if they separate. This had been the subject of constitutional challenges to several provincial statutes. The problem was resolved nationally when a Nova Scotia case was appealed to the Supreme Court of Canada, which ruled that persons who choose not to be married have elected a different property regime than those who choose to be married.

Parties who live together *may* have property rights against each other based on the same legal principles that govern property rights between any unrelated people. This law is founded on the idea of compensating a person for the contribution he or she makes to the property of another, by imposition of a constructive or implied trust from the recipient in favour of the contributor. The idea is that if the contributor is not compensated, the recipient of the contribution will be "unjustly enriched." This topic is dealt with in Chapter 7, "Property Rights."

In a landmark decision, the Supreme Court of Canada considered the case of a couple who lived together unmarried for about twenty years, during which they worked together to build a successful and prosperous beekeeping business, registered in the name of the man. The Court found that the woman's contribution in equal work and effort gave rise to a constructive trust in her favour for one-half of the property and business assets. Since then there have been many other cases where the Court has awarded a constructive trust, which may be a share of property or a monetary amount. Parties who live together can create their own support obligations and property regime by signing a "cohabitation agreement." *The Family Law Act* (FLA) specifically permits this, in the following words:

> Two persons of the opposite sex or the same sex who are cohabiting or intend to cohabit and who are not married to each other may enter into an agreement in which they agree on their respective rights and obligations during cohabitation, or on ceasing to cohabit or on death, including
> a) ownership in or division of property;
> b) support obligations;
> c) the right to direct the education and moral training of their children, but not the right to custody of or access to their children; and
> d) any other matter in settlement of their affairs.

To be valid, a cohabitation agreement must be in writing, signed by the parties, and witnessed. Under the FLA if the parties to a cohabitation agreement subsequently marry, in the absence of specific words to the contrary, their agreement becomes a marriage contract, as discussed in Chapter 10, "Domestic Contracts."

The Same-Sex Marriage Litigation[3]

Fundamental to the understanding of the litigation is the legal fact that there was no statutory definition of marriage in Canada as between persons of the opposite sex. It was legally taken for granted, or relied on a British decision in the House of Lords, where in connection with the legal effect of a polygamous marriage in Utah, it was stated that

3. See Joanna Radbord's, "Lesbian Love Stories: How We Won Equal Marriage in Canada," (2005) 17 Yale *J.L. & Feminism* 99. Ms. Radbord, along with Martha McCarthy, were the leading co-counsel in the Ontario litigation. Ms. Radbord's article is a rare combination of legal scholarship and autobiography. I have truncated and revised some material about the litigation from that article with her permission.

marriage is the union of one man and one woman. As we will see, the opponents of same-sex or, as its proponents prefer to say, equal marriage, often argue that marriage "just is" between one man and one woman. This is often referred to as "definitional preclusion."

In the spring and summer of 2000, three groups pursued same-sex marriage in Canada. Their cases were *Halpern* in Ontario, *EGALE* in British Columbia, and *Hendricks* in Quebec.

In Toronto the eight applicant couples applied for marriage licences, which were summarily rejected by the City Clerk. In response to a demand for written reasons for the rejection the Clerk forwarded the issue to the City legal department. The legal department said it was unsure whether licences should be granted to the couples. There was no statutory impediment to equal marriage. A Divisional Court decision excluding same-sex couples from marriage, *Layland v. Ontario*, predated *M. v. H.*, the Supreme Court precedent that strongly suggested that same-sex couples were entitled to equal relationship recognition. The Province had issued a directive not to issue licences. The Clerk decided to seek directions from the Court whether the City should issue licences. The applicants filed for directions on the same day as the City did.

The Court ruled that the applicants would have carriage of the case. The British Columbia and Quebec equal marriage cases started shortly after that.

In all three provinces, the applicant couples faced formidable opposition from the federal government. The government was joined by two intervener coalitions opposing equal marriage, The Interfaith Coalition on Marriage and the Family and The Association for Marriage and the Family. The federal government and these interveners made similar arguments. They alleged there was no discrimination in excluding same-sex couples from marriage—marriage just is the union of one man and one woman. A philosopher of language deposed that the marriage of a same-sex couple was an oxymoron. In the same way as applying the descriptor "women" does not discriminate against men, limiting the application of the word "marriage" to the unions of men and women did not discriminate against same-sex couples.

The government also argued that there was no substantive inequality. There was no offence to dignity. Same-sex couples had access to all the same rights and obligations as married couples, at least at a federal level. The provinces could cure any remaining differences in treatment. All that same-sex couples lacked was identical nomenclature. A formal difference in language, without more, did not create discrimination in a substantive sense. The federal government also proposed that each province ought to introduce registered domestic partnerships, while the federal government would preserve marriage for heterosexuals only. The applicants argued that the discriminatory impact of exclusion from marriage was clearly revealed "in the context of the place of the group in the entire social, political and legal fabric of our society." In this context, the exclusion of same-sex couples from the institution of marriage was a denial of equal membership and full participation in Canadian society. It attacked self-respect, self-worth, psychological integrity, and empowerment. It denied substantive equality.

All of the applicant couples emphasized that the denial of the freedom to marry stigmatized gay and lesbian relationships. It promoted a culture of intolerance. Marriage is "the institution that accords to a union the profound social stamp of approval and acceptance of the relationship as being of the highest value." They argued that only full and equal inclusion in marriage would promote substantive equality; that if they won equivalent rights and obligations, but were denied the status of marriage itself, the case would be lost.

The Courts' Decisions

With litigants seeking equal marriage in three provinces, the British Columbia decision, *EGALE*, was released first. Justice Pitfield held that there was an invisible yet constitutionally entrenched meaning to marriage, so that recognizing the marriages of same-sex couples would require a constitutional amendment. Constitutional scholars immediately rejected his reasoning.

The Ontario and Quebec decisions followed shortly after. The three-judge panel in Ontario found that the common-law definition of marriage discriminated in a manner that could not be justified in a free and democratic society. The Quebec Court declared that the opposite-sex requirement for marriage in its *Civil Code* was invalid. The Ontario Divisional Court was divided on the appropriate remedy, but a majority of that Court and Justice Lemelin in Quebec suspended their declarations for two years to give the government time to pass appropriate legislation.

On May 1, 2003, the British Columbia Court of Appeal rejected the frozen rights argument adopted by Justice Pitfield. The B.C. Court of Appeal held that the common-law definition of marriage discriminated on the basis of sexual orientation and the rights violation could not be justified. The Court adopted the same remedy as the Ontario and Quebec lower courts, reformulating the common-law rule and suspending the remedy for two years.

One month later, and less than two months after argument, the Ontario Court of Appeal upheld the Divisional Court decision in *Halpern*, and held that the common-law definition of marriage was unconstitutional. The Court also allowed the applicants' cross-appeal and gave its judgment immediate effect. Marriage, as of June 10, 2003, was now "the voluntary union for life of two persons to the exclusion of all others." The City Clerk was ordered to commence issuing licences immediately.

A week later, the Prime Minister announced there would be no appeal to the Supreme Court of Canada. He and the Minister of Justice noted that marriage is a fundamental right and that discrimination is intolerable under the *Charter*. The government said it would introduce legislation to make equal marriage available across the country.

The B.C. and Quebec Courts of Appeal came to the same conclusion. Same-sex couples across the country continued to litigate for the freedom to marry and won province by province, first in the Yukon, and then without opposition by the federal Attorney General in Saskatchewan, Nova Scotia, Manitoba, and Newfoundland.

No Ontario statutes were changed to recognize equal marriage for same-sex couples until March 9, 2005, when Bill 171, an act to amend various statutes in respect of spousal relationships, received Royal Assent. This omnibus legislation amended all Ontario legislation so that all married couples are treated the same, regardless of sexual orientation. At the same time, as part of this legislation the government eliminated all "same-sex partner" language from the statute books. Now, same-sex couples are spouses in exactly the same way as heterosexual couples.

Same-sex divorce is now available (see Chapter 8).

The Federal Government Reference

After announcing its intention not to appeal, the federal government asked the Supreme Court of Canada to hear a Reference on its proposed equal marriage legislation.

The Reference initially posed three questions with respect to the government's draft equal marriage legislation:

1. Whether the proposed legislation was within the exclusive legislative authority of the Parliament of Canada?
2. Whether extension of the capacity to marry to persons of the same sex was consistent with the *Canadian Charter of Rights and Freedoms*?
3. Whether freedom of religion under the *Charter* protected religious officials from being compelled to perform a marriage between two persons of the same sex that is contrary to their religious beliefs?

After Paul Martin replaced Jean Chrétien as Prime Minister and shortly before he called an election, a new question was added:

4. Whether the opposite-sex requirement for marriage for civil purposes was consistent with the *Charter*?

Some observers construed the addition of the fourth question as an attempt to re-litigate *Halpern*. The Court of Appeal had ruled on the unconstitutionality of exclusion of lesbians and gays from marriage, the appeal period had expired, and the government had publicly affirmed the correctness of the decision. The government was a party to the ruling that finally determined that issue. It should be bound.

A Supreme Court bench ordinarily interested in strictly limiting interveners granted leave to twenty-eight interest groups, more than in any case ever before the Court. The Court heard from civil liberties associations, a group of seven people interested in civil unions, human rights commissions, faith groups supporting and opposed to equal marriage, gay and lesbian equality rights groups, and the Canadian Bar Association. Even one Martin Dion, a resident of Quebec and heterosexual married father, was granted leave to intervene. He argued that marriage for same-sex couples demeaned his marriage and submitted that all marriages of same-sex couples that have occurred in Canada should be declared illegal.

On December 9, 2004, the Supreme Court of Canada issued its advisory opinion in *Reference re Same-Sex Marriage*. The Court affirmed that marriage for same-sex couples flows from the equality guarantee of the *Charter*. The Court ruled that the meaning of marriage is not a frozen concept limited to heterosexual unions, but has evolved to include the marriages of same-sex couples.

The Court answered that the power to define marriage to include same-sex couples is exclusively within federal jurisdiction, that equal marriage for same-sex couples is not contrary to the *Charter*, and that religious officials cannot be compelled to perform marriages for same-sex couples contrary to their religious beliefs. The Court refused to answer the fourth question, whether the old common-law definition of marriage was constitutional, on the basis that the federal government had promised to introduce equal marriage legislation regardless of the Court's answer and because the couples who had already married had vested interests that ought not be brought into question.

The Court confirmed that any alternative forms of partnership recognition such as civil unions were different from equal marriage and outside of federal jurisdiction. It also made it clear that no province has the power to legislate to deny same-sex couples the freedom to marry, even through the use of the override clause of the *Charter*. The Reference opinion gave the federal government the green light to proceed with its equal marriage legislation.

The federal *Civil Marriage Act* is now in force. The legislation states:

1. This Act may be cited as the *Civil Marriage Act*.
2. Marriage, for civil purposes, is the lawful union of two persons to the exclusion of all others.
3. It is recognized that officials of religious groups are free to refuse to perform marriages that are not in accordance with their religious beliefs.
4. For greater certainty, a marriage is not void or voidable by reason only that the parties are of the same sex.

The *Civil Marriage Act* includes a number of consequential amendments to seventy statutes. Among other things it amends the definition of "spouse" under the *Divorce Act* to read, "[E]ither of two persons who are married to each other" may apply for divorce. The *Marriage (Prohibited Degrees) Act* now provides that "no person shall marry another person if they are related lineally, or as brother or sister or half-brother or half-sister, including by adoption." In the *Income Tax Act*, the concept of natural or adoptive parent is replaced by the phrase "legal parent."

Same-sex marriage is now available in every province and territory of Canada. Outside of Canada, same-sex marriage is accepted and recognized in very few jurisdictions. This leaves same-sex married partners with a legal quandary. If they are ordinarily resident in, say, Colorado, and come to Alberta to get married, they are validly married under the laws of Canada, but when they return they are not validly married under the laws of their home state.

2

THE LEGAL REMEDIES

A range of alternative or cumulative remedies is available in matrimonial disputes. Roughly in order of severity or finality, they are:

(a) A separation agreement, which is a voluntary contract between the parties. It is a private matter, not needing court sanction or approval. A marriage contract, entered into before or during marriage, may also contain terms effective on the separation of the spouses.

(b) An application by either spouse for support in a "family court." This includes applications to a court set up under provincial law, not in connection with divorce proceedings. The actual name of the court varies from province to province, as do the rights of the parties. Typically, the court has power to make orders for custody, access, and support. In Ontario, the Ontario Court of Justice has these powers under the *Family Law Act*, referred to below.

(c) An application by either parent (or sometimes by another "interested party," perhaps a grandparent or uncle) for custody of children, with or without child support, and subject to awarding or refusing visiting rights (access) to the other parent. The court always has the power to look at arrangements for the children, even if there is a separation agreement or a previous court order. In that sense, a custody order is never final but is always open to review because the court never loses its power to make an order in the best interests of a child. An application for custody can be made independently of any other legal remedy or can be combined with a claim for divorce or support. Usually, the location of the habitual residence of the child determines which court has exclusive jurisdiction to deal with custody, but an exception may be made in favour of another court when, in extreme circumstances, the court must act to protect the child.

(d) An application for spousal support, with or without a claim for custody and child support. In Ontario, all jurisdiction to award support not linked to a divorce application for either husband or wife is governed by the *Family Law Act*, in force as of March 1, 1986. The right to support is independent of conduct, and is determined principally by the need of the applicant, the applicant's ability to provide self-support, and the respondent's capacity to pay, although there are many other factors that the court can consider in accordance with section 33(9) of the *Family Law Act*. There are roughly similar support provisions in statutes of every province.

The Superior Court of Justice, the Unified Family Court, and the Ontario Court of Justice all have power to award support and custody under the *Family Law Act* and the *Children's Law Reform Act*. The significant difference in jurisdiction is between the Ontario Court and the others. While all these courts have a broad power to make orders for periodic payments or lump sums of support or combinations of these, the Ontario Court has no jurisdiction over divorce or property matters.

(e) A claim in respect of "property rights," for example, to equalize the net worth accumulated during the marriage, force the sale of a home, divide its contents, or recover property in the hands of the other spouse. This is provincial rather than federal law. In Ontario, it is all under the *Family Law Act*, and is covered in Chapter 7. The jurisdiction to deal with matrimonial property is in the Superior Court of Justice or the Unified Family Court, and not in the Ontario Court. There are some such property statutes in every province of Canada. It is beyond the scope of this book to analyze and comment fully on the similarities and differences, but the wording of each individual provincial statute may create significant differences in the rights and obligations of the parties.

A claim for property rights can be made in several forms, either independently or combined with a claim for support, custody, or divorce.

(f) An application for divorce, with or without claims for support, custody, and property rights or, more rarely, a claim for annulment of marriage, which might also include claims for custody, support, and property rights. The law of divorce is under the federal *Divorce Act*. Jurisdiction under that Act is given exclusively to the superior court of each province; in Ontario it's the Superior Court of Justice or the Unified Family Court.

A separation agreement may settle between the parties any of the above matters that otherwise would be dealt with in the courts, except for divorce or annulment, which can be granted only by a court. You can't get a divorce or annulment by agreement or consent; there must be some kind of court process, which in undefended divorces usually does not require a hearing or trial. A valid, subsisting separation agreement is conclusive as to property rights between the parties, but is not strictly binding in matters of support, custody, and access.

You don't need a separation agreement in order to proceed with an application for divorce, but in most cases the existence of an agreement will greatly simplify divorce proceedings because the only remaining issue will be dissolution of the marriage, and people rarely argue about that.

In Ontario since 1978, and, I believe, now in every province of Canada, there is no longer any right to claim damages for seduction or breach of promise to marry. An offended husband can no longer sue for damages for "criminal conversation," which was neither criminal nor conversation, but was a claim for money damages against another man arising from adulterous intercourse with one's wife. It required a jury trial, and usually the wife would willingly testify on behalf of her paramour.

3

SEPARATION

Separation Agreements

Many people first approach a lawyer because they want a "legal separation."

What they usually mean is a separation agreement. This is a voluntary written contract between husband and wife, much like any other contract in law, in which they agree to live apart and on other matters referred to below. Nobody can be forced to sign a separation agreement or have one imposed on him or her by a court or any other authority.

The amount that should be paid under an agreement must necessarily be determined by negotiation, but in considering the amount and advising the client, a lawyer will be thinking what a court might award in the circumstances of the case. What you pay must somehow be related to what you might be ordered to pay. For this reason, and to avoid repetition, this difficult question has been included in Chapter 4, "Spousal Support"; Chapter 6, "Child Support"; and Chapter 7, "Property Rights."

In Ontario until 1978, spouses could not validly enter into an agreement in contemplation of future separation. Such an agreement was considered to be destructive of family relationships, and was void as against public policy. It was possible to enter into a prenuptial agreement, but this had to be very carefully worded as a property settlement in contemplation of marriage, not separation.

The *Family Law Act* permits three classes of "domestic contract" available to two persons of the same or opposite sex,[1] and similarly in all provinces.

(a) a "marriage contract," entered into in anticipation of marriage or during marriage, in which two persons agree on their respective rights and obligations under the marriage or upon separation, divorce, annulment, or death, dealing with ownership in or division of property, support obligations, the right to direct the education and moral training of children (but not custody), and any other subject matter. A marriage contract cannot validly limit the rights of a spouse to possession of a matrimonial home.

(b) a "cohabitation agreement," entered into between two persons who are living together or intend to live together but who are not married, covering exactly the same subject matter as a marriage contract. If they subsequently marry, the document automatically becomes a marriage contract unless they specifically agree otherwise.

(c) a "separation agreement," entered into between two persons who have cohabited, married or unmarried, and who are now living separate and apart, covering all of the subject matter of a marriage contract, plus custody of and access to children.

A domestic contract must be in writing, signed by the parties, and their signatures must be witnessed. The court has the power to disregard terms of a domestic contract dealing with children where the court is of the opinion that to do so would be in the best interests of the children. Chastity clauses in separation agreements or in marriage contracts to take effect on separation are invalid.

Notwithstanding a domestic contract, the court can make any appropriate support order under the *Family Law Act* where a provision in the contract for waiver of support is unconscionable, or the spouse is receiving welfare payments, or there has been default in payment of support under the terms of the contract itself. But properly drafted release clauses in a separation agreement are conclusive as to property rights under the *Family Law Act*.

A separation agreement (or any domestic contract) may be set aside or repudiated, like any other contract, if it was procured by

---

1. The *Ontario Family Statue Amendment Act, 2005*, will add family arbitration agreements as another class of domestic contract (see Chapter 12, "Alternate Dispute Resolution").

fraud, duress, misrepresentation, or coercion, and under the *Family Law Act* (a) if a party failed to disclose to the other significant assets or significant debts or other liabilities existing when the domestic contract was made; or (b) if a party did not understand the nature of consequences of the domestic contract.

There is no presumption of any of these just because the parties are married. On the other hand, it has been frequently stated that in negotiations toward a separation agreement, the parties must act in utmost good faith, meaning that they have an obligation to make total financial disclosure. This may extend to making detailed financial disclosure even where it is neither requested nor needed by the other party.

Sometimes one party to a separation agreement will try to invalidate it on the basis of fundamental unfairness (unconscionability). In a 1992 Ontario case, the trial judge set aside a separation agreement because of the unequal bargaining position of the spouses and the unconscionable result of the agreement, even though the wife had independent legal advice, was reasonably aware of her true entitlement, and entered into the contract entirely on her own volition. When the case came to the Court of Appeal in 1994, the trial judge was reversed, and the wife was held to the bargain she had made. The Court said that the validity of the agreement should depend on two general principles:

(a) It is desirable that parties settle their own affairs. Parties will enter into settlement agreements only if they expect the terms to be upheld. Therefore, as a general rule, courts should uphold agreements reached between the parties.

(b) The proper test of unconscionability, as set out in an earlier decision, is the equitable rule that if [a party] is in a situation in which he is not a free agent and is not able to protect himself, a Court ... will protect him, not against his own folly or carelessness, but against his being taken advantage of by those in a position to do so.... If the bargain is fair, the fact that the parties were not equally vigilant of their interest is immaterial. Likewise, if one was not preyed upon by the other, an improvident or even grossly inadequate consideration is no ground upon which to set aside a contract freely entered into. It is the combination of inequality and improvidence which alone may evoke this jurisdiction. Then the onus is placed upon the party seeking to uphold the contract to show that his conduct throughout was scrupulously considerate of the others interests.

But please note the very different approach taken by the courts in considering variation of spousal support under the *Divorce Act*. This very important topic is discussed in the Chapter 4 section "Spousal Support and Variation under the *Divorce Act*."

In Ontario, there is no requirement of independent legal advice in connection with a separation agreement, but that requirement exists in Alberta. This is just another example of statutory differences from province to province. Whether required or not, independent legal advice is strongly indicated, since it effectively prevents either party from later claiming that he or she didn't really understand the agreement. Sometimes a party simply refuses to get independent legal advice, and if this occurs, he or she should expect to be asked to sign a specific acknowledgment to that effect.

Many judgments establish that what a separation agreement says about support cannot bind the divorce court. The court may make any appropriate order in a divorce decree or on an application to vary a support provision under the *Divorce Act*; however, separation agreements are not lightly disregarded. This principle has extended to situations where the judge felt that she would have ordered somewhat more for the support of the wife than the separation agreement provided, but thought she should prefer to follow the contract that the parties had worked out for themselves. This is as it should be because our courts always tell litigants that they should settle their own disputes if possible, rather than leave the result to be imposed on them by a judge. Also, there may be all kinds of consideration for a separation agreement that are not apparent on the surface. A simple clause might cover the release of a valuable claim to share in property. Ownership of a house or other property may have been transferred as part of the agreement. A well-meaning attempt to change the terms of a separation agreement might be like trying to unscramble an omelette. However, rulings from the Supreme Court of Canada say that on an application for support or variation of a support order under the *Divorce Act*, the weight to be given to a separation agreement will depend on the extent to which it carries out the provisions of sections 15 and 17 of the Act (see Chapter 4).

In a British Columbia case, the wife was applying for divorce and claimed support greater than provided in a separation agreement. The court decided that in all the circumstances she was entitled to somewhat less than the agreement called for. At that point the wife tried to withdraw her claim, preferring to rely on the separation agreement, but the court held that once she had invoked the jurisdiction of the divorce court she was bound by its award, and could no longer go back to the terms of the separation agreement. The first matter to be covered in a separation agreement is the covenant of the parties to live apart from each other. This can be expressed at greater or lesser length, but essentially it will say that the spouses intend to live apart and be free from each other's control and authority as if they were unmarried, and that neither will molest or harass the other, for example, by seeking unilaterally to restore the married relationship.

The *Family Law Act* (Ontario) empowers the court to make an order restraining the spouse of the applicant from molesting, annoying, or harassing the applicant or children in the lawful custody of the applicant, and for exclusive possession of a matrimonial home and its contents.

Financial Provisions

Usually a separation agreement will contain financial provisions, perhaps a covenant by the husband to pay support for the wife and children, or it may contain a release of any claim for such payments. Payments may run for a fixed term of years, or may be expressed to continue while both parties are alive and so long as the wife does not remarry. It used to be the style to include a clause that the wife would be entitled to payments only while she remained chaste, but would lose her right to payments if she had a sexual relationship with another man. Chastity clauses are no longer valid. If a husband who enters into a separation agreement really wants to limit his financial obligations, he should encourage his wife toward remarriage.

Now separation agreements more often obligate the husband to pay support for the wife as long as she is not remarried or living with another man in a husband-and-wife type of relationship.

Some interesting cases have arisen involving separation agreements that, perhaps defectively, lacked any limiting clause. In one, the wife was living in what judges used to call "open adultery" and the husband applied to be relieved of his obligations to pay her under the separation agreement. The effect of the judgment was that he had made a deal and it was his own fault if he failed adequately to protect himself, so the payments continued. The effect of remarriage in these circumstances has led to different results in different cases. In some, it has been held that a woman should not be supported by two men, and the ex-husband was excused from support on public policy grounds. In other cases, the ex-husband has been held to the strict terms of the agreement, especially where the wife has remarried a man far less able to support her.

Support and Custody of Children

Support for children is usually fixed until the children reach an agreed age. Often this age is eighteen, with a provision that the children are entitled to support after age eighteen and until age twenty-one or possibly longer as long as the children are ordinarily living at home and attending school and have not themselves married. The *Child Support Guidelines* are very often followed in an agreement, and if they are not, it is prudent to say why the parties chose terms of child support that are at variance with the Guidelines (see Chapter 6).

Custody of the children can be either to one parent or jointly to both. The latter arrangement is strongly indicated when the children are in their early teens or older, and both parents are involved and concerned with supervision and guidance. Sometimes a separation agreement won't refer to custody at all, but will set out a "parenting plan."

Older children usually make their own decisions. They just aren't going to be controlled by the agreement of their parents that one or the other has custody. Also, as children grow up, there's a better chance that the relationship between parent and child can survive the separation. If the parents split when the child is, say, three years old and the parent with custody remarries, often the new spouse will completely replace the natural parent. But if the child is older, the step-parent may never become a full substitute. And if the children are old enough to truly understand what's happening, they may be extremely upset that one parent has, so to speak, given them up. An agreement for joint custody would be indicated in such a situation.

Access

Visiting rights can be undefined, often called "reasonable access," or defined, so that the parent who doesn't have custody is entitled to visit and have the children with him or her at specifically agreed-upon periods. Reasonable access often works well, but it depends on reasonable people. Where the parents are hostile to each other, access had better be defined. An agreement for reasonable access can contain a clause to permit either parent to invoke mediation or apply to court for a definition of access in the event of trouble. But the court probably has power to make an access order on whatever terms may be appropriate, even if the agreement omits this provision.

Alternatively, the agreement may contain terms that access be reasonable, but not less than some specific visiting rights, effectively combining the two forms of access.

Other Possible Provisions

The separation agreement may contain clauses covering division of property, possession of a home and contents, payment of debts, responsibility for carrying insurance, release of any interest in each other's estate, and anything else that the situation may require. A great advantage of a separation agreement is to make a creative and mutually advantageous, perhaps tax-driven, deal that a court, simply following the statutes, will not do for the parties.

If you need a separation agreement, don't try to do it yourself, even if you and your spouse agree (or think you agree) on all the terms. You may have to live with your agreement for many years. Only a skilled lawyer has the competence to handle this job, if only by pointing out possible rights and obligations that the parties may have overlooked.

Alteration of the Terms

Can the terms of a separation agreement be altered afterwards? The answer, like so many answers to legal problems, is that it depends.

Quite apart from the power of a court to modify or disregard a separation agreement in appropriate circumstances, as noted above, the answer is yes, if the agreement contains clauses that permit variation, as many do. Variation provisions may require the husband to pay an additional percentage of his income if it rises above an agreed level, and may allow him to reduce payments if it falls below that level. Fluctuation of payments, up or down, may be tied to the official cost-of-living index. The agreement may contain broad and general variation provisions, recognizing the potential need to make other arrangements for the benefit of the parties and their children as circumstances change. A modern tendency is to include a clause stating that in the event of a material change, either party has the right to apply to the other to renegotiate; if the parties can't agree on a variation, then either has the right to submit the problem to a mediator or arbitrator or to a judge, who will hear the submissions of the parties and make a decision.

Yes, a separation agreement may be altered also if a court needs to make an order contrary to the terms of the agreement for the benefit of the children. The parties can agree on custody, access, and maintenance, but no court is bound by this if, on hearing evidence, the judge concludes that the welfare of the children demands some other arrangement.

Also, under the provisions of the *Family Law Act* (Ontario), on the application of the dependent party, the Ontario Court has the power to impose cost-of-living indexing on support payments in a separation agreement.

The provisions of a valid separation agreement for sharing of property are conclusive.

Why Is a Separation Agreement a Good Idea?

There seems to be a common misconception that husband and wife must have a separation agreement before they can embark on a divorce. Even so, it's a good idea to work out a separation agreement if divorce is contemplated. Parties who have an agreement usually have nothing left to fight about when the divorce application is launched, so that the divorce can proceed as an undefended case. The clauses of the separation agreement that deal with corollary relief can be incorporated right into the divorce judgment or, if the parties choose, those terms can be omitted from the divorce judgment and the parties will simply rely on their contract. It's quicker and far less expensive to settle corollary relief by negotiation and a resulting separation agreement than it is to fight it out in court. And it's very important to note that a separation agreement can cover areas beyond the jurisdiction of a court that grants support or corollary relief, areas such as insurance, providing a car, club memberships, use of charge accounts, and anything else that the needs and imaginations of the parties may suggest.

Duration of the Terms

The terms of a separation agreement generally are expressed to continue after the parties are divorced, so that the divorce as such will not end, say, the husband's obligation to pay support, provide life insurance, etc. Also, if the corollary relief provisions of the agreement are included in the divorce decree—that is, support, custody, and access—the other terms are severable and survive in full force.

Even if it doesn't say so specifically, a separation agreement ends in all its terms if the parties effect a genuine reconciliation. If they break up after that, the agreement is not revived. They must go back to square one and start again. So as to avoid any wrangling over the genuineness of a reconciliation, many separation agreements provide that if the parties at any time resume cohabitation for a given period, for example, more than ninety days, the agreement will be void.

If the husband wants out, especially where there's another woman waiting for him, the best separation agreement is likely to be the quickest one. A husband who feels guilty about leaving his family often wants to ease his conscience by paying the maximum support and agreeing to all sorts of fringe benefits. Wait a few weeks and he'll realize that he loathes his wife and can do without his children. Guilt turns to relief, and he's tougher about money.

4

SPOUSAL SUPPORT

This chapter is a survey of the rights and obligations of spousal support. Child support is very different in principle, and is treated in Chapter 6.

First we will put spousal support in historical context by reviewing the old common-law rights of alimony, replaced in each province by a statutory code. Next we'll deal with spousal support under provincial statutes. Then we'll review spousal support under the federal *Divorce Act*. We'll also look at variation of spousal support where there is a previous order or dismissal of a claim for support, or an existing agreement between the parties under both provincial statutes and the *Divorce Act*; there are differences.

The reader is again warned that these rights and obligations vary from province to province, although the underlying principles are similar across the country. If you are concerned about financial support, by all means consult a lawyer or an intake worker at a family court. If legal fees are a problem, don't hesitate to take advantage of whatever legal-aid assistance is available in your province, and don't assume that you can't get legal aid if you have some income and assets. Legal Aid may still help you, although this assistance may be conditional on your making some contribution.

Alimony

Alimony was the allowance awarded by a court to a wife for her own support, payable by the husband. The power to award alimony stemmed from common law, deriving in turn from ecclesiastical law of England prior to 1857 when the church still had jurisdiction over marital disputes.

The award of alimony was limited to cases where it was proved that (1) the parties were living separate and apart; and (2) that the husband had been guilty of adultery, cruelty, or desertion. If there was a separation agreement, a wife could sue for alimony only if the husband was in breach of its terms. In Canada, only a wife could sue for alimony, but curiously enough, if a husband had been awarded alimony under the special laws of some other country, he was entitled to enforce his judgment in Canada.

In order to be entitled to alimony, an absolute requirement was a valid and subsisting marriage. Sometimes a claim for alimony could be defended where the marriage appeared on the surface to be valid, but where an annulment was available. Some years ago I was consulted by a man whose wife had just served him with a claim for alimony. There was no question about the validity of the marriage in the sense that the parties both had the capacity to marry and had gone through a proper form of solemnization, nor was there any question that the husband had deserted his wife—he had simply walked out on her, making no financial provisions for her at all. But in the course of our first interview, in groping for some explanation, the husband in great embarrassment told me that although he and his wife had lived together for nearly five years, their marriage had never been consummated. Apparently she had an aversion or repugnance to sex that she simply could not overcome. The lawsuit was quickly withdrawn when the wife's lawyer heard about this—his client hadn't bothered to tell him. Later, the husband obtained an annulment.

Alimony was awarded on the basis of financial need. This meant that if the wife had assets and income sufficient to maintain herself, the court would either refuse to award alimony or might make a nominal award, regardless of the husband's conduct, assets, or income.

Alimony actions were fraught with technical traps and difficulties. For many years, it was believed that a demand for "restitution of conjugal rights," meaning, roughly, a reconciliation, was necessary before the wife could be awarded alimony. Supposedly the wife had to make this demand in writing, and, of course, sincerely and in good faith, and to keep the offer open. There were exceptions to this rule and exceptions to the exceptions.

The wife also had to prove the husband's adultery, cruelty, or desertion. Proof of adultery followed the same principles as in divorce proceedings. Cruelty had to be proved to a higher standard than for a divorce. The wife had to prove that the husband subjected her to treatment likely to produce, or that did produce, physical illness or mental distress of such a nature calculated to affect permanently her bodily health or endanger her reason, and that there was a reasonable expectation that such treatment would continue. This derived from an 1897 decision that set the standard followed until 1978. Cruelty in one marriage might have been unobjectionable in another, and the line of demarcation was blurred. Of course, there were obvious cases of physical cruelty, but many situations presented subtle and difficult problems. In some cases, one isolated act of cruelty was held to be an insufficient ground, where the parties continued to live together for a time afterward. No doubt an isolated act of, say, stabbing would not be so lightly regarded.

Mental cruelty was often very difficult to prove sufficiently to satisfy the 1897 rule. Certainly if the husband's conduct had caused the wife to have a nervous breakdown or become a patient in a mental hospital, the lawyer's job was made easier, so to speak; in such a case there likely was available psychiatric evidence. But mental cruelty might have existed where the wife felt degraded or tyrannized and had to get out. She would need a sympathetic psychiatrist to testify that the husband's conduct was actionable mental cruelty, and not every judge would have agreed.

Desertion existed in law when the husband was living separate and apart from the wife, without sufficient cause, and at least theoretically, when she had a genuine desire for reconciliation. "Sufficient cause" for the husband to leave included the wife's adultery, cruelty, or desertion of him. Forgiveness of the husband's misconduct by the wife, called "condonation" (meaning resumption of the marriage relationship with knowledge of his misconduct), was a complete defence to an action of alimony. So was the existence of a separation agreement.

A wife's desertion of a husband might occur, in an obvious case, where she just walked out for no good reason known to law, or for reasons not arising from his misconduct. In more subtle cases (constructive desertion), desertion was said to have occurred where the wife persistently refused sexual relations or otherwise failed to carry out her "domestic duties." As in cases of cruelty, the facts of each alleged desertion were critical to a correct assessment of liability and responsibility. The wife might have committed adultery, but justified it as a result of the husband's misconduct—her defence to his defence. An alimony judgment was always subject to a chastity clause, the very same medieval survival that we discussed in connection with separation agreements. Otherwise, the judgment ordinarily ran during the joint lives of the parties, or until further order of the court. The judgment could be altered on the application of either party, who was expected to show a material change in circumstances, the exact nature of which, like so many problems in family law, depended on the facts of the individual case.

In Ontario, the right of a married woman to claim alimony was abolished in 1978 by the predecessor of the *Family Law Act*, 1986, in favour of gender-neutral support entitlement that is independent of conduct. A judgment for alimony granted under the pre-1978 law is effective, and treated as if it were a support order made under the *Family Law Act*.

Spousal Support and Variation under Provincial Statutes

The *Divorce Act* is a federal statute that provides for spousal support and child support linked to divorce. In every province and territory there is as well a provincial or territorial statute that provides for spousal support and child support not linked to divorce.

This section deals with the rights and obligations of spousal support (which completely replace the former rights of alimony), using as an example the *Ontario Family Law Act* (FLA) in force as of March 1, 1986. Under the FLA these rights and obligations apply in same-sex and opposite-sex relationships equally, and similarly across Canada except in P.E.I. and Nunavut. In the latter province and territory the support statutes have not yet been amended to include same-sex couples.

For the purpose of support applications, the definition of a "spouse" includes either of two persons who

(a) are married to each other; or
(b) have entered into a marriage that is voidable or void, in good faith on the part of the person asserting a right under the FLA (for further discussion of this, please see Chapter 9, "Annulment").

For purposes of support obligations (but not property rights), the definition of "spouse" also includes either of two persons not married to each other who have cohabited

(a) continuously for a period of not less than three years; or
(b) in a relationship of some permanence, if they are the natural or adoptive parents of a child.

"Cohabit" means to live together in a conjugal relationship, whether within or outside marriage.

"Child" means a person under the age of eighteen, and includes, in the words of the statute, "a person whom a parent has demonstrated a settled intention to treat as a child of his or her family, except under an arrangement where the child is placed for financial consideration in a foster home by a person having lawful custody." And "parent" is defined to conform to this.

Note particularly the limitation periods established by the FLA:

1. No action or application for an order for the support of a spouse shall be brought under this part after two years from the day the spouses separate.

2. If the spouses provided for support on separation in a domestic contract, subsection (1) does not apply and no application for an order for the support of a spouse shall be brought after default under the contract has subsisted for two years.

The FLA is expressed to be retroactive in the sense that it applies to any marriage, whenever solemnized, and even if the parties separated before the FLA came into force. The retroactivity of the FLA means that these periods became operative as of March 1, 1986. There is no such limitation period on claims for support as "corollary relief" under the *Divorce Act*.

These limitations may be flexible, since the FLA provides that

The court may, on motion, extend a time prescribed by this Act if it is satisfied that
a) there are prima facie grounds for relief;
b) relief is unavailable because of delay that has been incurred in good faith; and
c) no person will suffer substantial prejudice by reason of the delay.

Pursuant to the FLA, every spouse has an obligation to provide support for himself or herself and for the other spouse, in accordance with need, to the extent that he or she is capable of doing so. Note the wording here; the primary obligation of support rests on oneself. As well, every parent has an obligation to provide support, in accordance with need, for his or her unmarried child who is a minor or is enrolled in a full-time program of education, to the extent that the parent is capable of doing so. This potentially extends the obligation of support for a child well beyond age eighteen, but it is not clear where it stops. The FLA says nothing about continuing obligations for a disabled child over eighteen years of age. It does, however, state that the obligation of child support does not extend to a child who is sixteen years of age or older and has withdrawn from parental control. Under section 32 of the FLA there is also an obligation for a child who is not a minor to provide support, in accordance with need, for his or her parent who has cared for or provided support for the child to the extent that the child is capable of doing so.

The power to order support under the FLA is concurrent in the Superior Court, the Unified Family Court, and the Ontario Court, regardless of the amount claimed. Depending on the nature of the case, the claim for support may be asserted together with or independently of claims for custody, equalization of property, and divorce in the higher courts, but the Ontario Court has no jurisdiction in divorce or equalization of property. In the context of divorce proceedings, support is usually claimed as "corollary relief" to dissolution of the marriage. The court may order a person to provide support for his or her dependants and determine the amount of support. A dependant is defined as a person to whom another has an obligation of support.

An application for support may be made by the dependant or the dependant's parent, or by the Ministry of Community and Social Services or a municipal corporation if the dependant is receiving or has applied for welfare assistance. The purpose of bringing agencies in is that welfare assistance is made subject to whatever the agency can recover to defray its expenses from a person who has a support obligation, and the proceeds of the support order will be assigned to the agency.

In determining the amount of support in relation to need, the court is directed to consider an array of facts and circumstances, at least some of which will apply to anybody, so that the effect is to give the court the broadest and most flexible discretion.

Among these factors are the assets and means of the parties; the capacity of each of them to provide for his or her own support and the support of the other; their age, physical and mental health; the length of time they cohabited; the dependant's capacity to become financially independent; the accustomed standard of living while the parties resided together; and the obligation of the respondent to provide support for any other person. For the full text of these provisions, please see section 33(9) of the FLA.

The conduct of the respondent is not a factor in determining the entitlement to support, but the FLA says, "conduct that is so unconscionable as to constitute an obvious and gross repudiation of the relationship" may be considered in determining the amount of support. Of course, it is very difficult to distinguish between entitlement and amount of support, and no reliable precedents exist as to the interpretation and administration of this rule, although it is a very high threshold, calling for something outrageous, or, at a minimum, the formation of an economic union between that claimant and a third party.

Note that the statutory criteria for a spousal support award are different under section 15 of the *Divorce Act*.

Under the FLA, "compensatory support" has been awarded for the economic loss suffered by a claimant because she stayed home to care for children and thus lost working income or career advancement. In one case the compensatory support award was one-half of the economic loss (less tax as if it were income) on the theory that because the claimant agreed to stay home, she should bear one-half of the risk of loss. In other cases, compensatory support was granted to redress the contribution made by the wife to the husband's career. As a result of a decision in the Ontario Court of Appeal, the award of lump-sum compensatory support may be regarded as exceptional, but it does happen. Periodic support, without an element of "compensation," is far more common.

Support does *not* automatically terminate on the recipient's remarriage or cohabitation. The court has the power to order financial support in the form of periodic payments, for example, so much per week or month, either for an indefinite period or until a specified event occurs, together with a lump sum to be paid directly to the dependant or held in trust for the dependant, or any combination of these awards. There is also power to order the transfer of property as an element of support; to give exclusive possession of a matrimonial home and contents; to make the order effective to any retroactive date; to order that the payments be made to a welfare agency or municipal corporation; to order payment of expenses for prenatal care and birth of a child; to order that a dependant be designated the irrevocable beneficiary of an insurance policy; and to order that the payments be secured as against any property or asset, including a pension fund. The court may make the payments variable in accordance with the cost-of-living index either at the date the order is granted, or at some future time.

In the absence of a specific order to the contrary, support obligations automatically continue to be binding on the estate of the payor after death. This is not so under the *Divorce Act*, although one can apply during the lifetime of the payor to have the support order binding on his estate. Absent such an order, after the death of the payor, one must apply as a dependant under the provincial *Succession Law Reform Act* (see below).

It follows that each case must be individually weighed. There is no rule of law that income be divided in accordance with any fraction or percentage or formula for spousal support, although there is some case law that speaks of presumptively equalizing income after a long marriage. An advisory attempt to establish a spousal support formula is within the draft *Spousal Support Advisory Guidelines*, discussed at the end of this chapter. In contrast, there is a statutory formula when determining child support, where both federal and provincial *Child Support Guidelines* apply (see Chapter 6).

As well as the power to make permanent orders (subject to review or variation), the court may make interim orders of support until a full hearing or disposition of the matter, and may restrain any disposal or wasting of assets that would impair or defeat the claim or the order for payment.

The terms of a domestic contract, such as a marriage contract or separation agreement, are not necessarily binding on the court that considers a support application, even if the contract says they are. The court can make any order it thinks appropriate where a contract contains an unconscionable waiver of support, or where the applicant qualifies for welfare assistance, or where there has been a default in the payment of support under the contract.

One will often see in a newspaper a classified ad that purports to inform the world that a husband will not be responsible for his wife's debts thereafter. This follows from an old common-law principle, now part of the *Family Law Act*, that during cohabitation a spouse has authority to render himself or herself (since it cuts both ways) and the spouse liable to a third party for necessities of life, unless he or she has notified the third party that this authority has been withdrawn. A specific notice delivered to that third party would therefore be effective, but it is doubtful if a classified ad has any reliable legal effect.

An application for support can be made in a number of ways:

(a) in the Ontario Court by filling out an application and form of financial statement, in documents as provided by the Clerk of the Court. These documents are served on the respondent, together with a Notice of Hearing specifying the date when the matter will come before the court. The application can be commenced in the local court where either of the parties resides. The respondent is required to file an answer to the application and a form of financial statement. In default of an answer, the matter may be heard and decided without further notice to the respondent. The court has power to make whatever interim orders may be necessary, and to order that there be a pre-trial examination or disclosure of facts material to the case; and

(b) in the Superior Court or in Unified Family Court by application with some difference in the form of presentation. The applicant has to fill out and swear a financial statement, a comprehensive schedule of assets and liabilities, present and proposed expenses and will give notice to the other party requiring him or her to file a similar statement. At the end of this book, among the forms you will find a financial statement and a typical letter of instruction that we give to clients to assist them in filling out the financial statement.

The application is usually served by physical delivery to the respondent, who must respond and file financial information as required, or suffer the consequences of default. With permission of a judge the parties may be questioned about the contents of their financial statements and other aspects of the claim or defence before the case is heard, and may have to deliver an affidavit that sets out every document they now or ever had that bears upon the issues in the case. The financial statements must be accurate, up-to-date, and meaningful, so that nothing less than full financial disclosure will suffice.

A party need not have a lawyer to proceed with an application for support—a person can always represent himself or herself—but in the Superior Court or Unified Family Court the complexities are likely to baffle all but the most resourceful and resolute. In the Ontario Court, the organization includes intake and support staff, so that a lawyer is not necessary, but of course may contribute greatly to the effectiveness of the application, since parties rarely know what evidence should be presented, or how to do it properly.

The Ontario *Family Law Act*, and similar statutes in each province, contain provisions for the variation of spousal support. The FLA states that a support order may be discharged, varied, or suspended, prospectively or retrospectively, if there has been a material change in the circumstances of either of the parties, or new evidence has become available. An application is made to the level of court from which the order originated, although the locale may change as the residence of the parties changes. Except with leave of the court, no such application shall be made within six months of the original order or another variation application, so trivial or multiple applications are discouraged. An application for variation may include indexing the order to the cost-of-living index, if this was not previously provided.

The FLA also gives power to the Ontario Court and the Unified Family Court to vary the terms of an agreement: see sections 35, 37, and 38. Under section 33(4) of the FLA, a court may set aside a provision for support or a waiver of the right to support in a domestic contract and may determine and order support, although the contract agreement contains an express provision excluding the application of this section,

(a) if the provision for support or the waiver of support results in unconscionable circumstances;

(b) if the provision for support is in favour of or the waiver is by or on behalf of a dependant who qualifies for an allowance for support out of public money; or

(c) if there is default in payment of support under the contract or agreement at the time the application is made.

By way of comparison, and to emphasize that the principles differ from one province to another province, the British Columbia statute empowers its court to vary an agreement if it is found to be unfair, having regard to

(a) the duration of the marriage;
(b) the duration of the period during which the spouses have lived separate and apart;
(c) the date when property was acquired or disposed of;
(d) the extent to which property was acquired by one spouse through inheritance or gift;
(e) the needs of each spouse to become or remain economically independent and self-sufficient; or
(f) any other circumstance relating to the acquisition, preservation, maintenance, improvement, or use of property or the capacity or liabilities of a spouse.

The presumptive entitlement to spousal support runs from the date a person gave notice of the claim. This is not considered a retroactive claim. A spousal support claimant does not have to show that he or she had to encroach on capital or incur debt in order to be entitled to spousal support for the period of time when it was first requested to the disposition of the claim. The situation will be different if the claim is for a period *before* notice was given.

Same-Sex Spouses: The Decisions in *M. v. H.*

M. v. H. is the case that directly raised constitutional challenges to the definition of the word "spouse" in Part III of the *Family Law Act*, involving a claim for spousal support by one woman who had co-habited with another for many years. The Act allowed opposite-sex couples to claim support if they had cohabited for more than three years or, in a relationship of some permanence, if they are the natural or adoptive parents of a child. In the case, the applicant asserted that the lengthy period of cohabitation and the inherent sharing of roles and responsibilities created the same pattern of dependency and need for support that results from opposite-sex relationships.

The applicant told the Court

- sexual orientation is a personal characteristic, and that people involved in same-sex relationships constitute a discrete and insular minority which suffers discrimination by stereotyping, historical disadvantage and vulnerability to political and social prejudice, and that accordingly, sexual orientation is an analogous ground of discrimination to those enumerated in section 15(1) of the *Charter of Rights and Freedoms*;

- the then existing definition of "spouse" in section 29 of the *Family Law Act* creates a regime of differential treatment and discriminates against the applicant as a member of a same-sex spousal relationship by imposing a disadvantage which is not imposed on members of opposite-sex spousal relationships and by withholding opportunities, benefits and advantages which are available to members of opposite-sex spousal relationships, and that accordingly, the definition of "spouse" in section 29 of the *Family Law Act* is unconstitutional and offensive to her rights to equal treatment or benefit under or before the law pursuant to section 15(1) of the *Charter*; and
- the definition of "spouse" in section 29 of the *Family Law Act* is underinclusive and should be read to include two persons who are not married to each other and have cohabited continuously for a period of not less than three years.

The responding party said that there was no section 15 infringement; that alternatively any infringement was justifiable under section 1 of the *Charter*; and further that the remedy proposed by the plaintiff was inappropriate considering many factors, including the recommendations that had been made by the Ontario Law Reform Commission for a system of "Registered Domestic Partners."

The Attorney General for Ontario first took a position that the applicant was correct, but, with a change in government from NDP to Conservative, reversed that position and supported the responding party.

All of the parties agreed that the then present definition of "spouse" was discriminatory, but the responding party argued that any change was better left to the legislature.

In February 1996, the trial judge ruled that the definition was indeed discriminatory and that the legislative remedy was inappropriate. She said that the proper course is to "read in" to the *Family Law Act* the phrase "two persons" instead of "a man and a woman" in the extended definition of "spouse." Therefore, two persons in a same-sex relationship that resulted in continuous cohabitation for a period of at least three years would have rights and obligations of spousal support. The responding party spouse and the Attorney General both appealed this decision to the Court of Appeal.

In December 1996, the Ontario Court of Appeal released its reasons in *M. v. H.* Two of the three judges agreed with the trial judge and upheld her decision, with the additional provision that the effect of the decision would be deferred for one year to give the legislature a last chance to act, and if there was no legislative action, the new definition of "spouse" would automatically come into force, subject, of course, to the possibility of an application for leave to appeal to the Supreme Court of Canada. In his dissenting judgment, one of the judges expressed his dismay that the parties had conceded that the statute was discriminatory. He would not have so found, and would have overruled the trial judge completely.

The Attorney General appealed to the Supreme Court of Canada. In May 1999, the S.C.C. released a judgment in which it declared that the definition of "spouse" in section 29 of the FLA infringes section 15 of the *Charter*, insofar as it denies the right of same-sex spouses to seek support from each other after the relationship ends. The opportunity to gain access to a court-enforced process is a "benefit" under the law for the purposes of section 15 of the *Charter*. There is no justification for the infringement under section 1 of the *Charter* because there is no rational connection between the objectives of the spousal support provisions and the means chosen to further these objectives. They gave the province six months to re-enact section 29 of the FLA to comply with the *Charter*.

In response to this, the Ontario legislature passed a package of statutory amendments that came in to force on March 1, 2000, to define "spouse" to include same-sex partners, a new legal category of person, with the same rights as an unmarried person who already qualifies as a spouse under the statutes. Among the statutes amended were the FLA, the *Children's Law Reform Act*, the *Family Responsibility and Support Arrears Enforcement Act*, and the *Succession Law Reform Act*. Similar legislation was enacted soon after in all provinces and territories except P.E.I. and Nunavut.

The Part I property provisions of the FLA were not amended. In Ontario, neither same-sex spouses nor unmarried heterosexual spouses have the right to equalize net family property on the breakdown of their relationship. In the case of unmarried heterosexual spouses, this distinction has been the subject of *Charter* challenges. A Nova Scotia case was appealed to the Supreme Court of Canada, where it was held that couples who choose to remain unmarried do not have the same property rights as those who choose to be married.

Spousal Support and Variation
under the *Divorce Act*

As noted previously in connection with spousal support under a provincial statute the presumptive entitlement to spousal support runs from the date a person gave notice of the claim. This is not considered a retroactive claim. A spousal support claimant does not have to show that he or she had to encroach on capital or incur debt in order to be entitled to spousal support for the period of time when it was first requested to disposition of the claim. The situation will be different if the claim is for a period *before* notice was given.

The entitlement to and amount of interim or "permanent" spousal support will depend on a number of factors set out in section 15.2 of the *Divorce Act*. These are the conditions, means, and other circumstances of each spouse, including the length of time the spouses cohabited and the functions performed by each spouse during cohabitation, and any order, agreement, or arrangement relating to the support of a spouse or child. A spouse's misconduct is *not* a factor. Section 15.2(6) of the *Divorce Act* sets out in language unusual for a statute the objectives of an order for support of a spouse. The order should

(a) recognize any economic advantages or disadvantages to the spouses arising from the marriage or its breakdown;

(b) apportion between the spouses any financial consequences arising from the care of any child of the marriage;

(c) relieve any economic hardship of the spouses rising from the breakdown of the marriage;

(d) insofar as practicable, promote the economic self-sufficiency of each spouse within a reasonable period of time.

These ideas have been considered in a number of appeal court decisions. The Manitoba Court of Appeal put it this way:

Economic self-sufficiency may be appropriate for a wife who has had the same opportunities as her husband, but it surely leads to inequality for one who lacked them. Most women who married 30 years ago were encouraged to think of marriage as a way of life in which the husband provided for the family. A woman might be expected to help out in the early years, or even longer, but she was conditioned to think of her earning role as secondary. Although it may seem wrong to those who have been taught to think of woman as man's equal, it is a fact that for many women who were married in the past, a woman's own economic independence was neither a consideration about which she gave much thought nor a goal for which she planned.

* * *

The present divorce law, designated with the equality of women very much in mind, places emphasis on the attainment of economic self-sufficiency as the goal for both of the former spouses. But Parliament has recognized that each marriage must be judged according to its own circumstances.

* * *

A wife who has spent her entire married life in a traditional relationship with her husband is likely, from that fact alone, to be economically disadvantaged when divorced.

An Ontario decision contains these passages:

The support scheme established by Parliament seems to me to reflect the judgment that valid support needs arise from the economic aspects of the division of responsibilities within the marriage, not from the fact of the marriage itself. Merely because workforce participation results in the wage earning spouse (usually the husband) receiving an easily measured concrete benefit in the form of wages or salary, does not mean that the assumption of child care and household management responsibilities are to be viewed as having an economic value subservient to the role of financial provision.

In my view there is an almost presumptive economic disadvantage arising upon the breakdown of a long-term marriage, where the claimant spouse has been absent from the workforce for a lengthy period. There is an element of economic disadvantage arising out of the rules assumed in the marriage and a further economic disadvantage arising from the breakdown of the marriage.

* * *

In very general terms, it is likely that in marriages of short duration, particularly when there are no children, the self-sufficiency objective of s. 15.2(6)(d) will be given priority. In marriages of longer duration, where one spouse has been out of the workforce for an extended period of time while discharging child care and household management responsibilities, the self-sufficiency objective may be an objective which cannot be attained, and will not be given priority. Among other things, courts must consider what functions the spouses performed during the marriage to determine the extent to which a spouse in need of support has a real capacity to be self-sufficient.

The question of the appropriate standard of living to be considered if means are available is, in my view, a reasonable standard of living having in mind the circumstances of the marriage. In a long-term marriage a reasonable standard of living should be assessed in the context of the material standard of living, assuming ability to pay, and taking into account the financial result of the determination of property issues.

* * *

The objective of self-sufficiency must be assessed in the context of the marriage, particularly in a marriage involving a long period of cohabitation. To do otherwise is to recognize inadequately the economic value of the functions of child care and household management and the economic disadvantages accruing as a result of a long-term absence from the workforce. Defining self-sufficiency in the context of a wife's employment some 24 years before separation does not adequately recognize the economic advantages accruing to the husband. Nor does that approach adequately recognize the economic disadvantages accruing to a wife who has been substantially out of the workforce while undertaking child care and household management responsibilities for an extended period.

Then in 1992, the Supreme Court of Canada released its judgment in a case called *Moge v. Moge*. This lengthy judgment sets out a number of principles applicable to the award of spousal support under the *Divorce Act*. Some of these are complementary, and some of them seem paradoxical. It has been observed that you can find justification in *Moge* for any position you want to take. My esteemed colleague, Philip Epstein, using extracts from the *Moge* judgment, formulated a *catalogue raisonné* of these principles from which the following list has been taken:

1. An inability to become self-sufficient is not the only basis for spousal support. (Therefore, need is relative.)
2. The level of self-sufficiency set by courts in previous cases often demonstrated unmitigated parsimony. (Therefore, awards should be higher.)
3. The focus when assessing spousal support after the marriage has ended must be the effect of the marriage in impairing or improving each party's economic prospects. Support ought to be based on principles of compensation since a division of functions between spouses where one is a wage earner and the other remains at home will almost invariably create an economic need

in one spouse. (Therefore conduct in the sense of roles or contributions during the marriage will be an element.)

4. The absence of accumulated assets may require that one spouse pay support to the other in order to effect an equitable distribution of resources. (One would think that this can be done under a provincial "property" statute. Also it conflicts with the often-stated principle that the purpose of a support award is *not* the redistribution of property.)

5. As a starting point, the courts must develop parameters within which to assess the respective advantages and disadvantages of the spouses as a result of their roles in the marriage.

6. The Act requires a fair and equitable distribution of resources to alleviate the economic consequences of marriage or marriage breakdown for both spouses. (Divorce or separation should not lead to impoverishment of the parties.)

7. There has been a shift away from the means and needs test in the previous statute as the exclusive criterion for support, to a more encompassing set of objectives which requires the courts to accommodate to a much wider spectrum of considerations. The four policy objectives in section 15.2(6) of the *Divorce Act* are not necessarily independent of each other. They may overlap or operate independently, depending on the circumstances of the case.

8. All four of these objectives must be taken into account when dealing with the issue of support or variation. The fact that one objective, such as economic self-sufficiency, has been attained, does not necessarily dispose of the matter. (Does this mean there can be support awarded in the absence of need?)

9. Anyway, the objective of self-sufficiency is a goal "only insofar as is practicable." (This discourages unrealistic expectations of employability when one has been out of the workforce for a number of years.)

10. In cases where relatively few advantages or disadvantages are incurred, transitional support allowing for full and unimpaired reintegration back into the labour force might be all that is required. In many cases a former spouse will continue to suffer economic disadvantages of marriage breakdown while the other spouse reaps its economic advantages. In such cases, the proper compensatory award would be long-term support.

11. The equitable sharing of the economic consequences of marriage or breakdown is not a general tool of redistribution which is

activated by the mere fact of marriage. Marriage per se does not automatically entitle a spouse to support. In cases where neither spouse has made an economic sacrifice for the other, or they have made sacrifices equally (said to be "a Utopian scenario"), there might be no call for compensation.

12. In cases where a spouse is sick or disabled, as well as spousal support, the state may have a role to play.

13. The ultimate goal of any support order is to alleviate the disadvantaged spouse's economic losses as completely as possible, taking into account all of the circumstances of the parties, including the advantages conferred on the other spouse during the marriage, but also recognizing that the disadvantages may not be fully compensated in every case since, clearly, the ability of the debtor to pay must be considered.

14. Financial consequences of marriage breakdown extend beyond the simple loss of future earning power or losses directly related to the care of children. Loss of seniority, missed promotions, lack of access to fringe benefits such as pension plans, life, disability, dental and medical insurance are matters that must be considered, as is the fact that persons outside the workforce lose opportunities to upgrade their skills through on-the-job training.

15. The birth of children and the consequent devotion by the wife to most of the child-care responsibilities jeopardizes her ability to ensure her own income security and independent well-being, and, in such cases, spousal support may be a way to compensate such economic disadvantage. If child-care responsibilities continue after marriage breakdown, the existing disadvantages continue to be exacerbated by the need to accommodate and integrate child-care needs with the requirements of paid employment.

16. Even in childless marriages, a decision that one spouse will stay at home may lead to an economic disadvantage that should be regarded as compensable.

17. Where a spouse has contributed to the operation of a business or has taken on increased responsibilities, domestic or financial, that enabled the other spouse to pursue licences or degrees, then to the extent that those activities have not already been compensated for in the division of assets, they are factors that should be considered in granting spousal support.

18. Although the doctrine of spousal support, which focuses on equitable sharing, does not guarantee to either party the standard

of living enjoyed during marriage, this standard is far from irrelevant.

19. Great disparities in the standard of living that would be evident in the absence of support are often a revealing indication of the economic disadvantages inherent in the role assumed by one party. (Therefore, projected lifestyle after the breakdown of marriage will be an important factor.)

20. The courts, in the exercise of their discretion, must be alert to a wide variety of factors and decisions made during the marriage which have had the effect of disadvantaging one spouse or benefiting the other.

21. Since spousal support orders remain a function of the evidence in each particular case, such evidence will frequently come in the form of highly specific expert evidence. However, such evidence will not be required, nor will it be possible in most cases, and creative lawyers and courts will have to create different alternatives. (Actually, one can hardly establish economic loss without expert evidence. Its absence may lead to inaccurate and inappropriate assessments.)

22. The court should take judicial notice (traditionally, common knowledge, something that does not have to be specifically proved) of economic studies as background information. The general impact of divorce on women is a phenomenon that can no longer be reasonably questioned. Judges must be aware of the social reality in which support decisions are experienced when engaging in the examination of the support objectives of the *Divorce Act*. A judge must not close his or her eyes to the daily realities of present-day life.

But compare this with the view of the Ontario Court of Appeal that, at least under the *Family Law Act*, lump-sum compensatory support is generally inappropriate, especially because of the virtual impossibility of accurate assessment and the fact that a lump sum cannot be later varied if circumstances change. Thus, "compensation" should usually be in the form of periodic support, tapping into the income stream that is often the significant remaining resource after breakdown of marriage. This reinforces the idea that our courts will retain jurisdiction to vary a previous support order in the event of a material change in circumstances, rather than cut off support after some fixed period, which is inherently a leap in the dark.

Under the *Divorce Act*, it is not necessary to make a claim for corollary relief at the same time as the petition for dissolution of marriage. Either spouse or former spouse can assert a claim for corollary relief at any time during the original proceedings, or later, after the divorce has been granted, or even, as we will see below, after a claim for spousal support has been heard and dismissed.

The court can order support for a definite or indefinite term, "and may impose such other terms, conditions or restrictions in connection therewith as it thinks fit and just." The form of payment can be periodic or lump sum or any combination of these, to the spouse and any children, and payment can be secured against assets.

The end result is that the judge can do anything by way of interim or permanent corollary relief that she thinks—based on the individual facts—will be appropriate for the spouses. This is as it should be, the range and variability of human conduct and affairs being what it is.

If there are arrears under a previous support order made under a provincial statute, the divorce court can deal with this when making an order under the *Divorce Act*. Also, if you already have a support order under a provincial statute and your divorce decree doesn't deal with support, the previous order continues.

There is a long line of legal authority to the effect that when the court is determining rights in divorce proceedings, a separation agreement is not a bar to granting corollary relief. On the other hand, a separation agreement is not lightly disregarded. It is strongly persuasive, as it should be, because public policy dictates that the court should respect and encourage the right of the spouses to settle their own affairs.

It may happen that the spouses are content to rely on the terms of a separation agreement, and will not ask the court to make any order for corollary relief, but that's another matter. The separation agreement will continue as a contract between the spouses, and will be enforceable on its own terms. Or maybe on the court's terms.

In the Supreme Court of Canada, in a case called *Bracklow*, the now Chief Justice McLachlin reviewed the history of spousal support obligations and entitlement. She said it is critical to distinguish between the roles of the spouses during marriage, and the different roles on marriage breakdown. Absent indications to the contrary, during marriage the spouses owe a mutual duty of support. There is no presumption of support when a marriage breaks down. She puts the problem, and answers it this way:

> Is a sick or disabled spouse entitled to spousal support when a marriage ends, and if so, when and how much? More precisely, may a spouse have an obligation to support a former spouse over and above what is required to compensate the spouse for loss incurred as a result of the marriage and its breakdown (or to fulfill contractual support agreements)? I would answer this question in the affirmative.

She continues:

> The lower courts implicitly assumed that, absent a contractual agreement for post-marital assistance, entitlement to support could only be founded on compensatory principles, i.e., reimbursement of the spouse for opportunities foregone or hardships accrued as a result of the marriage. I conclude, however, that the law recognizes three conceptual grounds for entitlement to spousal support: (1) compensatory; (2) contractual; and (3) non-compensatory. These three bases of support flow from the controlling statutory provisions and the relevant case law, and are more broadly animated by different philosophies and theories of marriage and marriage breakdown thoroughly considered in this judgment.
>
> Contractual support obligations, while not new, were given new emphasis by statutory stipulations that the courts take into account support agreements, express or implied, between the parties.

Take them into account, but, of course, not be bound by them. There is no form of agreement, no spousal support release, nothing, that can prevent a court from reviewing and, if it thinks fit, awarding support in its discretion.

Compensatory support refers back to the S.C.C. decision in Moge, said to be the first comprehensive articulation of the view that when marriage ends, support criteria extend beyond needs and capacity to pay; and spouses are entitled to be compensated for contributions to the marriage and for losses sustained as a consequence of the marriage. Compensatory considerations are not the only basis for support.

The basic premise of contractual and compensatory support is that the parties are equal. As such, when the relationship ends, the parties are entitled to what they would receive in the commercial world—what the individuals contracted for and what they have lost due to the marriage, and its breakdown. Insofar as the marriage may have created dependencies, it is the duty of the dependent spouses to free themselves from their dependencies and to assume full self-sufficiency, thereby mitigating the need for continued compensation.

By directing the judge to consider factors like need and ability to pay, as in the *Divorce Act*, the Act left in place the possibility of non-compensatory, non-contractual support. Marriage *per se* does not automatically entitle a spouse to support, but on the breakdown of marriage, the court is directed to consider under section 15.2(6) of the *Divorce Act* the objectives of a spousal support order. The first two—to recognize the economic consequences of the marriage and its breakdown and to apportion between the spouses financial consequences of child care over and above child-support payments—are primarily related to compensation. The third and fourth objectives are broader: to relieve any economic hardship of the spouses arising from the breakdown of marriage, and insofar as practicable, to promote the economic self-sufficiency of each spouse within a reasonable period of time. The latter objectives speak to non-compensatory entitlement to support. From *Moge*: "... an equitable sharing of the economic consequences of divorce does not exclude other considerations, particularly when dealing with sick or disabled spouses." As Madame Justice McLachlin puts it in *Bracklow*, "To permit the award of support to a spouse disabled by illness is but to acknowledge the goal of equitably dealing with the economic consequences of marital breakdown that this Court in *Moge* ... recognized as lying at the heart of the *Divorce Act*." She reiterates the three conceptual bases for entitlement to spousal support, as "the starting position." She summarizes:

> Support agreements are important (although not necessarily deci-
> sive), and so is the idea that spouses should be compensated on
> marriage breakdown for losses and hardships caused by the mar-
> riage. Indeed, a review of cases suggests that in most circumstances
> compensation now serves as the main reason for support. However,
> contract and compensation are not the only sources of a support
> obligation. The obligation may alternatively arise *out of the marriage
> relationship itself*. Where a spouse achieves economic self-sufficiency
> on the basis of his or her own efforts, or on an award of compensatory
> support, the obligation founded on the marriage itself lies dormant.
> But where need is established that is not met on a compensatory or
> contractual basis, the fundamental marital obligation may play a vital

role. Absent negating factors, it is available, in appropriate circumstances, to provide just support. [emphasis added]

Then came the much-publicized case of *Bailey v. Paxton*. The parties had been married and divorced, and the husband had paid a lump sum and time-limited support in accordance with an agreement. Some ten years after the support and her money had run out, the wife applied for revival of spousal support. The judge ruled not only that the agreement was no bar to her claim, but, further, that the wife was entitled to interim support pending trial of the issue. She sensibly expedited the trial in the circumstances, but it was settled before the trial. That was followed by another decision called *Leopold*, which came to the opposite conclusion.

Compare all of this with the decision in *Gates*. In that case, the parties married in 1963, separated in 1990, and divorced in 1991. They signed an agreement that made no provision for spousal support, even if there were a material, profound, or catastrophic change in circumstances. In 1996 the wife was diagnosed with chronic myeloid leukemia. Unable to work, she subsisted on Canada Pension disability payments. She applied to add spousal support to the divorce judgment. The parties acknowledged that the disease was a radical change in circumstances, that the husband was capable of paying support, and that the wife's condition was not related to or causally connected to the marriage or its breakdown or to economic dependency engendered by the marriage. The trial judge noted a divergence of opinions between those who want agreements to be final and predictable, and those concerned about imposing unintended conditions on statutory entitlements. The judge ruled that in order to override the agreement, there must be a radical, unforeseen change in circumstances, *which must relate to the economic consequences of the roles of the parties in the marriage*. In this case the wife's condition had nothing to do with the pattern of economic dependency engendered by marriage, and her claim was dismissed. There have been a number of cases that have applied the same reasoning. These controversial and much-debated principles derive from three cases known as the *Pelech* trilogy, all decided by the Supreme Court of Canada in 1987, but under the provisions of the 1968 *Divorce Act*.

In 1995, the Supreme Court of Canada released an important decision, *L.G. v. G.B.*, on variation of spousal support under the

Divorce Act, an appeal from the Court of Appeal for Quebec. The parties married in 1960, and divorced in November 1986. They had signed a separation agreement that provided for $2,600 a month in spousal support, and $100 a month support for a minor child. Spousal support would not be reduced unless the appellant (wife) earned wages of more than $15,000 a year, then reduced dollar for dollar. At the date of the agreement, the wife was "seeing" a friend with whom she had cohabited since May 1989. Her companion was providing her with a monthly allowance, and had advanced money for her to buy a condominium. In July 1989, the respondent (husband) filed a variation application under section 17 of the *Divorce Act*, claiming custody of the minor child, cancellation of the child support (the child was then living with him), and cancellation of the spousal support. The trial judge only varied physical custody of the child. The trial judge held that there was no material change in circumstances, since the wife's cohabitation was foreseeable at the time of the divorce, and the spousal support in the agreement would have ordinarily taken this into account. There was no stipulation reducing or cancelling the support in those circumstances. Furthermore, as that relationship offered no guarantee of any permanence, it could not secure the wife's financial independence. The husband appealed.

The Quebec Court of Appeal held that the wife's new union had achieved sufficient stability for the support obligations imposed on the husband at the time of the divorce to be reassessed. The agreement was not a final settlement of all obligations pertaining to the marriage and its breakdown. Relying on the so-called presumption of self-sufficiency according to which the recipient of spousal support who is living in a cohabiting relationship has the burden of showing that, notwithstanding the cohabitation, she still needed the support, the Court of Appeal reduced the support to $1,250 a month, as of the date of its judgment in April 1993, and cancelled the child support retroactive to July 1989. The wife appealed.

Seven judges heard the appeal in the Supreme Court of Canada. The majority of them referred to the material change provisions of section 17 of the *Divorce Act*, i.e., a change that, if known at the time, would likely have resulted in different terms (the definition in the *Willick* case). If the matter that is relied on as constituting a material change was known at the relevant time, it cannot be relied on as a basis for variation. The wife was "seeing" her present companion, so it was foreseeable that they would cohabit, although, in *Willick* one judge had said "... the fact that a change was objectively foreseeable does not necessarily mean that it was contemplated by the parties." The trial judge correctly concluded that there was no material change of circumstances. There was no basis in fact or law for the Quebec Court of Appeal to reverse this conclusion. Child support was cancelled from the date of hearing this appeal.

The minority of three judges agreed with the majority in the result, with different reasons. They held that since this case was decided under the 1985 *Divorce Act*, variation principles under the 1968 *Divorce Act* could not be applied: The 1985 *Divorce Act* moved away from the "clean break" idea under the previous statute and emphasized the substantive rather than formal equality of the spouses in the marriage and at the time of divorce. The 1985 Act rejected the presumption of economic self-sufficiency and substituted for it a number of criteria that would take into account the advantages and disadvantages to spouses accruing from the marriage for its breakdown. The objective of economic self-sufficiency can only be pursued "insofar as practicable."

For the initial support to be varied, there must be a material change as defined above under section 17(4) of the *Divorce Act*. Once the sufficiency of a change has been established, the court must determine the extent of the variation, and to do so it generally has to make an assessment of the entirety of the present circumstances of the parties. If the parties have an agreement, the court must assess the agreement in the light of the factors and objectives that govern spousal support under sections 15.2(4), 15.2(5), 15.2(6), 17(4), 17(4.1), 17(7), and 17(10) of the *Divorce Act*. At the time of the divorce, the separation agreement is only one of the factors to be considered. In a variation application, although there is no mention of an agreement as a factor in section 17, the agreement should not be ignored when applications to vary support orders are made, especially when they were intended to be a final settlement and were ratified by the original support order. *The weight to be given to the agreement will depend, first, on the extent to which the agreement reflects the principles and objectives stated in section 17, and, second, on the scope and nature of the change that has occurred, taking into account all of the circumstances of the parties.* The more the agreement or support order takes the overarching principle of the 1985 Act into account in promoting an equitable distribution of the economic consequences of the marriage and its breakdown, the more likely it will be to influence the outcome of the variation application. For the minority, the judge criticizes the agreement for not mentioning the criteria in the 1985 Act, and she says, "In drafting future agreements, counsel would be well advised to articulate the bases on which both spousal and child support covenants have been negotiated."

Under the *Divorce Act* courts retain a discretionary power that will be exercised in accordance with the factors and objectives of the Act. The existence of an agreement, final or otherwise, should not have the effect of precluding such analysis.

The evidence disclosed no change that would be sufficient to justify a variation of spousal support. The wife's cohabiting relationship does not mean that she can be presumed to be financially independent. Anyway, that is only one of the objectives to be pursued insofar as practicable. Self-sufficiency is *not* to be presumed; it must be proved. There was no such evidence. The Court of Appeal could not properly start from a presumption of financial self-sufficiency that is not supported by either the 1985 Act or its interpretation. Also, the possibility that the wife would become economically self-sufficient was illusory on the facts. The minority also cancelled child support from the date of this hearing.

L.G. v. G.B. creates a lot of problems. Neither the date of the separation nor the agreement are stated in the judgment, but since the divorce was granted in November 1986, it seems likely that the separation agreement predates the *Divorce Act*. If that is correct, it seems unreasonable for that agreement, or any agreement entered into before the *Divorce Act*, to have anticipated the language of the statute.

The latest word on the threshold test to vary the terms of spousal support in an agreement comes from the Supreme Court of Canada in *Miglin*. This extremely important case deserves full consideration.

The parties in *Miglin* had a 1994 separation agreement. They divorced in 1997, but since they had an agreement, they chose not to put the financial terms in the divorce judgment. The (ex)wife applied for spousal support, and since no previous order had been made, it was treated as a first application for spousal support, which was granted by the trial judge. One of the issues on appeal was the effect of the agreement, and on what principles the court would modify its terms. In 1991 the Ontario Court of Appeal ruled definitively that the test in the *Pelech* trilogy is stone-cold dead. The threshold for variation of a previous order is simply a material change in circumstances, so why should it be higher in the case of an agreement? Therefore, "The threshold I would impose for the variation of a subsisting support agreement in an application for corollary relief under s. 15.2 [*Divorce Act*] is whether there has been a material change of circumstances from the time the agreement was made." The court referred to the definition of "material change" in the *Willick* case, below.

Also from *Miglin* in the Court of Appeal:

> The existence of a valid separation or settlement agreement under the … *Divorce Act* results in a two-stage inquiry designed to protect the parties' reasonable expectations from spurious challenge by requiring a material change before a judicial review of support takes place, while at the same time promoting, where warranted, the objectives of equitable spousal support set out in s. 15.2(6) and echoed in s. 17(7) of the 1985 *Divorce Act*. The first and threshold stage is to determine whether there has been a material change in circumstances. If the threshold of a material change has been met, the second stage is to determine what amount of spousal support, if any, is justified under the statutory principles set out in s. 15 of the *Divorce Act* and refined in leading cases from the Supreme Court of Canada.
>
> Any variation will, of course, be a matter of discretion depending on the facts of the particular case. The following are some of the factors to consider at the second stage in deciding whether and to what extent to vary the terms of an agreement: the extent, source and impact of the change in circumstances; whether the agreement reflects a clear and unequivocal intention to insulate it from review or variation; the extent to which the agreement satisfies the objectives of the [*Divorce*] *Act*; and, where there is an agreement to waive support or limit its duration to a fixed event or time, how lengthy a period has elapsed since the waiver, event or expiration of the time limit. This is not an exhaustive list, but represents the view that a valid agreement, while clearly not determinative, ought to be given significant weight.

The principles are different where a previous spousal support order runs for a definite period or until a specified event occurs: see section 17(10) of the *Divorce Act* at Appendix B, and note that this section speaks of a spousal support order, not an agreement. In *Miglin* the court said:

For the purposes of this appeal, it is unnecessary to decide whether, in the interests of consistency, the higher threshold for varying expired spousal support orders found in s. 17(10) of the Act should also apply to expired agreements, or whether this is an area where the different route to agreements and orders argues for leaving the variation threshold for agreements as being a material change. What is clear, however, is that the legislature has highlighted an intention in s. 17(10) that expired responsibilities should be significantly more difficult to reinstate. At the very least, it seems to me, the length of time which has elapsed since the parties last expected to receive or provide support under their agreement, and the extent to which they have reasonably relied in the interim on its absence in organizing their subsequent financial arrangements, is relevant in determining whether a variation should be ordered, and, if so, to what extent.

Miglin was appealed to the Supreme Court of Canada. In a 2003 decision, the S.C.C. ruled that in this case the Ontario Court of Appeal erred in finding that the wife was entitled to spousal support in the face of a spousal support release in the separation agreement. An application for spousal support that is inconsistent with a pre-existing separation agreement requires a two-stage consideration of all the circumstances surrounding the agreement, firstly at the time the agreement was made, and secondly, at the time of the application for support. In the first stage, the court should review the circumstances in which the agreement was negotiated and signed to determine if there is any reason to discount it, and whether the agreement substantially complies with the spousal support objectives in the Divorce Act. In the second stage, the court must assess whether the agreement still reflects the original intention of the parties, and the extent to which it still substantially complies with the spousal support objectives in the Divorce Act. A separation agreement that is created in "unimpeachable circumstances" is not likely to be varied. Miglin has been followed and applied in a number of cases at trial and appeal, notably a B.C. decision called Hartshorne where the wife unsuccessfully sought to vary the support releases in a prenuptial contract.

The ink was hardly dry on the Miglin decision in the Court of Appeal when the trial judgment in Marinangeli was released. The former wife applied under the Divorce Act for variation of child and spousal support that had been established in a 1996 agreement after some years of litigation. The agreement provided for variation in the event of material change in circumstances. The husband had said in a pre-trial conference memo that he expected his income to be reduced, but soon after he signed off on the settlement, he cashed in about $1 million worth of stock options, and his annual income otherwise increased substantially after that (this summary is a bit different from the judgment, and derives from discussion with the lawyers in the case). The variation of *Guideline* child support was conceded. In the unusual circumstances of this case, the trial judge ordered the increase of both child and spousal support back to 1997, and included in income the amount received for the stock options (there are cases where that hasn't happened). An extraordinary and unprecedented passage in the trial judgment says:

> I find that Mr. Marinangeli was *at fault in failing to recognize his obligation to notify Mrs. Marinangeli of the material change in circumstances* which occurred when he exercised his vested stock options in 1997. . . . A further material change in circumstances resulted when his income from employment substantially increased. *Mr. Marinangeli was obliged to notify Mrs. Marinangeli of each material change.* While the [agreement is] silent on this point, that obligation is implicit, given the agreement that spousal and child support may be varied in the event of a material change in circumstances. Furthermore, in that just prior to the execution of the [agreement] Mr. Marinangeli had taken the position that he anticipated a reduction in his income, there was no reason for Mrs. Marinangeli to believe otherwise. I weigh Mr. Marinangeli's presettlement statement heavily in that regard. It would be unreasonable to expect Mrs. Marinangeli to have commenced a variation application immediately after the [agreement was] executed in order to determine whether or not Mr. Marinangeli's financial circumstances had improved materially. The parties had just engaged in 4 years of litigation. [emphasis added]

This trial decision was upheld on appeal. As we will see in connection with *Guideline* child support, there is a statutory right to annual financial disclosure on demand. If the trial judge was correct in *Marinangeli*, then, as to spousal support, the obligation of disclosure must be bilateral. Can it be correct, for instance, that the recipient of support must notify the other if she gets a raise or her rent is reduced?

In a 2005 decision, *Murray*, the Ontario Court of Appeal sought to limit the principles in *Marinangeli* to the particular limited facts of the earlier case. The ruling was that before a court can imply a term into an agreement or minutes of settlement, it must be satisfied that the implied term is reasonable and equitable; capable of clear expressions; and not contradictory of an express term of the contract. The court also states that it cannot imply an obligation to disclose annual income when the wife had released spousal support. This is an application of *Miglin* to hold the parties to their bargain. In December 2005, the Supreme Court of Canada refused leave to appeal the *Murray* decision.

Section 17 of the *Divorce Act* contains a complete code for varying a spousal support order. Before making a variation order the court "shall satisfy itself that a change in the condition, means, needs or other circumstances of either former spouse has occurred since the making of the spousal support order or the last variation." Once that "material change" is established, a variation order of spousal support should consider exactly the same factors as in determining an original support order under section 15.2(6) of the Act. If the support order was for a definite period or until a specified event occurs, the court may not, on a variation application made after that period or event, make a variation order for the purpose of resuming support unless satisfied that it is necessary to relieve economic hardship resulting from a material change that is related to the marriage, and that the changed circumstances, if they had existed at the time of the last order or variation of it, would likely have resulted in a different order. Obviously, if one has an order for some kind of time-limited spousal support, it is much better to apply for a variation before the support runs out, when the threshold will simply be material change.

The application for a variation order under the *Divorce Act* need not be made to the court of the same province that made the original order. A court in a province has jurisdiction to make a variation order if either former spouse is ordinarily resident there, or if both former spouses accept the jurisdiction of the court, no matter where in Canada the divorce was granted. The court has no power under the *Divorce Act* to vary a support order made in a foreign court, but on an attempt to enforce a foreign order under a provincial statute, there may be a power to vary it: see, for example, section 7 of the *Reciprocal Enforcement of Support Orders Act* (Ontario).

On a variation application, the court may have to decide whether pension income is available to satisfy a spousal support claim.

The core problem is that the value of the pension may have been equalized, so the argument goes, if I have already shared the capital value of the pension, why should I now have to share the income? Isn't that "double-dipping"? The weight of authority is that the court will not exclude pension income from consideration of the payer's means, for example, it is "inappropriate to disregard the real needs of a spouse solely because of the assets received or retained at the time of the divorce," but, of course, the prior receipt of an equalizing payment is a factor in the financial circumstances of the parties.

This had been the subject of at least twenty reported decisions, with widely different results. Then, in 2001, the Supreme Court of Canada released its judgment in a case called *Boston*. The Court considered entitlement to spousal support where a retired payor applied to reduce or terminate his obligation of support on the primary basis that his pension was previously considered in the distribution of property. The majority ruled that you first look to the portion of pension payments attributable to the period after separation, not the amount attributable to the portion of the pension that has already been equalized. But that's not the end of it. The majority states:

> Double recovery cannot always be avoided, and a pension previously divided can also be viewed as a maintenance asset, where the payer has the ability to pay, where the payee has made a reasonable effort to use equalized assets in an income-producing way and despite this, economic hardship from the marriage or its breakdown persists. Double recovery may also be permitted in spousal support orders/ agreements based on need as opposed to compensation.

In a case called *Willick*, the Supreme Court of Canada defined a "material change in circumstances" as one that, if the court had known of it at the time of the original order or previous variation, likely would have resulted in different terms. Something that was known at the time of the original order cannot be relied on as a material change. This definition, which was referred to in the *Miglin* case, covers a lot of ground. As an example, suppose a former husband applies for a reduction of spousal support because he has now retired and has reduced income. Wasn't it known and foreseeable that at some point he would retire? The original order could have provided, as many separation agreements do, that retirement will be treated as a material change in circumstances, entitling a party to apply for variation of support. If that isn't provided in the original order, is the variation application doomed?

When the *Child Support Guidelines* came into force in 1997, the *Divorce Act* was amended to state that the reduction or elimination of child support payments is itself a material change sufficient to justify an application for increased spousal support.

There are a multitude of cases, including some in the Supreme Court of Canada, stating that parties must be encouraged to settle their own affairs by agreement, and that courts should respect those agreements. The jurisdiction under the *Divorce Act* no doubt extends to the variation of support but not the resolution of property settlements. Still, the property and support elements of a separation agreement are often interlinked and inextricable. This decision may discourage settlements if parties feel they can't rely on agreements, and thus actually promote litigation.

Is it really foreseeable that because the wife is "seeing" someone in 1986, she will cohabit with and be supported by that someone (or maybe another someone) in 1989? What is not foreseeable, even though it may not be contemplated? How does one unscramble a separation agreement in order to establish (or justify) its conformity to the ideals of the *Divorce Act*? What changes should be made to separation agreements to cover the warning from the court, set out above? Would it matter, anyway?

For many years, relying on two decisions in the Ontario Court of Appeal in 1986 and 1995, it was understood that if under the *Divorce Act* a spouse claimed support at a trial and the claim for support was dismissed, there was no right later to apply for variation. There was nothing to vary. Then in 2005 a five-judge panel of the same Court of Appeal heard the case of *Tierney-Hynes*. The variation provisions of the *Divorce Act* had been slightly amended in 1997. The court ruled that because of this amendment, even a judgment that dismisses a support claim at trial may be varied to allow support based on a material change of circumstances, although one may argue that because of *Miglin* it is more difficult to vary spousal support in the face of a separation agreement than if a support claim had been heard and dismissed at a trial under the *Divorce Act*.

In December 2005, the Supreme Court of Canada refused leave to appeal the *Tierney-Hynes* decision. This creates (or perpetuates) a legal conundrum. If parties have a separation agreement, an application for variation of spousal support is subject to the high threshold of the two-stage *Miglin* test, but if a claim for spousal support has been dismissed at a trial, the test for variation is simply material change, a lower threshold. Well, suppose there is a separation agreement, and an application for variation of spousal support is dismissed applying the *Miglin* test. Would the dismissal itself enable a further application for variation, applying the material change test?

As matters now stand there is no finality, certainty, or autonomy of agreement in spousal support.

Income Tax Considerations

In any determination of the appropriate amount of spousal support under a court order or separation agreement, the impact of taxation is a vital consideration. The same was true as to child support prior to May 1, 1997, but the changes to the *Income Tax Act* and the *Divorce Act* with the new *Child Support Guidelines* eliminate the taxability and deducibility of child support in orders or agreements made after that date (see "The Amount of Child Support under the *Guidelines*" in Chapter 6).

The *Income Tax Act* (Canada) contains sections that permit the party paying periodic spousal support to deduct the full amount of these payments from taxable income. The party receiving the payments must add the full amount of these payments to taxable income. These rules apply to any amount received by the taxpayer in the year pursuant to a decree, order, or judgment of a competent tribunal or pursuant to a written agreement, as alimony or other allowance payable on a periodic basis for the maintenance of the recipient thereof if the recipient was living apart from and was separated pursuant to a divorce, judicial separation, or written separation agreement from the spouse or former spouse required to make the payment at the time the payment was received and throughout the remainder of the year.

These rules are rather strictly construed as to form. The payments to a spouse or former spouse include those arising from a "common-law" relationship. Payments made to a third party for the benefit of the dependant may also be taxable and deductible, but only if the agreement or order specifically says so. The agreement or court order may be retrospective in effect, and the payments will be deductible or taxable for one year retroactively.

To take a typical example, the husband may be the only wage

earner. If the husband and wife separate, and he pays spousal support to the wife in accordance with a written separation agreement or court order in periodic amounts, he can deduct these payments from his taxable income in the year in which the payments were made. The wife will have to declare the payments as taxable income. The husband will not have the tax credit for the wife as a dependant on his return, but this will be offset by the deduction of the payments, which may amount to far more than that credit. The wife will deduct for tax purposes the basic personal credit and any other credits and deductions she is properly entitled to, including a tax credit for dependent children with her, although she will not declare any child support she receives under an agreement or order made after May 1, 1997. (She may be taxable on child support under an agreement or order made before May 1, 1997.)

The effect is to split income, so that unless both parties are in the highest or lowest tax brackets, the total tax payable is less than if the husband were the sole taxpayer. The savings can be substantial. In a case where the husband earns taxable income of $50,000 a year and pays $15,000 of this to the wife as periodic support under a written separation agreement or court order, his tax would be reduced by about $5,000. The wife's tax on that $15,000, if that is her only taxable income, would be about $2,500, so the absolute saving would be approximately $2,500.

These rules apply if both parties are tax residents of Canada. The rules may be very different if they are not. In some places, there is no tax or deduction for any support payments, and in others only spousal support has tax consequences. In some places, both lump-sum and periodic spousal support may be taxable and deductible. Foreign tax rates are likely to be different from Canadian rates. If you are paying support to a person who is not a resident of Canada, or receiving support from a person who is not a resident of Canada, you should get legal or accounting advice on the tax consequences.

Canada Pension Plan Benefits
Under regulations of the federal department of Health and Welfare, where parties have been married for at least three years, a spouse is entitled to apply for a share of the spouse's Canada Pension Plan benefits. The amount of payment will vary in each individual case. You can get an application form through any Canada Pension Plan office. You must send in with the application a marriage certificate

and a certified copy of the divorce decree. The right to share CPP benefits cannot be released by a clause to that effect in a separation agreement.

Support from an Estate

The *Family Law Act* says that support is binding on the estate unless otherwise provided, but under the *Divorce Act* a support order ends with the death of the payor unless otherwise provided. Since one never knows what may be left in an estate, separation agreements often provide for life insurance coverage, so that there will be a fund to look after support after death of the payor.

Under Part V of the Ontario *Succession Law Reform Act* (SLRA) and similar legislation across the country, a dependant can apply for a support order against the estate. Where a deceased has not made adequate provision for the proper support of dependants, the court "may order that such provision as it considers adequate be made out of the estate of the deceased for the proper support of the dependants or any of them." "Dependant" is defined to include a spouse (married or unmarried, including a same-sex partner), a parent, a child, or a brother or sister of the deceased to whom the deceased was providing support and was under a legal obligation to do so immediately prior to his or her death.

The limitation period for an application is six months from the grant of letters probate or letters of administration, which ties in to the requirement that (usually) the estate not be distributed for six months. That time may be extended by the court, but then the applicant is limited to whatever may be left in the estate. There are special provisions to include in the calculation of the fund that may be charged with the obligation of support, a clawback of certain assets, notably insurance that the deceased owned and that was left to a designated beneficiary, and certain property that the deceased may have disposed of prior to death, the idea being that a dependant's claim should not be defeated because an estate was stripped of assets. This is set out in section 72 of the SLRA.

The principles governing an award of support to a dependant are pretty much the same as for spousal support under section 33 of the FLA.

The *Spousal Support Advisory Guidelines*

In January 2005, after more than three years of study, research, and consultation, the Department of Justice released a draft of *Spousal Support Advisory Guidelines* (SSAG). There is ongoing discussion and consultation; the final version is expected to be released in late 2006 or early 2007. In view of that, this will alert the reader to the proposed principles of the SSAG, but is not meant to be a full analysis.

The SSAG "are intended to bring more certainty and predictability to the determination of spousal support under the federal *Divorce Act*." The operative word here is "advisory." These guidelines will never be legislated, in contrast to the *Child Support Guidelines*, which are law. As stated in the executive summary[1] :

> They are informal guidelines that will operate on an advisory basis only. The proposed advisory guidelines will be used to determine the amount and duration of spousal support within the existing legal framework of the *Divorce Act* and the judicial decisions interpreting its provisions. The guidelines are not legally binding and their adoption and use will be voluntary. They are intended as a practical tool to assist spouses, lawyers, mediators and judges in typical cases.

The SSAG deal with amount of spousal support, not entitlement. They do not deal with the effect of a prior agreement. They do not take into account differences in principle between spousal support under the federal *Divorce Act* and the various provincial and territorial statutes.

The SSAG propose two formulas for determining not a precise amount, but a range of spousal support: the *without child support* formula, and the *with child support* formula.

The *without child support* formula proposes spousal support around two factors: the gross income difference between the spouses and the length of the marriage. It is not based on budget. The amount would range from 1.5 to 2 percent of the difference between the spouses' gross incomes for each year of the marriage or cohabitation up to a maximum of 50 percent. Thus, for marriages of twenty-five years or longer, the rate would be fixed at between 37.5 and 50 percent of the gross income difference. The duration of spousal support would range from .5 to one year for each year of

---

1.www.justice.gc.ca/en/dept/pub/spousal/project/exec.html

marriage. The duration would be indefinite for a marriage of twenty years or longer, or if the marriage has lasted five years or longer, when the years of marriage and the age of the support recipient at date of separation total sixty-five or more.

The amount or duration within the ranges will be affected by, for example, a strong claim for compensatory support, the recipient's needs, property division (a large amount of capital may reduce or obviate the need for support), the needs and limited ability to pay of the payor spouse, and incentives to establish self-sufficiency, all of which are factors that can be found or implied in the objectives of spousal support under the *Divorce Act*.

The proposal envisions possibly swapping off amount for duration: take more support for a shorter time, or less for a longer time.

The *with child support* formula gives priority to the obligation of child support, usually leading to reduced ability to pay, and tax and benefit issues. As stated in the executive summary:

> Where there are dependent children, the primary rationale is compensatory. . . . What drives support is not the length of the marriage, or marital interdependency, or merger over time, but the presence of dependent children and the need to provide care and support for those children. This parental partnership rationale looks at not just past loss, but also at the continuing economic disadvantage that flows from present and future child care responsibilities, anchored in s. 15.2(6)(b) of the *Divorce Act*.
>
> There are three important differences between the *without child* support formula and the *with child support* formula. First, the *with child support* formula uses the net incomes of the spouses, not their gross incomes. Second, this formula divides the pool of combined net incomes between the two spouses, not the gross income difference. Third, the upper and lower percentage limits of net income division in the *with child support* formula do not change with the length of the marriage.

This is the basic *with child support* formula:

1. Determine the individual net disposable income (INDI) of each spouse, income as would be used under the *Child Support Guidelines* minus child support minus taxes and deductions. That is the payor's INDI. For the recipient the INDI is income as would be used under the *Child Support Guidelines* minus notional child support minus taxes and deductions plus government benefits and credits.
2. Add together the individual net disposable incomes. Determine

the range of spousal support amounts that would be required to leave the lower income recipient spouse with between 40 and 46 percent of the combined INDI.

The proponents observe that the calculation of the *with child support* formula will require computer software. As explained by the proponents, there will be two tests for duration of spousal support under the *with child support* formula, and whichever produces the longer duration will apply. First is the longer-marriage test, which is modelled on the maximum duration under the *without child support* formula, that is, one year of support for every year of marriage, and which will likely govern for most marriages of ten years or more. The second test is the shorter-marriage test, which sets the outside time limit for support at the time that the last or youngest child finishes high school and which will typically apply for marriages under ten years. In these shorter-marriage cases, there will likely be review conditions attached. Relatively few cases will reach this outside time limit and those that do will likely involve reduced amounts of top-up support by that time.

Situations of shared and split custody, and where the custodial parent is paying spousal support will require variation of the INDI. Quebec has different guidelines for child support, which will affect the application of the SSAG.

The advisory guidelines will not apply at all where the payor has gross annual income of more that $350,000 or less than $20,000.

The SSAG are intended to be used for initial orders and agreements, not to the full range of issues that may arise on variation and review applications.

Since their introduction in January 2005, the draft SSAG have been considered or mentioned in more than fifty decisions across the country, at trial and on appeal. The most important decision is considered to be *Yemchuk* in the B.C. Court of Appeal, where the *Guidelines* were approved "as a useful tool to assist judges in assessing the quantum and duration of spousal support," and "are intended to reflect the current law rather than change it" and "to build upon the law as it exists." The cases typically characterize the *Guidelines* as a "useful tool" or "check" or "bench mark" or "litmus test" or "starting point." In each case where the *Guidelines* were considered, the court used its discretion to award support in the range or to go above or below the range on the facts of the case.

5

CUSTODY AND ACCESS

The *Ontario Children's Law Reform Act* (CLRA) is a codification of the law of custody and contains as well many important provisions dealing with procedure, jurisdiction, and incidents of custody. The principles will be roughly the same in every province, but as said so often in this book, statutory differences may produce very different results on similar facts. Everything about custody and access applies equally whether the parents are married or unmarried.

The CLRA confers concurrent jurisdiction on the Superior Court of Justice and the Ontario Court of Justice. We start with the idea of equality: the father and mother are equally entitled to custody. But where the parents are separated and the child lives with one of them with the consent, implied consent, or acquiescence of the other, the right of the other to exercise the entitlement to custody and the incidents of custody, but not entitlement to access, is suspended until a separation agreement or order provides otherwise.

Entitlement to access includes the right to visit and be visited by the child and the right to make enquiries and be given information as to the health, education, and welfare of the child. No longer should there be any litigation over the right of a parent to receive a copy of the child's report card or medical reports.

The courts' jurisdiction is based on the habitual residence of the child in a province or on the child's physical presence in a province in addition to what I will call "special circumstances" that make it appropriate for a court to take jurisdiction. We won't ordinarily do it if another application is pending in the habitual residence or if an order has already been granted in another place and been recognized by our courts. In an overriding way, we retain jurisdiction if satisfied on a balance of probabilities that the child might otherwise suffer serious harm.

The CLRA enlarges the range of parties to a custody application. They include the father and mother, of course; a same-sex partner; "a person who has demonstrated a settled intention to treat the child as a child of his or her family"; "a person who had the actual care and upbringing of the child immediately before the application," which might include a grandparent or the live-in help who looks after the child while both parents work; and "any other person whose presence is necessary to determine the matters in issue."

The merits of an application for custody are generally determined in accordance with the best interests of the child. The court considers the following:

(a) the love, affection, and emotional ties between the child and the parties, other members of the family who reside with the child, and persons involved in the care and upbringing of the child;
(b) the views and preferences of the child, where these can reasonably be ascertained;
(c) the length of time the child has lived in a stable home environment;
(d) the ability and willingness of each applicant to provide the child with guidance and education, the necessities of life, and any special needs of the child;
(e) any plans proposed for the care and upbringing of the child;
(f) the permanence and stability of the family unit within which it is proposed that the child will live; and
(g) any blood or adoptive relationship with any party.

A Bill introduced in the Ontario legislature on November 15, 2005 will add the requirement, in assessing a person's ability to act as a parent, to consider whether that person has at any time committed violence or abuse against his or her spouse, a parent of the child to whom the application relates, a member of the person's household, or any child. Note the phrase "any child," meaning not only the child who is the subject of the application.

Very important: Past conduct is not a factor unless relevant to the ability of the person to act as a parent, so that will include domestic violence and abuse.

The court has specific power to direct an assessment of the child and the parties by appointing a qualified person, such as a psychiatrist, to do this and to report to the court. The report is admissible as evidence. The "qualified person" may be required to testify at the hearing. If a party fails to attend the assessment as ordered, the court is entitled to draw a "negative inference," that is, to assume that the assessment would have been unfavourable to that party. The court usually follows the recommendations of an assessment report. Therefore, unless the report is seriously flawed, parties will usually settle the matter in accordance with its terms, and no trial will actually be needed.

Many professionals who conduct assessments are members of the Association of Family and Conciliation Counsellors. The AFCC Task Force on Child Custody Evaluation Model Standards posted the Draft Model Standards of Practice for Child Custody Evaluation for comment on the AFCC Web site during the summer and fall of 2005. More than 300 comments were submitted and, as a result, the Task Force made numerous changes. The current Draft Model Standards are now posted at http://www.afccnet.org/about/child_cust_tf.asp.

There are tough new enforcement provisions, including power to compel disclosure of information about the child. There is a specific power to order the police to assist in the enforcement of an order. And the entire Hague Convention *On the Civil Aspects of International Child Abduction* is included in the CLRA.

The Hague Convention may be applicable if a child has been wrongfully removed from Canada, to expedite the return of the child from the foreign country, or it may operate in Canada to send a child back to the home country. The Hague Convention is partly or fully in force in about 45 countries. Among the contracting states where it is fully in force are the United States, the United Kingdom, and most countries in Western Europe. Since the Convention operates between nations, a custody order granted by the court of a particular province may present an enforcement problem. For help on this point, get in touch with Justice Legal Services, Department of Foreign Affairs, 125 Sussex Drive, Ottawa, ON, K1A OG2, or telephone (613) 992-6302.

There is also a federal statute, the *Family Orders and Agreements Enforcement Assistance Act*, which may be helpful. Its two main purposes are the establishment of an agency to assist a custodial parent in tracing a child who has been abducted by the other parent, and to trace a payor spouse who is in breach of a support order. The agency, called the Federal Orders and Agreements Enforcement Unit, has access to information in some otherwise confidential data banks. You can refer to a booklet published by the Department of Justice, *Family Orders and Agreements Enforcement Service*, or contact Family Orders and Agreements Assistance Unit, Department of Justice, P.O. Box 2730, Postal Station "O," Ottawa, ON, KIP 5W7, or telephone 1-800-267-7777. See also Chapter 11, "Enforcement."

The "incidents of custody" mentioned earlier include matters of health, education, and welfare. This means that the court has the power, for example, on the application of a parent or any other interested party, to determine whether the child should go to a public or parochial school; whether summer vacations should be spent at a camp and which one; and, I suppose, whether a child should have cosmetic surgery to change the shape of his ears. Fortunately, this has not encouraged a flood of novel and intimate litigation.

There are other provisions for children's property and guardianship, and there is an important part that now permits testamentary custody and guardianship. Before the CLRA, you could say in your will whom you wanted to have custody after your death, but this wasn't binding on the child, the person appointed, or any court. Now the CLRA specifically permits appointing by will one or more persons to have custody of the child after the death of the appointer. For it to be valid, you must have the consent of the person appointed. Of course this doesn't prevent anyone else from claiming custody or guardianship as set out before, but I think it would be a strongly persuasive factor in the determination.

An unmarried parent who is a minor can't validly make a will, so a simple written appointment will be sufficient.

How to Apply for Custody

There are three ways to bring an application for custody before a court in Ontario. These procedures are essentially similar in each province.

1. *Children's Law Reform Act* (Ontario)

Under Part III of the CLRA, the court may order that either parent or any person may have custody of or access to a child. In every province there is a statute permitting such an application to be made, often in a provincial court or family court. Alternatively, a claim for custody or access can be combined with a claim for support or division of property, in Ontario under the *Family Law Act*, and in other provinces under whatever statute prevails for support and property rights. Note that any interested person, not just a parent, can apply for custody under the CLRA, but such a person may first require permission of the court.

2. Divorce Application
A claim for custody can be made by either parent as corollary relief in a divorce application or counter-application. The *Divorce Act* says that corollary relief can be awarded upon or after the granting of a divorce decree, but in a few cases the court has dismissed the divorce application and yet granted custody and maintenance for the children anyway, exercising its general jurisdiction over infants, or utilizing the statutory powers contained in equivalents of the CLRA. For procedure, see Chapter 8.

3. General Jurisdiction
An application for custody can be made by anyone, whether a parent or not, invoking the general jurisdiction of the Superior Court to make orders for the welfare of infants. Also, this application is specifically enabled by the CLRA and arises because of a power that the Superior Court acquired when given the same jurisdiction as the courts of England.

The procedure starts by issuing an application in the Superior Court claiming custody, and then following the formal steps to bring the suit on for hearing, just like any other lawsuit. A complete survey of this procedure would amount to a law-school course, and is too technical and various for the scope of this book. It rarely happens because the CLRA contains all the powers and procedures that any interested person might need.

The Guiding Principle in Custody Cases
If the welfare of the children is the paramount consideration governing an award of custody, then the practical statement of that principle must be this: "He who has custody, gets custody."

You won't find that in the law books, but it's true. You will find in the law books an expression of that principle where an award of interim custody is concerned. An application for interim custody arises in connection with a claim for interim support, or with an application for interim corollary relief in a divorce application, or at any time when the matter of custody can't be dealt with right away but must be deferred for some reason. That's where a lot of custody cases are determined, on the application for interim custody. Here's why.

She who has custody, gets custody: the leading case on interim custody says that in the absence of very cogent evidence to the contrary, the children should stay where they are, pending a final disposition of the custody claim.

Suppose, for example, that the mother leaves the father, taking the children with her. She starts a claim for custody under one of the procedures already outlined, for example, under the CLRA in the Superior Court or the equivalent statute in her home province. She arranges some sort of home for the children. Maybe it's not materially as good as the one before the parents split, but the children are decently fed, clothed, and aren't being neglected. Let's say her application for custody is opposed by the father and turned into a directed trial of a custody issue. The mother has the established rule governing award of interim custody going for her, so the judge rules that the mother should have interim custody of the children pending trial. Under *ideal* conditions it will take several months for this case to be heard and the final disposition of custody to be made, and it may take a lot longer. During this time, the mother has stabilized the situation for the children. They've adjusted. They're at a new school, with new friends. The mother has a job. Daycare arrangements appear satisfactory. The father has been paying interim support for the children and seeing them regularly.

Well, if you were the trial judge, what would you do? Why uproot the children now, after they've been through so much? Agreed, the mother isn't perfect; maybe the father could buy more for the children. But the kids are doing all right. Better the devil you know than the devil you don't know. Result: custody to the mother with access to the father; support of so much a month for the children payable by the father.

The mother had custody, and she got custody. There are exceptions, of course, but typically, in a case like this it was over when the mother was granted interim custody.

Kidnapping Is No Solution

If you think the way to solve the problem is to "kidnap" the children, you're absolutely wrong. The courts have consistently ruled against this kind of attempt at self-help. No judge wants to see the children shuffled from one hiding-place to another because of the competing claims of the parents.

Attempts at self-help sometimes reach extremes. Believing that the courts of a given province will not rule on the custody of a child unless the child is resident in that province, a parent will sometimes snatch the child and flee to another province (or country), in the hope that custody proceedings in the home province will be defeated. It's very unlikely to work. The court of the home province will usually rule that the child is ordinarily resident in that province, and take jurisdiction to make a custody order.

In one Ontario case, while the mother's claim for interim custody was pending, the father called his lawyer from the airport on a Saturday morning, saying that he had the child, and was just getting on a plane for Saskatchewan. It didn't help him. The court subsequently ruled that he couldn't defeat the court's power to make a custody order by running away, and granted custody to the mother.

In another decision—and there are many cases like this—the ordinary residence of the children was in Ontario. The father had grabbed the children and taken them to northern British Columbia, where he left them in the care of the woman with whom he was living. The wife brought a claim for custody in Ontario. The judge ruled that since the children were ordinarily resident in Ontario, he had jurisdiction, and he awarded the mother custody of the children and ordered the father to return them.

If an applicant gets a custody order, but the children are not physically resident in the province where the order was granted, the applicant still has the problem of enforcing the order in another place. Generally, the courts of that other place will give "grave consideration" to the custody order. But they are not bound by it, unless the award of custody derives from the corollary relief provisions of the *Divorce Act*, because an order made under the *Divorce Act* has legal effect throughout Canada.

Please note also the provisions of the *Family Responsibility and Support Arrears Enforcement Act* (Ontario) (see Chapter 11, "Enforcement").

A distinction should be made between these "kidnap" cases and a situation where a previous custody order has been largely disregarded by the parents by agreement. In the latter case, the court must rule on the effect of a custody order that was made in another jurisdiction, but that is now perhaps obsolete because of changed circumstances. The court will certainly give consideration to that order, but will in no way be bound by it.

No matter how earnest and well-meant the motivation, a parent who "kidnaps" a child will rarely receive judicial sympathy when the case eventually comes before a court. Also, a parent who deprives another of lawful custody can be charged with the very serious criminal offence of abduction.

Review of Custody Orders

No custody order is ever final. Any custody order is open to review, simply because the welfare of the children may from time to time demand that another order be made. Parents can certainly agree on custody, as they often do in separation agreements, but no such agreement is strictly binding on a court.

Guiding Sub-principles

There are other sub-principles that guide the court in awarding custody:

- When other things between the parents are equal, it is presumed that children of "tender years" need the care of the mother more than that of the father. This applies up to the age of five, approximately. Beyond this age, custody of sons might more likely be given to the father, and custody of daughters to the mother, if there is no other basis for making a choice.
- The court will lean away from separating siblings.
- The court will consider the wishes of older children as to which parent should have custody. A judge would probably listen to a child of ten, certainly to a teenage child. As a practical matter, custody fights rarely occur over older children anyway. What are you going to do if a fourteen-year-old simply doesn't want to live with you? That's why the wishes of an older child might as well be considered because an order made contrary to his wishes is likely to be ignored by the child himself, or else enforced by compulsion, creating increased misery. The real knock-down, drag-out custody fights take place over younger children for just this reason: custody of a six-year-old can be enforced no matter what the child wants.
- Natural parents of a child can only lose custody against the claims of other interested parties by abandoning the child, or

so misconducting themselves that in the opinion of the court it would be improper for the child to remain with them. This will depend entirely on the facts of the individual case.

Lawyers have often observed that there's no more bitter and difficult case than hard-fought custody trial. Partly that's because of the incalculably high stakes. But partly it results from the belief that one way to bolster your case is to make the other parent look as destructive and incompetent as possible.

Fortunately, in Ontario (and similarly in other provinces) the *Children's Law Reform Act* states specifically that the conduct of the parents between themselves is irrelevant unless it bears directly upon the welfare of the child.

Custody by Agreement

Relatively few custody disputes get to trial. Most are settled by agreement because, having regard to the principles that motivate the court, the result is highly predictable. If, for example, the mother has had interim custody of the children for a year while the trial was pending, the father has little hope of winning permanent custody at trial. Why waste the time, money, and emotional energy in a trial?

Unless the father is so stubborn or self-righteous that he doesn't care what it costs him (not only financially but psychologically), he'd be better off to forget about custody, and concentrate on working out a sensible parenting arrangement. In order to avoid the pain and expense of a trial the mother may be willing to agree on far more generous access than a court would award. Also, if they settle, both parents can probably live with the deal, since it is of their own making, and their future relationship with each other and the children isn't poisoned by the traumatic memory of the trial.

Joint Custody

The idea of custody implies that one parent will have sole care and control of the child, and thus be responsible for all the decisions affecting the child's welfare. This is not always appropriate. It may be that such an order or agreement is simply unbearable for the non-custodial parent. In the case of older children (teenagers, for instance), sole custody may not reflect the true quality of the relationship with two devoted parents. In recent years, with increasing frequency, separation agreements express that the children will remain in the joint custody of the parents, thus giving both input into decisions concerning the children, but that the children will ordinarily *reside* with one parent.

Since joint custody implies agreement and co-operation between the parents, our courts have mostly ruled that joint custody should not be imposed on quarrelling parents; if they can agree on joint custody, that is just fine, and the court will likely go along with it. The court, however, will rarely order joint custody in the absence of an agreement by the parties themselves.

At trial, an Ontario case in 2005 actually imposed joint custody in a high-conflict case in the hope that this would compel the parents to co-operate. The judge ordered the parents to attend for parental counselling, and empowered the counsellor to decide if the parents could not agree on a parenting issue. The Court of Appeal held that while it may be desirable to appoint a parenting counsellor, the trial exceeded her jurisdiction because:

1. there was no evidence that the parties would agree whom to appoint;
2. there was no agreed process for appointing the counsellor if the parents could not themselves agree;
3. there was no evidence that the parties were willing to submit their disputes to a counsellor outside of the court process; and
4. the court cannot order the parties to engage in a process that forecloses their right to have recourse to the court.

Effect of Adultery

There is a common belief that a mother who commits adultery deprives herself of custody of the children. I'd like a nickel for every woman who has been terrified by a threat from her husband that he'll take the children away and she'll never see them again because she has been unfaithful. Even where the husband and wife have been separated for years, this threat still arises. It simply isn't true, but it once was, and the belief lingers today. Consider this statement, written in 1910:

> One of the saddest aspects in man-made divorce laws and which most deeply affects women, is the custody of children. The cruelest punishment of wrong-doing on the part of a woman is the deprivation of her children. According to law, a guilty mother is entirely deprived of

their custody, and even access which, however, is allowed to a faithless father. In no circumstances, if she is found guilty, can she have the custody of the children, however young one of them may be. It is opposed to every legal principle. She loses everything: income, custody and access to children, reputation, and even, in some cases, her husband's name.

The harshness of this rule may explain why divorces were often furiously contested in those years. The modern rule of law is that a mother who commits adultery is not disentitled to custody on that ground, and will be granted custody when to do so is in the best interests of the child. This applies even if the mother is living with another man. The welfare of the child governs. The courts no longer assume that an unfaithful wife is an unfit mother. For that matter, homosexuality, as such, is not a reason to refuse custody.

Visiting Rights (Access)

Access includes the right to visit the child and take the child away from the home under certain conditions. It's almost always granted. About the only way to bar a parent from access is to convince the court that physical, emotional, moral, or spiritual harm will result if that parent has access to the child. Obviously, that's hard to do. Often a custody case ends in an atmosphere of hostility and bitterness. If the mother is granted custody, she's likely to be terribly upset that the father has been granted access. But in many cases, whether for good or bad, the parent who loses custody just drifts off the scene after a few months, and seldom or never exercises the access he is entitled to.

Access can be undefined, so-called reasonable access, meaning, in effect, let the parents work it out themselves. As stated earlier, reasonable access depends on reasonable people. If the parents are on fairly good terms, the flexibility of reasonable access works just fine, and is to be preferred.

Naturally, in many cases the parents hate each other, and try to interfere with access so as to be as punitive as possible. Then "defined access" is indicated, the kind of order that specifies the precise days and times that the non-custodial parent may have the child. Sometimes access starts as reasonable, but that doesn't work out, and the parties have to go back to court to have access defined. Like a custody order, an access order is always open to review.

Sometimes the best interests of the children and parents are served by combining the two forms of access. For example, it might be agreed or ordered that a parent have reasonable access, but not less than alternate weekends and three weeks during the summer school vacation, plus other times as may be worked out.

Access has a practical base similar to custody. A six-year-old will go with the visiting parent whenever access is exercised, but a twelve-year-old often has her own time organized in a way that may not suit an access order. Well, what can you do? There's no effective way to compel an older child to submit to a visiting arrangement if she doesn't want to do it.

The reverse of that problem sometimes arises. There's no way you can compel a parent to take access, no matter how much the custodial parent and child may want it.

It's not easy to enforce an access order. Our courts have usually ruled that it's improper to withhold support payments in an attempt to gain access, just as it's improper to withhold access in an attempt to gain support payments. If the access is in accordance with a court order, about all you can do is try to cite the custodial parent for contempt of court, in wilfully disobeying the order. The penalty for contempt of court is usually a jail sentence, so the courts are reluctant to impose this. However, it has been held that persistent interference with or obstruction to access may place that parent's custody of the child in jeopardy, so in an extreme case the best remedy may be to apply for custody.

Because the law provides only drastic and unwieldy remedies, access problems are usually better resolved by referring the parties to mediation, assuming a vestige of goodwill remains.

A spouse who is entitled to access to a child is also entitled to get information about the health, education, and welfare of the child. A custody order can run for a definite or indefinite time or until the occurrence of a specified event. If the custodian intends to change the residence of the child, she must give thirty days' notice to anyone who is entitled to access. As to the underlying principles in a custody award, the *Divorce Act* says only that the court shall "take into consideration the best interests of the child of the marriage as determined by reference to the condition, means, needs and other circumstances of the child." Past conduct is irrelevant unless it relates to the ability of a person to act as a parent of that child. As to access, "the court shall give effect to the principle that a child of the marriage should have as much contact with each spouse as is consistent with the best interests of the child and, for that purpose, shall take into consideration the willingness of the person for whom custody is sought to facilitate such contact." This suggests strongly that if one parent persistently obstructs and interferes with the other's access, custody will be changed.

A particularly painful problem may arise when non-parent relatives of a child want access. Most frequently this involves grandparents, who are in conflict with one or both parents of the children. Although grandparents may offer unconditional love and resources, if they actually have to apply for access, whether against a custodial parent or both parents, it strongly suggests some underlying pathology, unilateral or bilateral, and is not likely going to be solved by either mediation or legal process and the imposition of an access order.

A grandmother was in conflict with both parents. She applied for access, and the trial judge granted it, although it had to be in the presence of the children's uncle, and it involved about a sixty-mile trip to the grandmother's home. The parents appealed that order. The following passages, which adumbrate access principles in general, are extracted from the judgment of the Court of Appeal:

> Although it may appear to be insensitive to the grandmother's needs for the parents to resist her efforts to decide how access is to be exercised, this case is not about the needs—or even the wishes—[of the grandmother]. It is about the needs and best interests of the children. The issue must be looked at from their, not the grandmother's perspective. The essence of the grandmother's submission is that, in general, it is in the best interests of children to maintain contact with members of their extended family. The test, however, is not what, in theory, is best for children in general, but what is in the best interests of the particular children before the court.
>
> In the particular circumstances of this case, the children are being forced to travel some distance on a regular basis to visit a grandparent with whom they do not, at the moment, have a positive relationship. It is difficult to see how this disruptive situation could be said to be in the best interests of the children. A relationship with a grandparent can—and ideally should—enhance the emotional well-being of a child. Loving and nurturing relationships with members of the extended family can be important for children. When those positive relationships are imperiled arbitrarily, as can happen, for example, in the reorganization of a family following the separation of the parents, the court may intervene to protect the continuation of the benefit of the relationship.

In this case, however, the issue is not about preserving a positive relationship, but about whether the disruption and stress generated by the grandmother's insistent attempts to get access on her own terms are in the children's best interests.

The trial judge acknowledged that the right of (the parents) "to independently raise their children should not be lightly interfered with," yet he defers that right to the speculative hope that continued imposed access to the grandmother will one day produce a positive relationship for these children.

This speculation, it seems to me, is an insufficient basis for overriding the parents' right to protect the children's interests and determine how their needs are best met. These are loving, devoted parents committed to their children's welfare. In the absence of any evidence that the parents are behaving in a way which demonstrates an inability to act in accordance with the best interests of their children, their right to make decisions and judgments on their children's behalf should be respected, including decisions about whom they see, how often, and under what circumstances they see them.

[The parents, not the grandmother] are responsible for the welfare of the children. They alone have this legal duty. [The grandmother] loves her grandchildren and, understandably, wants to maintain contact with them. Nonetheless, the right to decide the extent and nature of the contact is not hers, and neither she nor a court should be permitted to impose their perception of the children's best interests in circumstances such as these where the parents are so demonstrably attentive to the needs of their children. The parents have, for the moment, decided that those needs do not include lengthy, frequent visits with their grandmother. Although the parents' conflict with [the grandmother] is unfortunate, there is no evidence that this parental decision is currently detrimental to the children. It should therefore be respected by the court and the children's best interests left in the exclusive care of their parents.

The trial judge's articulated purpose was to create a close relationship between two children and a grandmother who loves them. There can be no criticism of this goal. But any duty to create such a relationship lies with the children's parents. The failure to do so does not warrant judicial intervention, especially in circumstances such as these where the immediate family is functioning well and the children's best interests are being assiduously nurtured by dedicated parents.

The appeal is allowed, the order of [the trial judge] is set aside, and the application for access is dismissed. This does not mean that the grandmother will be unable to have access; it means that the nature and frequency of the access will be at the discretion of the parents who, it is assumed, will make that determination based on the best interests of the children.

Adoption

Where the parents have divorced and the parent with custody remarries, adoption proceedings may arise. Let's say that the mother has custody after the divorce and remarriage, and her new husband wants to adopt the child. This may be done with the consent of the natural father, and may be done without his consent if he has in effect abandoned the child, for instance, by not paying support or visiting the child. In any event, the natural father must be consulted, and if the adopting parents seek to dispense with his consent, he must be given notice of the application to do so. Once the child is adopted, the natural parent has no further obligation to support the child. This may be the selling point in getting the required consent: if you let us adopt, you won't have to pay any more.

The legal effect of adoption varies somewhat from province to province.

Probably the idea in each province is to put the adopted child in *exactly* the same position as a natural and legitimate child of the parents. But the language of statutes and the ingenuity of lawyers being what they are, other interpretations have crept in. The problem usually arises in a fight over money: for example, if in a will the deceased left his estate "to my grandchildren," the question arises whether adopted children of his own children are included. From Ontario west to British Columbia, and in Nova Scotia, the statutes say that for all purposes an adopted child becomes upon adoption the child of the adopting parent, and the adopting parent becomes the parent of the child, as if the child had been born to that parent in lawful wedlock. The other provinces make it less clear. In Quebec the provision is that the adopted child becomes the legitimate child of the adopter and his consort, if the latter joined in the motion for adoption.

All provinces have procedures for amending the child's original birth certificate after adoption, so that the birth records show the adopting parents as if they were the natural parents, without any reference to the child's pre-adoption name.

Death of a Custodial Parent

A parent who has custody may wonder what would happen in the event of his or her death. Would the surviving parent have an absolute right to claim custody of the child?

In Ontario, the CLRA now permits testamentary custody and guardianship. You can appoint by will one or more persons to have custody of a child after your death. To make it valid, you must have the consent of the person appointed. But even this can't prevent anyone else from claiming custody or guardianship as set out above.

If there is no such statutory provision in your province, the answer is that the surviving parent would certainly have a considerable claim to custody, but no exclusive right. The court is always empowered to make whatever custody order best serves the welfare of the child. In cases of this sort, it is not at all unusual for another relative or a new spouse to gain custody instead of the surviving natural parent.

Mobility Rights

What are the rights and obligations when a custodial parent wants to relocate? This extremely difficult and controversial problem has been the subject of many decisions. This topic is treated at length because it has caused so much litigation, and the results, as we shall see are fact-driven and inconsistent.

The Ontario Court of Appeal had said in the 1990 decision of *Carter v. Brooks* that each case must be determined on its own facts and circumstances in accordance with the best interests of the child(ren). The 1995 case of *MacGyver v. Richards* is a philosophical exegesis of that doctrine by the Court of Appeal.

These are the facts in *MacGyver*. The parents had met in 1983 when they were students at Memorial University in Newfoundland. The father, MacGyver, left university to work in Ontario. The mother, Richards, soon followed. They eventually moved to North Bay, where these trial proceedings took place. In early 1989, when she was four months pregnant, Richards moved back to Newfoundland to live with her mother. The relationship with MacGyver had ended by then, largely as a result of his drug and alcohol addiction. The child, Vanessa, was born in Newfoundland in December 1989. Richards remained with Vanessa in Newfoundland until the child was seven months old. Her subsequent return to North Bay was prompted by a desire to give the relationship with the father another chance, in the hope of providing a "family" environment for the child. This time, however, his addiction was compounded by abusive behaviour toward the mother. They lived together for a total of only six months. In January 1991, the mother moved with Vanessa into Nipissing Transition House for two months, then into her own apartment. She started a claim for custody subject to supervised access, child support, and a restraining order.

On June 20, 1991, in accordance with a written settlement dated the previous day, a judge of the Ontario Court ordered that the mother be given custody of Vanessa and that the father be given access on alternate weekends, from noon on Saturday until noon on Sunday, in addition to two hours during the week. The mother abandoned her claims for child support, supervised access, and a restraining order. In March 1993, the father's access was expanded from twenty-four to forty-eight hours every other weekend.

Early in 1992, the mother had become involved with White, a Master Corporal with the Department of National Defence. In July 1993, White was transferred for four years to Tacoma, Washington. The couple made plans to marry in December 1993, with Vanessa and her mother then moving to Washington to form a new family unit.

In January 1993, the father had applied to vary the June 20, 1991, consent order from the mother's sole custody to joint custody. He sought to have Vanessa living with him from Wednesdays at 4:00 p.m. until Sundays at 4:00 p.m., to have an equal sharing of all holidays, and to prevent either parent being able to remove the child from the jurisdiction of Nipissing without the other parent's consent. The basis for the father's application was his assertion that he had changed his behaviour and was no longer abusive or alcoholic.

On December 7, 1993, after a two-day trial, the judge who had made all the previous orders in connection with the child ordered that the mother retain sole custody of Vanessa, who was by then almost four years old. The father was allowed to continue seeing his daughter for forty-eight hours every second weekend, but because of the mother's fears over the father's continued abusive and threatening behaviour, which occasionally resulted in calls to the police for assistance, the child was to be picked up from and delivered to the Supervised Access Centre.

The most contentious part of the judge's decision was an order that the child "shall reside in the City of North Bay until further Order of the Court." The mother successfully appealed to the Superior

Court. The resulting order, made on October 18, 1994, confirmed the mother's sole custody, stipulated that access to the father be as agreed between the parties, and deleted the requirement that the child remain in North Bay. The father appealed from that order to the Court of Appeal, seeking to have the order of the trial judge restored.

In the Court of Appeal, Madame Justice Abella dismissed the father's appeal. In the course of an extensive review of the facts and jurisprudence, she made a number of comments that will have broad application to future mobility problems:

> It is, in my view, a quantum leap from the observation that a child has a good relationship with a non-custodial parent to the conclusion that the preservation of this relationship is the determinative factor in deciding what is in the child's best interests. In a dispute over mobility, the certainty of a good relationship between the parent with access and the child is known. The decision to move, on the other hand, contains uncertainty. But this does not mean that it will not be best for the child. . . .
>
> Clearly, there is an inherent indeterminacy and elasticity to the "best interest" tests which makes it more useful as legal aspiration than as legal analysis. It can be no more than an informed opinion made at a moment in the life of a child about what seems likely to prove to be in that child's best interests. Deciding what is in a child's best interests means deciding what, objectively, appears most likely in the circumstances to be conducive to the kind of environment in which a particular child has the best opportunity for receiving the needed care and attention. . . .
>
> [T]he custodial parent must be understood as bearing a disproportionate amount of responsibility. The reality and constancy of that responsibility cannot be said to be the same as the responsibilities imposed on the parent who exercises access and sees the child intermittently. During those days or hours when parents without custody are not with their child, they are largely free to conduct their lives in any way they choose. The same cannot be said for parents with custody, most of whose decisions and choices are restricted by their role as the only adult legally responsible for the child. . . .
>
> We must also forcefully acknowledge that the custodial parent's best interests are inextricably tied to those of the child. The young child is almost totally dependent on that parent, not on the parent seen during visits. While it would always be preferable to attempt to find a solution which protects the child's relationship with both parents, this ideal is simply not always possible. It is practically inevitable, when two parents no longer live together, that the child's relationship with each will be different. This means that the child,

and each of its parents, must adjust to the new realities. The adjustments may be painful, including the adjustment of a parent seeing a child less often than anticipated. However painful, that parent's desires cannot be paramount. . . . [O]nce the parties themselves or a court decide that a particular person is primarily responsible for protecting a child and promoting the environment that best facilitates adjustments to change, that responsible parent should largely be free to carry on with parental decisions and duties. Unfortunately, this may affect the parent with access, but in the long run it may not affect the child.

And it is the child, after all, who is at the centre of the exercise. . . . When, therefore, a court has been asked to decide what is in a child's best interests, and a choice must be made between the responsible wishes and needs of the parent with custody and the parent with access, it seems to me manifestly unfair to treat these wishes and needs as being on an equal footing. When one adds to this the dimension that a court's decision ought to favour the possibility that the former partners can get on with their lives and their responsibilities, one reaches the admittedly difficult conclusion that a parent with custody, acting responsibly, should not be prevented from leaving a jurisdiction because the move would interfere with access by the other parent with the child, even if the relationship between the child and the access parent is a good one. . . .

This argues, it seems to me, for particular sensitivity and *a presumptive deference to the needs of the responsible custodial parent* who, in the final analysis, lives the reality, not the speculation, of decision dealing with the incidents of custody. The judicial perspective should acknowledge the overwhelmingly relentless nature of the custodial responsibility, and respect its day-to-day demands. . . . [emphasis added]

To conclude otherwise may render custody a unilaterally punitive order. No court could—or would—prevent a parent with access from moving anywhere or at any time he or she chose. Lee MacGyver could, for example, anytime he chose, and for whatever reason he chose, decide to leave North Bay for anywhere he chose, whether or not a court deemed the move "necessary." Whether or not the motivation was benign, and whether or not the loss of the visits was harmful to the child, it is inconceivable that a court would insist that the parent with access remain in the jurisdiction for the sake of the child's best interests. To do so would be an unwarranted intrusion into an entirely personal decision. . . . [emphasis added]

I have difficulty understanding why, then, courts should not feel equally constrained in interfering with the right of a custodial parent to decide where to live. In my view, it is not for a court to pass judgment on whether a move is "necessary" for the custodial parent, any more than it would be for a court to pass judgment on a similar decision by the parent with access. It is hard enough for members of a former family to adjust to separation without courts telling them where they should live. . . .

Custody and access represent symmetrical relationships with a child, but not identical ones. The trial judge erred in giving priority to the imperatives of the access relationship over those of the custodial one, by requiring the child, and therefore the mother, to remain in North Bay. There was no evidence that a move would impair the child's best interests, only that it would impair access. The two are not synonymous interests, and "access" must defer to "best interests" rather than the other way around. . . .

After *Carter v. Brooks* and prior to *MacGyver v. Richards*, one would have advised that it makes no difference whether the child is in sole or joint custody, and no matter what agreement or previous order is in effect. Each case is decided on its own facts at the time it comes before the court. Did *MacGyver* change all that? Or is *MacGyver* easily distinguished? For example, if a custodial parent has a presumptive mobility right, what is the right of each parent under a joint custody order or agreement, especially an agreement that provides for specific access? If a parent concedes sole custody, it appears that he or she is virtually conceding unfettered mobility. Won't this provoke and encourage more contested custody actions? Or will it cause the courts to reconsider the meaning of joint custody? Let us examine subsequent decisions.

In a case called *Gernat v. Gernat* the issue was whether the custodial mother should be permitted to change her daughter's residence from Thunder Bay, Ontario, to New Zealand. The father opposed the move and sought joint custody, but with the child's primary residence to remain with the mother in Thunder Bay. In reaching its decision, the court both listed the factors outlined in *Carter v. Brooks* and considered the Court of Appeal's decision in *MacGyver v. Richards*, noting in particular that

> The Court must weigh the benefits of being with the mother in New Zealand as against the benefits of being near the access parent. And then again, there is the matter of virtually compelling the mother to return to Thunder Bay by ordering that the child not be removed from the jurisdiction, in this scenario the child would have the benefit of both parents in the same area, but would this be in the best interests of the child if such a move would not be in the best interests of the custodial mother?

The court's conclusion was reached after examining a range of case-specific facts establishing, in its view, that the child's best interests would be met by remaining with her mother in New Zealand. The facts considered included

- the mother's role as the child's primary caregiver;
- the mother's bona fide motive for moving. In particular, the move was not viewed as a calculated effort to deny the father access;
- the presence of family support in New Zealand;
- potential for improved financial status in New Zealand;
- quality of life enhancements available in New Zealand, including a better home, child care provided by the maternal grandmother, and improvements to physical and emotional well-being;
- the availability in New Zealand of better employment opportunities in the mother's chosen field;
- the availability of alternatives to access (telephone and videotape contact); and,
- the mother's willingness to facilitate access.

In *Pfohl v. Long*, the court used *MacGyver* to remove mobility restrictions contained in an existing custody order, even though a move was not yet contemplated. The custodial mother had remarried and argued that her new husband could be required to relocate in the future. The trial judge accepted that *MacGyver* compelled courts to recognize that the legitimate mobility interests of a custodial parent were generally supportive of the child's best interests. The judge added to his own proviso, holding that custodial parents did not have licence to leave without making a reasonable and honest attempt at explaining the reason for the move to the access parent. Further, according to the trial judge, custodial parents are obliged to at least attempt to renegotiate an equitable variation of access, taking into account the distance and the expense involved in the continuation of access.

In *Dufour v. Dufour* the mother was granted custody subject to a provision in the divorce judgment that gave both parents equal authority, rights, and responsibility with respect to decisions bearing on the child's health, education, and religion. Mrs. Dufour remarried and, when she and her new husband lost their jobs in Regina, moved to Aurora, Ontario. The child's father sought a change in custody. In permitting the mother's move to Ontario, the Saskatchewan court made the following observations:

- while *MacGyver* does not operate to give custodial parents an absolute right to relocate, the court should defer to a custodial parent's decision unless it is clearly detrimental to the child's long-term well-being;
- the child's basic physical needs would be met in Ontario, although the material advantages he enjoyed in Regina were superior;
- employment was no longer available in Regina;
- the custodial mother was not attempting to restrict access;
- the child had spent his whole life with his mother. To reverse this situation would cause greater turmoil than a move to Ontario;
- with the custodial parent, the child is part of a two-parent family. It would be regressive to place him in a single-parent home.

Mobility in relation to interim custody has been considered in several decisions.

In *Charette v. Poisson*, it was held on a motion by the mother for interim custody that the best interests of the child would be served by giving her custody and allowing her to move to Pennsylvania to join her fiancé. The judge noted that the move offered the child an opportunity to live in a stable home environment, something the court was not convinced would result if the father was given custody. Further, the mother had indicated a willingness to facilitate the father's access. *MacGyver* and *Carter* were cited as "useful navigational aids," but the judge concluded that each case must be decided on its facts.

In *Kanellakos v. Kanellakos*, the judge who decided *Charette* released a parallel judgment, again granting the mother interim custody of the children and permitting her move to Michigan, where her mother and extended family lived. In reaching this conclusion, the court noted that

- the mother was the children's primary caregiver;
- there were employment opportunities and the prospect of financial and family support for her parenting;
- the children's grandmother and extended family resided in Michigan; and,
- her access proposal was reasonable.

In contrast, in *Filipe v. Filipe*, the British Columbia Supreme Court rejected the interim custodial mother's attempt to change the children's place of residence. The Court held that to establish a new residence in a new community would establish a *status quo* well in advance of a trial on the custody issue and would clearly skew *status quo* considerations toward the mother. There were no economic reasons to justify a move, nor had the mother offered to accept reduced child support to facilitate access in the face of significant travel costs. In particular the Court noted that, where custody is contested, one parent's agreement that the best interests of the children for an interim period would be best met by remaining with the *de facto* caregiver should not be treated by the Court as invoking all the broad policy considerations regarding mobility rights as set out in *MacGyver*.

In *Young v. MacDonald*, the Court examined mobility issues in the face of a separation agreement with joint custody provisions. In this case, the custodial father was given a lucrative promotion that required a two-year move to California. The father travelled to California prior to the move to assess its suitability for the children. He offered to provide financial assistance to underwrite the cost of the mother's access. The Court rejected the mother's motion to restrain the father from leaving the jurisdiction, noting that "mobility is a fact of modern day life." The Court approved the approach taken in *MacGyver*, stating that

> In deciding what restrictions, if any, should be placed on a parent with custody, the court should be weary [sic] about interfering with the parents' capacity to decide, daily, what is best for the child. That is the very responsibility a custody order imposes on a parent, and it obliges—and entitles—the parent to exercise judgment which may range from the trivial to the dramatic. . . . Each of those significant judgments may affect the child in some way, but that does not mean that the court has the right to prevent the change.

Similarly, in *Luckhurst v. Luckhurst* the custodial mother applied to the court for an order that would allow her to move with her children and partner of five years from London to Cobourg, Ontario. Mrs. Luckhurst's partner had accepted a new position in Cobourg and she was offered employment in the area if she chose to follow him. The Luckhursts' separation agreement provided for joint custody but, at all times, the children's primary residence was with their mother, who was their primary caregiver. The court allowed the move, noting that it was "consonant with the approach of our Court of Appeal in *Carter v. Brooks* and *MacGyver v. Richards.*" The factors considered included

- the stability of the second family's home environment. The family had been together for five years in a relationship marked by "love and affection";
- the permanency of the custodial parent's new relationship;
- the motivation for the move, career advancement, and monetary reward, although not necessary, were "entirely reasonable when viewed in the overall best interests of [the] family"; and
- the distance between the cities and the ease with which access could still be exercised.

In *D.A.S. v. T.J.S.*, the parties entered a child-care agreement in which both parties were restricted from moving out of the Lower Mainland in British Columbia. In the application for divorce, the wife, who shared interim joint custody with her husband, sought an order for custody and permission to move to Trail, British Columbia. In granting custody to the mother and permitting her move, the court rejected an assessment report that recommended that she be permanently restricted from moving. The court was swayed by the wife's evidence that

- she would be able to find equivalent work;
- she would have the support of other extended family;
- reasonably priced housing was available;
- the size of the community was more conducive to raising small children; and
- the reasons for moving were sensible and considered and not motivated by malice.

The court also undertook a *MacGyver* analysis, balancing the obvious benefit to the children that arose from being in close proximity to their father against the benefit of being in the care of a custodial parent who is leading her life in a fashion she considers best for the children she must care for and best for herself.

In *Drayton v. Drayton* the parties entered into a separation agreement that provided for joint custody, with primary care and control remaining with the father. The agreement also contained a non-mobility provision requiring consent before the children could be removed from the jurisdiction. When the custodial father approached the children's mother regarding his plans to remarry and relocate, she agreed verbally. On this basis the father terminated his existing employment and accepted a new position in Michigan. The wife then withdrew her consent and obtained an *ex parte* (without notice) order prohibiting the removal of the children from the jurisdiction. In granting the father an interim order permitting his move to Michigan, the court considered the move in the context of *MacGyver* and was persuaded by

- the fact that the custodial father considered the move and took into account the needs and best interests of the children. The move was bona fide and reasonable;
- the father considered the children's educational, health, housing, and economic needs and made reasonable plans;
- the father considered the importance of the children maintaining a close relationship with their mother and was prepared to make concessions with respect to access.

In *K.A.M.F. v. L.G.F.* a separation agreement gave the parties joint custody, with the wife having primary care and control. Each party agreed not to remove the children from the jurisdiction nor to change their residence from Vancouver Island. In requiring the mother, as a condition of custody, to remain on Vancouver Island, the court considered

- the fact that she had, with the benefit of legal advice, entered into an agreement which contained a mobility and residency restriction. There was no change in circumstances relating to the children's best interests that would compel a court to vary the Order;
- after a very acrimonious marriage breakdown, including unsubstantiated allegations of sexual abuse of the children, the children were beginning to enjoy their visits with their father. The children's relationship with their father would be seriously jeopardized by a move;
- the move presented no particular advantage to the children as

the sole reason for relocating appeared to have been to acquire a home;
- the children have extended family and friends in British Columbia;
- the wife was "duplicitous in failing to disclose her plans to move to Ontario" to the children's father; in so doing, the mother had put her own best interests ahead of those of the children and had not behaved as a "reasonable parent" as contemplated by Madam Justice Abella in *MacGyver*.

Problems in the co-existence of *Carter* and *MacGyver* are emphasized by the decision of the Ontario Court in *Harpur v. Belmore*. In *Harpur*, the parents had entered into a separation agreement, which provided for joint custody and gave the mother day-to-day care of the children. The agreement also required the mother to give notice of any proposed change in the children's residence and required the father's consent if a move out of province was contemplated. Following remarriage, the mother gave notice of her intention to move to British Columbia. A few days later the move was called off. She was advised by the father that, in the event the move was reactivated, a fresh notice would be required. In February 1995, without giving any notice, the mother and her new husband moved to British Columbia. The trial judge noted the decision in *MacGyver*, but applied the criteria from *Carter v. Brooks* in ordering the mother to return to Cornwall pending a trial of the issue. The custodial parent's actions were described by the court as a "perfect example of the respondent deciding what is best for her, with no consideration given to her legal obligations." In particular, the court was persuaded by

- the presence of a joint custody agreement. The judge felt that, if the custodial parent wanted the legal rights and privileges that arose from custody, including the mobility rights afforded by *MacGyver*, she should have brought a court application, alleged a change in circumstances, and requested custody of the children, as required by the parties' separation agreement;
- the mother's remarriage and the presence of a new family unit were considered by the court, but constituted "only one factor";
- the nature of the relationship between the children and the access parent;

- the reason for the move and the distance of the move. The court found that the economic rationale that seemingly compelled the move did not stand up, as the mother remained in the home and her new husband was employed in a position that would have been equally available in Cornwall;
- the financial resources of the access parent.

The Saskatchewan case of *Gordon v. Goertz* starts with a detailed and lengthy decision in February 1993, granting sole custody to the mother of a daughter born in November 1986. Apparently, in a subsequent proceeding, the father sought an injunction to restrain the mother from taking the child to live in Australia. The trial judge refused the injunction; this judgment is not reported at all. Then the father appealed to the Court of Appeal. In January 1995, the appeal was dismissed with brief reasons that do not speak to mobility criteria. The Court only says:

> We appreciate that access in such circumstances inevitably poses problems but the parties are in more fortunate financial circumstances than most litigants. Accordingly, they should be able to work out reasonable arrangements for the appellant to visit his child in Australia.

When *Gordon v. Goertz* was heard in the Supreme Court of Canada, the ruling said that *no previous order or agreement is effective to permit or refuse relocation. Instead, each case must be decided in accordance with the best interests of the child in accordance with the individual facts and evidence of the case.*

It follows that it is difficult to find consistency in fact-driven mobility (relocation) cases, although more, but by no means all, appellate decisions support a move by the primary caregiver.

Several decisions of the New Jersey Supreme Court have produced a set of guidelines in relocation cases, which, although not binding on Canadian courts, may be helpful. The court will consider these factors:

1. The reasons given for the move;
2. The reasons for the opposition;
3. The past history of dealings between the parties insofar as it bears upon the reasons for and opposition to the move;
4. Whether the child will receive educational, health, and leisure opportunities at least equal to what is available prior to the move;

5. Any special needs or talents of the child that require accommodation, and whether the accommodation or equivalent is available at the proposed new location;
6. Whether visitation and communication schedules can be developed that will allow the non-custodial parent to remain in a full and continuous relationship with the child;
7. The likelihood that the custodial parent will continue to foster the child's relationship with the other parent if the move is allowed;
8. The effect of the move on extended family relationships in the present and proposed locations;
9. If the child is old enough, his or her preference;
10. Whether the child is about to graduate from high school, in which event the child should not be moved without his or her consent;
11. Whether the non-custodial parent has the ability to relocate;
12. Any other factor bearing on the child's best interests.

The court then determines if the custodial parent's evidence has made out a *prima facie* case and, if so, the other parent has the burden of showing evidence to the contrary. A mere change or reduction in the non-custodial parent's access is one important consideration, but not an independent basis to deny relocation.

6

CHILD SUPPORT

The basic statutory provisions in Ontario governing child support are found in the *Family Law Act*, and similar legislation exists in every province. The Act states that every parent has an obligation, to the extent the parent is capable of doing so to provide support, in accordance with need, for his or her child who is unmarried and under eighteen years of age, but this obligation does not extend to a child at least sixteen years old who has withdrawn from parental control. A dependent child has a right to sue his parents for support.

The *Family Law Act* defines "child" to include a person whom a parent has demonstrated a settled intention to treat as a child of his or her family, but does not include a child placed in a foster home for financial consideration by the person who has lawful custody of the child. Therefore, to take one example, where a man marries a woman who has a child by a previous marriage or no marriage at all, the man may still have a support obligation for the child, even though there is no blood or adoptive relationship.

Also, under the *Criminal Code*, everyone is under a duty as a parent, foster parent, guardian, or head of a family to provide necessities of life for a child under the age of sixteen, with penalties ranging up to imprisonment for two years for failure to do so.

An order directing payment of support, or interim support, while legal proceedings are going on, can be made in several ways:

- In Ontario, under the *Family Law Act*, in the Superior Court, the Ontario Court, or the Unified Family Court, and in other provinces under similar legislation. Any such order can continue for an unmarried child so long as the child is engaged in a full-time program of education.
- In the Superior Court, exercising its inherent power to make orders for the benefit of infants, the court can order either parent to pay support on the application of any interested person. Support can continue to age eighteen.
- In the Superior Court, or the Unified Family Court, as corollary relief in the context of a divorce application, support can be ordered to continue to age sixteen, to an unspecified age if the child is dependent but able-bodied—a student, for example—and possibly to any age at all so long as the child remains dependent because of a disability.

It follows from the above that the rights and obligation of child support are the same whether the parents are married or unmarried.

Frequently a separation agreement provides that each child will be entitled to support up to age twenty-one (or even longer), provided that the child is living at home or is in full-time attendance at an educational institution, unless the child marries, which tracks statutory principles. Such an agreement is enforceable in accordance with its own terms. There are a number of decisions on child support after completion of an undergraduate degree, while a child is in post-graduate or professional education, but there is no consistency in the rulings.

The *Family Law Act* also makes children financially responsible for their parents in certain circumstances, in these words: "Every child who is not a minor has an obligation to provide support, in accordance with need, for his or her parent who has cared for and provided support for the child, to the extent that the child is capable of doing so."

Under section 59 of the *Family Law Act* if a man and a woman who are not spouses enter into an agreement for

(a) the payment of expenses of a child's prenatal care and birth;
(b) support of a child; or
(c) funeral expenses of the child or mother,

on the application of a party or a children's aid society to the Ontario Court or to the Unified Family Court, the court may incorporate the agreement into a support order. The court must be satisfied that the agreement is reasonable having regard to the child support guidelines (see below), as well as to any other provision relating to the support of the child in the agreement. A minor has capacity to enter into a paternity agreement. A paternity agreement is another type of domestic contract (see Chapter 10).

The *Child Support Guidelines*

In June 1995, the Supreme Court of Canada ruled constitutional the provisions of the *Income Tax Act* that made child support taxable to the recipient. The message from the Court was that if this were to be changed, it should be done by amending the *Income Tax Act*. In February 1996, the federal budget contained proposed changes to the *Income Tax Act* and the *Divorce Act*, which came into force on May 1, 1997.

The tax treatment of child support changed so that it is neither taxable to the recipient nor deductible to the payor.[1] The child support provisions of the *Divorce Act* changed so as to set up a schedule of presumptive payments under *Federal Child Support Guidelines* and to establish a complex set of regulations to administer that schedule. All of this is dealt with in more detail below.

These changes are specific to child support under the federal *Divorce Act*, and to child support under similar provisions of provincial statutes enacted after the federal *Guidelines* to conform to them.

The fundamental purpose of the *Guidelines* is to regularize child support awards and make the awards highly predictable. This should encourage settlement of child support, particularly in those cases where the payor's income is no more than $150,000 annually, which, of course, covers the vast majority of the population.

The *Divorce Act*, with all the latest amendments, and the *Guidelines* are reproduced at the end of the text. There is a schedule of *Guidelines* amounts for each province. For example, effective May 1, 2006, the table amount of child support for a Nova Scotia resident who earns $40,000 annually and has one child is $348 a month; for $60,000 and three children, it's $1,113 a month. For a Manitoba resident, the amounts are respectively $337 and $1,095. By way of

---

1. Periodic spousal support paid pursuant to an agreement or court order continues to be taxable for the recipent and deductible for the payor.

comparison, amounts under the tables in the 1997 *Guidelines* are for the Nova Scotia situation above $334 and $1,051, and for the Manitoba situation $328 and $1,023. All of the *Guidelines* tables for each province and territory can be obtained from the Federal Child Support Information Line at 1-888-373-2222 or connect to http://canada.justice.gc.ca on the Internet. There is a kit available from the Child Support *Guidelines* Implementation Project, 2nd floor, 720 Bay Street, Toronto, ON, M5G 2K1, or from Child Support Team, Department of Justice Canada, 239 Wellington Street, Ottawa, ON, K1A 0H8.

If You Have a Child Support Agreement or Court Order Made Prior to May 1, 1997

Any child support orders or agreements in force on May 1, 1997, continue to be in force in the same amount, and the amounts continue to be deductible from the payor's income and includable in the recipient's taxable income, until they are varied or terminated.

The provisions that made child support deductible for the payor and taxable for the recipient were, in their time, intended to create a tax "subsidy" by diverting income to the spouse with (presumably) the lesser income and thus the lower tax rate. Ideally, agreements and orders would gross up the child support to look after the tax at the lower rate. This would make more money directly available for child support.

Since any order or agreement in force on May 1, 1997, is "grand-fathered" (subject to later variation), it makes sense to continue any such arrangement that contains a tax benefit. It is an individual decision whether to do so or to apply for variation of an existing order or agreement after May 1, 1997. Good accounting or legal advice is strongly indicated.

The coming into force of the *Guidelines* is, in itself, a "material change in circumstances," sufficient to justify an application for variation of the amount of child support. Any agreement or order for child support that was in force on May 1, 1997, but is subsequently varied will automatically be subject to the new tax treatment.

The changes do not affect spousal support, which continues to be deductible by the payor and taxable to the recipient. There is some incentive after May 1, 1997, to create tax-efficient income splitting by an agreement that loads up the spousal support component and reduces the child support component. The tax rules before May 1,

1997, applied only to periodic child support, usually a weekly or monthly amount. Since child support is not deductible by the payor after May 1, 1997, the distinction between periodic support and lump-sum support disappears, and there is more incentive to agree on lump-sum or capital payment for child support. Under the former tax regime, the child support was taxable and deductible only if paid to a parent and not directly to the child. That distinction also disappears, so there is more incentive to make support payments directly to the child, for example, a child attending university.

Any deviation from the table amount of *Guidelines* child support should be in a carefully worded agreement that explains why the *Guidelines* amount is not being paid.

The Amount of Child Support under the *Guidelines*

The *Guidelines* are the result of years of contemplation, weighing, and sifting similar systems that are in force in many countries and states. The underlying philosophy or policy is that regardless of his or her own income, the recipient will spend a fairly predictable amount on the children. Therefore, subject to the important distinctions set out below, child support is fundamentally based on the income of the payor. The obligation of support will be, in most cases, the amount in the tables plus possible add-ons for child-care expenses, medical and dental costs and health-related expenses, extraordinary primary or secondary school expenses, post-secondary education expenses, and extraordinary expenses for extracurricular activities; see section 7 of the *Guidelines* in the statutes at the end of this text.

As previously stated, there is a slightly different table for each province. The applicable table is the one for the province in which the payor resides, or if the payor doesn't live in Canada, the province in which the recipient resides. The table is specific and virtually conclusive as a *minimum* amount where the payor's income is up to $150,000 annually. The amount of add-ons is determined as a proportion based on the respective incomes of the parents after deducting any contribution to those add-on expenses that the child contributes. For example, as of May 1, 2006, based on the tables, if the payor has an income of $70,000 annually, resides in Quebec, and has two children, the amount is $926 net monthly for both children, subject to possible add-ons. A child may be biological, adopted, or one with whom a person has a parental relationship.

For incomes over $150,000 there is a choice between a per-

CHAPTER 6: CHILD SUPPORT

centage increment or some other amount at the discretion of the judge. If the payor's income is $200,000, as of May 1, 2006, the base amount in Ontario for two children is $1,992 on the first $150,000 of income, plus either 1.16 percent per month of the other $50,000, for a total of $2,572, or something other as to the amount over the base (i.e., instead of a percentage of that "excess" $50,000, taking into account the recipient's ability to contribute and the means of the children themselves). Again, that is subject to add-ons determined as a proportion based on the respective incomes of the parents after deducting any contribution to those add-on expenses that the child contributes.

It's a bit different if the child is of the age of majority or over. In that case, child support is either the same as for a child under the age of majority or, if a judge thinks that is inappropriate, some other appropriate amount having regard to the means of the child and the ability of each parent to contribute to the support of the child.

The amount of child support in high-income cases has generated a lot of litigation right up to the Supreme Court of Canada. Many would think it absurd to award $17,000 a month in child support for a two-year-old child (an actual case), applying the tables to the father's annual income of about $2,500,000. Others would say that the father can afford it.

Section 4 of the *Guidelines* tells the court, in the case of annual income over $150,000, to award either the table amount, or if the court considers that to be inappropriate, award the table amount based on the first $150,000 and, as to the balance of the income, "the amount that the court considers appropriate, having regard to the condition, means, needs and other circumstances of the children who are entitled to support and the financial ability of each spouse to contribute to the support of the children" plus any add-on under section 7 of the *Guidelines*. In one case, "inappropriate" was held to mean "inadequate" so that the discretion of the court would only be to increase the table amount, but this interpretation was corrected in the Supreme Court of Canada; "inappropriate" means "unsuitable." While there is a presumption in favour of the table amount, section 4 gives discretion to increase or reduce it, for example, where the table amounts are so much in excess of the child's reasonable needs that the payments no longer qualify as child support. But the sheer size of the *Guidelines* amount does not *per se* make it inappropriate. Parliament did not choose to create a cap on child support awards.

Because the table amount is presumptively appropriate, the party who wants to depart from it must provide clear and compelling evidence that it is appropriate to do so in the particular case. The current trend seems to be in favour of a needs-driven award in an extreme high-income case, rather than a simple and reflexive use of the table amount.

A high amount of child support under the tables or in the court's discretion will likely affect the amount allocated to add-ons. Suppose the table amount of support in a given case is $5,000 a month for one child. Then there are, say, private school fees of $15,000 a year. The argument goes that from $5,000 a month (non-taxable), the custodial parent should easily be able to pay the school fees, or at least that the amount of add-on for school fees should be reduced.

In 2005, the Ontario Court of Appeal stated that in a case where children who attend a university or college program reside away from home for most of the year, the application of the *Guidelines* is inappropriate within the meaning of section 3(2)(b). It is more appropriate to calculate the actual costs of providing for the child in the other residence, factoring in a contribution to the cost of maintaining the family home for weekends and school breaks, and apportion the expense between the parents in accordance with income after considering the child's ability to contribute.

There have been many cases on the meaning and effect of some of the provisions of section 7 of the *Guidelines*. The court should take into account "the necessity of the expense in relation to the child's best interests and the reasonableness of the expense, having regard to the means of the spouses and those of the child and to the family's spending pattern prior to separation." One category of add-on is "extraordinary expenses for extracurricular activities."

The interpretation of "extraordinary" has taken two branches in the decided cases. There is the "subjective test," adopted in Alberta, B.C., Ontario, P.E.I., and Saskatchewan, which says that what is extraordinary depends on the income of the family. One case says that "extraordinary" means activities that are disproportionately expensive in relation to the payor's income, and thus not part of the recreation component that is built into the table amount. Another statement is that the relevant question is what expenditures would be expected to be absorbed by the custodial spouse's total income (including table child support); anything over that would be extraordinary. What may be an extraordinary expense for a family with total income of $25,000 may be routine for a family with income of $100,000.

The "objective test," adopted in Manitoba and Nova Scotia, says that income of the parties is irrelevant. The court should look at the nature of the activities and the nature of the expenses. Another case says that if the expense is unusual or exceptional according to an objective standard, then one considers the incomes of the parties to determine whether the expense is reasonable and in accord with the spending patterns of the parties prior to separation.

Ordinary extracurricular expenses are deemed to be included in the table amount. A custodial parent does not have a licence to enroll children in expensive activities and then demand an automatic contribution from the other parent. To qualify as an add-on, the extracurricular activity must meet the threshold test of necessity and reasonableness, and unusual cost.

Effective May 1, 2006, section 7 of the *Guidelines* will have a new explanatory provision:

"extraordinary expenses" means

(a) expenses that exceed those that the spouse requesting an amount for the extraordinary expenses can reasonably cover, taking into account that spouse's income and the amount that the spouse would receive under the applicable table or, where the court has determined that the table amount is inappropriate, the amount that the court has otherwise determined is appropriate; or

(b) where paragraph (a) is not applicable, expenses that the court considers are extraordinary taking into account

(i) the amount of the expense in relation to the income of the spouse requesting the amount, including the amount that the spouse would receive under the applicable table or, where the court has determined that the table amount is inappropriate, the amount that the court has otherwise determined is appropriate,

(ii) the nature and number of the educational programs and extra-curricular activities,

(iii) any special needs and talents of the child or children,

(iv) the overall cost of the programs and activities, and

(v) any other similar factor that the court considers relevant.

Obviously, these cases are individually fact-driven. Some examples of expenses held to be *not* extraordinary in a given case are summer and day camp; swimming lessons; YMCA membership; the cost of birthday parties; soccer; hockey; field hockey; basketball; martial arts; holidays: horseback riding lessons; and child care to enable the custodial parent to have a holiday.

In other cases, expenses have been held to be extraordinary, but were not allowed: horseback riding; dancing and swimming lessons and ski club; baseball travel expenses; and "respite" for mother and child. Examples of expenses that were extraordinary and were allowed include private school tuition; private school tuition for a learning-disabled child; figure skating lessons; hockey, baseball, and music lessons and modelling for three children; riding lessons; field trips, sporting activities and music lessons beyond the school's curriculum; gymnastics; bowling; art; and Cub Scouts.

Remember the definition of "child of the marriage" in subsection 2(1) of the *Divorce Act*. It includes a child under the age of majority, or over that age if the child is under the parents' charge, "but unable, by reason of illness, disability, or other cause, to withdraw from their charge or obtain the necessaries of life." Other cause includes pursuit of education. This is a strong message that child support does not simply stop at age twenty-one or even on completion of an undergraduate degree in an appropriate case.

But how do you determine the income of either the payor or the recipient? One simple solution is that income is whatever the parties themselves agree on, in writing, although this may have to pass the test of reasonableness in the view of a judge. Otherwise, the starting point is "total income," as shown on Line 150 in the bottom right-hand corner of the first page of the T1 General income tax return. This amount is adjusted in accordance with subsection 12(2) and Schedule III to the *Guidelines*. Some of these adjustments—for example, those in section 1 of Schedule III—will not have broad application. Some of the other adjustments will be commonly applied.

The "total income" includes income (or losses) from all sources, and dividend income and capital gains. Since we have to declare more dividends than we actually receive, and we declare less capital gains than we actually receive, the total income figure is adjusted to reflect actual amounts. Then we deduct interest and carrying charges as shown on the second page of the tax return and actual business losses. We deduct child support (that would have to be "grandfathered" child support) that is included in the income of the recipient. We deduct spousal support payments only from the recipient's income in any determination of a table amount of child support. We deduct spousal support payments from the payor's income only for the purpose of calculating the proper amount of add-ons to the table amount of child support. There are other Schedule III adjustments that may apply to self-employment income, capital cost allowance, partnership income, and stock options. Of course, none of these adjustments affects the determination of income tax liability.

As set out in sections 15, 16, and 17 of the *Guidelines* regulations, a judge has a broad power to determine what income really is for these purposes, to deal with situations where income may not be fairly expressed, as could happen where the payor is self-employed, or underemployed, or has non-recurring income or expenses, or has capital that is not working reasonably efficiently to produce income, among other reasons.

Split Custody

If each parent has custody of one or more of the children of the marriage, the child support order will be the difference between the amount each parent would pay to the other, as provided in section 8 of the *Guidelines*. This applies both to the table amount and the add-ons.

Shared Custody

Under section 9 of the *Guidelines*, where a spouse exercises a right of access to, or has physical custody of, a child for not less than 40 percent of the time over the course of a year, the amount of the child support order must be determined by taking into account:

(a) the amounts set out in the applicable tables for each of the spouses;

(b) the increased costs of shared custody arrangements; and

(c) the conditions, means, needs, and other circumstances of each spouse and of any child for whom support is sought.

In practical terms, how much access or physical custody is 40 percent? Over the course of a year, that would be not less than 146 days. That could be forty-two weekends from Friday evening to Sunday evening (eighty-four days), forty-two mid-week overnights, each counting as half a day (twenty-one days), four weeks during the summer vacation (twenty-eight days), and half of the Christmas and spring vacations (fourteen days), for a total of 147 days. There have been a number of cases that wrestled with the calculation of that 40 percent. In a 2005 Ontario decision called *Froom*, the two judges ruled one way and the other dissented. The majority said it was correct to count days, not hours; the dissenting judge said that counting hours produces the more accurate result.

If the court makes such an order, when can it be varied? Suppose that one month after the order, the access arrangements change. It appears that one would have to wait for a full year of experience to determine whether section 9 applies. Suppose one has a right of access that is frustrated or obstructed by the other spouse, or the children refuse to co-operate. In many cases, by the time the application to vary is heard, the facts will have changed again.

The "increased costs" idea is that one parent may have greater ability to provide the facilities that the child or children need. Of course, this may simply be a reflection of greater income, which is already taken into account in the *Guidelines* tables, but it could be something else. Suppose the mother remarries and her new husband provides a large home, while the father is in a one-bedroom apartment. Does the mother then have greater financial ability? But suppose she is unemployed in her new marriage. Does she then have any financial ability at all?

The Supreme Court of Canada had to deal with this in a 2005 decision called *Contino*. By the time it got to the S.C.C., three other court levels had come up with three different results. The S.C.C. declined to provide a formula such as the simple set-off that arises from split custody. Instead, the Court said that the correct amount will depend on the evidence in each case as to increased costs, condition, and means as set out in section 4, and that the parties should be prepared to present detailed evidence. There is an element of absurdity in this when one considers the costs of the process. In *Contino* the three awards were $100, $688, and $399 monthly before our highest court determined that $500 was the appropriate amount. The Justice Department has recommended the enactment of regulations that would create predictability, so that, as one lawyer told the S.C.C., "we wouldn't have the rather bizarre situation in which three different courts came to widely varying views on the application of [section 4], all in an attempt to apply and promote predictability."

Undue Hardship

Under section 10 of the *Guidelines*, a court may make an order for child support in a different amount altogether if otherwise a parent or child would suffer "undue hardship." Obviously, this application will arise much more often in a claim for a reduction rather than an increase.

The circumstances that may cause a parent or child to suffer undue hardship are set out in section 10(2):

- responsibility for an unusually high level of debts reasonably incurred to support the spouse and their children prior to the marriage breakdown or to earn a living (before or after marriage breakdown);
- a legal duty under a judgment, order, or written separation agreement to support any person, e.g., a former spouse, children of a previous marriage, children born out of wedlock, or, possibly, a dependent parent;
- a legal duty to support any person who is unable to obtain the necessaries of life due to a disability or illness, without reference to a judgment, order, or written separation agreement, e.g., a disabled child, or disabled (present) spouse, or an infirm parent.

But the undue hardship application must be denied if the household of the spouse who claims undue hardship would, after child support is determined as if no such claim were made, have a higher standard of living than the household of the other spouse. The standard of living test is a lengthy formula set out in Schedule II to the *Guidelines*. A glance at Schedule II will convince you that this is a very complex process, well suited to computerized determination. The necessary software has been developed. Anyone who believes he or she has an undue hardship claim can probably get a reasonably quick and inexpensive assessment from any lawyer or accountant who has the software, so ask about this before you arrange consultation.

Disclosure Requirements on Application

Where you are applying for an original order or a variation, your obligation of disclosure is set out in section 20 of the *Guidelines*.

It includes:

- a copy of every personal income tax return and notice of assessment or re-assessment for the three most recent taxation years;
- if you are an employee, the most recent statement of earnings including the earnings year-to-date, or a letter from your employer setting out that information including your rate of annual salary and remuneration;
- if you are self-employed, for the three most recent taxation years, financial statements from your business or professional practice, and further statements showing a breakdown of all salaries, wages, management fees, or other payments paid to, or on behalf of, persons or corporations with whom you do not deal at arm's length;
- if you are a partner in a partnership, confirmation of your income and draw from, and capital in, the partnership for the partnership's three most recent taxation years;
- if you control a corporation, for the three most recent taxation years, financial statements of the corporation and its subsidiaries, and a statement showing a breakdown of all salaries, wages, management fees, or other payments paid to, or on behalf of persons with whom the corporation, and every related corporation, does not deal at arm's length;
- if you are a beneficiary under a trust, a copy of the most recent trust agreement and copies of the trust's three most recent financial statements.

If you are served with an application for, or variation of, child support, and your income information is necessary to determine the amount, you have the same disclosure obligation as an applicant. You must supply these documents within thirty days after the application is served on you if you live in Canada or the United States, or sixty days if you reside elsewhere.

In every case where one party claims the add-on expenses, pleads undue hardship, or has annual income over $150,000, the disclosure documents must be provided to the other party. The disclosure obligation does not specifically extend to other members of your household, although some information about other members might be revealed within the documents set out above.

If one party fails to comply with the disclosure requirements, the other may ask for determination of child support without disclosure, at a hearing or on a motion made to a judge, or may ask for an order compelling disclosure. A support order made in default of disclosure must include costs that fully compensate the applicant for legal fees and disbursements incurred in the application. At a hearing or on a motion in default of disclosure, the judge may draw "an adverse inference" against the defaulter, and impute income in whatever amount appears to be appropriate.

Annual Disclosure Requirements

Under section 25 of the *Guidelines*, every spouse against whom a child support order has been made must, at the written request of the other spouse or by anyone (such as welfare authorities) to whom the order has been assigned, make annual disclosure of the same documents that are required on an application (see above), within the same time limits, and with the same consequences for non-disclosure. This disclosure must also be made if the responding spouse is not now subject to a child support order because his or her income is below the minimum amount required for application of the tables. If the child support order includes the add-ons or was modified because of the undue hardship provisions, the disclosure extends as well to current expenses incurred for the child.

This annual disclosure on request is mandatory. Section 25(8) of the *Guidelines* says that a provision in a judgment, order, or agreement purporting to limit a spouse's obligation to provide the disclosure is unenforceable.

Form of Payments and Security

The tables express monthly amounts of support, but a court does not have to order support in that form. Under section 11 of the *Guidelines*, the order may be in periodic payments, probably monthly but possibly weekly or any other period, or in a lump sum or in a combination of lump-sum and periodic payments. A lump-sum order will not be the norm, but may be appropriate where the payor has a history of default or where the payor has a lot of capital but relatively little income. The court may also impose security for the payment. This is not defined or restricted in the *Guidelines*, but could take the form of insurance, a deposit of capital into a trust account, a mortgage or real estate, a lien on an investment or RRSP account, or anything else that the situation may dictate.

Any court order or agreement should specify how much is

child support and how much is spousal support. If the order or agreement, made before May 1, 1997, just sets out a blended amount of child support and spousal support, an order made on a variation application will rescind the previous arrangement and impose separate amounts for each. Under section 15.3 of the *Divorce Act*, child support has priority, and if the court is unable to order spousal support because of the imposition of child support, the reasons for doing so must be recorded. However, when child support is reduced or terminated, that will be a material change in circumstances entitling a spouse to revive the claim for spousal support. Also, the breakdown is needed for accurate tax calculation, since only the spousal support portion will be taxable/deductible.

Can You Make an Agreement for Child Support That Is Not in Accordance with the *Guidelines*?

When periodic support paid to a parent was taxable/deductible, agreements rarely provided for lump-sum support. Now that child support is neither taxable nor deductible, there may be more incentive for arrangements that provide for lump-sum support, or support payable directly to the children, as one can imagine to satisfy the obligation of a child engaged in post-secondary education.

What is the effect of such an agreement or any agreement that provides for child support that is different from the entitlement under the *Guidelines*?

Clearly, the policy of the legislation does not favour such agreements. Section 15(5) of the *Divorce Act* says:

> a court may award an amount that is different from the amount that would be determined in accordance with the applicable *Guidelines* if the court is satisfied
>
> (a) that *special* provisions in an order, a judgment or a written agreement respecting the financial obligations of the spouses or the division or transfer of their property, *directly or indirectly benefit a child*, or that special provisions have otherwise been made for the benefit of the child; *and*
>
> (b) that the application of the applicable *Guidelines* would result in an amount of child support that is inequitable given those *special* provisions. [emphasis added]

In that event, the court must record the reasons for departing from the *Guidelines* amount. Even so, the court would still be open to a variation application, discussed below, and the mandatory annual disclosure requirements would still be in effect.

Variation of Child Support

Exactly the same principles of disclosure as on an original application will apply if a spouse (or former spouse) applies to vary a previous agreement or order for child support. All of the same principles will apply in the new determination of the amount of child support, including the add-ons. Note the annual disclosure requirements set out above, which should lead to negotiated variations without court intervention in most cases. In those cases where parties come to an agreement, they should express that they are doing so in accordance with the *Guidelines*, and that they are both satisfied that the terms carry out the objectives of the *Guidelines*.

Again, note that every agreement or order for child support made before May 1, 1997, is exposed to variation to bring it into accordance with the Guidelines.

The Problem of Retroactive Child Support

At date of writing there is a stark conflict between the approaches to retroactive child support taken by the appeal courts of Alberta and Ontario. The matter will be heard and resolved in due course by the Supreme Court of Canada.

Three 2005 decisions in the Alberta Court of Appeal ("the Alberta trilogy") hold that in determining the issue of retroactive child support, courts should start with the premise that a payor who does not pay the proper amount of child support should be ordered to do so retroactively unless he or she can show why such an order would be unfair and unreasonable in the circumstances. The date the obligation arose should be the presumptive starting date for commencement of the retroactive order. One can easily find out what the correct amount should be. Any requirement that the recipient must give notice as a prerequisite for a retroactive order shifts the responsibility to the parent who is without information and often with less resources, and delays fulfilment of a parent's obligation to the child.

The Alberta court set out these considerations as relevant in the exercise of discretion to award retroactive child support:

1. A child is entitled to child support. Need is presumed.
2. The *Guidelines* presume an ability to pay on the part of the payor in accordance with his or her income.
3. Blameworthy conduct on the part of the payor is not a factor. The recipient does not have to show an encroachment on capital or incurring of debt.
4. Notice of an intention to pursue child support is not a prerequisite to a retroactive award.
5. One should not assume that an unreasonable burden is placed on the payor by a retroactive award. Any such burden must be balanced against the corresponding deprivation to the recipient and the child.
6. A lump-sum payment is not precluded because it "redistributes capital."
7. The date of the payor's increased income is the presumptive date for commencement of the retroactive award unless the payor has satisfied the additional financial obligation in some other manner, has taken all reasonable steps to fulfill the obligation, had a previous arrangement for child support that contemplates the provisions of the *Guidelines*, or the payee fails to act diligently without reasonable excuse.
8. The child need not be a "child of the marriage" at the time the retroactive order is made. The recipient is still entitled to reimbursement for having carried a heavier burden when the child was a "child of the marriage." The retroactive support may go directly to the child.
9. Retroactive awards may be made at trial or at interim or variation proceedings.

In Ontario, three decisions in the Court of Appeal affirm that there is no presumption in favour of awarding child support retroactive to some date prior to the commencement of the application, and that the jurisdiction to award retroactive child support should be sparingly exercised. In the latest of these cases, *Park v. Thompson*, the Court of Appeal reiterated the factors to be considered on an application for retroactive child support:

1. Need on the part of the child and a corresponding ability to pay on the part of the non-custodial parent;

2. Some blameworthy conduct on the part of the non-custodial, such as incomplete or misleading financial information;
3. Need on the part of the custodial parent to encroach on capital or incur debt;
4. Any excuse for delay in bringing the application; and
5. Notice to the payor parent of an intention to pursue support.

The factors that would mitigate against retroactive support are:

1. The order would cause an unreasonable or unfair burden to the non-custodial parent, especially to the extent that such a burden would interfere with ongoing support obligations; and
2. A significant, unexplained delay in bringing the application.

7

PROPERTY RIGHTS

Property rights differ significantly from province to province. As previously stated, no proprietary rights are created by marriage, in the sense that no spouse becomes the owner of the other's property in whole or part just because of marriage. Depending on the laws of the province in which you reside, and subject to the personal arrangement you may have made in a domestic contract (see Chapter 10), marriage does create a statutory right to share in the value of property acquired during the marriage, and a right of possession (not ownership) of the matrimonial home. In Ontario, property rights are codified in the *Family Law Act*. A brief summary of property rights in all provinces is in Appendix B.

The 1986 Ontario *Family Law Act* (FLA) created a new property regime in the province. It replaced the *Family Law Reform Act* (FLRA), itself a radical statute that was in force for only eight years. The FLA also deals with spousal and child support rights and obligations, and possession, sale, and mortgaging of a matrimonial home. This chapter deals only with property rights. It should not be used as a substitute for proper legal advice: as complex as it may appear, it is only an overview.

Equalization of Net Family Property (Part I, *Family Law Act*, Ontario)

Retroactivity
The FLA is retroactive in several aspects:
  (a) It covers every case that was not settled or adjudicated as of June 4, 1985, the date when the FLA was introduced in the legislature.
  (b) It applies to property owned by spouses regardless of the date of the marriage and whether the property was acquired before or after the FLA came into force.

Limitations
There are limitation periods that *may* be extended by the court for claiming a share of the value of matrimonial property:

  (a) two years after the day the marriage is terminated by divorce or judgment of nullity;
  (b) six years after the day that spouses separate and there is no reasonable prospect they will resume cohabitation; or
  (c) six months after the death of the first spouse to die.

The Basic Idea
The basic idea is that "net family property" (NFP) should be equalized between the spouses on breakdown of marriage, unless an equal division would be unconscionable in the view of a judge. Virtually the same provisions apply on the death of one spouse.

The spouses may enter into a "domestic contract" that alters this regime to suit themselves. A valid domestic contract made before the FLA is valid as to rights under the FLA, with the necessary changes in terminology (see Chapter 10, "Domestic Contracts").

The FLA does *not* create proprietary rights as such, nor does any proprietary right or lien on property arise simply because of marriage. Except as to a matrimonial home, and except where there is fear of an improvident depletion of a spouse's property, prior to breakdown of marriage, a spouse as owner of property may freely deal with it in any way he or she chooses. You don't own one-half or any other share of your spouse's property just because you are married.

Nor does the FLA create a proprietary right in a matrimonial home. The right is *possessory* under the FLA, Part II. This means that one spouse cannot dispose of or encumber a matrimonial home without the consent of the other spouse, unless pursuant to a domestic contract or court order. This is emphasized in decisions of the Court of Appeal. In one case, the husband and wife owned the matrimonial home as joint tenants, with right of survivorship, meaning that if one died, the survivor would become the sole owner. Their relationship was hostile. The husband was terminally ill. With the intention to sever the joint tenancy and defeat his wife's right of survivorship, he signed and registered a deed transferring a half-share of the home from himself to himself! His idea was to create a "tenancy in common," another form of joint ownership that enables each owner to dispose of the property by will in any way he or she chooses. Of course he didn't leave his share of the home to his wife. The Court ruled this was permissible. The husband had done nothing to interfere with his wife's possessory right to the matrimonial home, and the transfer was held not to be a "disposition" within the meaning of the FLA. The Court of Appeal has ruled that the result is completely different if the transfer is from one spouse to a third party.

Definitions

The FLA introduced some new concepts and definitions:

"Property," as defined in the FLA, includes "any interest, present or future, vested or contingent, in real or personal property." It includes property held in trust for a spouse. It includes pension funds of all sorts, a pension in pay, and if the pension is vested, it includes the employer's contributions to the spouse's pension.

"Net family property" is something else. It is the value of all the property that each spouse individually owns on the "valuation date" (description to follow), after deducting

(a) the spouse's debts and other liabilities as of the valuation date; and

(b) the value of property, other than a matrimonial home, that a spouse owned on the date of the marriage, after deducting the spouse's debts and liabilities, calculated as of the date of the marriage.

Note the difference between bringing, say, money into the marriage as against bringing in a matrimonial home. The former is deductible from NFP, and the latter isn't. Note also that a matrimonial home—there may be more than one matrimonial home—is defined in the FLA as the place where the spouses ordinarily resided just before separation. So one spouse could bring in a home to the marriage; then if it is sold, the character of the asset changes (it is no longer a matrimonial home), and the value becomes deductible on breakdown of marriage.

Each spouse has his or her individual NFP. If an asset is jointly owned, such as a matrimonial home in joint tenancy, each spouse includes half the market value, and deducts half the mortgage.

"Valuation date" is the earliest of the following: the date of separation with no reasonable prospect of resumption of cohabitation, divorce, or annulment; or the date when one spouse commences an application to equalize NFP because of the improvident depletion of property by the other (dealt with below); or the date before the date when one of the spouses dies, leaving the other surviving (dealt with under "Estate Rights," below). There is a subjective element to this, since spouses may differ on their view of the prospect of reconciliation. There have been a number of cases dealing with this problem because a difference in the valuation date may have a profound effect on the value of NFP. The valuation date will probably be determined by the date that the spouses physically separate, and no amount of unilateral wishful thinking, as one case puts it, will create a reasonable prospect of reconciliation. Physical separation was also held to determine the valuation date even where the husband positively misled the wife into believing a reconciliation was possible.

There are other exclusions from NFP, as set out in the FLA. The value of the following property that a spouse owns on the valuation date does not form part of the spouse's NFP:

(a) Property other than a matrimonial home that was acquired by gift or inheritance from a third person after the date of the marriage. Note that if the matrimonial home is physically inherited, it is part of the NFP.

(b) Income from such an inheritance or gift, but only if the testator or donor has expressly stated that it is to be excluded from the recipient's NFP. Therefore, the capital enhancement or income on an inheritance or gift will often be included. Any new or revised will or trust agreement should consider this point; the testator or donor may well want to exclude income on the gift or inheritance from the recipient's NFP.

(c) Damages or a right to damages for personal injuries.

(d) Death benefits from a life insurance policy.

(e) Property other than a matrimonial home with which the above excluded property can be traced.

(f) Property that the spouses have agreed by domestic contract is not to be included in NFP.

The burden of proving the right to a deduction or exclusion lies on the spouse who claims it.

"Value" is undefined in the FLA and may be highly controversial. There are many concepts and views of value, and experts may disagree. It should be relatively easy to determine the value of a matrimonial home, since most experts will agree that one should apply "fair market value," typically within a narrow range. The problem of value is vastly more difficult in the case of, say, a minority interest in a private company. The minority interest may have no fair market value because there is no market, or because of a shareholders' agreement that restricts the transfer of shares. But the shares must have some value, perhaps liquidation value, perhaps "value to owner," or whatever.

The valuation of pensions has spawned a sub-industry for actuaries. Unfortunately, the decided cases suggest a number of what seem to be equally legitimate ways to determine pension values, with many variations depending on whether the pension is vested or not; locked in or not; with or without allowance for inflation; with or without a discount for the tax payable on the pension at some time in the future at some rate or other (estimated tax is usually deducted). Under a Supreme Court of Canada decision, the pension contributions are prorated over the term of the marriage, without an allowance for weighing the pension at the far end for likely greater contributions after marriage. All of this is variable depending on the retirement date, which may be normal retirement or some earlier date and determination of life expectancy. Then one must determine whether the equalizing payment for the pension should be paid up front, or as a portion of the payments if and when they start to flow. The possible range of variation in value of a pension is remarkable.

For instance, expert actuarial evidence has valued the pension of a senior Ontario civil servant from $44,000 to $155,000, depending on the relevance and weight of the factors set out above.

If you can resolve the value of a pension, there may still be a problem in the sharing of its value. A person who is employed in an industry governed by federal legislation, such as banking, interprovincial transportation, or a federal Crown corporation, has a pension under a federal statute, called the *Pension Benefits Standards Act* (military pensions are another matter). This Act permits sharing of the pension credits in the hands of the pension trustee. Sharing of pensions under provincial legislation is subject to different rules of appalling complexity, leading to the practical conclusion that provincial pensions should nearly always be paid out "up front" rather than on an "if and when" basis.

The leading case on dividing a federal pension on an "if and when" method applied a formula by awarding to the wife one-half of the amount calculated in this way:

> The number of months during
> which pension contributions
> were made during cohabitation
> _____ x pension benefit payable
> Total number of months
> during which pension contributions
> were or would be made

The phrase "debts and other obligations" (a deduction from NFP) is left undefined in the FLA. It includes contingent liabilities such as guarantees, which may never be called on. It includes unpaid taxes, but may or may not include the impact of taxes attracted if an asset were liquidated. It may or may not include realtor's commission on the sale of a home. It may or may not include the tax costs of collapsing an RRSP. There were two streams of judicial authority on the point.

One stream stated that in order to determine the value of NFP we must assume that all assets were liquidated as of the valuation date, and all taxes and costs of disposition paid in full. This approach would clearly benefit the major asset holder, who may have no intention whatever of liquidating the assets, but who gets credit as if he did. This approach has now been overruled in the Court of Appeal.

The leading judgment now says that we examine the situation on a case-by-case basis to determine what is fair and reasonable in the individual circumstances. We deduct for the impact of taxation and costs of disposition if the property in question must be (or is likely to be) liquidated in the reasonably near future, or in order to fund the equalization payment, but not if the impact of taxation and costs of disposition are "remote and speculative." We apply (or try to apply) a calculation of the present value of the future tax. So, if we assume that the future tax rate will be 40 percent, we may deduct 20–25 percent as the present value of the tax.

Even the fundamental idea of ownership had produced conflicting decisions, now resolved by the Supreme Court of Canada. The ruling is that the idea of ownership extends to a property interest that one spouse claims against the other. For instance, a matrimonial home may be registered in the name of only one spouse, but the other may claim that it's really owned jointly as a matter of law. This becomes important in the case of an asset that has substantially appreciated or depreciated since the valuation date. Please refer to the section "Trust Interests," below.

Whatever the deductions and exclusions may be, NFP cannot be a negative number. It will never be deemed less than zero.

Equalizing Payment
Once the NFP is determined for each of the spouses, the FLA says: "When a divorce is granted or a marriage is declared a nullity, or when the spouses are separated and there is no reasonable prospect that they will resume cohabitation, the spouse whose net family property is the lesser of the two net family properties is entitled to one-half the difference between them." The same applies when one spouse dies, as a right of election against the will or intestacy (see "Estate Rights," below). The same right of equalizing NFP also arises when legally married spouses are cohabiting, if there is serious danger that one spouse may improvidently deplete his or her NFP, as may occur where one spouse is mentally incapacitated or simply reckless. An application to equalize NFP commenced before the death of a spouse may be continued against the estate of a deceased spouse.

The entitlement to equalize NFP results in a payment obligation from one spouse to the other. *It does not mean that one spouse has specific rights to specific property.*

This can lead to some remarkable results. Let's suppose the husband comes into the marriage with $200,000 in cash, which he uses to buy a matrimonial home after the date of the marriage. Let's suppose that at the valuation date—the date of separation—the home is worth $250,000, and it's the only asset. The sharing depends on registration of title. If the home is in his name alone, his net family property is the value of the home ($250,000) minus the amount he brought in ($200,000), so he and the wife have $25,000 each as net family property, but the husband gets back the original $200,000. If title is in the wife's name alone, then her net family property is $250,000, and the husband's is negative $200,000, which is deemed to be zero. They split the proceeds of the home $125,000 each. But if the title is held jointly, each of them has a half-share worth $125,000. The husband can then deduct the amount of $200,000 that he brought to the marriage from his $125,000, so his net family property is negative $75,000, deemed to be zero. Because her share is $125,000 the wife has to pay him an equalizing payment of $62,500. So in the result, the $250,000 is divided $187,500 to the husband and $62,500 to the wife.

The FLA provides that a judge may set terms of payment over a period not exceeding ten years, usually with, but sometimes without, interest on the unpaid balance, and that every effort should be made to preserve an existing farm or business. Yet it is inescapable that in many cases assets will have to be sold to fund an equalizing payment. Where the NFP has considerable value but produces little cash flow—a family farm would be a good example—it is hard to imagine what else one could do. The powers of the court provide for such a sale, or specific transfer of property, or securing an award against property, or any combination of these to satisfy the equalizing payment. A judge may also order that the recipient is entitled to prejudgment interest on the equalizing payment, back to the date when it was first claimed and post-judgment interest until it is paid.

The court may award an amount that is more or less than half the NFP only if equal sharing would be unconscionable. This is a very high threshold, something that is shocking to the conscience of the court. It is clear that the fundamental legislative intent is equal sharing except in extraordinary circumstances. A number of factors are set out in the FLA, but the case law rightly does not define what facts would support such a conclusion. While each case will depend on its own facts, the factors are as follows:

(a) a spouse's failure to disclose to the other spouse debts or other liabilities existing at the date of the marriage;
(b) the fact that debts or other liabilities claimed in reduction of a spouse's net family property were incurred recklessly or in bad faith;
(c) the part of a spouse's net family property that consists of gifts made by the other spouse (since these gifts would ordinarily be part of the net family property);
(d) a spouse's intentional or reckless depletion of his or her net family property;
(e) the fact that the amount a spouse would otherwise receive is disproportionately large in relation to a period of cohabitation (which may be before actual marriage) that is less than five years (so that if cohabitation lasts more than five years, it's not a factor);
(f) a written agreement between the spouses that is not a domestic contract (because a valid domestic contract is itself conclusive as to those property rights it covers);
(g) any other circumstance relating to the acquisition, disposition, preservation, maintenance, or improvement of property.

Marital misconduct, such as adultery or cruelty, will not ordinarily affect the right to equalize NFP, nor does it matter which spouse leaves the other or why. But there is some room for consideration of another kind of personal conduct. The FLA states its purpose:

> to recognize that child care, household management and financial provision are the joint responsibilities of the spouses and that inherent in the marital relationship there is equal contribution, whether financial or otherwise, by the spouse to the assumption of these responsibilities, entitling each spouse to the equalization of the net family properties, subject only to the [unconscionable] considerations. . .

This raises the question of the effect of a failure to make a contribution by child care, household management, and financial provision. Our courts are extremely reluctant to weigh the relative contributions of the spouses, but in an extraordinary case, where one spouse makes virtually no contribution at all, a judge may rule that he or she has no entitlement to share in the value of the other's property. The starting point is a New Brunswick case that went to the Supreme Court of Canada. Although property rights in New Brunswick are different under its statute than those under the FLA, a recent judgment of the Ontario court has ruled that this principle applies as well in Ontario.

Statement of NFP: Concepts of Value

In a very simplified form, the statements of NFP might look like this:

		Husband	Wife
___	Jointly owned matrimonial home; half-share	$200,000	$200,000
___	Contents of home	40,000	40,000
___	Automobiles	15,000	15,000
___	Cash on deposit	50,000	20,000
___	Term deposits	70,000	
___	Common stocks	35,000	
___	RRSPs	80,000	10,000
___	Share of business	500,000	
___	Pension fund, present value	85,000	
___	Personal account receivable	15,000	
Total:		**$1,005,000**	**$370,000**
Less:			
___	Mortgage on matrimonial home; half-share	$40,000	$40,000
___	Personal loans	25,000	
___	Income tax owing	20,000	
___	Inheritance resulting in term deposits	70,000	
___	Cash savings at date of marriage	25,000	5,000
Net family property:		**$895,000**	**$255,000**

The equalization payment is one-half the difference between the NFPs: $895,000 – $255,000 = $640,000 x 1/2 = $320,000. The husband must pay $320,000 to the wife, on terms to be agreed or imposed by a court. As noted above, if that equalization payment would be "unconscionable," a court may adjust the payment up or down.

If we examine the example above, it will be clear that some of the property is easy to value; some is problematic.

There should be no dispute about actual values of deposits, savings, securities, mortgages, bank loans, and outstanding income tax. The value of a residence can be easily appraised, or if it is sold, the market determines value. In our example, each of the parties would probably just keep his or her car.

Contents of a home are a problem. We are supposed to use "market value" for these, what the sale of used furniture would produce. But "replacement value"' and "value to owner" are usually higher than market value, so the parties typically agree on physical division of contents.

Already we see at least five concepts of value: present, actual, fair market, replacement, and value to owner. The concept to be applied to each item is whatever produces a fair result, again a matter of considerable argument.

Space does not permit a full exposition of the various concepts of value. That already fills books and has caused a tremendous expansion of valuation services by accountants, actuaries, and appraisers.

Let's just raise (without always answering) some of the questions that might arise from our simple example.

1. Suppose the wife is going to keep the matrimonial home, and credit the husband for half its value. Should there be an adjustment for real estate commission and legal fees that will likely be incurred whenever she ultimately sells it?

2. Should we deduct the tax that will be attracted whenever the RRSP is cashed in? Isn't that a "debt or other liability"? (Probably no, if the parties plan to retain the RRSPs, or take off the estimated present value of the tax. Yes, if they have to be cashed in to fund the equalization payment. Solve the problem by rollover: the husband transfers an equalizing portion of his RRSP to the wife, without immediate tax consequences.)

3. The present value of the pension is an actuarial calculation of the husband's entitlement to the payments he anticipates receiving. But should he equalize this now? Suppose either party dies before the pension payments start to flow. How do you take into account the present value of the tax on the future pension payments as income? Alternatively, should the pension payments be divided on some "if and when" basis, i.e., the wife gets some portion of the pension payments only when they are actually received?

4. The husband's share of the business is a minority interest that can't be transferred or sold without the consent of the majority.

There is no "fair market value" because there is no market, and "book value" seems insufficient. Should you apply a minority or illiquidity discount?

5. The husband is a physician. Is his professional licence part of the property? How do you value it? Does it have value, since it can't be sold or assigned? It has no "value in exchange." (The Court of Appeal has ruled that a professional licence is not "property" at all.)

6. The husband is in a manufacturing business. Both the husband and wife have personally signed for a business bank loan of $300,000. How do you treat this contingent debt?

7. If the husband sells the business, there will be immediate, significant tax consequences. Are these contingent "debts or other liabilities"? Suppose he has to sell the business to fund the equalization payment. Suppose he plans to keep the business. Suppose the forced liquidation of the business will put twenty people out of work and cut off the husband's income.

8. Suppose the value of a particular item of property has substantially increased or decreased since the valuation date. Is there some adjustment for that?

9. The wife's account receivable is a loan to her brother that she never expects to collect. Part of the husband's personal loans includes $10,000 from his mother that he never expects to repay. How do you treat these?

10. The husband inherited $30,000, but it was just spent, or it was used to reduce the mortgage on the matrimonial home. Does he get any credit for this? (No.)

"Suppose I win the lottery?"

Lottery winnings are property, and if acquired before breakdown of marriage will be subject to equalization. In a remarkable Ontario case, the husband won $2,500,000 one month before the parties separated, and made strenuous attempts to conceal it from his wife. He had his brother claim the prize, and paid the brother $375,000 for his co-operation. He gave various other substantial sums to his siblings for deposit or for purchase of real estate. The wife claimed and received equalization on the whole amount. The court held that the husband had recklessly depleted his property in an attempt to deprive the wife of her entitlement. The transfers to the husband's siblings were set aside. The wife was also awarded

$50,000 as punitive damages for the husband's calculated and malicious conduct.

There are penalties against a party who has not "removed all barriers that are within his or her control and that would prevent the other spouse's remarriage within that spouse's faith."

Section 3 of the FLA is a complete code for the appointment of a mediator, on an application to the court. The mediator must be a person selected by the parties, and who has consented to act and has agreed to file a report within the period of time specified by the court. Usually when the parties want mediation, they simply agree on it.

Rights under the FLA may be enforced by an application in the Superior Court or Unified Family Court. The applicant must file with the court and serve on the respondent spouse a comprehensive financial statement, setting out assets and liabilities, income and expenses (there is a form of financial statement in Appendix A). The respondent spouse then files similar documents by way of answer. Please see further notes on procedure in Chapter 8, "Divorce."

The parties usually go through some form of pre-trial disclosure and questioning involving delivering an affidavit that sets out every document the party has or ever had bearing on any of the issues in the case, and personal attendance for examination by the other spouse's lawyer.

At an early stage there will be a case conference and later a pre-trial conference with a judge or judicial officer, attended by all parties and lawyers in an attempt to at least narrow the issues in dispute, and maybe settle the case then and there. If it doesn't settle, the next step is a trial, with witnesses before a judge in open court.

Never forget that a dispute can be settled at any stage.

Estate Rights

The FLA created entirely new estate rights and obligations arising from the death of a spouse after the FLA came into force.

Under the FLA, when a spouse dies, if the NFP of the deceased spouse exceeds the NFP of the surviving spouse, the latter is entitled to one-half the difference between them.

An application for an equalizing payment of NFP commenced before a spouse's death may be continued against the deceased spouse's estate.

An application to recover an equalizing payment of NFP from

an estate should be made within six months of the spouse's death, although this may be extended by a court order.

The right to equalize NFP after the death of a spouse may create conflict with the will of the deceased or the rights on an intestacy. Therefore the FLA provides as follows:

1. When a spouse dies leaving a will, the surviving spouse has a right to elect to take what the will provides, or may elect to take an equalizing payment. In many cases, one spouse leaves all the estate to the survivor, so this right of election can be academic. But in a case where a spouse has attempted to cut the other out of the estate, it will be very meaningful.

   In the unlikely event that the will states that the surviving spouse should receive bequests under the will and an equalizing payment, the will prevails. In the more probable case, where the will says nothing specific about the surviving spouse receiving both the bequests and the equalizing payment, if the survivor elects to take the equalizing payment, *any bequests in the will are treated as revoked.*

2. When a spouse dies intestate—without a will—the survivor may elect to receive the entitlement under Part II of the *Succession Law Reform Act*, that is, the amount payable on an intestacy, or to receive an equalizing payment of NFP.

3. When a spouse dies testate as to some property and intestate as to other property, the survivor may elect to take what the will provides and the entitlement under Part II of the *Succession Law Reform Act*, or to receive an equalizing payment of NFP.

None of this affects entitlement that may arise on the death of a spouse where the property is outside the estate. A common example of this is a matrimonial home registered in joint tenancy. The surviving joint tenant takes all of the home by operation of law. The same would apply to a joint bank account. Also, if the survivor owned life insurance on the life of the deceased spouse, that would be the property of the survivor and would not be part of the estate. Since the valuation date for determining NFP is the date before the date of death, the death benefits under the policy would not form part of the survivor's NFP, although the cash surrender value, if any, would form part of the deceased's NFP.

There is a special rule if your spouse dies and you receive death benefits under a life insurance policy or a lump sum under a pension plan. The amount of this payment is credited against your entitlement if you elect equalization, unless your spouse has specifically provided by written designation to the contrary. Suppose a wife has an estate of $100,000 that she has left entirely to charity, precisely because she knows that her husband will receive life insurance proceeds of $500,000. This sensible rule means that the husband, although excluded from her will, has no reason to challenge its terms by electing equalization.

But note that unless the will or a designation in an insurance policy provides specifically to the contrary (very unlikely), a surviving spouse who elects to take his or her entitlement to an equalizing payment of NFP is deemed to have disclaimed as well:

(a) any entitlement to receive payment of support as a dependant under the *Succession Law Reform Act*; and

(b) the right to receive payment under an insurance policy owned by the deceased spouse, or to pension-plan death benefits or proceeds of a group insurance policy taken out on the deceased's life.

It follows that an election to take one's entitlement to an equalizing payment of NFP takes priority over

(a) gifts made by the will to any person, except insofar as these may be in accordance with a contract that the deceased entered into with the survivor (very unlikely);

(b) any person's right to a share of the estate on intestate succession; and

(c) an order made under the *Succession Law Reform Act* in favour of a dependant except such an order in favour of a child of the deceased spouse.

The election to take an equalizing payment of NFP should be filed in the office of the Superior Court of Ontario within six months after the death of the spouse. If no such election is filed, the surviving spouse is deemed to have elected to take under the will or intestacy, as the case may be, unless a judge orders otherwise. This time may be extended by court order.

For all of these reasons, an estate must not be distributed within six months of a spouse's death unless the surviving spouse authorizes the distribution, or a judge orders it. If an application is made for an equalizing payment of NFP, the estate must not be distributed at all unless the applicant consents or a judge orders it. However, the FLA says that these provisions do not prohibit reasonable advances to the dependants of a deceased spouse for their support.

This also means that within six months of the death of a spouse, the survivor will have to determine the amount of NFP so as to make an informed election whether to take under the will or intestacy or get an extension of time from the court to do so. This may present a problem, since the personal representative of the deceased may be reluctant to make full disclosure except in the context of litigation.

Trust Interests

There are two types of trust interests that may arise: "resulting trusts" and "constructive trusts." These are not statutory rights under the FLA or any other statute. They are rights in common law. As such, they apply equally to married and unmarried persons. Unmarried couples, even if they qualify under the expanded definition of "spouse" for the purpose of support rights and obligations, have no statutory property rights. Unmarried partners may have rights arising from trust interests, or of course they may be registered owners of property together. These trust interests, as determined by a court or by agreement, have the effect of making the beneficiary party an owner, in whole or part, of property registered or recorded in the name of the other party.

A "resulting trust" can arise in two ways:

1. By the common intention of the parties, as manifested in their conduct. This could be by words spoken or written, or simply by a course of behaviour that makes their intention clear.
2. By a direct contribution of money or money's worth to the acquisition of the subject property. An example of this arose where a jointly owned matrimonial home was sold and the proceeds used to purchase a business that was registered in the name of the husband. There was no doubt that a resulting trust arose from the wife's contribution of her half-share of the proceeds of sale of the home, and that the husband was holding a half-share of the business in trust for the wife. He was a trustee for her, and

she was the beneficiary of that trust, represented by a half-share of the business.

A "constructive trust" arises despite the intention of the parties. In Canadian law, a constructive trust is "remedial." It may be imposed where there has been an unjust enrichment, characterized by some deprivation to the claimant party, a corresponding enrichment to the other party, and no legal (juristic) reason for the enrichment. It is most often seen where one party contributes work, money, money's worth, services, or some combination of these to the other, resulting in the acquisition or maintenance of the other's property, in the reasonable expectation by the claimant that he or she was acquiring a share of some property. The contribution must be something substantial, and should have some connection or "nexus" to the property in question. A constructive trust might be imposed, for example, where parties lived together for a considerable period, had children together, and the claimant contributed her household management, child care, and earnings to the household in the reasonable expectation that she was a part owner of their home, although it was registered in the name of her companion, who may have made all the direct payments for the acquisition and maintenance of the home. A court might rule that she "lightened his burden," or enabled him to acquire and maintain the home, which he never could have done without her assistance. A court could declare that she is entitled to a half-share, or some other proportion of the home, as a remedy for "unjust enrichment," so that by operation of a constructive trust as imposed by the court, he is a trustee holding a share of the home for her as beneficiary. The court could instead quantify the amount of her entitlement, which may be far more convenient, and simply say that she is entitled to a specific amount of compensation rather than an unquantified fractional share of the subject property. Something similar could arise where the claimant has worked in a business owned by the other, without any (or with insufficient) compensation.

8

DIVORCE

A divorce is the legal process by which a valid marriage is dissolved. The same term is often used to mean the judgment that dissolves the marriage. The party who starts the divorce proceedings is called the applicant and the other spouse is called the respondent.

The current federal *Divorce Act*, in force as of June 1, 1986, greatly simplifies the grounds for divorce, and compatible provincial rules of procedure have made the entire process of an uncontested divorce relatively simple. Even so, the system places all divorce proceedings in the context of a formal lawsuit. Here's an outline of the steps in taking a typical divorce to completion. We'll take the point of view that the wife is applicant and the husband is respondent to avoid clumsy multiple pronouns. Also, we'll ignore joint applications, since an application by one spouse is simpler and far more common. Everything in the *Divorce Act* is gender-neutral.

Since the advent of same-sex marriage, it follows that there should be same-sex divorce, and there is. The first same-sex divorce was granted in 2005, before the *Divorce Act* was amended to provide specifically for it. It involved at that time (as in so many other same-sex issues) a constitutional challenge, but the outcome was never really in doubt.

There are also faith-based divorces and annulments granted by religious authorities that may be prerequisites to marriage within the faith, and may be treated as binding by adherents within that faith. These are not valid divorces and have no legal effect under the secular law of Canada.

Procedure

In order to deal with an application for divorce, the court must have jurisdiction (legal power) to do so. In all provinces of Canada, only the superior court of the province has this jurisdiction. In Ontario, this is the Superior Court of Justice. In British Columbia, the judges of the district courts are specially empowered to hear divorce applications. It is a great convenience to empower judges who hear cases within a local area because they are much more easily available to preside than judges of a higher court, who might conduct assizes in a small population centre for only a few weeks in each year.

The requirement of jurisdiction under the *Divorce Act* is easily satisfied: "A court in a province has jurisdiction to hear and determine a divorce proceeding if either spouse has been ordinarily resident in the province for at least one year immediately preceding the commencement of the proceeding."

If the spouses cannot meet these requirements of jurisdiction, the application for divorce will be refused, even though the grounds may be perfectly valid.

The applicant starts proceedings by "presenting" an application for divorce. The application is a document that sets out information and vital statistics about the marriage and any children, and a statement of the claims and the facts on which the applicant relies. The application also lets the respondent know what he must do if he wants to dispute any of the claims in the application.

An application is presented when a copy is filed at the appropriate court office, in the form prescribed by the rules of the superior court of the province where the application has been commenced, and on payment of a filing fee, currently $170 in Ontario, which includes $10 to pay for a clearance certificate issued from a central registry in Ottawa to establish that there is no duplication of the proceedings. A certified copy of the marriage certificate can be filed along with the application, or if not immediately available, it can be filed later.

The application is then "served," usually by mail or by physical delivery of a copy to the respondent or his lawyer. It sometimes happens that the respondent cannot be personally served with these papers, so the rules of court provide a procedure for ordering "substitutional service," perhaps by serving a relative, or by advertising.

The rules under the *Divorce Act* say that the applicant does not have to name the person with whom adultery occurred, but if named, that person must be served with the application.

In addition to claiming dissolution of marriage, the application may also include claims for "corollary relief," which include financial support for the applicant and child support, custody of children, and access (visiting rights) to children. Also, in Ontario, property claims under the *Family Law Act* can be joined in the application (please see Chapter 7, "Property Rights"), and similarly in all provinces. If there is a claim for corollary relief, the applicant will have to fill out and serve along with the application a comprehensive financial statement, showing all assets and liabilities, income and expenses (please see Forms for an example of a financial statement).

After the application has been served, the respondent usually has twenty days (more if served outside the home province) to deliver an "answer." This is a document that may admit parts of the application and deny others, dispute the application in whole or in part, and may contain a counter-application, that is, a claim by the respondent for a divorce and corollary relief. The answer and counter-application are delivered by serving a copy of the document on the applicant or the applicant's lawyer, and by filing a copy at the court office where the application was launched. The respondent spouse should expect to prepare, serve, and file a financial statement. The original applicant has the right to deliver a "reply," but that's generally the end of the documentation. The application, answer, counter-application, and reply are collectively called "the pleadings." The filing fee for this is $125.

Some problems may arise in figuring out just who is a "child" or "child of the marriage" within the meaning of the *Divorce Act*. The definition includes any child of two spouses or former spouses to whom they both stand in the place of parents. A "child of the marriage" is under the age of sixteen years, or older and under the charge of the parents but unable, because of illness, disability, or other cause, to withdraw from their charge or to obtain the necessities of life. This is interpreted to include a child engaged in a full-time program of education, up to completion of an undergraduate degree, or to a specific age, often twenty-one. Some cases have granted child support under the *Divorce Act* for a child engaged in post-graduate education; some have refused it. The *Divorce Act* is federal legislation, so a person may be over the age of minority under provincial law, but still a "child" in divorce proceedings.

When the pleadings have all been delivered, the case may be entered on a list of divorces awaiting hearing. If the respondent doesn't deliver an answer, that's fine—the application is undefended, and may be entered for hearing when the time for delivering an answer has expired. The case is entered for hearing by "passing a record," filing with the now-familiar court office copies of all the pleadings in the format prescribed for use by the trial judge, and by paying another fee of $280.00. Then you wait your turn, and the registrar of the court will inform you of progress; or you can apply for an immediate judgment.

In most disputed cases, each of the parties is questioned under oath on his or her affidavit(s) and financial statement by a procedure that brings the party and the opposing lawyers to the office of a court reporter chartered for this purpose. The transcripts of the examinations, together with copies of all the papers filed with the court in that case, are then used to present and argue any motion for interim corollary relief, heard by a judge. Often, either combined with or conducted separately, there may be a further pretrial questioning of each of the parties at a later stage, again taken under oath at the office of a chartered court reporter. Both kinds of examinations explore the evidence to be presented at trial, and are also used to secure admissions from the other side that may be helpful later on. The transcripts of any examinations under oath can be used as evidence at the hearing by reading into the trial record such portions of them as are wanted, or by invoking them as an aid to cross-examination of a person whose testimony at the hearing differs from previous testimony.

Each party is obliged to deliver an affidavit to the other listing all the documents that bear upon any of the issues in the case, and to make these documents available as far as possible for inspection by the other side. This can be onerous. Also, potential witnesses may have to attend for a form of pre-trial questioning in circumstances too various to be dealt with here.

Corollary Relief

As also noted above, in addition to claiming dissolution of marriage, the application may also include claims for "corollary relief," which include financial support for the applicant and child support, custody of children, and access (visiting rights) to children. Also, in Ontario, property claims under the *Family Law Act* and similarly in all provinces can be joined in the application (please see Chapter 7, "Property Rights"). If there is a claim for corollary relief, the applicant will have to fill out and serve along with the application a comprehensive financial statement, showing all assets and liabilities, income and expenses (please see Appendix A for an example of a financial statement).

Either spouse may need to get an order for corollary relief while the hearing is pending. This is done by a motion for "interim corollary relief," started by a notice in the prescribed form served on the opposite party or his lawyer. The notice is almost invariably accompanied by an affidavit (a written, signed, sworn statement), setting out the facts in support of the claim for interim corollary relief. The other spouse may file his own affidavit opposing the claim for interim corollary relief, by denying, contradicting, or clarifying the applicant's affidavit. These affidavits may also be the subject of questioning before the hearing as noted above.

Grounds for Divorce

Under the *Divorce Act*, there is only one ground for divorce: marriage breakdown. This is established if

1. The spouses have lived separate and apart for at least one year immediately prior to the determination of the divorce and were living separate and apart when the proceedings were commenced; or
2. The spouse against whom the divorce is claimed (the respondent) has committed adultery; or
3. The respondent spouse has treated the other with physical or mental cruelty of such a kind as to render intolerable the continued cohabitation of the spouses.

A divorce application can be commenced any time after separation. If the idea is to obtain it on the basis of one year of separation, then although the application can proceed, the decree of divorce will not be granted until one year of separation has actually elapsed. If the parties have already been separated for one year, or if the applicant is relying on adultery or cruelty, the divorce can be granted as soon as the matter can be brought before the court.

Adultery
Adultery has been defined as voluntary sexual intercourse of a married person with one of the opposite sex, and has become more

broadly construed to include the voluntary surrender to another person of the reproductive powers or faculties of the guilty person and any submission of these powers to "the service or enjoyment of any person not the spouse." In one case, it was held that the wife committed adultery when she had herself artificially inseminated without her husband's consent. The modern definition of adultery goes beyond ordinary heterosexual intercourse.

Many people seem to believe that adultery must be proved by direct observation. This is simply untrue. The court will usually be satisfied with evidence from which adultery can be inferred, based on familiarity of the respondents and opportunity to commit the offence. That's why evidence that the respondents spent a night together in a motel will be accepted as inferential proof of adultery, especially in the absence of any denial from the respondents themselves.

The correct principles covering proof of adultery were established in two cases decided in 1810 and 1894. This is the kernel of the later decision:

> It is not necessary to prove the direct fact of adultery, nor is it necessary to prove a fact of adultery in time and place, because . . . if it were otherwise, there is not one case in a hundred that that proof would be obtainable; it is very rarely indeed that the parties are surprised at the direct act of adultery. In every case almost the fact is inferred from circumstances which lead to it by a fair inference as a necessary conclusion; and unless this were the case, and this were so held, no protection whatever could be given to marital rights. To lay down any general rule, to attempt to define what circumstances would be sufficient and what insufficient upon which to infer the fact of adultery, is impossible. Each case must depend on its own particular circumstances. It would be impractical to enumerate the infinite variety of circumstantial evidentiary acts, which of necessity are as various as the modifications and combinations of events in actual life.

The evidence from which adultery can be inferred may arise from the applicant's own observations, but it's preferable to have corroboration from another witness. Anyone can be a witness—the testimony of a relative or friend will do fine.

The use of private investigators to gather evidence has diminished in recent years. When adultery was the only ground for divorce, and the erring spouse wouldn't reveal his or her misconduct, there was often no choice but to call in a private investigator. Today, expanded grounds for divorce and the high costs of investigators' services make this need far less frequent. Still, there's no reason why an investigator can't be used, and his or her testimony is as entitled to credibility as anyone else's.

The overwhelming majority of divorces are undefended simply because both parties want the marriage ended and they have nothing to argue about. Defended divorce cases rarely have anything to do with an attempt to hold the marriage together. Rather, the fight is about money or custody of children.

Most divorces based on adultery ultimately require the co-operation of the parties. This is partly necessitated by a statutory protection against "self-incrimination" where adultery is alleged. The law states that the parties to proceedings instituted in consequence of adultery, and the husbands and wives of these parties, are not liable to be asked or bound to answer questions that could tend to show he or she is guilty of adultery. This protection exists at the pre-trial questioning as well as at the trial, and will be enforced by the trial judge without the need to ask for the protection. The parties may consent to be asked such questions, and may answer such of them as they wish, but unless the person has already given evidence in the same proceedings in *disproof* of adultery, the protection holds. The effect of this is to make it difficult or impossible to *compel* an unwilling party to provide admissions needed in proof of adultery. So where an applicant seeks to impose a divorce based on adultery on a reluctant respondent, the applicant better have some independent evidence of adultery available at trial.

Some judges will grant a divorce on the ground of adultery after hearing the uncorroborated admission of the respondent spouse. Although it has been ruled that the testimony of a respondent spouse confessing adultery is not an "admission" within the meaning of the *Divorce Act*, there is a string of older authority to the effect that a divorce should not be granted on this kind of testimony, and anyway, it depends on the attitude of the individual judge. Since most divorces are both undefended and co-operative in the sense that both parties want the divorce, it is usually simple to have the respondent spouse bring a corroborating witness to the trial, especially in a case where there has been a continuing relationship with the co-respondent.

Cruelty

Cruelty as a ground for divorce has produced the largest volume of precedent and controversy. For some time after the 1986 *Divorce Act* came into force, lawyers and judges were not sure just what was meant by the phrase "cruelty of such a kind as to render intolerable the continued cohabitation of the spouses." Some thought it referred to the standard of cruelty established in 1897 as applicable to claims by the wife for alimony, and others thought it set up a new standard within the words of the Act itself. As a result, conflicting opinions and authorities abounded, and quite a few undefended applications were dismissed on strict interpretations of the Act. A decision of the Ontario Court of Appeal in 1970 went far to resolve the difficulty, in these words:

> Over the years the Courts have steadfastly refrained from attempting to formulate a general definition of cruelty. As used in ordinary parlance, "cruelty" signifies a disposition to inflict suffering; to delight in or exhibit indifference to the pain or misery of others; mercilessness or hard-heartedness as exhibited in action. If in the marriage relationship one spouse by his conduct causes wanton, malicious or unnecessary infliction of pain or suffering upon the body, the feelings or emotions of the other, his conduct may well constitute cruelty which will entitle an applicant to dissolution of the marriage in the Court's opinion, if it amounts to physical or mental cruelty "of such a kind as to render intolerable the continued cohabitation of the spouses." That is the standard which the Courts are to apply, and in the context . . . of the Act, that standard is expressed in language which must be taken to exclude the qualifications laid down in [the 1897] rule . . . and in the numerous other cases which have followed and applied [that] rule in matrimonial disputes. . . .
>
> Care must be taken . . . that conduct relied upon to establish cruelty is not a trivial act, but one of a "grave and weighty" nature, and not merely conduct which can be characterized as little more than a manifestation of incompatibility of temperament between the spouses. The whole matrimonial relationship must be considered, especially if the cruelty consists of reproaches, complaints, accusations or constant carping criticism. A question most relevant for consideration is the effect of the conduct complained of on the mind of the affected spouse. The determination of what constitutes cruelty must, in the final analysis, depend on the circumstances of the particular case having regard to the physical and mental condition of the parties, their character and their attitude towards the marriage relationship.

So the test of cruelty is subjective, "whether *this* conduct by this man to this woman or vice versa is cruelty," because, as one case puts it, "The same conduct may amount to abominable cruelty in one set of circumstances, to the enjoyable rough and tumble of a happily married life in another."

Many cases present facts that so clearly constitute cruelty that nobody could doubt it. A series of beatings, until the wife can take no more; a single savage attack, such as in one case where the parties had separated because of the husband's indifference, and when he came to the wife's residence supposedly to discuss reconciliation, fractured her skull with a hammer he had brought along; harassment, abuse, and degradation, driving the spouse to seek psychiatric help or hospitalization for a nervous breakdown: these create no legal problem. But other marginal cases will turn on the subjective test and the attitude of the individual judge.

Cruelty sufficient for divorce has been found in these less obvious situations:

- the practice of *coitus interruptus* adversely affecting the health of the wife
- a husband's wilful refusal to recognize the wife's right to his society
- transvestism of the husband causing continual stress to the wife
- husband's pedophilia
- adoption by the husband of a hippie lifestyle and use of soft drugs despite disapproval by the wife
- husband ignored wife, neglected her medical needs, and made unreasonable sexual demands
- chronic alcoholism of the husband (although there are cases that say that addiction to alcohol is not cruelty as such)
- applicant wife forced by her husband to engage in fellatio
- persistent refusal of sexual relations. There have been cases both ways—husband's refusal and wife's refusal—but there have also been cases where it was ruled that refusal of sexual intercourse as such was not cruelty. The successful cases have been those in which it could be demonstrated that refusal of sexual relations had an adverse effect on the physical or mental health of the applicant.
- wife habitually and continually ridiculed the husband's sexual

performance and compared him to a previous husband and lovers. On the evidence, the wife's conduct caused the husband such anxiety that the judge said, "There is little doubt in my mind that if he had not left he would have become a prime candidate for the mental hospital."

- husband's domineering, tyrannizing, or abusive conduct, particularly where it causes the wife to need psychiatric help

The fact that the respondent was insane at the time of committing the acts of cruelty is no bar to granting a divorce. Cruelty need not be intentional; a divorce can be granted where the conduct that rendered continued cohabitation intolerable was founded in delusions.

Although cruelty as a ground for divorce is more liberally construed now than in the first few years of the previous *Divorce Act* (and often much more liberally in undefended cases), the ease with which a divorce may be granted on this ground seems to vary tremendously from province to province and, precisely because of the "subjective test," from judge to judge.

Separation

The simplest and most common way by far to obtain a divorce is to proceed on the ground of separation. The *Divorce Act* states that the right to a divorce is established if "the spouses have lived separate and apart for at least one year immediately prior to the determination of the divorce and were living separate and apart when the proceedings were commenced."

There is no element of desertion by either party in this, and no need to allege or prove any fault at all. A spouse can start the application at any time after actual separation and the divorce will issue immediately following the anniversary of the separation. If the spouses have already been separated for a year when one of them starts the application, and there's no argument about it or anything else, a divorce should be available immediately. This emphasizes the importance of settling any controversial matters, preferably by a separation agreement, before anyone starts a divorce application. If you already have a separation agreement, there shouldn't be anything left to argue about, so the divorce is completely uncontested.

There need not be a mutual intention of the spouses to separate. The *Divorce Act* provides that the period of separation is not considered to have been interrupted or terminated "by reason only that either spouse has become incapable of forming or having an intention to continue to live separate and apart or of continuing to live separate and apart of the spouse's own volition, if it appears to the court that the separation would probably have continued if the spouse had not become so incapable . . ."

Nor is the period of separation interrupted or terminated if "the spouses have resumed cohabitation during a period of, or periods totaling, not more than ninety days with reconciliation as its primary purpose."

It is sometimes less than clear whether the parties were living separate and apart within the meaning of the *Divorce Act*. There are two elements to this: the spouses must be physically separated, and they, or one of them, must have the intention of terminating the marriage relationship. There are situations where the husband and wife have been held to be living separate and apart although they continued to reside under the same roof, but such cases have been subjected to extremely careful scrutiny. Mere lack of sexual relationship will not qualify; there must be a complete removal from every aspect of the marriage relationship. In the cases where this has been successfully invoked, there was no sexual, social, or domestic relationship between the parties. For one example, the wife did not sleep with the husband, went nowhere with him, did not cook or keep house for him, but shared a residence with him through financial necessity.

The converse is that the parties can be physically separated for a long period of time, but not be living "separate and apart" because they did not intend to destroy the marriage relationship. An obvious instance might arise where the husband is posted overseas on military service.

Reconciliation

There are several ways in which the *Divorce Act* encourages reconciliation.

In the first place, it imposes a duty on the lawyer for the prospective applicant, "except where the circumstances of the case are of such nature that it would clearly not be appropriate to do so," to discuss the possibility of reconciliation, and inform the client of marriage counselling or guidance facilities known to the lawyer. Naturally, in the overwhelming majority of cases, the client isn't interested in reconciliation, or else he or she wouldn't be in the lawyer's office.

But the statutory hope of reconciliation persists. At the trial, it's the duty of the judge, before he hears any evidence, to ask the parties if there's any possibility of reconciliation. If one or both of them say there isn't, the trial can proceed. There have been a few cases where one of the spouses wanted to reconcile, but the other was adamant in refusing to try, and it has been ruled that both parties must be willing to make the attempt.

If both parties want to try, either before any evidence is heard, or at any later stage of the trial if the judge feels there is a possibility of reconciliation, the case must be adjourned to give the parties an opportunity of being reconciled. With the consent of the parties, the judge can appoint a counsellor to help them. If, after an adjournment of fourteen days, the parties are not reconciled, either of them may apply to the court to resume the proceedings. It's very rare that a husband and wife decide in the courtroom that they want to try to work things out, and rarer still that a judge will seek to impose his view of the possibility of reconciliation on them after he has started to hear the evidence.

If the court actually does adjourn the hearing and appoint a person to assist the spouses in an attempt at reconciliation, that person cannot be compelled to testify in later divorce proceedings as to any communication or admission made to him or her in that capacity by anyone, and no such evidence is admissible at all, whatever the source.

Furthermore, the *Divorce Act* requires every lawyer who undertakes a divorce case to discuss with his client the advisability of negotiating the matters that might be the subject of a corollary relief order, and to inform the client of mediation facilities known to the lawyer that might assist in the negotiations.

The Hearing and Judgment

Most undefended divorces are granted based on affidavits filed with the court, so that there is no need for a live hearing. If there is a hearing, a judge presides and listens to the evidence, ordinarily presented in the form of live testimony and documents, with full rights of counsel, examination, and cross-examination as at any other trial. If the judge is satisfied that the applicant is entitled to a divorce, she will grant the judgment and may make other orders for corollary relief and sharing of property.

There are several bars to divorce:

(a) The court must dismiss the application if it finds there has been collusion in presenting it. Collusion means some kind of fraud, an attempt to fabricate or suppress evidence, to subvert the administration of justice, or to deceive the court. This is an absolute bar to divorce.

(b) It is the duty of the court "to satisfy itself that reasonable arrangements have been or can be made for the support of any children of the marriage and, if such arrangements can be made, to stay the granting of the divorce until such arrangements are made or, if no such arrangements can be made, to dismiss the application for a divorce."

(c) If the application is based on adultery or cruelty, the court must be satisfied that there has been no *condonation* or *connivance* on the part of the spouse bringing the proceeding. If not satisfied of this, the court must dismiss the application "unless, in the opinion of the court, the public interest would be better served by granting the divorce."

Condonation is forgiveness, in the special sense of restoration of the marriage relationship after the adultery or cruelty occurred. Condonation does not arise if the spouses continue or resume cohabitation for a period or periods up to ninety days, in the aggregate, with reconciliation as the primary purpose.

Connivance may arise where, for example, there has really been adultery, so there is no fraud in that sense, but the spouses encouraged it in an attempt to obtain a divorce.

The ease with which an undefended divorce is available based on separation for one year suggests that the elaborate subterfuges of an earlier and more restrictive era will rarely trouble our judiciary.

The judgment must be prepared in proper form, signed by a registrar of the court, and a copy filed at the court office. Usually, the judgment must be served on the respondent.

The divorce takes effect on the thirty-first day after the date on which the judgment was given. The waiting period is for the purpose of exhausting any rights of appeal, and to permit a last-ditch attempt at reconciliation. The court office issues a "final certificate" of divorce. The fee for this is $19.

The waiting period may be shortened or eliminated if the judge thinks it appropriate to do so, provided the spouses agree, and promise not to appeal.

In Ontario, it is often unnecessary for the parties to attend at court for the hearing because a divorce can be granted on affidavit evidence, and most undefended divorces proceed just that way, with the parties submitting written statements to the judge in which they swear to the truth of the facts that they rely on.

Divorce can be granted on motion by either or both spouses to the court, in advance of the resolution of complex financial disputes. This is a process of splitting off the uncontroversial divorce—the grounds for divorce are admitted—from the other issues that may take months or even years to determine, and could be the subject of extended appeals, so as to permit the parties to get on with their lives. Sometimes there is initial opposition to this, but the opposition typically evaporates before (maybe just before) the motion is heard.

The judge may award court costs to either spouse, at her discretion. There will usually be no award of costs unless the case presents some substantial dispute, in which one of the spouses is perceived to be both successful and deserving. An award of costs is not appropriate in a simple undefended divorce, and is not often made if the only substantial dispute is custody of or access to children.

If awarded, the amount of costs is in the discretion of the court, and should not be expected to cover the entire bill for fees and disbursements between lawyer and client. Many women still apparently believe that their husbands are automatically responsible for paying their legal fees, and although that was often true at one time, it is no longer so.

Appeals

Any aspect of a divorce judgment, whether the dissolution of the marriage, or an order granting or refusing interim or permanent corollary relief, may be appealed. An appeal from an order concerning interim corollary relief tends to be a cumbersome and wasteful process, so the interests of the aggrieved spouse are often far better served by just pushing the case on to the hearing.

The Court of Appeal has a full power of review, and may grant the judgment it thinks should have been given at trial, or may order a new trial. Of course it may also dismiss the appeal, and will do so unless it thinks the trial judge made a reversible error. The appeal court may find that the trial judge made a number of mistakes, but if the court agrees in a general way with her conclusion, it will refuse to alter the trial judgment. Except in very unusual circumstances, the Court of Appeal will base its decision on the testimony and documents that the trial judge used, so an appeal is not an opportunity to put before the court all the things one neglected to say at the hearing. Furthermore, the Court of Appeal will rarely interfere with a finding of fact made by the trial judge as long as there was some evidence to support it. In effect the Court of Appeal says, "The trial judge heard and weighed the evidence of the witnesses, and came to certain conclusions. Why should we substitute our perceptions for hers?"

Thus, a judgment based on the exercise of a trial judge's discretion, and especially on findings of credibility of witnesses, will only be upset on appeal if the trial judge made a serious and reversible error in the application of the law.

It is possible to appeal from a decision of a provincial Court of Appeal to the Supreme Court of Canada on a point of law, but first, as a screening process, the appellant must gain permission to do so at a preliminary application. Permission is hard to achieve; among other things the applicant must demonstrate that the matter in appeal goes beyond the interests of the spouses themselves, and presents a problem of national importance and public interest.

Once a divorce judgment is "final," there is perhaps only one way to have it set aside and that is if the judgment was procured by some kind of fraud or perjury. As a matter of public policy, it should be and is extremely difficult to reverse a divorce judgment, since parties are free to remarry once the judgment (apparently) becomes final.

Recognition of Divorce Judgments

There should be no problem in any jurisdiction that accepts civil marriage and divorce in the recognition of a divorce granted in any Canadian province no matter where the marriage took place. There are, of course, a number of countries where strict ecclesiastical law applies, so that some form of religious marriage and divorce is all they will recognize.

Any Canadian province will recognize a divorce granted by any jurisdiction with which either of the spouses have a substantial connection, in accordance with the internal laws of that place. This general rule is supplemented by specific statutory provisions:

1. Canada will acknowledge jurisdiction if either former spouse was ordinarily resident in that place for at least one year before starting the divorce proceedings;
2. for purposes of determining foreign jurisdiction, the spouses have individual domiciles (legal residences).

9

ANNULMENT

An annulment is a judgment declaring that a marriage, apparently valid in form, is for some reason void in law. The result is called a declaratory judgment, one that declares the existence of legal status and as such is considered binding on the whole world, provided only that the court that gave the judgment is considered by other courts to have the power to do so. An annulment differs from a divorce, since a divorce dissolves a valid marriage. The *Divorce Act* makes no change in the jurisdiction of the superior courts in each province to grant annulments. Annulment is a matter of common law, not statute. Since we have same-sex marriage in Canada, one may assume we have same-sex annulment, but apparently no same-sex annulment case has come before our courts.

There are also ecclesiastical annulments, most often encountered within the Roman Catholic church, as a prerequisite to remarriage within the church. These are outside the scope of secular law in this text.

There are really two types of annulments: (a) those where the marriage is void *ab initio* (from the beginning) because the parties never had the legal capacity to marry, for example, where one of the parties is still legally married to someone else; and (b) those where an incapacity arises or is revealed after the marriage, but where the parties may, if they wish, go on indefinitely in a married state, as in a case of sexual incapacity, which creates a marriage that is not void from the beginning, but merely voidable at the instance of one of the parties.

The distinction between the two types of annulment is not academic. Generally, only the courts of the domicile have the jurisdiction to annul a voidable marriage, while any court wherever the suit may be brought has the jurisdiction to declare a marriage void *ab initio*. The problems of "domicile" no longer trouble us in connection with divorce proceedings because divorce jurisdiction depends on residence. However, domicile is something more than just residence. This may lead to tricky problems of annulment jurisdiction, deriving from old common-law rules that domicile is determined by the physical residence of the husband and his intention to make a permanent home in that place. At common law, the wife has the domicile of her husband, no matter where she may be resident. She might be living in Saskatchewan, but if her husband is domiciled in Zimbabwe, the courts of Saskatchewan will not have jurisdiction to annul her voidable marriage, although they would have jurisdiction if the marriage were void *ab initio*. It is anyone's guess how this would apply to a male same-sex relationship: who is the husband? And in a female same-sex relationship, is there a husband for the purpose of determining domicile?

There may be, in a given case, compelling reasons to proceed with an annulment rather than a divorce. A spouse may have strong religious convictions against divorce. Also, if the marriage is invalid, a court won't grant a divorce at all: a divorce dissolves a valid marriage.

Grounds for Annulment

In Chapter 2, "Marriage," we discussed capacity to form a valid marriage. Lack of that capacity may arise through a prior subsisting marriage; absence of consent to the solemnization of the marriage; mental incapacity rendering a party unable to understand the nature of the marriage contract; forbidden blood relationship (consanguinity); or the fact of being just too young. All of these confer a right to apply for an annulment.

Most of the cases in which a marriage is void *ab initio* arise because of a prior subsisting marriage. Some of these cases involve families torn apart by war or political upheaval. Such a case might arise where a man fled his homeland in Eastern Europe, leaving his wife and children behind. Later, in Canada, he contracts another "marriage" without bothering to determine whether his first marriage has been validly dissolved by death or divorce. Where the new "wife" has been deceived into entering a "marriage" that is of no legal effect, she may also have a right to claim for damages for his misrepresentation and deceit, and for assault in the form of sexual relations consented to in the mistaken belief she was his wife, as well as for annulment. However, these cases mostly arise as a result of ordinary all-Canadian bigamy.

Absence of consent may occur where there has been duress or threats inducing the marriage. Duress implies the exertion of force that induces fear, and not just physical force; there may be threats or terrorizing acts that nullify apparent consent. Fear is a necessary ingredient, whether for the person coerced or for some other person. The legal concept of duress is pretty clear and well defined, but as you might expect, the difficulty comes from applying it to the facts of each individual case. The age, strength of character, impressionable nature, and mental capacity of the person influenced, and his or her relations with whoever attempted the coercion must be taken into consideration and measured, as must the qualities and capacity for influencing and importuning possessed by the persons charged with having exerted the undue influence.

In addition, the court may grant an annulment where there has been a basic mistake as to the nature and effect of the marriage ceremony ("It's just a joke! He's not really a minister."), particularly where the parties never lived together as husband and wife.

There have been a number of cases where marriage was contracted in order to assist one of the parties to stay in Canada as an immigrant, but where one or both of the parties never intended a real marriage to endure. There was a precedent that where one of the parties had induced the other to marry for this purpose, an annulment might be granted. That was overruled in a later decision, and as the law now stands such conduct will not render a marriage void unless an operative mistake, for instance, as to the nature of the ceremony, is also found.

Mental incapacity to marry may be found where one of the parties was incapable of understanding the nature of the marriage contract, and the duties and responsibilities that it creates. The person seeking to prove mental incapacity has an uphill fight, since there is a legal presumption in favour of a valid marriage, and also a presumption that all persons are sane until the contrary is proved.

Sexual impotence sufficient to obtain an annulment is the incurable inability or incapacity of one of the parties to have normal sexual intercourse with the other, and must exist at the time of solemnization of the marriage. An annulment isn't granted if the parties *don't* have sexual relations, but rather because they *can't*. Permanent inability on the part of the husband to emit semen constitutes impotence sufficient for an annulment, even if he is capable both of erection and penetration. Impotence of the wife usually takes the form of an invincible repugnance or aversion to sexual intercourse with her husband. Some years ago, there was a case in which the husband applied for an annulment because his wife refused to have sexual relations with him because, as she put it, she didn't like him. Both were perfectly capable of sexual relations, and by her own admission the wife had had relations with other men prior to marriage. Result: no annulment. But in view of the principles set out above, this case was probably wrongly decided. The fact that the wife had a repugnance to sex with her husband should have tipped the case in his favour.

Nobody yet knows what non-consummation means in a same-sex marriage.

How can sexual incapacity be proved? In some (rare) cases the wife is able to obtain a medical certificate in proof of her virginity, but generally the court must rely on the testimony of one or both of the parties. The court may also draw an inference of impotence arising from illness, disability, or refusal to consummate where the defendant has refused to submit to a medical examination. It is a question whether the court has power to order a party to submit to a medical examination as to sexual capacity.

An annulment action based on sexual incapacity may be started by either spouse.

Another problem is how long the marriage must have lasted before it can be said that it's impossible to consummate. There's no definite answer to that question. But the *Divorce Act* goes a long way toward eliminating the problem entirely by permitting a divorce where the parties have been separated for one year. Also, in a number of cases, persistent refusal of sexual relations has been held to be cruelty sufficient for a divorce.

A party to a void or voidable marriage may have the same rights to financial support and sharing of property just as if he or she had been validly married. In Ontario, all spouses have these rights, and the *Family Law Act* defines "spouse" to include either two persons who (a) are married to each other; or (b) have entered into a marriage that is voidable or void, in good faith on the part of the person asserting a right under this Act.

A "spouse" includes a person who entered into a marriage actually or potentially polygamous, if the marriage was celebrated in a jurisdiction whose system of law recognizes it as valid.

Children of an invalid marriage have the same rights and obligations as children of a valid marriage.

10

DOMESTIC CONTRACTS

The Ontario *Family Law Reform Act* of 1978 and the *Family Law Act, 1986*, greatly enlarged the scope of contracts between spouses or unmarried persons.

Before the *Family Law Reform Act* (FLRA), these agreements were severely limited. A couple could enter into a separation agreement, but not an agreement that provided for *future* separation. An unmarried couple might make an agreement about property rights and support in contemplation of marriage, but could not provide for future separation. If the couple didn't intend to marry, they couldn't validly make a domestic contract at all. Agreements for future separation were considered void on public policy grounds because they were thought to undermine the stability of marriage and the family. Agreements between unmarried persons were void as encouraging immorality. These principles still apply to any such contract entered into before the FLRA came into force on March 31, 1978, since a domestic contract must be valid in form and content as of the date it was executed.

Under the FLRA, and then under the *Family Law Act* (FLA), there are four types of domestic contract: separation agreements[1] (discussed in Chapter 3); marriage contracts; cohabitation agreements; and paternity agreements. As a result of amendments to the FLA, family arbitration agreements will become another form of domestic contract (see Chapter 12).

---

1. For paternity agreements see Chapter 6, "Child Support."

Two persons (who could be of the same sex) who are married to each other or intend to marry may enter into a domestic contract in which they agree on their respective rights and obligations under the marriage or on separation, on the annulment of the marriage or on death, including

(a) ownership in or division of property;
(b) support obligations;
(c) the right to direct the education and moral training of their children, but not the right to custody of or access to their children; and
(d) any other matter in settlement of their affairs.

There is one further exception in a marriage contract: a provision purporting to limit a spouse's rights to possession of a matrimonial home is unenforceable.

Two persons who are cohabiting or intend to cohabit may enter into a domestic contract that covers exactly the same points as a marriage contract. Cohabitation agreements are specifically authorized by statute in Alberta, Manitoba, New Brunswick, Newfoundland, Nova Scotia, Nunavut, Ontario, P.E.I., Yukon, and are recognized in B.C. and Saskatchewan. Under some of the statutes—Ontario is one—if a man and a woman subsequently marry, the cohabitation agreement automatically becomes their marriage contract unless they specifically stipulate to the contrary. In Ontario, "domestic contract" inclues a family arbitration agreement.

A domestic contract is not strictly binding on a court when dealing with support obligations under the FLA. The court may disregard the contract if the provision for support or the waiver of support results in "unconscionable circumstances"; if the provision for support or the waiver of support is by or on behalf of a dependant who qualifies for public assistance; and if there is default in the payment of support under the domestic contract. Also, when hearing a claim for spousal support under the *Divorce Act*, the court may disregard a domestic contract and make any order that seems reasonable. However, domestic contracts are persuasive, and not lightly dismissed. As previously noted, public policy demands that parties must be able to settle their own affairs by private contract, and to depend on the courts to uphold these contracts other than in egregious circumstances. As a further general principle, the court can disregard a domestic contract pertaining to any matter concerning a child, where to do so is in the best interests of the child.

The weight given to domestic contracts got a huge boost in the *Miglin* decision in the Supreme Court of Canada, and later decisions that applied *Miglin*. This is discussed in Chapter 4, "Spousal Support."

Any domestic contract, and any agreement to amend a domestic contract, must be in writing, signed by the parties, and witnessed. A minor who is capable of marrying may enter into a domestic contract subject to approval of the court, which may be given before or after the minor enters into the contract. Some provinces require independent legal advice for a valid domestic contract. Alberta does, Ontario doesn't, although in every case independent legal advice is strongly recommended. It is a kind of insurance against one party saying later on that he didn't understand what he was signing. In our practice, if a party absolutely refuses to get independent legal advice, we recite that in the agreement. If a party says he can't afford it or doesn't want to spend the money, we will sometimes offer to pay the legal fees incurred by the other party to obtain independent legal advice from the lawyer of his choice.

As in a separation agreement, any term of a domestic contract that purports to make future support after separation dependent on continued chastity is void, but the contract can state that support stops on remarriage or cohabitation with another.

The subject matter of a cohabitation agreement or marriage contract may be matters of behaviour—who will do the dishes, what independent activities each may engage in, such as hobbies, education, travel, or, for that matter, extramarital relationships—but in my opinion these are legally dubious. Although it is *theoretically* possible to ask a court to issue an order directing a party to behave in a certain way, the courts are extremely reluctant to do so. First, there is a principle that a contract for personal service will not be specifically enforced; second, the court will not issue any futile order, that is, an order it cannot enforce. Of course, there is no reason why a couple should not make such an agreement as an expression of their wishes or policy, but they should be aware that it has little or no legal effect.

A young couple is likely to see their relationship exclusively as a matter of trust and love, not as a matter of contract. This has a certain wistful charm, but since lovers do grow apart, and marriages do break down, a contract might prevent bitterness, expense, and legal proceedings. In saying this, I realize that a serious discussion of a marriage contract may be anti-romantic, and, as a practical matter, impossible for some people. In cases where the older generation has conferred wealth on the younger, the parents are often protective of what they have created, and they urge (insist on) a marriage contract. In my experience, the attitude of the less-endowed party is usually that he didn't work for it, and understands the attitude of his future in-laws.

A couple who have previously been through divorce are more likely to be pragmatic, so a marriage contract is especially appropriate for parties entering a second marriage. Each may have property that is to be kept individually and not shared in the event of separation or for estate purposes. For instance, a man may be moving into the home that the woman owned prior to their marriage; they may want to agree that the man has no property right in the house, or acquires none unless the marriage lasts a specified term. Or they may want to prevent sharing of property by agreeing that some items will always remain separate property.

They may want to limit support obligations; for example, if they separate within a certain period, the husband will not have to pay maintenance, or only a fixed amount or a lump sum. They may want to agree that neither will ever have any financial obligation for the support of the other's children. They may want to define or limit estate obligations, to provide for life insurance coverage or bequests, or release each other's estates completely.

A domestic contract can be attacked like any other contract, for example, because of fraud, duress, or misrepresentation, but also for improvidence in the result (manifest unfairness) and passive non-disclosure of assets. Our courts have said that in entering into a domestic contract, the parties must act in utmost good faith.

It is not a simple matter to set aside a domestic contract for undue influence or unconscionability of its terms. These cases are highly individual and fact-driven. The distinction between these two claims, undue influence and unconscionability, was summarized in an appeal decision in these words:

> The equitable principles relating to undue influence and relief against unconscionable bargains are closely related, but the doctrines are separate and distinct. . . . A plea of undue influence attacks the sufficiency of consent; a plea that a bargain is unconscionable invokes relief against an unfair advantage gained by an unconscientious use of power by a stronger party against a weaker. On such a claim, the material ingredients are proof of inequality in the position of the parties arising out of the ignorance, need or distress of the weaker,

which left him in the power of the stronger, and proof of substantial unfairness of the bargain obtained by the stronger. On proof of those circumstances, it creates a presumption of fraud which the stronger must repel by proving that the bargain was fair, just and reasonable . . . or perhaps by showing that no advantage was taken.

The FLA and other provincial statutes also provide that a domestic contract or a provision in it may be set aside

(a) if a party failed to disclose to the other significant assets, or significant debts or other liabilities, existing when the domestic contract was made; or
(b) if a party did not understand the nature or consequences of the domestic contract,

or similar words, thus reinforcing the importance of independent legal advice, whether or not it is a statutory requirement in your province.

Of course our courts lean in favour of written contracts; the onus of proof is on the person seeking to set aside the contract or a provision in it.

A valid domestic contract is conclusive as to property rights (but not strictly as to support rights: see above). The Ontario Court of Appeal has ruled that with one exception, only a domestic contract can release property rights under the FLA. The exception is an actual transfer of property between separated spouses, which the Act says operates as equivalent to a domestic contract.

There have been a number of cases where a Canadian resident imports a spouse from a foreign country. Just before marriage, at the insistence of the Canadian, they enter into a marriage contract in which they mutually release all support and property claims. They separate and the imported spouse asserts a claim for spousal support. But as part of the immigration process, the Canadian spouse has signed a sponsorship agreement with Immigration Canada with an undertaking to support the imported spouse for ten years. The sponsorship agreement trumps the marriage contract.

Each marriage contract will depend on the particular needs of the couple, so there is no "standard form." If you want a marriage contract, prepare a memo of the points for agreement or discussion, and consult your lawyer. The fees will be modest, especially as compared with the costs of litigation.

11

ENFORCEMENT

The enforcement of family law rights and remedies is a complex mixture of statutory and common-law rights. This subject alone is enough to fill a book. This chapter is organized along the lines of the legal remedies and the statutes applicable to each of them. There are yet other methods of enforcement, where criminal or quasi-criminal conduct is involved. Domestic assault may lead to summons or arrest. Bail or probation terms may include an order that the offending party must stay away from the matrimonial home and the victim spouse or children. Allegations of child physical or sexual abuse will lead to intensive investigation by a Children's Aid Society, and possible criminal and child-welfare proceedings. These offences are not taken, or to be taken, lightly. The mere allegations of assault or abuse often have a devastating effect on the accused party and on any other legal process in which he or she is engaged. Unfortunately, sometimes these accusations are used as a tactical weapon in the context of a bitter dispute about custody or money, which debases their gravity and general credibility.

The bankruptcy of a debtor party will not wipe out "domestic obligations," usually construed to mean periodic or lump-sum support orders. Bankruptcy, which is federal law, will probably have the effect of eliminating an obligation to make an equalizing payment under the *Family Law Act* (Ontario) or a similar property-sharing order in another province, since an order or agreement for an equalizing payment is legally like an obligation between a creditor and debtor, rather than like a support obligation.

Support orders can be reciprocally enforced from province to province, in the United Kingdom, in the Australian states, in a number of American states, and in some other places under the provisions of the *Reciprocal Enforcement of Support Orders* acts across the country, wherein each reciprocating province or state agrees to enforce orders of the other provinces or states as if they were their own. It gets a bit cumbersome, though, and in many cases geographical separation of the parties spells the effective end of a support order or agreement. Often, if the custodial parent moves away, or stays and obstructs access, the other parent will complain that he's being asked to pay for the children when he can't effectively have a relationship with them. This argument is frequently received with sympathy in court, and the support order is varied or discharged. One method of variation, where the custodian has moved away, is to deduct the travel costs of access from child support by an agreement between the parties.

Enforcement of arbitration awards is dealt with separately in Chapter 12, "Alternate Dispute Resolution."

Enforcement of Separation Agreements

A separation agreement can be enforced just like any other contract. This also applies to a marriage contract or cohabitation agreement. If payments are in default, you can sue on the contract for a judgment entitling you to collect by seizure of assets including wages. If, for example, the husband harasses his wife despite his promise to leave her alone, the wife can apply for an injunction restraining the husband from continuing his harassment. If he persists, he runs the risk of a citation for contempt of court, a fine, and a possible jail term. A wife who violates the terms of a separation agreement may disentitle herself to payment of support or other benefits under the agreement.

Under the *Family Law Act* (Ontario), if there is default in payment of support as provided in a separation agreement, the dependant can ask a court to disregard the terms of the contract and make an order for support. If there is a "fundamental breach" (ask a lawyer), it is usually open to a party to make any claim that would have been available if there had never been an agreement at all.

Even better, under the *Family Law Act* (Ontario), the support obligations may be enforced in the Ontario Court as if these were an order of the court by filing the agreement and requesting enforcement. The court can also order cost-of-living indexing if this was not provided in the agreement.

The provisions of a separation agreement can also be enforced under the *Family Responsibility and Support Arrears Enforcement Act* (Ontario): see below.

There is a strong judicial trend to interpret the terms of separation agreements as "severable," meaning that the entire agreement does not stand or fall as a unit. For instance, if the husband is in breach of the agreement in not paying support as promised, this would give the wife the right to claim support in court in any amount she likes, not just the amount stipulated in the agreement, but the rest of the terms of the agreement will continue as valid and subsisting.

Enforcement of Custody and Access

An order or agreement for custody may be enforced under the *Family Responsibility and Support Arrears Enforcement Act* (Ontario): see below. Other aspects of the enforcement are dealt with in Chapter 5, "Custody and Access."

Canadian provinces are signatories to the Hague Convention *On the Civil Aspects of International Child Abduction*. The full text of this Convention is part of the *Children's Law Reform Act* (Ontario), and similarly in all provinces.

In the United States, there are statutes for the uniform enforcement of custody orders and agreements, effective in every state. In some cases where a child has been wrongfully taken from a Canadian province to an American state, the American state court has applied the uniform enforcement legislation by analogy. There is a statutory mandate in provincial and state legislation across Canada and the United States to confer primary custody jurisdiction on the place where the child has ordinary or usual residence, so as to discourage a parent from "kidnapping" a child and then seeking a custody order in the place where the child has been wrongfully taken. The recipient jurisdiction will typically act only if there is clear evidence of actual or grave potential harm to the child if he or she is returned to the usual place of residence.

Abduction of a child contrary to a custody order is a criminal offence under the Canadian *Criminal Code*.

There are also comprehensive statutes in each province dealing with child-welfare matters, which include child protection, Crown wardship, powers of Children's Aid Societies, and the like.[1]

---

1. This subject fills several books. See, for example, Wilson and Tomlinsion, *Children and the Law* (Butterworths, 1994); Berstein, Paulseth, Ratcliffe, and Scarcella, *Child Protection in Canada* (Carswell, 1990).

Enforcement under the *Family Responsibility and Support Arrears Enforcement Act*

The *Family Responsibility and Support Arrears Enforcement Act* (Ontario), hereafter the FRSAE, came into force on January 31, 1997. It completely repeals and replaces the *Family Support Plan Act*. It contains many of the enforcement provisions of its predecessor, and goes a lot further. These are the basic ideas.

Any support order now on file with the *Family Support Plan* is now enforceable under the terms of the FRSAE. The entire text of the new FRSAE is with the statutes at the end of this text.

Every support order made by an Ontario court, other than a provisional order (one that must be confirmed by another court), must state in its operative part that, unless the order is withdrawn from the FRSAE, it shall be enforced by the Director of the FRSAE, and that the payments go first to the Director and then to the person to whom they are owed. Some people prefer to have payments made directly, so they ask that the order be withdrawn from the Director. A judge may order that it cannot be withdrawn, probably where the judge senses that the recipient may be intimidated.

Every support order that goes to the Director, and any variation of a previous support order, must contain a support deduction order. The support deduction order is transmitted to the payor's "income source" as defined in section 1 of the FRSAE, who is required to deduct and remit to the Director the amount of support. The combined amount of the deduction, for an ongoing order and any arrears, will not exceed 50 percent of the net amount that the income source owes the payor, but if the deduction is only for an ongoing order (not arrears), it will be the amount of the ongoing order even if that exceeds 50 percent of the net income owed by the income source to the payor, although a judge has the power to modify this when making the support order. Up to 100 percent of an income tax refund can be deducted and paid over. The Director can apply to raise the 50 percent level.

Both the payor and the recipient must notify the Director of a change of address. A payor who does not comply faces a fine of up to $10,000.

Within ten days of the termination or interruption of payments from the income source to the payor—for example, layoff, unpaid sick leave, or loss of job—both the payor and the income source must inform the Director and supply certain specified information.

There is a potential fine of up to $10,000 for non-compliance.

There are provisions in sections 26 and 27 of the FRSAE to resolve disputes as to identity of the income source or the amount of the deduction. If there are arrears and the payor's financial circumstances improve, the Director may apply for an increase in the deduction. If the financial circumstances deteriorate, a judge may suspend the operation of the deduction order, provided the judge finds it would be unconscionable to continue the deduction order, or if the parties themselves agree to suspend it; see section 28 of the FRSAE.

Section 30(1) says that a support order and a deduction order have priority over the claims of other creditors "despite any other Act." This may create priority even over claims from Revenue Canada. The parties cannot validly contract not to enforce a support deduction order.

In addition:

- Default of support payments may lead to suspension of the payor's driver's licence (sections 34 to 38).
- If the payments are in default, the Director can demand delivery of a financial statement from the payor and from a person who is "financially connected" to the payor. Both default of compliance and default of payment can ultimately lead to arrest and imprisonment (sections 40 and 41) and a fine of up to $10,000.
- A support order may be registered against land or against personal property (a car, a boat) to create a lien (sections 42 and 43).
- The sheriff can be directed to seize any property, just as in the case of, but in priority to, any other creditor's claim.
- Any kind of deposit account, including any joint account, at a financial institution can be attached, and up to 50 percent of the amount on deposit paid out to satisfy a support order.
- If there are arrears, lottery winnings over $1,000 can be attached, and the arrears deducted and paid over.
- Workers' Compensation payments can be attached.
- A court can issue an injunction to restrain the disposition or wasting of assets that may hinder or defeat the enforcement of a support order or a support deduction order.
- If satisfied that a payor is about to leave Ontario, and there are reasonable grounds to believe that the payor intends to evade

his or her support obligations, a judge can order the payor to be arrested.

- The Director has access to a tremendous range of information from public and private and otherwise confidential records (see sections 54 to 61) to promote enforcement of a support order.

For more information about FRSAE and FRO enforcement, you can go to www.theFRO.ca. There is a twenty-four-hour automated information telephone service at 416-326-1818 or 1-800-267-7263. For account information and forms, the Customer Service Unit is at 416-243-1909 or 1-888-815-2757. The Enforcement Call Centre offers specific enforcement information: call 416-326-1817 or 1-800-267-4330.

Enforcement under the *Family Law Act*

Any order made under the *Family Law Act* (Ontario) can be the subject of enforcement under the FRSAE: see above. Alternatively, if one chooses individual enforcement, any such order can be enforced like any other judgment debt: by seizure and sale of assets; by examining the debtor under oath to determine his capacity to pay; and by examining under oath anyone who may be able to provide information about collecting on the order. There are some specific powers and penalties in the *Family Law Act*.

The court can order security, including a charge (lien) on property, to be given for the performance of an obligation imposed by the order. The court can also make an order for the preservation of property, or restraining the depletion of property pending the determination of a claim for an equalizing payment.

Contravention of an order for exclusive possession of a matrimonial home can lead to arrest without warrant and on conviction for a first offence, a fine of up to $1,000 or imprisonment for up to three months, or both. In the case of a second or subsequent offence, the penalties can be a fine of up to $10,000 or imprisonment for up to two years, or both.

The court has the power, before or after a support order is granted, to restrain the depletion of a spouse's property that would impair or defeat the rights of the claimant.

If one party applies for an order for support, or variation of a previous order for support, and the court is satisfied that the other party (the respondent) is about to leave Ontario with the intention of evading his or her responsibilities, the court may issue a warrant for the respondent's arrest for the purpose of bringing him or her before the court. This is not often invoked, but an order for arrest will usually result in some further order that the respondent stays in custody until the support is paid or secured. There are similar arrest powers to enforce an agreement between unmarried parents for expenses of prenatal care and birth, child support, or funeral expenses of the child or mother.

In connection with an application for support, or variation of a previous support order, the Superior Court of Justice and the Ontario Court both have power to order the employer of a party to the application to make a written return to the court showing the party's wages or other remuneration during the preceding twelve months. Also, in connection with an application for support, the court may require any person or public body to provide the court or the claimant with any information in any record under the person's or public body's possession or control that shows the other party's place of employment, address, or location.

The Ontario Court can punish wilful contempt of or resistance to its process by a fine of up to $1,000 or imprisonment for up to ninety days, or both. The court can make an order restraining the applicant's spouse or former spouse from molesting, annoying, or harassing the applicant or children in the applicant's lawful custody, or from communicating with the applicant except as the order provides. Contravention of such a restraining order can lead to arrest without warrant and on conviction for a first offence, a fine of up to $1,000 or imprisonment for up to three months, or both. In the case of a second or subsequent offence, the penalties can be a fine of up to $10,000 or imprisonment for up to two years, or both.

Enforcement under the *Divorce Act*

An order for corollary relief under the *Divorce Act*—that is, support, custody, or access granted in the context of a divorce judgment—has legal effect in every province of Canada. It will also have more or less legal effect in other parts of the world, depending on local statutes and regulations. Across Canada, in each province these statutes are called the *Reciprocal Enforcement of Support Orders Act*, or a similar title. In the absence of some such statutory recognition, if you need to enforce corollary relief in a foreign jurisdiction, you will likely find that your judgment has the status only of a sort of contract, and you must sue on the contract, subject to nearly any defence that could have been raised in the original proceedings. There is a fairly widespread rule in Canada and the United States that a court will only enforce a final judgment of a foreign court. Since judgments for corollary relief may be varied in accordance with material changes in circumstances, it is easy to argue that a variable judgment is not a final judgment.

The bankruptcy of the respondent does not relieve him of obligations under an order for corollary relief, though it may relieve him from paying a judgment for sharing of property under the *Family Law Act* or similar statute in any province.

Armed with an order for corollary relief, the petitioner can attach money due under a federal pension. The widow of a member of the armed forces, if entitled to financial support under a court order or separation agreement, can apply for the same pension as any widow would receive, or for the amount provided in the order of agreement. Please also see the note on rights to Canada Pension Plan benefits after divorce in Chapter 4.

Any order for corollary relief under the previous *Divorce Act* is valid and enforceable or variable as if made under the present Act.

A federal statute, the *Family Orders and Agreements Enforcement Assistance Act* (FOEA), came into force on June 1, 1986, the same date as the *Divorce Act*. It is subtitled "An Act to provide for the release of information that may assist in locating defaulting spouses and other persons and to permit, for the enforcement of support orders and support provisions, the garnishment and attachment of certain moneys payable by Her Majesty in right of Canada."

The major points of the FOEA are as follows:

- The FOEA is subject to agreements with the provinces for establishing safeguards for protection of information, and establishing provincial data banks.
- Any interested person or agency may apply to court for release of information from federal or provincial data banks to assist in the enforcement of "family provisions," meaning orders or agreements for support, custody, or access. The federal data banks are those of the Department of National Health and Welfare, and the Canada Employment and Immigration Commission.
- The information that may be searched and released is the address of the person in arrears under a support provision or who has

possession of a child who is the subject of a custody or access provision; the name and address of that person's employer or the employer of a subject child; and the address of the subject child.

- There is a procedure for garnishment (seizure or attachment) of Her Majesty, which means that the wages of a federal civil servant are exposed for the purpose of enforcing a "family provision."

12

ALTERNATE DISPUTE RESOLUTION

There is an increasing trend and considerable pressure from our judges and court administration to get cases settled through some form of alternate dispute resolution. This may take the form of voluntary or mandatory mediation in some jurisdictions, or rigorous, mediative case conferences and pre-trial conferences. Outside of, or parallel to, the court system, parties may choose to mediate or arbitrate. Mediation is a process of attempting to work out an agreement with the assistance of a person trained to facilitate agreement—a mediator—who has no power to impose any result on the parties if they are unable to agree. Mediation can occur with or without the involvement of lawyers.

Arbitration is the process of resolving a dispute by presenting evidence in some form to an arbitrator, who has the role of a private judge, appointed and paid by the parties. There will be some form of an "arbitration agreement" that sets out the issues in dispute and establishes the procedure, which may be rather formal, much like what would happen in a courtroom, or it may be much more casual. There is a statute in every jurisdiction that governs the conduct of arbitrations. Family arbitrations are available in every province except Quebec, where under the *Civil Code* family arbitrations are specifically forbidden and will not be enforced if they arise in other jurisdictions.

An arbitrator has the power to make an award, which can be enforced like a court judgment or order. Sometimes the mediation and arbitration processes are merged, so that the parties try to resolve the dispute with a mediator, and if this fails, the mediator then takes on the role of arbitrator and imposes a result on the parties. This combined mediation arbitration process requires specific agreement to do so. A mediation-arbitration agreement will be found at the end of this text.

The alternate dispute resolution process is usually expeditious and cost-effective. Most of the time it works well and to the satisfaction of the parties. As a unique example of the process gone wrong, a case is presented below in detail, as a cautionary tale.

There has been little jurisprudence on the duties and obligations of a mediator/arbitrator in a family dispute. It is often difficult to determine which role one is in at some stage of the process. *Hercus v. Hercus*, released in January 2001, is a lengthy decision of the Ontario Superior Court of Justice. The facts are complex and involve a process of mediation/arbitration entered into after divorce by agreement of the parties to resolve issues of custody, access, and child support for their two sons. The decision as arbitrator would be made under the *Arbitrations Act* and would be binding subject to possible judicial review, and the parties would be equally responsible for the costs of the "med/arb." In the court, the wife sought an order setting aside two arbitration awards and removing the arbitrator's firm and the arbitrator personally.

The wife opposed the arbitrator's acting because

- from inception, he was favourably disposed to the husband's solicitor;
- he did not respect her schedule when arranging appointments;
- he threatened to make an arbitral decision against her when she did not agree to his "mediation" recommendations, changing hats with impunity;
- he twice initiated new parenting plans at the husband's request and when she opposed him doing so and indicated she had no more money, the husband paid his fees in full;
- he issued an arbitral decision requiring her to pay the husband for the fees he had incurred as a result of a process she had no involvement in and strongly opposed;
- he had private conversations with the husband about custody issues;
- he continued to arbitrate after being expressly advised that she

had withdrawn her consent; and

- he used people in his employ to complete assessments of the children against her wishes.

She also submitted that the arbitrator treated her unfairly in that

- he withheld information from her as to the reason the husband sought a review of the parenting plan;
- he did not wait for the outcome of a CAS investigation before releasing his decision, even though his staff had reported her;
- he ordered the police to enforce his order with respect to the children after she had withdrawn her consent from continuing in the process;
- he complied with the husband's request as to the costs order; and
- he scheduled appointments without any input from her.

The husband argued that the wife was involved in every step of the process, that she was obstructive and dilatory, and that she was not entitled to enter into an agreement, and then unilaterally withdraw from it. He submitted that

- she had not satisfied the burden on her that she was not treated equally or fairly;
- it would not be in the best interests of the children to go through a trial or another arbitration process, and the children had expressed their preference in favour of their father;
- for public policy reasons, the awards under a mediation/arbitration agreement ought to be upheld. The courts ought not to allow a party to withdraw from an arbitration agreement simply because she doesn't like it any more; that would undermine confidence in the process.

The judge reviewed the provisions of the *Arbitration Act*. It is settled law that the right to a fair hearing is an independent and unqualified right. Arbitrators must listen fairly to both sides, give parties a fair opportunity to contradict or correct prejudicial statements, not receive evidence from one party behind the back of the other, and ensure that the parties know the case they have to meet. An unbiased appearance is, in itself, an essential component of procedural fairness. The legislature has given the courts clear instructions to exercise the highest deference to arbitration awards and arbitration disputes generally. Courts ought not to endorse withdrawal from a process entered into by the parties with the advice of counsel.

The parties adopted a combined process of mediation and arbitration, and these two concepts and procedures were inextricably linked in the minds of the parties. They expected that mediation would be drawn upon first, and, failing mediation, there would be resort to the arbitration process. The court referred to comments about mediation as a consensual process from which a party is free to withdraw at any time. In other words, said the trial judge, it appears at first blush that under the terms of this kind of agreement, in exercising the right to withdraw from mediation (a consensual process) with respect to any or all of the issues, a party may automatically invoke the process of arbitration (a non-consensual process) over which he or she has no control and from which he or she may not be able to withdraw unless both parties choose to do so. In this case, given the wording of the agreement, attempts to mediate were obligatory prior to moving to the arbitral process.

On the evidence, he found that there was an attempt to mediate some issues but not others. Further, the mediator/arbitrator moved to arbitration if not immediately when he determined that mediation was not possible, then within a time frame that he set but was not communicated to the wife, and without providing reasons for the urgency of the transition; as to some issues "mediation was given short shrift," and on some other issues, mediation was ignored. He adopted this opinion from an earlier decision:

> While it may be open to an arbitrator to devise and adopt a procedure for the arbitration under s. 20(1) of the *Arbitration Act* . . . I do not see why that authority should be read as allowing the arbitrator to insist on continuing with a process involving mediation that he has devised when one of the parties is no longer a willing participant . . . . I do not think that the mother should be bound by the result when the mediator, having heard that the mother now rejected mediation (something anyone who has agreed to mediation is free to do) and had lost confidence in his ability and impartiality, skipped over the mediation step and carried on as an arbitrator.
>
> If [the mediator/arbitrator] was abandoning the terms of the "dispute resolution agreement" as he called it, which called for mediation, or if he knew the mother now repudiated the agreement, I think it was incumbent on him to reach a new agreement with the parties before he proceeded to arbitrate.

The trial judge was critical of the mediator/arbitrator's scheduling of appointments; of his failure to communicate that his award was intended to be a temporary solution when the agreement mandated a final determination of the issues; and of his embarking on a "review" when there was no mandate to do so in the agreement nor in the *Arbitrations Act*. Then in undertaking a review without jurisdiction to do so, he withheld from the wife the husband's reasons for requesting a review. The wife was kept unaware that the husband was attempting to change custody, and this was not disclosed to her until after she had lost faith in the process. The conduct was not fair to the wife nor demonstrative of equal treatment. Nor was she treated fairly as to certain allegations of child abuse: an arbitral decision based on these allegations was made before the investigation was complete. The review was in the context of mediation, in which the wife was not compelled to participate. The judge was also critical of the arbitrator's handling of the costs issue.

In the result, the judge set aside the award, stating that this was not to be interpreted as comments or findings on the substantive decision of the arbitrator, removed the arbitrator and his firm from the case, and directed an expedited trial of the issues of custody and access.

Enforceability of Arbitration Agreements

Arbitration proceeds because parties agree to arbitrate. A court cannot delegate its powers and order parties to arbitrate unless the parties agree. Section 5(5) of the *Arbitration Act* provides that an arbitration agreement may be revoked only in accordance with the ordinary rules of contract law. Therefore, an arbitration agreement is enforceable like any other contract, even if one party changes his or her mind and decides against arbitration. Where there is a valid arbitration agreement, an arbitration can continue even where one party refuses to participate. Of course, like any other contract, an arbitration agreement can be amended, ignored, or terminated if both parties agree.

If there is an arbitration agreement in place, the *Arbitration Act* enforces it by requiring any court action brought on a dispute covered by the agreement to be stayed. You can't both litigate and arbitrate at the same time. But an arbitration agreement is enforceable only to the extent that any other contract is enforceable. The court may refuse to stay a proceeding where (i) a party entered into the arbitration agreement while under a legal incapacity, (ii) the arbitration agreement is invalid, or (iii) the subject matter of the dispute is not capable of being the subject of arbitration under Ontario law.

Enforceability of Arbitration Awards

An arbitration award has the same finality as a court order. Like a court order or judgment, an arbitration award binds the parties to an arbitration unless it is set aside or varied on appeal. In addition, a valid and binding arbitration award, like a court order, acts as both a shield and a sword. Where a new proceeding is brought and a party has previously been absolved of liability or the issues raised have otherwise been the subject of an arbitration award, the award forms the basis for a plea of *res judicata* or issue estoppel, principles that prevent a party from coming back for another try. The court has the same power of enforcement of arbitration awards as of its own judgments. Unlike many other provisions of the *Arbitration Act*, parties to an arbitration agreement may not agree to vary or exclude the court's power of enforcement.

Parties usually perform their obligations under an arbitration award. If they do not, under section 50(1) of the *Arbitration Act*, a person who is entitled to enforcement of an award may make an application to the Superior Court of Justice to that effect. The application must be made not more than two years after the day on which the applicant receives the award, on notice to the person against whom enforcement is sought and in accordance with the rules of court, and it must be supported by the original award or a certified copy. The party may ask the court for an order enforcing the award, so as to enable enforcement in the same manner as a judgment (for example, by such means as garnishment, seizure and sale, or through proceedings in contempt). The party may also ask for pre-judgment and post-judgment interest.

The court is required to make such an order unless (i) there is a pending appeal or application to set the award aside or for a declaration of invalidity; (ii) the thirty-day period for commencing such an appeal or application has not yet elapsed; or (iii) the award has been set aside or the arbitration has been the subject of a declaration of invalidity. If the period for commencing an appeal, an application to set the award aside, or an application for a declaration of invalidity has not yet elapsed, or if such a proceeding is pending, the court may (i) enforce the award or (ii) order, on such conditions as are just, that enforcement of the award is stayed until the period has elapsed without such a proceeding being commenced or until the pending proceeding is finally disposed of. If the court stays the enforcement of an award until a pending proceeding is finally disposed of, it may give directions for the speedy disposition of the proceeding.

An application to enforce the award does not provide a vehicle for an appeal from the award. It does not provide the judge with the opportunity to reopen the award and conduct a new hearing. The court should not hear evidence on the merits of the dispute in determining whether leave to enforce should be granted. The scope of the discretion to grant leave to enforce does not extend to inquiries that are appropriate to an application to set aside the award when no such application has been made. Mr. Justice Nelson made this point in the 2005 decision of *Shoval* when considering a father's motion to incorporate an award into an order pursuant to section 50 of the *Arbitration Act*:

> It could be said that the proper course of action for the mother to take would have been to launch an appeal of the arbitration award, under s. 46 of the *Arbitration Act*. However, she did not, and it now appears that time has expired on that option in any event. So, in making this decision, I must restrict myself to considering the motion [to enforce] brought pursuant to s. 50.

Of course, as Mr. Justice Nelson noted in *Shoval*, there are challenges one or both parties may make to an award if they take the proper steps, including under sections 45 and 46 of the *Arbitration Act* (see below).

Challenges to Arbitration Awards or Agreements

For the most part, the *Arbitration Act* has given parties to an arbitration the ability to conduct their affairs with little court intervention. Section 6 specifies that no court shall intervene in matters governed by the *Arbitration Act*, except for the following purposes, in accordance with the *Arbitration Act*:

1. to assist the conducting of arbitrations;
2. to ensure that arbitrations are conducted in accordance with arbitration agreements;

3. to prevent unequal or unfair treatment of parties to arbitration agreements; and
4. to enforce awards.

However, the court is entitled to vary or set aside arbitration awards and agreements on limited grounds, as set forth below.

Appeal under Section 45 of the *Arbitration Act*

At date of writing it is possible for parties to contract out of all rights to appeal under section 45 of the *Arbitration Act*, thereby limiting their exposure to threats to the finality of an arbitration award based on appellate review. This will change when Bill 27, the *Family Statute Amendment Act*, which received third reading on February 14, 2006, comes into force. The Bill provides that in family law arbitrations, the parties cannot waive a right of appeal; see below, and note this applies only to Ontario.

Under section 45 of the *Arbitration Act*, if the arbitration agreement so provides, a party may appeal an award to the Superior Court of Justice on a question of law, on a question of fact, or on a question of mixed fact and law. If the arbitration agreement does not deal with appeals on questions of law, pursuant to section 45(1) a party may appeal an award to the court on a question of law, with leave, where the court is satisfied that (i) the importance to the parties of the matters at stake in the arbitration justifies an appeal; and (ii) the determination of the question of law at issue will significantly affect the rights of the parties. Accordingly, as matters now stand, if the parties do not want rights of appeal on any basis, they should say so in the arbitration agreement.

If the parties to an arbitration agreement have not contracted out of all rights of appeal, there exists the possibility that one or both parties may seek appellate review of an award. On appeal the court may confirm, vary or set aside the award, or remit the award to the arbitrator with the court's opinion on the question of law (in the case of an appeal on a question of law), and give directions about the conduct of the arbitration. Pursuant to section 49 of the *Arbitration Act*, there is a further right of appeal from the court's decision in an appeal of an award to the Court of Appeal, with leave.

Very few arbitration awards are appealed. In those cases that have gone before the courts, it seems as though the courts are taking into account the well-recognized principle of both law and public policy that where parties have contracted to arbitrate a dispute, the courts should be loathe to intervene. For the most part, the courts have been reluctant to interfere in family law arbitration awards, and give deference to the arbitrator. The standard of review has been expressed like this:

> With respect to the standard that should be applied on a review of an Award by an Arbitrator, it is established that the court should not interfere with the arbitrator's award unless it is satisfied that the arbitrator acted on the basis of a wrong principle, disregarded material evidence or misapprehended the evidence.

In *Lalonde*, a 1994 appeal from a custody arbitration, the judge declined to interfere with an award, even though he found the arbitrator's decision not to order a family assessment troublesome. Mr. Justice Morin stated:

> I must also say that the arbitrator's decision not to order a family assessment before making a final decision as to custody is somewhat troublesome to me. In her reasons, the arbitrator listed a number of concerns that she had about the respondent's situation that might impact on the best interests of the children and the ultimate issue of custody. The arbitrator, in her reasons, listed as well concerns that she had about the appellant as they related to the same issues. Had I been sitting as arbitrator I might have been inclined to order a family unit assessment, as requested by the appellant, to assist me in arriving at a final decision as to custody. However, it is not my function on this appeal and review to substitute my decision for that of the arbitrator. I must, rather, determine whether the arbitrator has made an error in law in not ordering such an assessment, an error in law which would justify the setting aside of her award. I have concluded that no such error was committed by the arbitrator in deciding not to order a family unit assessment.

Setting Aside an Award: Section 46 of the *Arbitration Act*

The parties cannot contract out of section 46, which empowers the court to set aside an arbitration award in certain circumstances. The court may set aside an award on any of the following grounds:

1. a party entered into the arbitration agreement while under a legal incapacity;
2. the arbitration agreement is invalid or has ceased to exist;

3. the award deals with a dispute that the arbitration agreement does not cover or contains a decision on a matter that is beyond the scope of the agreement;
4. the composition of the arbitration tribunal was not in accordance with the agreement or, if the agreement did not deal with that matter, was not in accordance with the *Arbitration Act*;
5. the subject matter of the dispute is not capable of being the subject of arbitration under Ontario law;
6. the applicant was not treated equally and fairly, was not given an opportunity to present a case or to respond to another party's case, or was not given proper notice of the arbitration or of the appointment of an arbitrator;
7. the procedures followed in the arbitration did not comply with the *Arbitration Act*;
8. an arbitrator has committed a corrupt or fraudulent act or there is a reasonable apprehension of bias;
9. the award was obtained by fraud.

As to bias the court shall not set aside an award on these grounds if the party had an opportunity to challenge the arbitrator on these grounds under section 13 of the *Arbitration Act* before the award was made and did not do so, or if those grounds were the subject of an unsuccessful challenge to bias; and the court shall not set aside an award on a ground to which the applicant is deemed to have waived the right to object.

When the court sets aside an award, it may remove the arbitrator and give directions about the conduct of the arbitration. Alternatively, the court may decline to set aside an award and instead remit it to the arbitrator and give directions about the conduct of the arbitration. Pursuant to section 49 of the *Arbitration Act*, an appeal from the court's decision in an application to set aside an award may be made to the Court of Appeal, with leave.

Generally, as in the case of appeals under section 45 of the *Arbitration Act*, the courts are reluctant to set aside an arbitration award under section 46. For example, in *Lalonde*, the court declined to interfere with an award granting custody to the mother despite the fact that the arbitration had not been recorded as required under the arbitration agreement. Mr. Justice Morin stated:

To the extent that the procedure followed at the time of the arbitration hearing on June 9th, 1994, did not comply strictly with the procedure agreed to by the parties in the arbitration agreement, in all of the circumstances of this case, the parties must be deemed to have waived such strict compliance. Specifically, they must be deemed to have waived the requirement of the arbitration agreement that a recording be made of the proceeding. The absence of such a recording, therefore, does not, as argued by the appellant, render the arbitration award null and void.

In December 2005, an unhappy applicant sought to set aside a family law arbitration award on grounds of unfair procedure and perceived bias using a process called judicial review under the *Judicial Review Procedure Act.* This process may be used in challenging the decision of an arbitration tribunal set up under a statute, but not where the arbitration proceeds under the private contract of the parties. The Divisional Court held that judicial review had no application, and the remedy, if any, had to be found under section 46. The provisions of section 46 are pretty much what a court would consider on judicial review; the practical difference is that an application under section 46 goes to a single judge and not a three-judge panel of the Divisional Court.

The *Family Statute Law Amendment Act, 2005,* and Family Arbitrations

Up to now, Ontario law does not differentiate between family law arbitrations and other arbitrations under the *Arbitration Act.* Up to now, parties to an arbitration agreement can choose the law that will govern the arbitration, including the right to appeal or not to appeal.

Because of the controversy about the use of faith-based law in family arbitrations, the Ontario government commissioned a report in which the former Attorney General, Marion Boyd, made a series of recommendations about how family law arbitrations should be conducted.[1] The essential terms of that report have been rejected by the government in introducing a Bill on November 15, 2005, the *Family Statute Law Amendment Act, 2005,* and in particular in proposing amendments to the *Arbitration Act* and complementary amendments to the *Family Law Act.* This Bill creates a new regime for Ontario family law arbitrations by requiring that a family law arbitration can only be conducted exclusively in accordance with

---

1. For the full text or an executive summary of the Boyd Report, go to http://www.attorneygeneral.jus. gov.on.ca/english/about/pubs/boyd/

the law of Ontario or another Canadian jurisdiction. Parties will not only be denied the right to have an arbitration under their religious faith (i.e., a faith-based arbitration), they will also be denied the right to choose the law, such as New York or English law, to apply to their arbitration agreement. Arbitrations conducted on the basis of anything other than Ontario or Canadian law will not be enforceable in Ontario courts. The government wants to be sure that its citizens are not subjected to faith-based arbitration or arbitration that is not conducted under a secular legal system. Of course, one may assume that parties who want faith-based arbitration will continue to do it, and that they were never likely to seek enforcement outside of their communities anyway.

The amendments will include family arbitration agreements as another form of domestic contract (see Chapter 10). "Family arbitration" means an arbitration that:

(a) deals with matters that could be dealt with in a marriage contract, separation agreement, cohabitation agreement, or paternity agreement, and
(b) is conducted exclusively in accordance with the law of Ontario or of another Canadian jurisdiction.

Parties to arbitration agreements will have to ensure that the agreements are domestic contracts under Part IV of the *Family Law Act* and, accordingly, these agreements will need to be both signed by the parties and witnessed. The agreement must be in writing, and the parties must have had independent legal advice before making the arbitration agreement. The *Family Statute Law Amendment Act, 2005,* also provides for a series of regulations that will require family law arbitrators to (i) be members of a specified dispute resolution organization, (ii) undergo training, (iii) submit reports, (iv) inquire into matters such as power imbalances and domestic violence, and (v) keep records.

The *Family Statute Law Amendment Act, 2005*, would prohibit parties from agreeing to family law arbitration in advance of a dispute. An agreement in a marriage contract to go to arbitration in the event of a breakdown of the marriage will be void. Many separation agreements now provide for future arbitration in the event of a dispute about the terms. Those provisions may also be void.

Possibly the most important change in the *Family Statute Law Amendment Act, 2005*, is the elimination of the right to waive the right of appeal in family law arbitrations. The right of appeal from an arbitration award is limited, as noted above. As matters now stand, many parties want certainty and finality and confidentiality; they want never to appear before a court. Many parties opt out of the right of appeal and specifically waive any right of appeal (they do not waive, and indeed cannot waive their rights to apply to set aside an arbitration award under section 46, but that is not an appeal). *The Family Statute Law Amendment Act, 2005,* will prohibit such a waiver and make such a waiver ineffective. One wonders why parties should not have the right of waiver if that is their free choice.

The following is most of an explanatory note that accompanied third reading of Bill 27:

EXPLANATORY NOTE

1. The term "family arbitration" is applied only to processes conducted exclusively in accordance with the law of Ontario or of another Canadian jurisdiction. Other third-party decision-making processes in family matters are not family arbitrations and have no legal effect.

2. Both the *Arbitration Act, 1991,* and the *Family Law Act* apply to family arbitrations, and the *Family Law Act* governs in case of conflict between the two statutes.

3. Family arbitration agreements are domestic contracts under Part IV of the *Family Law Act* and are enforced under that Act, not under the *Arbitration Act, 1991.*

4. A family arbitration agreement must be in writing, and each party must receive independent legal advice before making the arbitration agreement.

5. Power is provided to make regulations under the *Arbitration Act, 1991,* to govern family arbitrations. For example, these regulations could require arbitrators who conduct family arbitrations to be members of a specified dispute resolution organization, to undergo training, to submit reports, to inquire into matters such as power imbalances and domestic violence, and to keep records.

6. A number of additional rules are provided for family arbitrations (for example, a party's failure to object to an irregularity in the arbitration will not be considered a waiver of the right to object later).

7. A family arbitration award may be enforced using a process similar to that set out in section 50 of the *Arbitration Act, 1991* (that is, by motion to a judge of the Family Court in the five Ontario judicial districts where it operates, and to a judge of the Superior Court in the rest of the Province).

Appendix A

WHAT YOUR LAWYER WILL PROBABLY WANT TO KNOW

The first meeting between a lawyer and a new client who has a matrimonial problem is something like the first meeting with a doctor. It's a fact-gathering session in which the lawyer is likely to ask a lot of questions to compile the history he or she needs as a basis for advising the client and planning tactics.

You can make it easier for your lawyer and yourself by putting together information before the first interview. The list that follows will cover most of the usual questions. Whenever possible, I like to get the information delivered before the first meeting, so I can be well prepared.

Personal Data

- Correct full names of the spouses and the date and place of the marriage. Try to bring along your marriage certificate.
- Addresses, telephone and fax numbers, and e-mail addresses of all parties, including residence addresses for at least the past year.
- Correct full names and birth dates of all children of the marriage; information about their past, present, and proposed residence, maintenance, and education.
- Information about any health problems, disabilities, or special needs.

- Information about education, work history, and current employment.
- Data about the prior marriage of either spouse. A certified copy of a divorce decree dissolving a previous marriage would be helpful.
- Date and duration of any previous separation.
- Particulars of any previous legal proceedings between the spouses or involving any of the children.
- Information about any domestic contract between the spouses. If you have such an agreement, bring along a copy.
- If adultery is a factor, as much information as possible about where, when, and with whom the adultery occurred.
- If cruelty or domestic violence is a factor, dates and places where it occurred; where and when any medical treatment was obtained; whether the police were ever involved and, if so, dates and places; details of psychiatric treatment for either spouse during the marriage or since separation.
- Information about any attempts at reconciliation or marriage counselling.

Financial Data

For the first interview, try to bring along at least your last year's income tax return (three years of tax returns if possible) information about current income, and a basic net-worth statement, showing the substantial assets and liabilities of the spouses.

You should expect to make full financial disclosure. This must be done accurately and in good faith. It's not always easy to do. The financial statement form used in Ontario is reproduced on the following pages. The complexity may be daunting; sometimes the assistance of an accountant is needed. This form includes a budget, which often reveals, for the first time, real cash-flow need. On page 189 you will find a typical instructional letter that we give to clients to assist in filling out the financial statement.

ONTARIO

Court File Number

(Name of court)

at _____

Court office address

Family Law Rules, O. Reg. 114/99
**Form 13.1: Financial
Statement (Property and
Support Claims)
sworn/affirmed**

Applicant(s)

Full legal name & address for service — street & number, municipality, postal code, telephone & fax numbers and e-mail address (if any).	*Lawyer's name & address — street & number, municipality, postal code, telephone & fax numbers and e-mail address (if any).*

Respondent(s)

Full legal name & address for service — street & number, municipality, postal code, telephone & fax numbers and e-mail address (if any).	*Lawyer's name & address — street & number, municipality, postal code, telephone & fax numbers and e-mail address (if any).*

INSTRUCTIONS

1. USE THIS FORM IF:
   - you are making or responding to a claim for property or exclusive possession of the matrimonial home and its contents; or
   - you are making or responding to a claim for property or exclusive possession of the matrimonial home and its contents together with other claims for relief.

2. DO NOT USE THIS FORM AND INSTEAD USE FORM 13 IF:
   - you are making or responding to a claim for support but NOT making or responding to a claim for property or exclusive possession of the matrimonial home and its contents.

1. **My name is** *(full legal name)* _____

   I live in *(municipality & province)* _____

   and I swear/affirm that the following is true:

   My financial statement set out on the following *(specify number)* _____ pages is accurate

   to the best of my knowledge and belief and sets out the financial situation as of *(give date for which information is*

   accurate) _____ for

   Check one or more boxes, as circumstances require.

   ☐ me

   ☐ the following person(s): *(Give name(s) and relationship to you.)*

   _____

   _____

FLR 13.1 (Rev. 04/03)

Continued on next sheet →
(Français au verso)

Form 13.1: **Financial Statement (Property and**   **(page 2)**
Support Claims)

Court file number

NOTE: When you show monthly income and expenses, give the current actual amount if you know it or can find out. To get a monthly figure you must multiply any weekly income by 4.33 or divide any yearly income by 12.

PART 1: INCOME

for the 12 months from *(date)* _____ to *(date)* _____

Include all income and other money that you get from all sources, whether taxable or not. Show the gross amount here and show your deductions in Part 3.

	CATEGORY	Monthly			CATEGORY	Monthly
1.	Pay, wages, salary, including overtime (before deductions)			9.	Rent, board received	
				10.	Canada Child Tax Benefit	
2.	Bonuses, fees, commissions			11.	Support payments actually received	
3.	Social assistance			12.	Income received by children	
4.	Employment insurance			13.	G.S.T. refund	
5.	Workers' compensation			14.	Payments from trust funds	
6.	Pensions			15.	Gifts received	
7.	Dividends			16.	Other *(Specify. If necessary, attach an extra sheet.)*	
8.	Interest					
				17.	**INCOME FROM ALL SOURCES**	

PART 2: OTHER BENEFITS

Show your non-cash benefits — such as the use of a company car, a club membership or room and board that your employer or someone else provides for you or benefits that are charged through or written off by your business.

ITEM	DETAILS	Monthly Market Value
	18. TOTAL	

19. **GROSS MONTHLY INCOME AND BENEFITS** *(Add* [17] *plus* [18].*)* $ _____

PART 3: AUTOMATIC DEDUCTIONS FROM INCOME

for the 12 months from *(date)* _____ to *(date)* _____

	TYPE OF EXPENSE	Monthly			TYPE OF EXPENSE	Monthly
20.	Income tax deducted from pay			25.	Group insurance	
21.	*Canada Pension Plan*			26.	Other *(Specify. If necessary, attach an extra sheet.)*	
22.	Other pension plans					
23.	Employment insurance					
24.	Union or association dues			27.	**TOTAL AUTOMATIC DEDUCTIONS**	

28. **NET MONTHLY INCOME** *(Do the subtraction:* [19] *minus* [27].*)* $ _____

FLR 13.1 (Rev. 04/03)

Continued on next sheet →
(Français au verso)

Form 13.1:   Financial Statement (Property and   (page 3)   Court file number
                Support Claims)

PART 4: TOTAL EXPENSES

for the 12 months from *(date)* _____ to *(date)* _____

NOTE: *This part must be completed in all cases. You must set out your TOTAL living expenses, including those expenses involving any children now living in your home. This part may also be used for a proposed budget. To prepare a proposed budget, photocopy Part 4, complete as necessary, change the title to "Proposed Budget" and attach it to this form.*

TYPE OF EXPENSE	Monthly		TYPE OF EXPENSE	Monthly
Housing			**Child(ren)**	
29. Rent/mortgage			57. School activities (field trips, etc.)	
30. Property taxes & municipal levies			58. School lunches	
31. Condominium fees & common expenses			59. School fees, books, tuition, *etc.* (for children)	
32. Water			60. Summer camp	
33. Electricity & heating fuel			61. Activities (music lessons, clubs, sports)	
34. Telephone			62. Allowances	
35. Cable television & pay television			63. Baby sitting	
36. Home insurance			64. Day care	
37. Home repairs, maintenance, gardening			65. Regular dental care	
			66. Orthodontics or special dental care	
Sub-total of items [29] to [37]			67. Medicine & drugs	
Food, Clothing and Transportation etc.			68. Eye glasses or contact lenses	
38. Groceries			**Sub-total of items [57] to [68]**	
39. Meals outside home			**Miscellaneous and Other**	
40. General household supplies			69. Books for home use, newspapers, magazines, videos, compact discs	
41. Hairdresser, barber & toiletries			70. Gifts	
42. Laundry & dry cleaning			71. Charities	
43. Clothing			72. Alcohol & tobacco	
44. Public transit			73. Pet expenses	
45. Taxis			74. School fees, books, tuition, *etc.*	
46. Car insurance			75. Entertainment & recreation	
47. Licence			76. Vacation	
48. Car loan payments			77. Credit cards *(but not for expenses mentioned elsewhere in the statement)*	
49. Car maintenance and repairs			78. R.R.S.P. or other savings plans	
50. Gasoline & oil			79. Support actually being paid in any other case	
51. Parking			80. Income tax and *Canada* Pension Plan *(not deducted from pay)*	
Sub-total of items [38] to [51]			81. Other *(Specify. If necessary attach an extra sheet.)*	
Health and Medical *(do not include child(ren)'s expenses)*				
52. Regular dental care				
53. Orthodontics or special dental care			**Sub-total of items [69] to [81]**	
54. Medicine & drugs				
55. Eye glasses or contact lenses			82. **Total of items [29] to [81]**	
56. Life or term insurance premiums				
Sub-total of items [52] to [56]				

SUMMARY OF INCOME AND EXPENSES

Net monthly income *(item* **[28]** *above)* =$ _____

Subtract actual monthly expenses *(item* **[82]** *above)* =$ _____

ACTUAL MONTHLY SURPLUS/DEFICIT =$ _____

Continued on next sheet →
(Français au verso)

FLR 13.1 (Rev. 04/03)

Form 13.1:	Financial Statement (Property and Support Claims)	(page 4)	Court file number

PART 5: OTHER INCOME INFORMATION

1. I am ☐ employed by *(name and address of employer)*

☐ self-employed, carrying on business under the name of *(name and address of business)*

☐ unemployed since *(date when last employed)*

2. I attach the following required information *(if you are filing this statement to update or correct an earlier statement, then you do not need to attach income tax returns that have already been filed with the court):*

☐ a copy of my income tax returns that were filed with the Canada Customs and Revenue Agency for the past 3 taxation years, together with a copy of all material filed with the returns and a copy of any notices of assessment or re-assessment that I have received from the Canada Customs and Revenue Agency for those years; or

☐ a statement from the Canada Customs and Revenue Agency that I have not filed any income tax returns from the past 3 years; or

☐ a direction in Form 13A signed by me to the Taxation Branch of the Canada Customs and Revenue Agency for the disclosure of my tax returns and notices of assessment to the other part for the past 3 years.

I attach proof of my current income, including my most recent

☐ pay cheque stub. ☐ employment insurance stub. ☐ worker's compensation stub.
☐ pension stub. ☐ Other. *(Specify.)*

3. ☐ *(check if applicable)* I am an Indian within the meaning of the *Indian Act* (Canada) and all my income is tax exempt and I am not required to file an income tax return. I have therefore not attached an income tax return for the past three years.

PART 6: OTHER INCOME EARNERS IN THE HOME

Complete this part only if you are making a claim for undue hardship or spousal support. Indicate at paragraph 1 or 2, whether you are living with another person (for example, spouse, same sex partner, roommate or tenant). If you complete paragraph 2, also complete paragraphs 3 to 6.

1. ☐ I live alone.

2. I am living with *(full legal name of person)* _____

3. This person has *(give number)* _____ child(ren) living in the home.

4. This person ☐ works at *(place of work or business)* _____
☐ does not work outside the home.

5. This person ☐ earns (give amount) $ _____ per _____
☐ does not earn anything.

6. This person ☐ contributes about $ _____ per _____ towards the household expenses.
☐ contributes no money to the household expenses.

FLR 13.1 (Rev. 04/03)

Continued on next sheet →
(Français au verso)

Form 13.1: **Financial Statement (Property and**   **(page 5)**
Support Claims)

Court file number

PART 7: ASSETS IN AND OUT OF ONTARIO

If any sections of Parts 7 to 12 do not apply, do not leave blank, print "NONE" in the section.

The date of marriage is: *(give date)* _____

The valuation date is: *(give date)* _____

The date of commencement of cohabitation is (if different from date of marriage): *(give date)* _____

PART 7(a): LAND

*Include any interest in land **owned** on the dates in each of the columns below, including leasehold interests and mortgages. Show estimated market value of your interest, but do not deduct encumbrances or costs of disposition; these encumbrances and costs should be shown under Part 8, "Debts and Other Liabilities".*

Nature & Type of Ownership *(Give your percentage interest where relevant.)*	Address of Property	Estimated Market Value of YOUR Interest		
		on date of marriage	on valuation date	today
	83. TOTAL VALUE OF LAND	$		

PART 7(b): GENERAL HOUSEHOLD ITEMS AND VEHICLES

Show estimated market value, not the cost of replacement for these items owned on the dates in each of the columns below. Do not deduct encumbrances or costs of disposition; these encumbrances and costs should be shown under Part 8, "Debts and Other Liabilities".

Item	Description	Indicate if NOT in your possession	Estimated Market Value of YOUR Interest		
			on date of marriage	on valuation date	today
Household goods & furniture					
Cars, boats, vehicles					
Jewellery, art, electronics, tools, sports & hobby equipment					
Other special items					
84. TOTAL VALUE OF GENERAL HOUSEHOLD ITEMS AND VEHICLES			$		

FLR 13.1 (Rev. 04/03)

Continued on next sheet →
(Français au verso)

Form 13.1: **Financial Statement (Property and Support Claims)** **(page 6)** | Court file number

PART 7(c): BANK ACCOUNTS, SAVINGS, SECURITIES AND PENSIONS

Show the items owned on the dates in each of the columns below by category, for example, cash, accounts in financial institutions, pensions, registered retirement or other savings plans, deposit receipts, any other savings, bonds, warrants, options, notes and other securities. Give your best estimate of the market value of the securities if the items were to be sold on the open market.

Category	INSTITUTION (including location)/ DESCRIPTION (including issuer and date)	Account number	Amount/Estimated Market Value		
			on date of marriage	on valuation date	today

85. TOTAL VALUE OF ACCOUNTS, SAVINGS, SECURITIES AND PENSIONS	$

PART 7(d): LIFE AND DISABILITY INSURANCE

List all policies in existence on the dates in each of the columns below.

Company, Type & Policy No.	Owner	Beneficiary	Face Amount	Cash Surrender Value		
				on date of marriage	on valuation date	today

86. TOTAL CASH SURRENDER VALUE OF INSURANCE POLICIES	$

PART 7(e): BUSINESS INTERESTS

Show any interest in an unincorporated business owned on the dates in each of the columns below. An interest in an incorporated business may be shown here or under "BANK ACCOUNTS, SAVINGS, SECURITIES, AND PENSIONS" in Part 7(c). Give your best estimate of the market value of your interest.

Name of Firm or Company	Interest	Estimated Market Value of YOUR Interest		
		on date of marriage	on valuation date	today

87. TOTAL VALUE OF BUSINESS INTERESTS	$

FLR 13.1 (Rev. 04/03)

Continued on next sheet →
(Français au verso)

Form 13.1:   **Financial Statement (Property and**   (page 7)
             Support Claims)

Court file number

PART 7(f): MONEY OWED TO YOU

Give details of all money that other persons owe to you on the dates in each of the columns below, whether because of business or from personal dealings. Include any court judgments in your favour, any estate money and any income tax refunds owed to you.

Details	Amount Owed to You		
	on date of marriage	on valuation date	today
88. TOTAL OF MONEY OWED TO YOU	$		

PART 7(g): OTHER PROPERTY

Show other property or assets owned on the dates in each of the columns below. Include property of any kind not listed above. Give your best estimate of market value.

Category	Details	Estimated Market Value of YOUR interest		
		on date of marriage	on valuation date	today
89. TOTAL VALUE OF OTHER PROPERTY		$		
90. VALUE OF ALL PROPERTY OWNED ON THE VALUATION DATE *(Add items [83] to [89].)*		$		

PART 8: DEBTS AND OTHER LIABILITIES

Show your debts and other liabilities on the dates in each of the columns below. List them by category such as mortgages, charges, liens, notes, credit cards, and accounts payable. Don't forget to include:

- *any money owed to the Canada Customs and Revenue Agency;*
- *contingent liabilities such as guarantees or warranties given by you (but indicate that they are contingent); and*
- *any unpaid legal or professional bills as a result of this case.*

Category	Details	Amount Owing		
		on date of marriage	on valuation date	today
91. TOTAL OF DEBTS AND OTHER LIABILITIES		$		

Continued on next sheet →
(Français au verso)

FLR 13.1 (Rev. 04/03)

Form 13.1: **Financial Statement (Property and** **(page 8)**
Support Claims)

Court file number

PART 9: PROPERTY, DEBTS AND OTHER LIABILITIES ON DATE OF MARRIAGE

Show by category the value of your property and your debts and other liabilities **as of the date of your marriage.** DO NOT INCLUDE THE VALUE OF A MATRIMONIAL HOME THAT YOU OWNED ON THE DATE OF MARRIAGE IF THIS PROPERTY IS STILL A MATRIMONIAL HOME ON VALUATION DATE.

Category and details	Value on date of marriage	
	Assets	Liabilities
Land		
General household items & vehicles		
Bank accounts, savings, securities & pensions		
Life & disability insurance		
Business interests		
Money owed to you		
Other property *(Specify.)*		
Debts and other liabilities *(Specify.)*		
TOTALS	$	$
92. NET VALUE OF PROPERTY OWNED ON DATE OF MARRIAGE *(From the total of the "Assets" column, subtract the total of the "Liabilities" column.)*	$	
93. VALUE OF ALL DEDUCTIONS *(Add items [91] and [92].)*	$	

PART 10: EXCLUDED PROPERTY

Show by category the value of property owned on the valuation date that is excluded from the definition of "net family property" (such as gifts or inheritances received after marriage).

Category	Details	Value on valuation date
94. TOTAL VALUE OF EXCLUDED PROPERTY		$

FLR 13.1 (Rev. 04/03)

Continued on next sheet →
(Français au verso)

Form 13.1: **Financial Statement (Property and** (page 9)
Support Claims)

Court file number

PART 11: DISPOSED-OF PROPERTY

Show by category the value of all property that you disposed of during the two years immediately preceding the making of this statement, or during the marriage, whichever period is shorter.

Category	Details	Value
	95. TOTAL VALUE OF DISPOSED-OF PROPERTY $

PART 12: CALCULATION OF NET FAMILY PROPERTY

	Deductions	BALANCE
Value of all property owned on valuation date *(from item [90] above)*		$
Subtract value of all deductions *(from item [93] above)* $		$
Subtract total value of excluded property *(from item [94] above)* $		$
96. NET FAMILY PROPERTY		$

☐ I do not expect changes in my financial situation.

☐ I do expect changes in my financial situation as follows:

☐ I attach a proposed budget in the format of Part 4 of this form.

NOTE: *As soon as you find out that the information in this financial statement is incorrect or incomplete, or there is a material change in your circumstances that affects or will affect the information in this financial statement, you MUST serve on every other party to this case and file with the court:*
- *a new financial statement with updated information, or*
- *if changes are minor, an affidavit in Form 14A setting out the details of these changes.*

Sworn/Affirmed before me at _____
municipality

in _____
province, state or country

on _____
date   _____
Commissioner for taking affidavits
(Type or print name below if signature is illegible.)

_____
Signature
(This form is to be signed in front of a lawyer, justice of the peace, notary public or commissioner for taking affidavits.)

FLR 13.1 (Rev. 04/03)

(Français au verso)

Instructional Memo for Financial Statement

To:
From:

Enclosed you will find a financial statement which we would like you to start working on. This will be needed in both negotiations and litigation. Careful and detailed completion of the statement will save a substantial amount of time which translates into lower legal fees. If you have difficulty preparing this, please call me and I will be pleased to help you. You can reach me at [number].

Income may be declared for the most recent taxation year, or you may project your income for the current taxation or calendar year. The choice of the appropriate period is very significant in that the form should state income which most accurately reflects your current financial position. You may be required to disclose income for various other periods in due course. However, the form should not reflect an unusually high or unusually low income. As the form specifies, please also show other money received, even it is not in the nature of income, for example, any gifts or receipts of capital.

The "Actual Budget" as it says in the form, should be "actual monthly expenses or your best estimates where you cannot ascertain actual amounts." Most people have some difficulty in estimating costs of clothing, entertainment, recreation, vacation, gifts and a number of other items that are not regular recurring expenses. Please give us your best estimate of these based on the standard of living you now have, even if it is not in accordance with the accustomed standard or your expectations. The "proposed budget" should be based upon the accustomed standard or your expectations, if your expenses will be changing. In some cases the completion of this portion of the form may not be necessary if it does not convey any real information. If you feel that comment applies to you, you should speak to us.

We suggest you use a notebook to annotate your expenses. It would be convenient if you used one page for each item. These annotations should be in the same numerical order as the list of expenses in the financial statement. Some of these are very easy to annotate; so, for example, if you are making mortgage payments or paying rent you can just put down a note to whom these items are being paid and, for example, if a mortgage, you could set out that the payments are so much a month including principal, interest, taxes, as the case may be. These annotations will be particularly useful as to the items referred to above, in which most people have difficulty in making estimates. Therefore, you should, for example, think about the amount of clothing you have bought in the past year, and what you may require in the near future, and write down some explanation of it. Similarly, when it comes to an item such as entertainment, set down your pattern of expenses and the individual items that make this up, whatever these may be. These annotations will be helpful if, at some point, you must justify or rationalize your expenses. You should retain this notebook and revise it and make further annotations from time to time as may be required. We may ask you to bring this notebook to conferences with us, and we suggest you treat it as confidential, being prepared for the purpose of instructing your solicitors.

This Financial Statement includes matters under Part I of the *Family Law Act*, leading to a calculation of "net family property." In each category please list all significant assets or "classes" of assets (furniture may be grouped, for instance). Each asset or class should be valued as at the date of marriage (if it existed at that time), on the "valuation date" (generally, the date you and your spouse separated), and as of the date you prepare the statement. The estimated market value of your interests should be your share without deduction of any encumbrances, the latter being shown under debts. For example, as to a matrimonial home, of which you are a joint owner or entitled to a share, put down one-half of the estimated market value, unless there is some good reason for deviating from this. If there is a mortgage, put down one half of the balance owing under "Debts." Again, we would be pleased to help you and, in any event, we will be editing your work.

Commencing on page 5 you will find a schedule of assets. As to Land, list all real estate of which you are a registered owner.

On page 6 in dealing with household items and vehicles, it is not necessary to provide a catalogue or inventory. You are asked to show the estimated market value or value(s) of these, which would be the value you are likely to get if you were to dispose of these items. This usually means something substantially less than replacement cost, but there may be some items that have appreciated since you bought them and should be treated accordingly.

On page 6, be sure to list under "Bank Accounts, Savings, Securities and Pensions" all bank accounts, even if there is a very small balance. Pensions are part of the "property" subject to an equalizing payment to a spouse. List any RSP at present value, without deducting the tax which would be paid if you cashed it in. If you have a pension entitlement, just show that but don't try to value it; please supply us with a copy of whatever information you can gather up as to your pension benefits package. Under "Life and Disability Insurance" set out the insurance in which you have any interest, whether as an owner or beneficiary.

On page 8 please list both your current debts and liabilities and those you had at the date of the marriage. In addition, in the lower box, list the property you owned at the date of the marriage, and its value as of that date. Remember that "property" means any kind of asset, present or future, vested or contingent.

On page 9, you are asked to list "excluded property", valued as of the "valuation date." Assume the valuation date is the date of actual or intended separation. You may exclude the value of property that you own on the valuation date:

(a) Acquired by gift or inheritance from a third person after the date of the marriage, other than the matrimonial home. This exclusion does not usually extend to the income that you may have earned on such a gift or inheritance. If this applies to you, please discuss it with us;

(b) Deriving from damages or a right to damages for personal injuries;

(c) Deriving from proceeds or a right to proceeds of a policy of life insurance payable on the death of the life insured;

(d) Traceable to the exclusions set out above; and

(e) If you have a marriage contract, whatever you and your spouse have agreed will be excluded.

A problem may arise where any of this excluded property changed its identity. An inheritance might have been received in cash, invested in bonds, and used on cashing the bonds to buy a car. You are entitled to trace excluded property right up to the valuation date, if you can. Of course, in may cases, this is impossible. Some of this becomes quite technical; we will review and discuss with you all aspects of any excluded property.

We look forward to the return of your "homework" at your earliest convenience. A hand-written form is satisfactory, since we will be entering it into a computer.

Please do not hesitate to ask for assistance.

Appendix B

COMPARATIVE ANALYSIS OF FAMILY PROPERTY LEGISLATION

Since the Ontario *Family Law Reform Act* was passed in 1978, each of the other provinces has passed a new family property statute. There is no uniformity to the legislation and thus tremendous potential for conflict of laws. All number references are to sections of the statute.

	ALBERTA
Statute	*Matrimonial Property Act*
Intent	Unstated
Jurisdiction	Supreme or District Court (1)
Who may apply	A spouse, if habitual residence of both spouses, or last joint habitual residence was Alberta; or a party to a divorce petition issued in Alberta (5)
When may order be made	If a decree nisi or declaration of nullity or a judgment of judicial separation is made; if spouses have been living separate and apart for at least one year before application, or less if there is no possibility of reconciliation; or if the defendant spouse transfers or dissipates

property or intends to do so. May be commenced not later than two years after decree nisi, declaration of annulment, or judgment of judicial separation, etc. (6)

Property included	All property owned by both spouses and by each of them (7.1)
Property excluded	Market value of property at time of marriage or acquisition, whichever is later, acquired by third-party gift, inheritance, damages for tort, insurance proceeds; or acquired before the marriage (7.2)
Basic entitlement	Just and equitable distribution, considering: contribution (including that of a homemaker or parent); income, earning capacity, liabilities, obligations, property and other financial resources; duration of marriage; date of acquisition; agreement; previous gifts or transfers; previous distribution between spouses; prior order; tax liability as a result of transfer or sale; dissipation of property; "any fact or circumstance that is relevant" (8)
Powers of court	Partition, sale, transfer, division, order for payment, declaration re title; order for charging, security, imposing trust, variation of prior order, "any other order that in the opinion of the court is necessary" (9)
Date of valuation	Not specifically stated, but probably the date of trial
Effect of agreement	Overrides statutory property rights; must contain written acknowledgment made before lawyer. (37, 38) Non-reviewable if valid

BRITISH COLUMBIA

Statute or source	*Family Relations Act*

Intent	Unstated
Jurisdiction	Supreme Court
Who may apply	Spouse or former spouse
When may application be made	Within two years of an order for dissolution of marriage, judicial separation, or declaring the marriage to be null and void (1)
Property included	"Family assets," i.e., property owned by one or both spouses and ordinarily used by a spouse or a minor child of either spouse for a family purpose. Includes a right of a spouse under an annuity or a pension, home ownership or retirement savings plan, or "a right share or interest of a spouse *in a venture* to which money or moneys worth was directly or indirectly contributed by or on behalf of the other spouse" (45.3)
Property excluded	Property owned by one spouse to the exclusion of the other and used primarily for business purposes where the spouse who does not own the property made no direct or indirect contribution to the acquisition of the property by the other spouse or to the operation of the business; but an indirect contribution includes savings through effective management of household or child-rearing responsibilities by the spouse who holds no interest in the property (46)
Basic entitlement	An undivided half interest in family assets as a tenant-in-common
Powers of court	Determine any matter respecting the ownership right of possession or division of property and make such orders as are necessary, reasonable, or ancillary to give effect to the determination, etc.; and interim orders (53)

Judicial discretion to create unequal sharing where provisions for division of property in accordance with a basic entitlement or under a marriage agreement would be unfair (51)

Date of valuation   Unstated

Effect of agreement   Parties may contract for management of family assets or other property during marriage or ownership in or division of family assets or other property during marriage or on the making of an order for dissolution of marriage, judicial separation, or declaration of nullity of marriage; this includes separation agreements, but apparently parties cannot contract in respect of support obligations. (48) Apparently, marriage agreements override statutory property rights.

MANITOBA

Statute   *Marital Property Act*

Intent   To provide for presumption in the event of the breakdown of the marriage of equal sharing of the family and commercial assets of the parties of the marriage acquired by them during the marriage

Jurisdiction   Queen's Bench or County Court

Who may apply   Spouses whether married before or after coming into force of the Act if the habitual residence of both spouses is in Manitoba or, where each of the spouses has a different habitual residence if the last common habitual residence of the spouses was in Manitoba. (2) The Act does not apply to spouses who were living separate and apart from each other on May 6, 1977, unless those spouses after that date resumed cohabitation for a period of more than ninety days. (2.4)

When may application be made	Any time up to sixty days after granting of decree absolute of divorce or decree of nullity or, as against estate, within six months after date of death (18)
Property included	Assets
Property excluded	Any article of personal apparel. Assets acquired after separation, while married to a former spouse or while unmarried, or disposed of by spousal agreement
Basic entitlement	Equal sharing of assets where spouses made a separation agreement in writing, an order for judicial separation, where spouses have been living separate and apart for a continuous period of at least six months, where Court has pronounced a decree absolute of divorce or decree of nullity or proceedings for same have been commenced, or where the other spouse has committed an act amounting to dissipation of assets
Powers of court	Unequal division of family assets if equal division would be grossly unfair or unconscionable having regard to any extraordinary financial or other circumstances of the spouses or the extraordinary nature or value of any of their assets
	Unequal division of commercial assets if equal division would be clearly inequitable having regard to any circumstances the Court deems relevant (13)
	Accounting and division of assets valued at fair market value, with payment made by lump sum or instalments or by transfer, conveyance, or delivery of asset(s) or any combination of this

Date of valuation	Date as agreed by spouses and in the absence of agreement the date when they last cohabited or where the application results from dissipation of assets, the date of the application to Court for an accounting and division
Effect of agreement	Overrides statutory property rights

NEW BRUNSWICK

Statute	*Marital Property Act*
Intent	Equal sharing of marital property, subject to equitable considerations and equal sharing of marital debts (2)
Jurisdiction	Court of Queen's Bench
Who may apply	A spouse (married person); a person whose marriage is declared a nullity shall be deemed to have been a spouse during the period between the purported solemnization of marriage and the declaration of nullity (3)
When may order be made	Where a decree nisi of divorce is pronounced, or the marriage is declared a nullity, or the spouses are living separate and apart and there is no reasonable prospect of the resumption of cohabitation, or the marriage is broken down, and there is no reasonable prospect of reconciliation whether or not the spouses are living separate and apart. The application must be made not later than sixty days after a spouse ceases to be a spouse by reason of a divorce or declaration of nullity. (3)
Property included	Marital property that includes family assets and property owned by one or both spouses that is not a family asset and acquired while the spouses cohabited (1)
Property excluded	A business asset; property that was a gift from one spouse to the other including income from

that property; property that was a gift from any other person to one spouse including income from that property; property that represents the proceeds of disposition of property that was not a family asset and that was not acquired while the spouses cohabited or in contemplation of marriage, or insurance proceeds from that property; property acquired by one spouse after cessation of cohabitation and that was acquired through the disposition of property that would have been marital property had the disposition not occurred (1)

Basic entitlement	Equal sharing of marital property
Powers of court	Partition, sale, payment out of proceeds of sale, transfer of property to or in trust for a child, posting of security, ancillary orders (10) Unequal division of marital property on equitable grounds (7) Division of property of either spouse that is not marital property on equitable grounds (8) Fair and equitable division of marital debts taking into account any tax consequences that may arise from the division of property (9)
Date of valuation	Unstated
Effect of agreement	Overrides statutory property rights (40) May be disregarded by the Court in matters involving the welfare of a child (38) May be disregarded by the Court if it was made before the Act came into force and not made in contemplation of the Act or if it was entered into without independent legal advice, if the agreement would be inequitable in all the circumstances (41)

NEWFOUNDLAND

Statute	*Matrimonial Property Act*
Intent	To reform the law with respect to matrimonial-property in order to recognize the contribution made by each spouse to a marriage, give a one-half interest in the matrimonial home to each spouse, provide for the deferred sharing of most other property acquired during the marriage, and provide for judicial discretion in sharing business assets built up by a spouse during the marriage.
Jurisdiction	Unified Family Court, Trial Division of the Supreme Court or the District Court (2.1)
Who may apply	A spouse, but not persons who have received a Decree Absolute of divorce or in relation to matrimonial assets provided for in a separation agreement before July 1, 1980 (2.3, 19)
When may order be made	Where divorce petition is filed, and marriage is declared a nullity, spouses have been separated and there is no reasonable prospect of the resumption of cohabitation, or one of the spouses has died (19)
Property included	"Matrimonial Assets," which includes all real and personal property acquired by either or both spouses during the marriage, and "Business Assets," meaning property primarily used or held for or in connection with a commercial, business, investment, or other income or profit-producing purpose (16)
Property excluded	Gifts, inheritances, trusts, or settlements received by one spouse from a person other than the other spouse and any appreciation in value of them during the marriage; personal injury awards except that portion that represents compensation for economic loss;

	personal effects; property exempted under a marriage contract or separation agreement; family heirlooms; and real and personal property acquired after separation
Basic entitlement	Equal division of matrimonial assets. Sharing of business assets where one spouse has contributed work money or money's worth in respect of the acquisition, management, maintenance, operation, or improvement of the business asset of the other spouse (19, 27)
Powers of court	Order–equal division of matrimonial assets or unequal division if satisfied that a division of these assets in equal shares would be grossly unjust or unconscionable (20) Order–title to specific property be transferred to or held in trust for a spouse; partition or sale; payment to be made out of proceeds of sale; transfer property to or held in trust for a child; order security; order of payment; make declaratory orders as to ownership or right of possession; all necessary interim orders (24, 25)
Date of valuation	Unstated
Effect of agreement	Varies or excludes the application of this Act (41)

NOVA SCOTIA

Statute or source	*Married Persons Property Act*, 1978 Value of Intent property to be divided equally between spouses on termination of marriage (2, 6)
Jurisdiction	Trial Division of Supreme Court (3)
Who may apply	Married persons both resident in the province at the time of termination of the marriage (4)

When may application be made	On termination of marriage by death; application for divorce or annulment; after separation agreement; or upon determination that marriage has terminated (7)
Property included	Real or personal property or any interest therein, wheresoever situated (3, 4)
Property excluded	Property of spouse who has been living apart at least three years before Act came into force, or where there is separation agreement; legacy, bequest, gift; property acquired before marriage (3, 5)
Basic entitlement	Equal sharing (9)
Powers of court	Valuation and distribution of property, except that the spouse in whose name an asset is shall have the right to retain that asset as part of the share in the value of the property of the marriage, if not interfering with other's share. No power to make unequal division (9)
Date of valuation	Date of termination of marriage (7)
Effect of agreement	Overrides statute. If valid as contract, non-reviewable

PRINCE EDWARD ISLAND

Statute	*Family Law Reform Act*
Intent	Unstated
Jurisdiction	Family Division of Supreme Court (2)
Who may apply	Spouse (5)
When may application be made	After separation, or in connection with divorce or annulment (5)
Property included	Real or personal property or any interest therein (4)

Property excluded	Net value of the equity of any property acquired by either spouse prior to date of marriage (5)
Basic entitlement	Equal division of family assets, i.e., matrimonial home and property owned by one or both spouses and ordinarily used . . . while residing together for household, educational, recreational, social and aesthetic purposes, except excluded property (4)
Powers of court	Unequal division of family assets based on equitable considerations (5) Sharing of non-family assets based on contribution (9), or on equitable considerations (5) Transfer of title, partition or sale, payment from proceeds of sale, transfer to trust for spouse or child, posting of security, ancillary orders (7)
Date of valuation	Unstated. Implicitly, family assets at date of hearing, non-family assets at date of separation
Effect of agreement	Overrides statutory property rights (3) May be disregarded by Court in matter involving welfare of a child (55) May be disregarded by Court as to provision for support or waiver of support if result is unconscionable, if dependent spouse qualifies for public support, or if there has been default in payment of support under the agreement (19)

QUEBEC

Statute	*Quebec Civil Code*, principally Articles 462.1 to 462.17, 482, 483, 485, 495, 500, 503, 504, 505, 514, 517, 524.1, and 607.1 to 607.11; in force January 1, 1991
Intent	(a) recognize that both spouses contribute to the family's wealth, whatever their spousal and parental assignments are during the marriage; (b) ... permit dissolutions to be completed as efficiently as possible ...

(c) [minimize post-divorce financial interaction] by giving each an immediate financial stake when the marriage is terminated "The object of this bill is to favour economic equity and to underline the character of marriage as a partnership."

Jurisdiction	Superior Court
Who may apply	Spouse; no provision for common-law relationships
When may application be made	Subsequent to separation, divorce, or annulment of marriage
Property included	Principal residence, secondary residence, household furniture, motor vehicles used for family travel, benefits accrued during marriage under a retirement plan, QPP pension plan
Property excluded	Business assets, and apparently all other property
Basic entitlement	Equal sharing of the included property, called the "family patrimony"
Powers of court	Order payment in currency in instalments spread over a period of not more than ten years; transfer of no more than half value of a pension plan; transfer other property as parties may agree; award ownership of property, particularly the family residence. Judicial discretion not to divide pension equally, considering brevity of marriage, waste of property by one spouse, or bad faith
Date of valuation	Date of institution of proceedings for separation, divorce, or annulment
Effect of agreement	These rights cannot be renounced by spouses married subsequent to July 1, 1989.

Note	These rights could be renounced by spouses married prior to July 1, 1989, if they did so by or before December 31, 1990. These provisions do not apply to parties who separated prior to 1989, and settled the consequences of their separation by agreement in writing; or to spouses who instituted proceedings for separation, divorce, or annulment prior to May 15, 1989.

SASKATCHEWAN

Statute	*Matrimonial Property Act*
Intent	To recognize that child care, household management, and financial provision are the joint and mutual responsibilities of spouses . . . that entitles each spouse to an equal distribution of the matrimonial property . . . (2)
Jurisdiction	Court of Queen's Bench, District Court or Unified Family Court
Who may apply	Spouse (1)
When may application be made	Apparently, any time, by a spouse (not former spouse); or within six months of a grant of probate or administration for estate of a deceased spouse
Property included	Any real or personal property whatsoever, viz. "matrimonial property"
Property excluded	Fair market value of property at time of marriage owned by a spouse before marriage or acquired by a spouse before marriage by third party gift or inheritance Award or settlement of damages; insurance proceeds; property acquired after decree nisi, declaration of nullity, or a judgment of judicial separation; property exchanged for these; appreciation on or income from these

Basic entitlement	"Subject to any exceptions, exemptions and equitable considerations mentioned in this Act, order that matrimonial property or its value be distributed equally between the spouses"
Powers of court	Include or exclude any property from "matrimonial property" (23.4) If satisfied that it would be unfair and inequitable to make an equal distribution of matrimonial property or its value, refuse to order any distribution; order that all the matrimonial property be vested in one spouse; or make any other order that it considers fair and equitable (21.2) Partition, sale, transfer, lump sum, installments vesting, any other necessary order, etc. (26)
Date of valuation	Unstated
Effect of agreement	If in writing, signed, witnessed; and if each spouse has independently acknowledged the nature and effect of the contract, overrides statutory property rights (38)

Statutes

Divorce Act
R.S., 1985, c. 3 (2nd Supp.)
An Act respecting divorce and corollary relief
[1986, c. 4, assented to 13th February, 1986]

SHORT TITLE

Short title

INTERPRETATION

Definitions

"age of majority"
« *majeur* »

"appellate court"
«*cour d'appel*»

"applicable guidelines"
« *lignes directrices
applicables* »

"child of the marriage"
«*enfant à charge*»

1. This Act may be cited as the *Divorce Act.*

2. (1) In this Act,

"age of majority", in respect of a child, means the age of majority as determined by the laws of the province where the child ordinarily resides, or, if the child ordinarily resides outside of Canada, eighteen years of age;

"appellate court," in respect of an appeal from a court, means the court exercising appellate jurisdiction with respect to that appeal;

"applicable guidelines" means

(a) where both spouses or former spouses are ordinarily resident in the same province at the time an application for a child support order or a variation order in respect of a child support order is made, or the amount of a child support order is to be recalculated pursuant to section 25.1, and that province has been designated by an order made under subsection (5), the laws of the province specified in the order, and (b) in any other case, the Federal Child Support Guidelines;

"child of the marriage" means a child of two spouses or former spouses who, at the material time, (a) is under the age of majority and who has not withdrawn from their charge, or (b) is the age of majority or over and under their charge but unable, by reason of illness, disability or other cause, to withdraw from their charge or to obtain the necessaries of life;

"child support order"
« *ordonnance*
alimentaire au
profit d'un enfant »

"child support order" means an order made under subsection 15.1(1);

"corollary relief
proceeding"
« action en mesures
accessoires »

"corollary relief proceeding" means a proceeding in a court in which either or both former spouses seek child support order, a spousal support order or a custody order;

"court" «*tribunal*»

"court", in respect of a province, means (a) for the Province of Ontario, the Superior Court of Justice, (a.1) for the Province of Prince Edward Island or Newfoundland, the trial division of the Supreme Court of the Province, (b) for the Province of Quebec, the Superior Court, (c) for the Provinces of Nova Scotia and British Columbia, the Supreme Court of the Province, (d) for the Province of New Brunswick, Manitoba, Saskatchewan or Alberta, the Court of Queen's Bench for the Province, and (e) for Yukon or the Northwest Territories, the Supreme Court, and in Nunavut, the Nunavut Court of Justice, and includes such other court in the province the judges of which are appointed by the Governor General as is designated by the Lieutenant Governor in Council of the province as a court for the purposes of this Act;

"custody"
«*garde*»

"custody" includes care, upbringing and any other incident of custody;

"custody order"
«*ordonnance de garde*»

"custody order" means an order made under subsection 16(1);

"divorce proceeding"
« *action en divorce* »

"divorce proceeding" means a proceeding in a court in which either or both spouses seek a divorce alone or together with a child support order, a spousal support order or a custody order;

"Federal Child
Support Guidelines"
« *lignes directrices*
fédérales sur les
pensions alimentaires
pour enfants »

"Federal Child Support Guidelines" means the guidelines made under section 26.1;

"provincial child
support service"
« service provincial
des aliments pour
enfants »

"provincial child support service" means any service,
agency or body designated in an agreement with a
province under subsection 25.1(1);

"spousal support
order"

"spousal support order" means an order made under
subsection 15.2(1);

"spouse" «époux»

"spouse" means either of a man or woman who are
married to each other;

"support order"
« ordonnance
alimentaire »

"support order" means a child support order or a
spousal support order;

"variation order"
«ordonnance
modificative»

"variation order" means an order made under sub-
17(1);

"variation proceeding"
«action en
modification»

"variation proceeding" means a proceeding in a
court in which either or both former spouses seek
a variation order.

Child of the marriage

(2) For the purposes of the definition "child of the
marriage" in subsection (1), a child of two spouses
or former spouses includes (a) any child for whom
they both stand in the place of parents; and (b) any
child of whom one is the parent and for whom the
other stands in the place of a parent.

Term not restrictive

(3) The use of the term "application" to describe
a proceeding under this Act in a court shall not be
construed as limiting the name under which and
the form and manner in which that proceeding
may be taken in that court, and the name, manner
and form of the proceeding in that court shall be
such as is provided for by the rules regulating the
practice and procedure in that court.

Idem

(4) The use in section 21.1 of the terms "affidavit"
and "pleadings" to describe documents shall not
be construed as limiting the name that may be
used to refer to those documents in a court and the
form of those documents, and the name and form
of the documents shall be such as is provided for

by the rules regulating the practice and procedure in that court.

Provincial child support guidelines

(5) The Governor in Council may, by order, designate a province for the purposes of the definition "applicable guidelines" in subsection (1) if the laws of the province establish comprehensive guidelines for the determination of child support that deal with the matters referred to in section 26.1. The order shall specify the laws of the province that constitute the guidelines of the province.

Amendments included

(6) The guidelines of a province referred to in subsection (5) include any amendments made to them from time to time. R.S., 1985, c. 3 (2nd Supp.), s. 2, c. 27 (2nd Supp.), s. 10; 1990, c. 18, s. 1; 1992, c. 51, s. 46; 1997, c. 1, s. 1; 1998, c. 30, ss. 13(F), 15(E); 1999, c. 3, s. 61; 2002, c. 7, s. 158(E).

JURISDICTION

Jurisdiction in divorce proceedings

3. (1) A court in a province has jurisdiction to hear and determine a divorce proceeding if either spouse has been ordinarily resident in the province for at least one year immediately preceding the commencement of the proceeding.

Jurisdiction where two proceedings commenced on different days

(2) Where divorce proceedings between the same spouses are pending in two courts that would otherwise have jurisdiction under subsection (1) and were commenced on different days and the proceeding that was commenced first is not discontinued within thirty days after it was commenced, the court in which a divorce proceeding was commenced first has exclusive jurisdiction to hear and determine any divorce proceeding then pending between the spouses and the second divorce proceeding shall be deemed to be discontinued.

Jurisdiction where two proceedings commenced on same day

(3) Where divorce proceedings between the same spouses are pending in two courts that would otherwise have jurisdiction under subsection (1) and werecommenced on the same day and neither proceeding is discontinued within thirty days after it was commenced, the Federal Court has exclusive

jurisdiction to hear and determine any divorce proceeding then pending between the spouses and the divorce proceedings in those courts shall be transferred to the Federal Court on the direction of that Court.
R.S., 1985, c. 3 (2nd Supp.), s. 3; 2002, c. 8, s. 183.

Jurisdiction in corollary relief proceedings

4. (1) A court in a province has jurisdiction to hear and determine a corollary relief proceeding if (a) either former spouse is ordinarily resident in the province at the commencement of the proceeding; or (b) both former spouses accept the jurisdiction of the court.

Jurisdiction where two proceedings commenced on different days

(2) Where corollary relief proceedings between the same former spouses and in respect of the same matter are pending in two courts that would otherwise have jurisdiction under subsection (1) and were commenced on different days and the proceeding that was commenced first is not discontinued within thirty days after it was commenced, the court in which a corollary relief proceeding was commenced first has exclusive jurisdiction to hear and determine any corollary relief proceeding then pending between the former spouses in respect of that matter and the second corollary relief proceeding shall be deemed to be discontinued.

Jurisdiction where two proceedings commenced on same day

(3) Where proceedings between the same former spouses and in respect of the same matter are pending in two courts that would otherwise have jurisdiction under subsection (1) and were commenced jurisdiction under subsection (1) and were commenced on the same day and neither proceeding is discontinued within thirty days after it was commenced, the Federal Court has exclusive jurisdiction to hear and determine any corollary relief proceeding then pending between the former spouses in respect of that matter and the corollary relief proceedings in those courts shall be transferred to the Federal Court on the direction of that Court.
R.S., 1985, c. 3 (2nd Supp.), s. 4; 1993, c. 8, s. 1; 2002, c. 8, s. 183.

Jurisdiction where two proceedings commenced on different days

(2) Where variation proceedings between the same former spouses and in respect of the same matter are pending in two courts that would otherwise have jurisdiction under subsection (1) and were commenced on different days and the proceeding that was commenced first is not discontinued within thirty days after it was commenced, the court in which a variation proceeding was commenced first has exclusive jurisdiction to hear and determine any variation proceeding then pending between the former spouses in respect of that matter and the second variation proceeding shall be deemed to be discontinued.

Jurisdiction where two proceedings commenced on same day

(3) Where variation proceedings between the same former spouses and in respect of the same matter are pending in two courts that would otherwise have jurisdiction under subsection (1) and were commenced on the same day and neither proceeding is discontinued within thirty days after it was commenced, the Federal Court has exclusive jurisdiction to hear and determine any variation proceeding then pending between the former spouses in respect of that matter and the variation proceedings in those courts shall be transferred to the Federal Court on the direction of that Court. R.S., 1985, c. 3 (2nd Supp.), s. 5; 2002, c. 8, s. 183.

Transfer of divorce proceeding where custody application

6. (1) Where an application for an order under section 16 is made in a divorce proceeding to a court in a province and is opposed and the child of the marriage in respect of whom the order is sought is most substantially connected with another province, the court may, on application by a spouse or on its own motion, transfer the divorce proceeding to a court in that other province.

Transfer of corollary relief proceeding where custody application

(2) Where an application for an order under section 16 is made in a corollary relief proceeding to a court in a province and is opposed and the child of the marriage in respect of whom the order is sought is most substantially connected with another province, the court may, on application by a former spouse or on its own motion, transfer the corollary relief proceeding to a court in that other province.

Transfer of variation proceeding where custody application

(3) Where an application for a variation order in respect of a custody order is made in a variation proceeding to a court in a province and is opposed and the child of the marriage in respect of whom the variation order is sought is most substantially connected with another province, the court may, on application by a former spouse or on its own motion, transfer the variation proceeding to a court in that other province.

Exclusive jurisdiction

(4) Notwithstanding sections 3 to 5, a court in a province to which a proceeding is transferred under this section has exclusive jurisdiction to hear and determine the proceeding.

Exercise of jurisdiction by judge

7. The jurisdiction conferred on a court by this Act to grant a divorce shall be exercised only by a judge of the court without a jury.

DIVORCE

Divorce

8. (1) A court of competent jurisdiction may, on application by either or both spouses, grant a divorce to the spouse or spouses on the ground that there has been a breakdown of their marriage.

Breakdown of marriage

(2) Breakdown of a marriage is established only if (a) the spouses have lived separate and apart for at least one year immediately preceding the determination of the divorce proceeding and were living separate and apart at the commencement of the proceeding; or (b) the spouse against whom the divorce proceeding is brought has, since celebration of the marriage,

(i) committed adultery, or
(ii) treated the other spouse with physical or mental cruelty of such a kind as to render intolerable the continued cohabitation of the spouses.

Calculation of period of separation

(3) For the purposes of paragraph (2)(a),
(a) spouses shall be deemed to have lived separate and apart for any period during which they lived apart and either of them had the intention to live separate and apart from the other; and (b) a period during which spouses have lived separate and apart

shall not be considered to have been interrupted or terminated

(i) by reason only that either spouse has become incapable of forming or having an intention to continue to live separate and apart or of continuing to live separate and apart of the spouse's own volition, if it appears to the court that the separation would probably have continued if the spouse had not become so incapable, or

(ii) by reason only that the spouses have resumed cohabitation during a period of, or periods totalling, not more than ninety days with reconciliation as its primary purpose.

Duty of legal adviser

9. (1) It is the duty of every barrister, solicitor, lawyer or advocate who undertakes to act on behalf of a spouse in a divorce proceeding

(a) to draw to the attention of the spouse the provisions of this Act that have as their object the reconciliation of spouses, and

(b) to discuss with the spouse the possibility of the reconciliation of the spouses and to inform the spouse of the marriage counselling or guidance facilities known to him or her that might be able to assist the spouses to achieve a reconciliation, unless the circumstances of the case are of such a nature that it would clearly not be appropriate to do so.

Idem

(2) It is the duty of every barrister, solicitor, lawyer or advocate who undertakes to act on behalf of a spouse in a divorce proceeding to discuss with the spouse the advisability of negotiating the matters that may be the subject of a support order or a custody order and to inform the spouse of the mediation facilities known to him or her that might be able to assist the spouses in negotiating those matters.

Certification

(3) Every document presented to a court by a barrister, solicitor, lawyer or advocate that formally commences a divorce proceeding shall contain a statement by him or her certifying that he or she has complied with this section.

Duty of court
— reconciliation

10. (1) In a divorce proceeding, it is the duty of the court, before considering the evidence, to satisfy itself that there is no possibility of the reconciliation of the spouses, unless the circumstances of the case are of such a nature that it would clearly not be appropriate to do so.

Adjournment

(2) Where at any stage in a divorce proceeding it appears to the court from the nature of the case, the evidence or the attitude of either or both spouses that there is a possibility of the reconciliation of the spouses, the court shall
(a) adjourn the proceeding to afford the spouses an opportunity to achieve a reconciliation; and
(b) with the consent of the spouses or in the discretion of the court, nominate
(i) a person with experience or training in marriage counselling or guidance, or
(ii) in special circumstances, some other suitable person,to assist the spouses to achieve a reconciliation.

Resumption

(3) Where fourteen days have elapsed from the date of any adjournment under subsection (2), the court shall resume the proceeding on the application of either or both spouses.

Nominee not competent or compellable

(4) No person nominated by a court under this section to assist spouses to achieve a reconciliation is competent or compellable in any legal proceedings to disclose any admission or communication made to that person in his or her capacity as a nominee of the court for that purpose.

Evidence not admissible

(5) Evidence of anything said or of any admission or communication made in the course of assisting spouses to achieve a reconciliation is not admissible in any legal proceedings.

Duty of court — bars

11. (1) In a divorce proceeding, it is the duty of the court
(a) to satisfy itself that there has been no collusion in relation to the application for a divorce and to dismiss the application if it finds that there was collusion in presenting it; (b) to satisfy itself that reasonable arrangements have been made for the support of any children of the marriage, having regard to the applicable guidelines, and, if such arrangements have not been made, to stay the granting of the divorce

until such arrangements are made; and (c) where a divorce is sought in circumstances described in paragraph 8(2)(b), to satisfy itself that there has been no condonation or connivance on the part of the spouse bringing the proceeding, and to dismiss the application for a divorce if that spouse has condoned or connived at the act or conduct complained of unless, in the opinion of the court, the public interest would be better served by granting the divorce.

Revival

(2) Any act or conduct that has been condoned is not capable of being revived so as to constitute a circumstance described in paragraph 8(2)(b).

Condonation

(3) For the purposes of this section, a continuation or resumption of cohabitation during a period of, or periods totalling, not more than ninety days with reconciliation as its primary purpose shall not be considered to constitute condonation.

Definition of "collusion"

(4) In this section, "collusion" means an agreement or conspiracy to which an applicant for a divorce is either directly or indirectly a party for the purpose of subverting the administration of justice, and includes any agreement, understanding or arrangement to fabricate or suppress evidence or to deceive the court, but does not include an agreement to the extent that it provides for separation between the parties, financial support, division of property or the custody of any child of the marriage.
R.S., 1985, c. 3 (2nd Supp.), s. 11; 1997, c. 1, s. 1.1.

Effective date generally

12. (1) Subject to this section, a divorce takes effect on the thirty-first day after the day on which the judgment granting the divorce is rendered.

Special circumstances

(2) Where, on or after rendering a judgment granting a divorce,
(a) the court is of the opinion that by reason of special circumstances the divorce should take effect earlier than the thirty-first day after the day on which the judgment is rendered, and
(b) the spouses agree and undertake that no appeal from the judgment will be taken, or any appeal from the judgment that was taken has been abandoned, the court may order that the divorce takes effect at such earlier time as it considers appropriate.

Effective date where appeal

(3) A divorce in respect of which an appeal is pending at the end of the period referred to in subsection (1), unless voided on appeal, takes effect on the expiration of the time fixed by law for instituting an appeal from the decision on that appeal or any subsequent appeal, if no appeal has been instituted within that time.

Certain extensions to be counted

(4) For the purposes of subsection (3), the time fixed by law for instituting an appeal from a decision on an appeal includes any extension thereof fixed pursuant to law before the expiration of that time or fixed thereafter on an application instituted before the expiration of that time.

No late extensions of time for appeal

(5) Notwithstanding any other law, the time fixed by law for instituting an appeal from a decision referred to in subsection (3) may not be extended after the expiration of that time, except on an application instituted before the expiration of that time.

Effective date where decision of Supreme Court of Canada

(6) A divorce in respect of which an appeal has been taken to the Supreme Court of Canada, unless voided on the appeal, takes effect on the day on which the judgment on the appeal is rendered.

Certificate of divorce

(7) Where a divorce takes effect in accordance with this section, a judge or officer of the court that rendered the judgment granting the divorce or, where that judgment has been appealed, of the appellate court that rendered the judgment on the final appeal, shall, on request, issue to any person a certificate that a divorce granted under this Act dissolved the marriage of the specified persons effective as of a specified date.

Conclusive proof

(8) A certificate referred to in subsection (7), or a certified copy thereof, is conclusive proof of the facts so certified without proof of the signature or authority of the person appearing to have signed the certificate.

Legal effect throughout Canada

13. On taking effect, a divorce granted under this Act has legal effect throughout Canada.

Marriage dissolved

14. On taking effect, a divorce granted under this Act dissolves the marriage of the spouses.

COROLLARY RELIEF

Interpretation

Definition of "spouse"

15. In sections 15.1 to 16, "spouse" has the meaning assigned by subsection 2(1), and includes a former spouse.
R.S., 1985, c. 3 (2nd Supp.), s. 15; 1997, c. 1, s. 2.

Child Support Orders

Child support order

15.1 (1) A court of competent jurisdiction may, on application by either or both spouses, make an order requiring a spouse to pay for the support of any or all children of the marriage.

Interim order

(2) Where an application is made under subsection (1), the court may, on application by either or both spouses, make an interim order requiring a spouse to pay for the support of any or all children of the marriage, pending the determination of the application under subsection (1).

Guidelines apply

(3) A court making an order under subsection (1) or an interim order under subsection (2) shall do so in accordance with the applicable guidelines.

Terms and conditions

(4) The court may make an order under subsection (1) or an interim order under subsection (2) for a definite or indefinite period or until a specified event occurs, and may impose terms, conditions or restrictions in connection with the order or interim order as it thinks fit and just.

Court may take
agreement, etc.,
into account

5) Notwithstanding subsection (3), a court may award an amount that is different from the amount that would be determined in accordance with the applicable guidelines if the court is satisfied
(a) that special provisions in an order, a judgment or a written agreement respecting the financial obligations of the spouses, or the division or transfer of their property, directly or indirectly benefit a child, or that special provisions have otherwise been made for the benefit of a child; and
(b) that the application of the applicable guidelines would result in an amount of child support that is inequitable given those special provisions.

Reasons

(6) Where the court awards, pursuant to subsection (5), an amount that is different from the amount that would be determined in accordance with the applicable guidelines, the court shall record its reasons for having done so.

Consent orders

(7) Notwithstanding subsection (3), a court may award an amount that is different from the amount that would be determined in accordance with the applicable guidelines on the consent of both spouses if it is satisfied that reasonable arrangements have been made for the support of the child to whom the order relates.

Reasonable arrangements

(8) For the purposes of subsection (7), in determining whether reasonable arrangements have been made for the support of a child, the court shall have regard to the applicable guidelines. However, the court shall not consider the arrangements to be unreasonable solely because the amount of support agreed to is not the same as the amount that would otherwise have been determined in accordance with the applicable guidelines. 1997, c. 1, s. 2.

Spousal Support Orders

Spousal support order

15.2 (1) A court of competent jurisdiction may, on application by either or both spouses, make an order requiring a spouse to secure or pay, or to secure and pay, such lump sum or periodic sums, or such lump sum and periodic sums, as the court thinks reasonable for the support of the other spouse.

Interim order

(2) Where an application is made under subsection (1), the court may, on application by either or both spouses, make an interim order requiring a spouse to secure or pay, or to secure and pay, such lump sum or periodic sums, or such lump sum and periodic sums, as the court thinks reasonable for the support of the other spouse, pending the determination of the application under subsection (1).

Terms and conditions

(3) The court may make an order under subsection (1) or an interim order under subsection (2) for a definite or indefinite period or until a specified

event occurs, and may impose terms, conditions or restrictions in connection with the order as it thinks fit and just.

Factors

(4) In making an order under subsection (1) or an interim order under subsection (2), the court shall take into consideration the condition, means, needs and other circumstances of each spouse, including
(a) the length of time the spouses cohabited;
(b) the functions performed by each spouse during cohabitation; and
(c) any order, agreement or arrangement relating to support of either spouse.

Spousal misconduct

(5) In making an order under subsection (1) or an interim order under subsection (2), the court shall not take into consideration any misconduct of a spouse in relation to the marriage.

Objectives of spousal support order

(6) An order made under subsection (1) or an interim order under subsection (2) that provides for the support of a spouse should
(a) recognize any economic advantages or disadvantages to the spouses arising from the marriage or its breakdown;
(b) apportion between the spouses any financial consequences arising from the care of any child of the marriage over and above any obligation for the support of any child of the marriage;
(c) relieve any economic hardship of the spouses arising from the breakdown of the marriage; and
(d) in so far as practicable, promote the economic self-sufficiency of each spouse within a reasonable period of time.
1997, c. 1, s. 2.

Priority

Priority to child support

15.3 (1) Where a court is considering an applica-cation for a child support order and an application for a spousal support order, the court shall give priority to child support in determining the appli-cations.

Reasons

(2) Where, as a result of giving priority to child support, the court is unable to make a spousal

support order or the court makes a spousal support order in an amount that is less than it otherwise would have been, the court shall record its reasons for having done so.

Consequences of reduction or termination of child support order

(3) Where, as a result of giving priority to child support, a spousal support order was not made, or the amount of a spousal support order is less than it otherwise would have been, any subsequent reduction or termination of that child support constitutes a change of circumstances for the purposes of applying for a spousal support order, or a variation order in respect of the spousal support order, as the case may be. 1997, c. 1, s. 2.

Custody Orders

Order for custody

16. (1) A court of competent jurisdiction may, on application by either or both spouses or by any other person, make an order respecting the custody of or the access to, or the custody of and access to, any or all children of the marriage.

Interim order for custody

(2) Where an application is made under subsection (1), the court may, on application by either or both spouses or by any other person, make an interim order respecting the custody of or the access to, or the custody of and access to, any or all children of the marriage pending determination of the application under subsection (1).

Application by other person

(3) A person, other than a spouse, may not make an application under subsection (1) or (2) without leave of the court.

Joint custody or access

(4) The court may make an order under this section granting custody of, or access to, any or all children of the marriage to any one or more persons.

Access

(5) Unless the court orders otherwise, a spouse who is granted access to a child of the marriage has the right to make inquiries, and to be given information, as to the health, education and welfare of the child.

Terms and conditions

(6) The court may make an order under this section for a definite or indefinite period or until the happening of a specified event and may impose such other terms, conditions or restrictions in connection therewith as it thinks fit and just.

Order respecting
change of residence

(7) Without limiting the generality of subsection (6), the court may include in an order under this section a term requiring any person who has custody of a child of the marriage and who intends to change the place of residence of that child to notify, at least thirty days before the change or within such other period before the change as the court may specify, any person who is granted access to that child of the change, the time at which the change will be made and the new place of residence of the child.

Factors

(8) In making an order under this section, the court shall take into consideration only the best interests of the child of the marriage as determined by reference to the condition, means, needs and other circumstances of the child.

Past conduct

(9) In making an order under this section, the court shall not take into consideration the past conduct of any person unless the conduct is relevant to the ability of that person to act as a parent of a child.

Maximum contact

(10) In making an order under this section, the court shall give effect to the principle that a child of the marriage should have as much contact with each spouse as is consistent with the best interests of the child and, for that purpose, shall take into consideration the willingness of the person for whom custody is sought to facilitate such contact.

Variation, Rescission
or Suspension of Orders

Order for variation, rescission or suspension

17. (1) A court of competent jurisdiction may make an order varying, rescinding or suspending, prospectively or retroactively,

(a) a support order or any provision thereof on application by either or both former spouses; or

(b) a custody order or any provision thereof on

application by either or both former spouses or by any other person.

Application by other person

(2) A person, other than a former spouse, may not make an application under paragraph (1)(b) without leave of the court.

Terms and conditions

(3) The court may include in a variation order any provision that under this Act could have been included in the order in respect of which the variation order is sought.

Factors for child support order

(4) Before the court makes a variation order in respect of a child support order, the court shall satisfy itself that a change of circumstances as provided for in the applicable guidelines has occurred since the making of the child support order or the last variation order made in respect of that order.

Factors for spousal support order

(4.1) Before the court makes a variation order in respect of a spousal support order, the court shall satisfy itself that a change in the condition, means, needs or other circumstances of either former spouse has occurred since the making of the spousal support order or the last variation order made in respect of that order, and, in making the variation order, the court shall take that change into consideration.

Factors for custody order

(5) Before the court makes a variation order in respect of a custody order, the court shall satisfy itself that there has been a change in the condition, means, needs or other circumstances of the child of the marriage occurring since the making of the custody order or the last variation order made in respect of that order, as the case may be, and, in making the variation order, the court shall take into consideration only the best interests of the child as determined by reference to that change.

Conduct

(6) In making a variation order, the court shall not take into consideration any conduct that under this Act could not have been considered in making the order in respect of which the variation order is sought.

Guidelines apply

(6.1) A court making a variation order in respect of a child support order shall do so in accordance with the applicable guidelines.

Court may take agreement, etc., into account

(6.2) Notwithstanding subsection (6.1), in making a variation order in respect of a child support order, a court may award an amount that is different from the amount that would be determined in accordance with the applicable guidelines if the court is satisfied
(a) that special provisions in an order, a judgment or a written agreement respecting the financial obligations of the spouses, or the division or transfer of their property, directly or indirectly benefit a child, or that special provisions have otherwise been made for the benefit of a child; and
(b) that the application of the applicable guidelines would result in an amount of child support that is inequitable given those special provisions.

Reasons

(6.3) Where the court awards, pursuant to subsection (6.2), an amount that is different from the amount that would be determined in accordance with the applicable guidelines, the court shall record its reasons for having done so.

Consent orders

(6.4) Notwithstanding subsection (6.1), a court may award an amount that is different from the amount that would be determined in accordance with the applicable guidelines on the consent of both spouses if it is satisfied that reasonable arrangements have been made for the support of the child to whom the order relates.

Reasonable arrangements

(6.5) For the purposes of subsection (6.4), in determining whether reasonable arrangements have been made for the support of a child, the court shall have regard to the applicable guidelines. However, the court shall not consider the arrangements to be unreasonable solely because the amount of support agreed to is not the same as the amount that would otherwise have been determined in accordance with the applicable guidelines.

Objectives of variation order varying spousal

(7) A variation order varying a spousal support order should

support order

(a) recognize any economic advantages or disadvantages to the former spouses arising from the marriage or its breakdown;
(b) apportion between the former spouses any financial consequences arising from the care of any child of the marriage over and above any obligation for the support of any child of the marriage;
(c) relieve any economic hardship of the former spouses arising from the breakdown of the marriage; and
(d) in so far as practicable, promote the economic self-sufficiency of each former spouse within a reasonable period of time.
(8) [Repealed, 1997, c. 1, s. 5]

Maximum contact

(9) In making a variation order varying a custody order, the court shall give effect to the principle that a child of the marriage should have as much contact with each former spouse as is consistent with the best interests of the child and, for that purpose, where the variation order would grant custody of the child to a person who does not currently have custody, the court shall take into consideration the willingness of that person to facilitate such contact.

Limitation

(10) Notwithstanding subsection (1), where a spousal support order provides for support for a definite period or until a specified event occurs, a court may not, on an application instituted after the expiration of that period or the occurrence of the event, make a variation order for the purpose of resuming that support unless the court is satisfied that
(a) a variation order is necessary to relieve economic hardship arising from a change described in subsection (4.1) that is related to the marriage; and
(b) the changed circumstances, had they existed at the time of the making of the spousal support order or the last variation order made in respect of that order, as the case may be, would likely have resulted in a different order.

Copy of order

(11) Where a court makes a variation order in respect of a support order or a custody order made by another court, it shall send a copy of the variation

order, certified by a judge or officer of the court, to that other court.
R.S., 1985, c. 3 (2nd Supp.), s. 17; 1997, c. 1, s. 5.

Variation order
by affidavit, etc.

17.1 Where both former spouses are ordinarily resident in different provinces, a court of competent jurisdiction may, in accordance with any applicable rules of the court, make a variation order pursuant to subsection 17(1) on the basis of the submissions of the former spouses, whether presented orally before the court or by means of affidavits or any means of telecommunication, if both former spouses consent thereto.
1993, c. 8, s. 2.

Provisional Orders

Definitions

18. (1) In this section and section 19,

"Attorney General"
«procureur général»

"Attorney General," in respect of a province, means
(a) for Yukon, the member of the Executive Council of Yukon designated by the Commissioner of Yukon,
(b) for the Northwest Territories, the member of the Council of the Northwest Territories designated by the Commissioner of the Northwest Territories,
(b.1) for Nunavut, the member of the Executive Council of Nunavut designated by the Commissioner of Nunavut, and
(c) for the other provinces, the Attorney General of the province,
and includes any person authorized in writing by the member or Attorney General to act for the member or Attorney General in the performance of a function under this section or section 19;

"provisional order"
«ordonnance
conditionnelle»

"provisional order" means an order made pursuant to subsection (2).

Provisional order

(2) Notwithstanding paragraph 5(1)(a) and subsection 17(1), where an application is made to a court in a province for a variation order in respect of a support order and
(a) the respondent in the application is ordinarily resident in another province and has not accepted

the jurisdiction of the court, or both former spouses have not consented to the application of section 17.1 in respect of the matter, and

(b) in the circumstances of the case, the court is satisfied that the issues can be adequately determined by proceeding under this section and section 19, the court shall make a variation order with or without notice to and in the absence of the respondent, but such order is provisional only and has no legal effect until it is confirmed in a proceeding under section 19 and, where so confirmed, it has legal effect in accordance with the terms of the order confirming it.

Transmission

(3) Where a court in a province makes a provisional order, it shall send to the Attorney General for the province

(a) three copies of the provisional order certified by a judge or officer of the court;

(b) a certified or sworn document setting out or summarizing the evidence given to the court; and

(c) a statement giving any available information respecting the identification, location, income and assets of the respondent.

Idem

(4) On receipt of the documents referred to in subsection (3), the Attorney General shall send the documents to the Attorney General for the province in which the respondent is ordinarily resident.

Further evidence

(5) Where, during a proceeding under section 19, a court in a province remits the matter back for further evidence to the court that made the provisional order, the court that made the order shall, after giving notice to the applicant, receive further evidence.

Transmission

(6) Where evidence is received under subsection (5), the court that received the evidence shall forward to the court that remitted the matter back a certified or sworn document setting out or summarizing the evidence, together with such recommendations as the court that received the evidence considers appropriate.

R.S., 1985, c. 3 (2nd Supp.), s. 18; 1993, c. 8, s. 3, c. 28, s. 78; 2002, c. 7, s. 159.

Transmission

19. (1) On receipt of any documents sent pursuant to subsection 18(4), the Attorney General for the province in which the respondent is ordinarily resident shall send the documents to a court in the province.

Procedure

(2) Subject to subsection (3), where documents have been sent to a court pursuant to subsection (1), the court shall serve on the respondent a copy of the documents and a notice of a hearing respecting confirmation of the provisional order and shall proceed with the hearing, in the absence of the applicant, taking into consideration the certified or sworn document setting out or summarizing the evidence given to the court that made the provisional order.

Return to Attorney General

(3) Where documents have been sent to a court pursuant to subsection (1) and the respondent apparently is outside the province and is not likely to return, the court shall send the documents to the Attorney General for that province, together with any available information respecting the location and circumstances of the respondent.

Idem

(4) On receipt of any documents and information sent pursuant to subsection (3), the Attorney General shall send the documents and information to the Attorney General for the province of the court that made the provisional order.

Right of respondent

(5) In a proceeding under this section, the respondent may raise any matter that might have been raised before the court that made the provisional order.

Further evidence

(6) Where, in a proceeding under this section, the respondent satisfies the court that for the purpose of taking further evidence or for any other purpose it is necessary to remit the matter back to the court that made the provisional order, the court may so remit the matter and adjourn the proceeding for that purpose.

Order of confirmation or refusal

(7) Subject to subsection (7.1), at the conclusion of a proceeding under this section, the court shall make an order

(a) confirming the provisional order without variation;
(b) confirming the provisional order with variation; or
(c) refusing confirmation of the provisional order.

Guidelines apply

(7.1) A court making an order under subsection (7) in respect of a child support order shall do so in accordance with the applicable guidelines.

Further evidence

(8) The court, before making an order confirming the provisional order with variation or an order refusing confirmation of the provisional order, shall decide whether to remit the matter back for further evidence to the court that made the provisional order.

Interim order for support of children

(9) Where a court remits a matter pursuant to this section in relation to a child support order, the court may, pending the making of an order under subsection (7), make an interim order in accordance with the applicable guidelines requiring a spouse to pay for the support of any or all children of the marriage.

Interim order for support of spouse

(9.1) Where a court remits a matter pursuant to this section in relation to a spousal support order, the court may make an interim order requiring a spouse to secure or pay, or to secure and pay, such lump sum or periodic sums, or such lump sum and periodic sums, as the court thinks reasonable for the support of the other spouse, pending the making of an order under subsection (7).

Terms and conditions

(10) The court may make an order under subsection (9) or (9.1) for a definite or indefinite period or until a specified event occurs, and may impose terms, conditions or restrictions in connection with the order as it thinks fit and just.

Provisions applicable

(11) Subsections 17(4), (4.1) and (6) to (7) apply, with such modifications as the circumstances require, in respect of an order made under subsection (9) or (9.1) as if it were a variation order referred to in those subsections.

Report and filing

(12) On making an order under subsection (7), the court in a province shall
(a) send a copy of the order, certified by a judge or officer of the court, to the Attorney General for that province, to the court that made the provisional order and, where that court is not the court that made the support order in respect of which the provisional order was made, to the court that made the support order;
(b) where an order is made confirming the provisional order with or without variation, file the order in the court; and
(c) where an order is made confirming the provisional order with variation or refusing confirmation of the provisional order, give written reasons to the Attorney General for that province and to the court that made the provisional order.
R.S., 1985, c. 3 (2nd Supp.), s. 19; 1993, c. 8, s. 4; 1997, c. 1, s. 7.

Definition of "court"

20. (1) In this section, "court," in respect of a province, has the meaning assigned by subsection 2(1) and includes such other court having jurisdiction in the province as is designated by the Lieutenant Governor in Council of the province as a court for the purposes of this section.

Legal effect throughout Canada

(2) Subject to subsection 18(2), an order made under any of sections 15.1 to 17 or subsection 19(7), (9) or (9.1) has legal effect throughout Canada.

Enforcement

(3) An order that has legal effect throughout Canada pursuant to subsection (2) may be
(a) registered in any court in a province and enforced in like manner as an order of that court; or
(b) enforced in a province in any other manner provided for by the laws of that province, including its laws respecting reciprocal enforcement between the province and a jurisdiction outside Canada.

Variation of orders

(4) Notwithstanding subsection (3), a court may only vary an order that has legal effect throughout Canada pursuant to subsection (2) in accordance with this Act.

R.S., 1985, c. 3 (2nd Supp.), s. 20; 1997, c. 1, s. 8.

Assignment of order

20.1 (1) A support order may be assigned to
(a) any minister of the Crown for Canada designated by the Governor in Council;
(b) any minister of the Crown for a province, or any agency in a province, designated by the Lieutenant Governor in Council of the province;
(c) any member of the Legislative Assembly of Yukon, or any agency in Yukon, designated by the Commissioner of Yukon;
(d) any member of the Council of the Northwest Territories, or any agency in the Northwest Territories, designated by the Commissioner of the Northwest Territories; or
(e) any member of the Legislative Assembly of Nunavut, or any agency in Nunavut, designated by the Commissioner of Nunavut.

Rights

(2) A minister, member or agency referred to in subsection (1) to whom an order is assigned is entitled to the payments due under the order, and has the same right to be notified of, and to participate in, proceedings under this Act to vary, rescind, suspend or enforce the order as the person who would otherwise be entitled to the payments.
1993, c. 28, s. 78; 1997, c. 1, s. 9; 1998, c. 15, s. 23; 2002, c. 7, s. 160.

APPEALS

Appeal to appellate court

21. (1) Subject to subsections (2) and (3), an appeal lies to the appellate court from any judgment or order, whether final or interim, rendered or made by a court under this Act.

Restriction on divorce appeals

(2) No appeal lies from a judgment granting a divorce on or after the day on which the divorce takes effect.

Restriction on order appeals

(3) No appeal lies from an order made under this Act more than thirty days after the day on which the order was made.

Extension

(4) An appellate court or a judge thereof may, on special grounds, either before or after the

expiration of the time fixed by subsection (3) for instituting an appeal, by order extend that time.

Powers of
appellate court

(5) The appellate court may
(a) dismiss the appeal; or
(b) allow the appeal and
(i) render the judgment or make the order that ought to have been rendered or made, including such order or such further or other order as it deems just, or
(ii) order a new hearing where it deems it necessary to do so to correct a substantial wrong or miscarriage of justice.

Procedure on appeals

(6) Except as otherwise provided by this Act or the rules or regulations, an appeal under this section shall be asserted, heard and decided according to the ordinary procedure governing appeals to the appellate court from the court rendering the judgment or making the order being appealed.

GENERAL

Definition of
"spouse"

21.1 (1) In this section, "spouse" has the meaning assigned by subsection 2(1) and includes a former spouse.

Affidavit re removal
of barriers to religious
remarriage

(2) In any proceedings under this Act, a spouse (in this section referred to as the "deponent") may serve on the other spouse and file with the court an affidavit indicating
(a) that the other spouse is the spouse of the deponent;
(b) the date and place of the marriage, and the official character of the person who solemnized the marriage;
(c) the nature of any barriers to the remarriage of the deponent within the deponent's religion the removal of which is within the other spouse's control;
(d) where there are any barriers to the remarriage of the other spouse within the other spouse's religion the removal of which is within the deponent's control, that the deponent
(i) has removed those barriers, and the date and circumstances of that removal, or

(ii) has signified a willingness to remove those barriers, and the date and circumstances of that signification;

(e) that the deponent has, in writing, requested the other spouse to remove all of the barriers to the remarriage of the deponent within the deponent's religion the removal of which is within the other spouse's control;

(f) the date of the request described in paragraph (e); and

(g) that the other spouse, despite the request described in paragraph (e), has failed to remove all of the barriers referred to in that paragraph.

Powers of court where barriers not removed

(3) Where a spouse who has been served with an affidavit under subsection (2) does not

(a) within fifteen days after that affidavit is filed with the court or within such longer period as the court allows, serve on the deponent and file with the court an affidavit indicating that all of the barriers referred to in paragraph (2)(e) have been removed, and

(b) satisfy the court, in any additional manner that the court may require, that all of the barriers referred to in paragraph (2)(e) have been removed, the court may, subject to any terms that the court considers appropriate,

(c) dismiss any application filed by that spouse under this Act, and

(d) strike out any other pleadings and affidavits filed by that spouse under this Act.

Special case

(4) Without limiting the generality of the court's discretion under subsection (3), the court may refuse to exercise its powers under paragraphs (3)(c) and (d) where a spouse who has been served with an affidavit under subsection (2)

(a) within fifteen days after that affidavit is filed with the court or within such longer period as the court allows, serves on the deponent and files with the court an affidavit indicating genuine grounds of a religious or conscientious nature for refusing to remove the barriers referred to in paragraph (2)(e); and

(b) satisfies the court, in any additional manner that the court may require, that the spouse has genuine grounds of a religious or conscientious nature for refusing to remove the barriers referred to in paragraph (2)(e).

Affidavits

(5) For the purposes of this section, an affidavit filed with the court by a spouse must, in order to be valid, indicate the date on which it was served on the other spouse.

Where section does not apply

(6) This section does not apply where the power to remove the barrier to religious remarriage lies with a religious body or official. 1990, c. 18, s. 2.

Recognition of foreign divorce

22. (1) A divorce granted, on or after the coming into force of this Act, pursuant to a law of a country or subdivision of a country other than Canada by a tribunal or other authority having jurisdiction to do so shall be recognized for all purposes of determining the marital status in Canada of any person, if either former spouse was ordinarily resident in that country or subdivision for at least one year immediately preceding the commencement of proceedings for the divorce.

Idem

(2) A divorce granted, after July 1, 1968, pursuant to a law of a country or subdivision of a country other than Canada by a tribunal or other authority having jurisdiction to do so, on the basis of the domicile of the wife in that country or subdivision determined as if she were unmarried and, if she was a minor, as if she had attained the age of majority, shall be recognized for all purposes of determining the marital status in Canada of any person.

Other recognition rules preserved

(3) Nothing in this section abrogates or derogates from any other rule of law respecting the recognition of divorces granted otherwise than under this Act.

Provincial laws of evidence

23. (1) Subject to this or any other Act of Parliament, the laws of evidence of the province in which any proceedings under this Act are taken, including the laws of proof of service of any document, apply to such proceedings.

Presumption

(2) For the purposes of this section, where any proceedings are transferred to the Federal Court under subsection 3(3) or 5(3), the proceedings shall be deemed to have been taken in the province specified in the direction of the Court to be the province with which both spouses or former spouses, as the case may be, are or have been most substantially connected. R.S., 1985, c. 3 (2nd Supp.), s. 23; 2002, c. 8, s. 183.

Proof of signature or office

24. A document offered in a proceeding under this Act that purports to be certified or sworn by a judge or an officer of a court shall, unless the contrary is proved, be proof of the appointment, signature or authority of the judge or officer and, in the case of a document purporting to be sworn, of the appointment, signature or authority of the person before whom the document purports to be sworn.

Definition of "competent authority"

25. (1) In this section, "competent authority," in respect of a court, or appellate court, in a province means the body, person or group of persons ordinarily competent under the laws of that province to make rules regulating the practice and procedure in that court.

Rules

(2) Subject to subsection (3), the competent authority may make rules applicable to any proceedings under this Act in a court, or appellate court, in a province, including, without limiting the generality of the foregoing, rules
(a) regulating the practice and procedure in the court, including the addition of persons as parties to the proceedings;
(b) respecting the conduct and disposition of any proceedings under this Act without an oral hearing;
(b.1) respecting the application of section 17.1 in respect of proceedings for a variation order;
(c) regulating the sittings of the court;
(d) respecting the fixing and awarding of costs;
(e) prescribing and regulating the duties of officers of the court;
(f) respecting the transfer of proceedings under

this Act to or from the court; and

(g) prescribing and regulating any other matter considered expedient to attain the ends of justice and carry into effect the purposes and provisions of this Act.

Exercise of power

(3) The power to make rules for a court or appellate court conferred by subsection (2) on a competent authority shall be exercised in the like manner and subject to the like terms and conditions, if any, as the power to make rules for that court conferred on that authority by the laws of the province.

Not statutory instruments

(4) Rules made pursuant to this section by a competent authority that is not a judicial or quasi-judicial body shall be deemed not to be statutory instruments within the meaning and for the purposes of the Statutory Instruments Act. R.S., 1985, c. 3 (2nd Supp.), s. 25; 1993, c. 8, s. 5.

Agreements with provinces

25.1 (1) With the approval of the Governor in Council, the Minister of Justice may, on behalf of the Government of Canada, enter into an agreement with a province authorizing a provincial child support service designated in the agreement to

(a) assist courts in the province in the determination of the amount of child support; and

(b) recalculate, at regular intervals, in accordance with the applicable guidelines, the amount of child support orders on the basis of updated income information.

Effect of recalculation

(2) Subject to subsection (5), the amount of a child support order as recalculated pursuant to this section shall for all purposes be deemed to be the amount payable under the child support order.

Liability

(3) The former spouse against whom a child support order was made becomes liable to pay the amount as recalculated pursuant to this section thirty-one days after both former spouses to whom the order relates are notified of the recalculation in the manner provided for in the agreement authorizing the recalculation.

Right to vary

(4) Where either or both former spouses to whom a child support order relates do not agree with the amount of the order as recalculated pursuant to this section, either former spouse may, within thirty days after both former spouses are notified of the recalculation in the manner provided for in the agreement authorizing the recalculation, apply to a court of competent jurisdiction for an order under subsection 17(1).

Effect of application

(5) Where an application is made under subsection (4), the operation of subsection (3) is suspended pending the determination of the application, and the child support order continues in effect.

Withdrawal of application

(6) Where an application made under subsection (4) is withdrawn before the determination of the application, the former spouse against whom the order was made becomes liable to pay the amount as recalculated pursuant to this section on the day on which the former spouse would have become liable had the application not been made.
1997, c. 1, s. 10; 1999, c. 31, s. 74(F).

Regulations

26. (1) The Governor in Council may make regulations for carrying the purposes and provisions of this Act into effect and, without limiting the generality of the foregoing, may make regulations
(a) respecting the establishment and operation of a central registry of divorce proceedings in Canada; and
(b) providing for uniformity in the rules made pursuant to section 25.

Regulations prevail

(2) Any regulations made pursuant to subsection (1) to provide for uniformity in the rules prevail over those rules.

Guidelines

26.1 (1) The Governor in Council may establish guidelines respecting the making of orders for child support, including, but without limiting the generality of the foregoing, guidelines
(a) respecting the way in which the amount of an order for child support is to be determined;
(b) respecting the circumstances in which

discretion may be exercised in the making of an order for child support;

(c) authorizing a court to require that the amount payable under an order for child support be paid in periodic payments, in a lump sum or in a lump sum and periodic payments;

(d) authorizing a court to require that the amount payable under an order for child support be paid or secured, or paid and secured, in the manner specified in the order;

(e) respecting the circumstances that give rise to the making of a variation order in respect of a child support order;

(f) respecting the determination of income for the purposes of the application of the guidelines;

(g) authorizing a court to impute income for the purposes of the application of the guidelines; and

(h) respecting the production of income information and providing for sanctions when that information is not provided.

Principle

(2) The guidelines shall be based on the principle that spouses have a joint financial obligation to maintain the children of the marriage in accordance with their relative abilities to contribute to the performance of that obligation.

Definition of "order for child support"

(3) In subsection (1), "order for child support" means

(a) an order or interim order made under section 15.1;

(b) a variation order in respect of a child support order; or

(c) an order or an interim order made under section 19.

1997, c. 1, s. 11.

Fees

27. (1) The Governor in Council may, by order, authorize the Minister of Justice to prescribe a fee to be paid by any person to whom a service is provided under this Act or the regulations.

Agreements

(2) The Minister of Justice may, with the approval of the Governor in Council, enter into an

agreement with the government of any province respecting the collection and remittance of any fees prescribed pursuant to subsection (1).

Review and report **28.** The Minister of Justice shall undertake a comprehensive review of the provisions and operation of the Federal Child Support Guidelines and the determination of child support under this Act and shall cause a report on the review to be laid before each House of Parliament within five years after the coming into force of this section. R.S., 1985, c. 3 (2nd Supp.), s. 28; 1997, c. 1, s. 12.

29. to 31. [Repealed, 1997, c. 1, s. 12]

TRANSITIONAL PROVISIONS

Proceedings based on facts arising before commencement of Act **32.** Proceedings may be commenced under this Act notwithstanding that the material facts or circumstances giving rise to the proceedings or to jurisdiction over the proceedings occurred wholly or partly before the day on which this Act comes into force.

Divorce Act, R.S. 1970, c. D-8

Proceedings commenced before commencement of Act **33.** Proceedings commenced under the *Divorce Act*, chapter D-8 of the Revised Statutes of Canada, 1970, before the day on which this Act comes into force and not finally disposed of before that day shall be dealt with and disposed of in accordance with that Act as it read immediately before that day, as though it had not been repealed.

Variation and enforcement of orders previously made **34.** (1) Subject to subsection (1.1), any order made under subsection 11(1) of the *Divorce Act*, chapter D-8 of the Revised Statutes of Canada, 1970, including any order made pursuant to section 33 of this Act, and any order to the like effect made corollary to a decree of divorce granted in Canada before July 2, 1968 or granted on or after that day pursuant to subsection 22(2) of that Act may be varied, rescinded, suspended or enforced in accordance with sections 17 to 20, other than subsection 17(10), of this Act as if

(a) the order were a support order or custody order, as the case may be; and

(b) in subsections 17(4), (4.1) and (5), the words "or the last order made under subsection 11(2) of the Divorce Act, chapter D-8 of the Revised Statutes of Canada, 1970, varying that order" were added immediately before the words "or the last variation order made in respect of that order".

Combined orders

(1.1) Where an application is made under subsection 17(1) to vary an order referred to in subsection (1) that provides a single amount of money for the combined support of one or more children and a former spouse, the court shall rescind the order and treat the application as an application for a child support order and an application for a spousal support order.

Enforcement of interim orders

(2) Any order made under section 10 of the *Divorce Act,* chapter D-8 of the Revised Statutes of Canada, 1970, including any order made pursuant to section 33 of this Act, may be enforced in accordance with section 20 of this Act as if it were an order made under subsection 15.1(1) or 15.2(1) or section 16 of this Act, as the case may be.

Assignment of orders previously made

(3) Any order for the maintenance of a spouse or child of the marriage made under section 10 or 11 of the *Divorce Act*, chapter D-8 of the Revised Statutes of Canada, 1970, including any order made pursuant to section 33 of this Act, and any order to the like effect made corollary to a decree of divorce granted in Canada before July 2, 1968 or granted on or after that day pursuant to subsection 22(2) of that Act may be assigned to any minister, member or agency designated pursuant to section 20.1. R.S., 1985, c. 3 (2nd Supp.), s. 34; 1997, c. 1, s. 14.

Procedural laws continued

35. The rules and regulations made under the *Divorce Act*, chapter D-8 of the Revised Statutes of Canada, 1970, and the provisions of any other law or of any rule, regulation or other instrument made thereunder respecting any matter in relation to which rules may be made under subsection 25(2) that were in force in Canada or any province immediately before the day on which this Act comes into force and that are not inconsistent with this Act continue in force as though made or enacted by or under this Act until they are repealed or altered by rules or regulations made under this Act or are, by virtue of the making of rules or regulations under this Act, rendered inconsistent with those rules or regulations.

Divorce Act, *R.S. 1985*, c. 3 (2nd Supp.)

Variation and enforcement of support orders previously made

35.1 (1) Subject to subsection (2), any support order made under this Act before the coming into force of this section may be varied, rescinded, suspended or enforced in accordance with sections 17 to 20 as if the support order were a child support order or a spousal support order, as the case may be.

Combined orders

(2) Where an application is made under subsection 17(1) to vary a support order made under this Act before the coming into force of this section that provides for the combined support of one or more children and a former spouse, the court shall rescind the order and treat the application as an application for a child support order and an application for a spousal support order.

Assignment of orders previously made

(3) Any support order made under this Act before the coming into force of this section may be assigned to any minister, member or agency designated pursuant to section 20.1.
1997, c. 1, s. 15.

COMMENCEMENT

Commencement

*36. This Act shall come into force on a day to be fixed by proclamation.

*[Note: Act in force June 1, 1986, see SI/86-70.]

Federal Child Support Guidelines

OBJECTIVES

Objectives
1. The objectives of these Guidelines are

(a) to establish a fair standard of support for children that ensures that they continue to benefit from the financial means of both spouses after separation;

(b) to reduce conflict and tension between spouses by making the calculation of child support orders more objective;

(c) to improve the efficiency of the legal process by giving courts and spouses guidance in setting the levels of child support orders and encouraging settlement; and

(d) to ensure consistent treatment of spouses and children who are in similar circumstances.

INTERPRETATION

Definitions
2. (1) The definitions in this subsection apply in these Guidelines.

"Act" « Loi »
"Act" means the *Divorce Act*. (Loi)

"child" « enfant »
"child" means a child of the marriage. (enfant)

"income" « revenu »
"income" means the annual income determined under sections 15 to 20. (revenu)

"order assignee" « cessionnaire de la créance alimentaire »
   "order assignee" means a minister, member or agency referred to in subsection 20.1(1) of the Act to whom a child support order is assigned in accordance with that subsection. (cessionnaire de la créance alimentaire)

"spouse" « époux »
   "spouse" has the meaning assigned by subsection 2(1) of the Act, and includes a former spouse. (époux)

"table" « table »
"table" means a federal child support table set out in Schedule I.
(table)

Income Tax Act
(2) Words and expressions that are used in sections 15 to 21 and that are not defined in this section have the meanings assigned to them under the *Income Tax Act.*

Most current information
(3) Where, for the purposes of these Guidelines, any amount is determined on the basis of specified information, the most current information must be used.

Application of Guidelines
(4) In addition to child support orders, these Guidelines apply, with such modifications as the circumstances require, to
(a) interim orders under subsections 15.1(2) and 19(9) of the Act;
(b) orders varying a child support order;
(c) orders referred to in subsection 19(7) of the Act; and
(d) recalculations under paragraph 25.1(1)(b) of the Act.

Recalculations
(5) For greater certainty, the provisions of these Guidelines that confer a discretionary power on a court do not apply to recalculations under paragraph 25.1(1)(b) of the Act by a provincial child support service.

AMOUNT OF CHILD SUPPORT
Presumptive rule
3. (1) Unless otherwise provided under these Guidelines, the amount of a child support order for children under the age of majority is
(a) the amount set out in the applicable table, according to the number of children under the age of majority to whom the order relates and the income of the spouse against whom the order is sought; and
(b) the amount, if any, determined under section 7.

Child the age of majority or over
(2) Unless otherwise provided under these Guidelines, where a child to whom a child support order relates is the age of majority or over, the amount of the child support order is
(a) the amount determined by applying these Guidelines as if the child were under the age of majority; or
(b) if the court considers that approach to be inappropriate, the amount that it considers appropriate, having regard to the condition, means, needs and other circumstances of the child and the financial ability of each spouse to contribute to the support of the child.

Applicable table

(3) The applicable table is

(a) if the spouse against whom an order is sought resides in Canada,

(i) the table for the province in which that spouse ordinarily resides at the time the application for the child support order, or for a variation order in respect of a child support order, is made or the amount is to be recalculated under section 25.1 of the Act,

(ii) where the court is satisfied that the province in which that spouse ordinarily resides has changed since the time described in subparagraph (i), the table for the province in which the spouse ordinarily resides at the time of determining the amount of support, or

(iii) where the court is satisfied that, in the near future after determination of the amount of support, that spouse will ordinarily reside in a given province other than the province in which the spouse ordinarily resides at the time of that determination, the table for the given province; and

(b) if the spouse against whom an order is sought resides outside of Canada, or if the residence of that spouse is unknown, the table for the province where the other spouse ordinarily resides at the time the application for the child support order or for a variation order in respect of a child support order is made or the amount is to be recalculated under section 25.1 of the Act. SOR/97-563, s. 1.

Incomes over $150,000

4. Where the income of the spouse against whom a child support order is sought is over $150,000, the amount of a child support order is

(a) the amount determined under section 3; or

(b) if the court considers that amount to be inappropriate,

(i) in respect of the first $150,000 of the spouse's income, the amount set out in the applicable table for the number of children under the age of majority to whom the order relates;

(ii) in respect of the balance of the spouse's income, the amount that the court considers appropriate, having regard to the condition, means, needs and other circumstances of the children who are entitled to support and the financial ability of each spouse to contribute to the support of the children; and

(iii) the amount, if any, determined under section 7.

Spouse in place of a parent

5. Where the spouse against whom a child support order is sought stands in the place of a parent for a child, the amount of a child support order is, in respect of that spouse, such amount as the court considers appropriate, having regard to these Guidelines and any other parent's legal duty to support the child.

Medical and dental insurance

6. In making a child support order, where medical or dental insurance coverage for the child is available to either spouse through his or her employer or otherwise at a reasonable rate, the court may order that coverage be acquired or continued.

Special or extraordinary expenses

7. (1) In a child support order the court may, on either spouse's request, provide for an amount to cover all or any portion of the following expenses, which expenses may be estimated, taking into account the necessity of the expense in relation to the child's best interests and the reasonableness of the expense in relation to the means of the spouses and those of the child and to the family's spending pattern prior to the separation:

(a) child care expenses incurred as a result of the custodial parent's employment, illness, disability or education or training for employment;

(b) that portion of the medical and dental insurance premiums attributable to the child;

(c) health-related expenses that exceed insurance reimbursement by at least $100 annually, including orthodontic treatment, professional counselling provided by a psychologist, social worker, psychiatrist or any other person, physiotherapy, occupational therapy, speech therapy and prescription drugs, hearing aids, glasses and contact lenses;

(d) extraordinary expenses for primary or secondary school education or for any other educational programs that meet the child's particular needs;

(e) expenses for post-secondary education; and

(f) extraordinary expenses for extracurricular activities.

Sharing of expense

(2) The guiding principle in determining the amount of an expense referred to in subsection (1) is that the expense is shared by the spouses in proportion to their respective incomes after deducting from the expense, the contribution, if any, from the child.

Subsidies, tax deductions, etc.

(3) In determining the amount of an expense referred to in subsection (1), the court must take into account any subsidies, benefits or income tax deductions or credits relating to the expense, and any eligibility to claim a subsidy, benefit or income tax deduction or credit relating to the expense. SOR/2000-337, s. 1; SOR/2000-390, s. 1(F).

Split custody

8. Where each spouse has custody of one or more children, the amount of a child support order is the difference between the amount that each spouse would otherwise pay if a child support order were sought against each of the spouses.

Shared custody

9. Where a spouse exercises a right of access to, or has physical custody of, a child for not less than 40 per cent of the time over the course of a year, the amount of the child support order must be determined by taking into account

(a) the amounts set out in the applicable tables for each of the spouses;

(b) the increased costs of shared custody arrangements; and

(c) the conditions, means, needs and other circumstances of each spouse and of any child for whom support is sought.

Undue hardship

10. (1) On either spouse's application, a court may award an amount of child support that is different from the amount determined under any of sections 3 to 5, 8 or 9 if the court finds that the spouse making the request, or a child in respect of whom the request is made, would otherwise suffer undue hardship.

Circumstances that may cause undue hardship

(2) Circumstances that may cause a spouse or child to suffer undue hardship include the following:

(a) the spouse has responsibility for an unusually high level of debts reasonably incurred to support the spouses and their children prior to the separation or to earn a living;

(b) the spouse has unusually high expenses in relation to exercising access to a child;

(c) the spouse has a legal duty under a judgment, order or written separation agreement to support any person;

(d) the spouse has a legal duty to support a child, other than a child of the marriage, who is

(i) under the age of majority, or

(ii) the age of majority or over but is unable, by reason of illness, disability or other cause, to obtain the necessaries of life; and

(e) the spouse has a legal duty to support any person who is unable to obtain the necessaries of life due to an illness or disability.

Standards of living must be considered

(3) Despite a determination of undue hardship under subsection (1), an application under that subsection must be denied by the court if it is of the opinion that the household of the spouse who claims undue hardship would, after determining the amount of child support under any of sections 3 to 5, 8 or 9, have a higher standard of living than the household of the other spouse.

Standards of living test

(4) In comparing standards of living for the purpose of subsection (3), the court may use the comparison of household standards of living test set out in Schedule II.

Reasonable time

(5) Where the court awards a different amount of child support under subsection (1), it may specify, in the child support order, a reasonable time for the satisfaction of any obligation arising from circumstances that cause undue hardship and the amount payable at the end of that time.

Reasons

(6) Where the court makes a child support order in a different amount under this section, it must record its reasons for doing so.

ELEMENTS OF A CHILD SUPPORT ORDER

Form of payments

11. The court may require in a child support order that the amount payable under the order be paid in periodic payments, in a lump sum or in a lump sum and periodic payments.

Security

12. The court may require in the child support order that the amount payable under the order be paid or secured, or paid and secured, in the manner specified in the order.

Information to be specified in order

13. A child support order must include the following information:

(a) the name and birth date of each child to whom the order relates;

(b) the income of any spouse whose income is used to determine the amount of the child support order;

(c) the amount determined under paragraph 3(1)(a) for the number of children to whom the order relates;

(d) the amount determined under paragraph 3(2)(b) for a child the age of majority or over;

(e) the particulars of any expense described in subsection 7(1), the child to whom the expense relates, and the amount of the expense or, where that amount cannot be determined, the proportion to be paid in relation to the expense; and

(f) the date on which the lump sum or first payment is payable and the day of the month or other time period on which all subsequent payments are to be made.

VARIATION OF CHILD SUPPORT ORDERS
Circumstances for variation

14. For the purposes of subsection 17(4) of the Act, any one of the following constitutes a change of circumstances that gives rise to the making of a variation order in respect of a child support order:

(a) in the case where the amount of child support includes a determination made in accordance with the applicable table, any change in circumstances that would result in a different child support order or any provision thereof;

(b) in the case where the amount of child support does not include a determination made in accordance with a table, any change in the condition, means, needs or other circumstances of either spouse or of any child who is entitled to support; and

(c) in the case of an order made before May 1, 1997, the coming into force of section 15.1 of the Act, enacted by section 2 of chapter 1 of the Statutes of Canada, (1997). SOR/97-563, s. 2; SOR/2000-337, s. 2.

INCOME
Determination of annual income

15. (1) Subject to subsection (2), a spouse's annual income is determined by the court in accordance with sections 16 to 20.

Agreement

(2) Where both spouses agree in writing on the annual income of a spouse, the court may consider that amount to be the spouse's income for the purposes of these Guidelines if the court thinks that the amount is reasonable having regard to the income information provided under section 21.

Calculation of annual income

16. Subject to sections 17 to 20, a spouse's annual income is determined using the sources of income set out under the heading "Total income" in the T1 General form issued by the Canada Customs and Revenue Agency and is adjusted in accordance with Schedule III. SOR/2000-337, s. 3.

Pattern of income

17. (1) If the court is of the opinion that the determination of a spouse's annual income under section 16 would not be the fairest determination of that income, the court may have regard to the spouse's income over the last three years and determine an amount that is fair and reasonable in light of any pattern of income, fluctuation in income or receipt of a non-recurring amount during those years.

Non-recurring losses

(2) Where a spouse has incurred a non-recurring capital or business investment loss, the court may, if it is of the opinion that the determination of the spouse's annual income under section 16 would not provide the fairest determination of the annual income, choose not to apply sections 6 and 7 of Schedule III, and adjust the amount of the loss, including related expenses and carrying charges and interest expenses, to arrive at such amount as the court considers appropriate. SOR/2000-337, s. 4.

Shareholder, director or officer

18. (1) Where a spouse is a shareholder, director or officer of a corporation and the court is of the opinion that the amount of the spouse's annual income as determined under section 16 does not fairly reflect all the money available to the spouse for the payment of child support, the court may consider the situations described in section 17 and determine the spouse's annual income to include

(a) all or part of the pre-tax income of the corporation, and of any corporation that is related to that corporation, for the most recent taxation year; or

(b) an amount commensurate with the services that the spouse provides to the corporation, provided that the amount does not exceed the corporation's pre-tax income.

Adjustment to corporation's pre-tax income

(2) In determining the pre-tax income of a corporation for the purposes of subsection (1), all amounts paid by the corporation as salaries, wages or management fees, or other payments or benefits, to or on behalf of persons with whom the corporation does not deal at arm's length must be added to the pre-tax income, unless the spouse establishes that the payments were reasonable in the circumstances.

Imputing income

19. (1) The court may impute such amount of income to a spouse as it considers appropriate in the circumstances, which circumstances include the following:

(a) the spouse is intentionally under-employed or unemployed, other than where the under-employment or unemployment is required by the needs of a child of the marriage or any child under the age of majority or by the reasonable educational or health needs of the spouse;

(b) the spouse is exempt from paying federal or provincial income tax;

(c) the spouse lives in a country that has effective rates of income tax that are significantly lower than those in Canada;

(d) it appears that income has been diverted which would affect the level of child support to be determined under these Guidelines;

(e) the spouse's property is not reasonably utilized to generate income;
(f) the spouse has failed to provide income information when under a legal obligation to do so;
(g) the spouse unreasonably deducts expenses from income;
(h) the spouse derives a significant portion of income from dividends, capital gains or other sources that are taxed at a lower rate than employment or business income or that are exempt from tax; and
(i) the spouse is a beneficiary under a trust and is or will be in receipt of income or other benefits from the trust.

Reasonableness of expenses
(2) For the purpose of paragraph (1)(g), the reasonableness of an expense deduction is not solely governed by whether the deduction is permitted under the *Income Tax Act*. SOR/2000-337, s. 5.

Non-resident
20. Where a spouse is a non-resident of Canada, the spouse's annual income is determined as though the spouse were a resident of Canada.

INCOME INFORMATION
Obligation of applicant
21. (1) A spouse who is applying for a child support order and whose income information is necessary to determine the amount of the order must include the following with the application:
(a) a copy of every personal income tax return filed by the spouse for each of the three most recent taxation years;
(b) a copy of every notice of assessment and reassessment issued to the spouse for each of the three most recent taxation years;
(c) where the spouse is an employee, the most recent statement of earnings indicating the total earnings paid in the year to date, including overtime or, where such a statement is not provided by the employer, a letter from the spouse's employer setting out that information including the spouse's rate of annual salary or remuneration;
(d) where the spouse is self-employed, for the three most recent taxation years
(i) the financial statements of the spouse's business or professional practice, other than a partnership, and
(ii) a statement showing a breakdown of all salaries, wages, management fees or other payments or benefits paid to, or on behalf of, persons or corporations with whom the spouse does not deal at arm's length;
(e) where the spouse is a partner in a partnership, confirmation of the spouse's income and draw from, and capital in, the partnership for its three most recent taxation years;
(f) where the spouse controls a corporation, for its three most recent taxation years

(i) the financial statements of the corporation and its subsidiaries, and

(ii) a statement showing a breakdown of all salaries, wages, management fees or other payments or benefits paid to, or on behalf of, persons or corporations with whom the corporation, and every related corporation, does not deal at arm's length;

(g) where the spouse is a beneficiary under a trust, a copy of the trust settlement agreement and copies of the trust's three most recent financial statements; and

(h) in addition to any income information that must be included under paragraphs (c) to (g), where the spouse receives income from employment insurance, social assistance, a pension, workers compensation, disability payments or any other source, the most recent statement of income indicating the total amount of income from the applicable source during the current year, or if such a statement is not provided, a letter from the appropriate authority stating the required information.

Obligation of respondent

(2) A spouse who is served with an application for a child support order and whose income information is necessary to determine the amount of the order, must, within 30 days after the application is served if the spouse resides in Canada or the United States or within 60 days if the spouse resides elsewhere, or such other time limit as the court specifies, provide the court, as well as the other spouse or the order assignee, as the case may be, with the documents referred to in subsection (1).

Special expenses or undue hardship

(3) Where, in the course of proceedings in respect of an application for a child support order, a spouse requests an amount to cover expenses referred to in subsection 7(1) or pleads undue hardship, the spouse who would be receiving the amount of child support must, within 30 days after the amount is sought or undue hardship is pleaded if the spouse resides in Canada or the United States or within 60 days if the spouse resides elsewhere, or such other time limit as the court specifies, provide the court and the other spouse with the documents referred to in subsection (1).

Income over $150,000

(4) Where, in the course of proceedings in respect of an application for a child support order, it is established that the income of the spouse who would be paying the amount of child support is greater than $150,000, the other spouse must, within 30 days after the income is established to be greater than $150,000 if the other spouse resides in Canada or the United States or within 60 days if the other spouse resides elsewhere, or such other

time limit as the court specifies, provide the court and the spouse with the documents referred to in subsection (1).

Making of rules not precluded
(5) Nothing in this section precludes the making of rules by a competent authority, within the meaning of section 25 of the Act, respecting the disclosure of income information that is considered necessary for the purposes of the determination of an amount of a child support order. SOR/2000-337, s. 6.

Failure to comply
22. (1) Where a spouse fails to comply with section 21, the other spouse may apply
(a) to have the application for a child support order set down for a hearing, or move for judgment; or
(b) for an order requiring the spouse who failed to comply to provide the court, as well as the other spouse or order assignee, as the case may be, with the required documents.

Costs of the proceedings
(2) Where a court makes an order under paragraph (1)(a) or (b), the court may award costs in favour of the other spouse up to an amount that fully compensates the other spouse for all costs incurred in the proceedings.

Adverse inference
23. Where the court proceeds to a hearing on the basis of an application under paragraph 22(1)(a), the court may draw an adverse inference against the spouse who failed to comply and impute income to that spouse in such amount as it considers appropriate.

Failure to comply with court order
24. Where a spouse fails to comply with an order issued on the basis of an application under paragraph 22(1)(b), the court may
(a) strike out any of the spouse's pleadings;
(b) make a contempt order against the spouse;
(c) proceed to a hearing, in the course of which it may draw an adverse inference against the spouse and impute income to that spouse in such amount as it considers appropriate; and
(d) award costs in favour of the other spouse up to an amount that fully compensates the other spouse for all costs incurred in the proceedings.

Continuing obligation to provide income information
25. (1) Every spouse against whom a child support order has been made must, on the written request of the other spouse or the order assignee, not more than once a year after the making of the order and as long

as the child is a child within the meaning of these Guidelines, provide that other spouse or the order assignee with

(a) the documents referred to in subsection 21(1) for any of the three most recent taxation years for which the spouse has not previously provided the documents;

(b) as applicable, any current information, in writing, about the status of any expenses included in the order pursuant to subsection 7(1); and

(c) as applicable, any current information, in writing, about the circumstances relied on by the court in a determination of undue hardship.

Below minimum income

(2) Where a court has determined that the spouse against whom a child support order is sought does not have to pay child support because his or her income level is below the minimum amount required for application of the tables, that spouse must, on the written request of the other spouse, not more than once a year after the determination and as long as the child is a child within the meaning of these Guidelines, provide the other spouse with the documents referred to in subsection 21(1) for any of the three most recent taxation years for which the spouse has not previously provided the documents.

Obligation of receiving spouse

(3) Where the income information of the spouse in favour of whom a child support order is made is used to determine the amount of the order, the spouse must, not more than once a year after the making of the order and as long as the child is a child within the meaning of these Guidelines, on the written request of the other spouse, provide the other spouse with the documents and information referred to in subsection (1).

Information requests

(4) Where a spouse or an order assignee requests information from the other spouse under any of subsections (1) to (3) and the income information of the requesting spouse is used to determine the amount of the child support order, the requesting spouse or order assignee must include the documents and information referred to in subsection (1) with the request.

Time limit

(5) A spouse who receives a request made under any of subsections (1) to (3) must provide the required documents within 30 days after the request's receipt if the spouse resides in Canada or the United States and within 60 days after the request's receipt if the spouse resides elsewhere.

Deemed receipt
(6) A request made under any of subsections (1) to (3) is deemed to have been received 10 days after it is sent.

Failure to comply
(7) A court may, on application by either spouse or an order assignee, where the other spouse has failed to comply with any of subsections (1) to (3)
(a) consider the other spouse to be in contempt of court and award costs in favour of the applicant up to an amount that fully compensates the applicant for all costs incurred in the proceedings; or
(b) make an order requiring the other spouse to provide the required documents to the court, as well as to the spouse or order assignee, as the case may be.

Unenforceable provision
(8) A provision in a judgment, order or agreement purporting to limit a spouse's obligation to provide documents under this section is unenforceable. SOR/97-563, s. 3(E).

Provincial child support services
26. A spouse or an order assignee may appoint a provincial child support service to act on their behalf for the purposes of requesting and receiving income information under any of subsections 25(1) to (3), as well as for the purposes of an application under subsection 25(7).

COMING INTO FORCE
Coming into force
27. These Guidelines come into force on May 1, 1997.

SCHEDULE I
(Subsection 2(1))
FEDERAL CHILD SUPPORT TABLES

Notes:
1. The federal child support tables set out the amount of monthly child support payments for each province on the basis of the annual income of the spouse ordered to pay child support (the "support payer") and the number of children for whom a table amount is payable. Refer to these Guidelines to determine whether special measures apply.

2. There is a threshold level of income below which no amount of child support is payable. Child support amounts are specified for incomes up to $150,000 per year. Refer to section 4 of these Guidelines to determine the amount of child support payments for support payers with annual incomes over $150,000.

3.Income is set out in the tables in intervals of $1,000. Monthly amounts are determined by adding the basic amount and the amount calculated by multiplying the applicable percentage by the portion of the income that exceeds the lower amount within that interval of income.

Example:

Province: British Columbia
Number of children: 2
Annual income of support payer: $33,760
Basic amount: $480
Percentage: 1.20%
Lower amount of the income interval: $33,000

The amount of monthly child support is calculated as follows:

$480 + [1.2% x ($33,760 – 33,000)]
$480 + [1.2/100 x $760]
$480 + [0.012 x $760]
$480 + $9.12 = $489.12

4.There are separate tables for each province. The amounts vary from one province to another because of differences in provincial income tax rates. The tables are in the following order:

(a) Ontario;
(b) Quebec;
(c) Nova Scotia;
(d) New Brunswick;
(e) Manitoba;
(f) British Columbia;
(g) Prince Edward Island;
(h) Saskatchewan;
(i) Alberta;
(j) Newfoundland;
(k) Yukon;
(l) Northwest Territories; and
(m) Nunavut.

5.*The amounts in the tables are based on economic studies of average spending on children in families at different income levels in Canada. They are calculated on the basis that child support payments are no longer taxable in the hands of the receiving parent and no longer deductible by the paying parent. They are calculated using a mathematical formula and generated by a computer program.*

6. *The formula referred to in note 5 sets support amounts to reflect average expenditures on children by a spouse with a particular number of children and level of income. The calculation is based on the support payer's income. The formula uses the basic personal amount for non-refundable tax credits to recognize personal expenses, and takes other federal and provincial income taxes and credits into account. Federal Child Tax benefits and Goods and Services Tax credits for children are excluded from the calculation. At lower income levels, the formula sets the amounts to take into account the combined impact of taxes and child support payments on the support payer's limited disposable income.*

FEDERAL CHILD SUPPORT TABLES
SOR/97-563, ss. 4 to 9; SOR/99-136, ss. 1, 2.

SCHEDULE II
(Subsection 10(4))
COMPARISON OF HOUSEHOLD STANDARDS OF LIVING TEST

Definitions
1. The definitions in this section apply in this Schedule.
"average tax rate" [Repealed, SOR/2000-337, s. 7]

"child" « enfant »
"child" means a child of the marriage or a child who
(a) is under the age of majority; or
(b) is the age of majority or over but is unable, by reason of illness, disability or other cause to obtain the necessaries of life. (enfant)

"household" « ménage »
"household" means a spouse and any of the following persons residing with the spouse
(a) any person who has a legal duty to support the spouse or whom the spouse has a legal duty to support;
(b) any person who shares living expenses with the spouse or from whom the spouse otherwise receives an economic benefit as a result of living with that person, if the court considers it reasonable for that person to be considered part of the household; and
(c) any child whom the spouse or the person described in paragraph (a) or (b) has a legal duty to support. (ménage)

"taxable income" « revenu imposable »
"taxable income" means the annual taxable income determined using

the calculations required to determine "Taxable Income" in the T1 General form issued by the Canada Customs and Revenue Agency. (revenu imposable)

Test

2. The comparison of household standards of living test is as follows:

STEP 1

Establish the annual income of each person in each household by applying the formula

$$A - B$$

where

A is the person's income determined under sections 15 to 20 of these Guidelines, and

B is the federal and provincial taxes payable on the person's taxable income.

Where the information on which to base the income determination is not provided, the court may impute income in the amount it considers appropriate.

STEP 2

Adjust the annual income of each person in each household by

(a) deducting the following amounts, calculated on an annual basis:

(i) any amount relied on by the court as a factor that resulted in a determination of undue hardship, except any amount attributable to the support of a member of the household that is not incurred due to a disability or serious illness of that member,

(ii) the amount that would otherwise be payable by the person in respect of a child to whom the order relates, if the pleading of undue hardship was not made,

(A) under the applicable table, or

(B) as is considered by the court to be appropriate, where the court considers the table amount to be inappropriate,

(iii) any amount of support that is paid by the person under a judgment, order or written separation agreement, except

(A) an amount already deducted under subparagraph (i), and

(B) an amount paid by the person in respect of a child to whom the order referred to in subparagraph (ii) relates; and

(b) adding the following amounts, calculated on an annual basis:

(i) any amount that would otherwise be receivable by the person in respect of a child to whom the order relates, if the pleading of undue hardship was not made,

(A) under the applicable table, or
(B) as is considered by the court to be appropriate, where the court considers the table amount to be inappropriate,
(ii) any amount of child support that the person has received for any child under a judgment, order or written separation agreement.

STEP 3
Add the amounts of adjusted annual income for all the persons in each household to determine the total household income for each household.

STEP 4
Determine the applicable low-income measures amount for each household based on the following:

(LOW-INCOME MEASURES)

Household Size	Low-income Measures Amount
One person	
1 adult	$10,382
Two persons	
2 adults	$14,535
1 adult and 1 child	$14,535
Three persons	
3 adults	$18,688
2 adults and 1 child	$17,649
1 adult and 2 children	$17,649
Four persons	
4 adults	$22,840
3 adults and 1 child	$21,802
2 adults and 2 children	$20,764
1 adult and 3 children	$20,764
Five persons	
5 adults	$26,993
4 adults and 1 child	$25,955
3 adults and 2 children	$24,917
2 adults and 3 children	$23,879
1 adult and 4 children	$23,879
Six persons	
6 adults	$31,145

5 adults and 1 child	$30,108
4 adults and 2 children	$29,070
3 adults and 3 children	$28,031
2 adults and 4 children	$26,993
1 adult and 5 children	$26,993

Seven persons

7 adults	$34,261
6 adults and 1 child	$33,222
5 adults and 2 children	$32,184
4 adults and 3 children	$31,146
3 adults and 4 children	$30,108
2 adults and 5 children	$29,070
1 adult and 6 children	$29,070

Eight persons

8 adults	$38,413
7 adults and 1 child	$37,375
6 adults and 2 children	$36,337
5 adults and 3 children	$35,299
4 adults and 4 children	$34,261
3 adults and 5 children	$33,222
2 adults and 6 children	$32,184
1 adult and 7 children	$32,184

STEP 5
Divide the household income amount (Step 3) by the low-income measures amount (Step 4) to get a household income ratio for each household.

STEP 6
Compare the household income ratios. The household that has the higher ratio has the higher standard of living.

SOR/97-563, ss. 10, 11; SOR/2000-337, s. 7.

SCHEDULE III
(Section 16)
ADJUSTMENTS TO INCOME

Employment expenses

1. Where the spouse is an employee, the spouse's applicable employment expenses described in the following provisions of the *Income Tax Act* are deducted:

(a) [Repealed, SOR/2000-337, s. 8]

(b) paragraph 8(1)(d) concerning expenses of teacher's exchange fund contribution;

(c) paragraph 8(1)(e) concerning expenses of railway employees;

(d) paragraph 8(1)(f) concerning sales expenses;

(e) paragraph 8(1)(g) concerning transport employee's expenses;

(f) paragraph 8(1)(h) concerning travel expenses;

(f.1) paragraph 8(1)(h.1) concerning motor vehicle travel expenses;

(g) paragraph 8(1)(i) concerning dues and other expenses of performing duties;

(h) paragraph 8(l)(j) concerning motor vehicle and aircraft costs;

(i) paragraph 8(1)(l.1) concerning Canada Pension Plan contributions and *Employment Insurance Act* premiums paid in respect of another employee who acts as an assistant or substitute for the spouse;

(j) paragraph 8(1)(n) concerning salary reimbursement;

(k) paragraph 8(1)(o) concerning forfeited amounts;

(l) paragraph 8(1)(p) concerning musical instrument costs; and

(m) paragraph 8(1)(q) concerning artists' employment expenses.

Child support

2. Deduct any child support received that is included to determine total income in the T1 General form issued by the Canada Customs and Revenue Agency.

Spousal support
3. (1) To calculate income for the purpose of determining an amount under an applicable table, deduct the spousal support received from the other spouse.

Special or extraordinary expenses
(2) To calculate income for the purpose of determining an amount under section 7 of these Guidelines, deduct the spousal support paid to the other spouse.

Social assistance
4. Deduct any amount of social assistance income that is not attributable to the spouse.

Dividends from taxable Canadian corporations
5. Replace the taxable amount of dividends from taxable Canadian corporations received by the spouse by the actual amount of those dividends received by the spouse.

Capital gains and capital losses
6. Replace the taxable capital gains realized in a year by the spouse by the actual amount of capital gains realized by the spouse in excess of the spouse's actual capital losses in that year.

Business investment losses
7. Deduct the actual amount of business investment losses suffered by the spouse during the year.

Carrying charges
8. Deduct the spouse's carrying charges and interest expenses that are paid by the spouse and that would be deductible under the *Income Tax Act*.

Net self-employment income
9. Where the spouse's net self-employment income is determined by deducting an amount for salaries, benefits, wages or management fees, or other payments, paid to or on behalf of persons with whom the spouse does not deal at arm's length, include that amount, unless the spouse establishes that the payments were necessary to earn the self-employment income and were reasonable in the circumstances.

Additional amount
10. Where the spouse reports income from self-employment that, in accordance with sections 34.1 and 34.2 of the *Income Tax Act*, includes an additional amount earned in a prior period, deduct the amount earned in the prior period, net of reserves.

Capital cost allowance for property

11. Include the spouse's deduction for an allowable capital cost allowance with respect to real property.

Partnership or sole proprietorship income

12. Where the spouse earns income through a partnership or sole proprietorship, deduct any amount included in income that is properly required by the partnership or sole proprietorship for purposes of capitalization.

Employee stock options with a Canadian-controlled private corporation

13. (1) Where the spouse has received, as an employee benefit, options to purchase shares of a Canadian-controlled private corporation, or a publicly traded corporation that is subject to the same tax treatment with reference to stock options as a Canadian-controlled private corporation, and has exercised those options during the year, add the difference between the value of the shares at the time the options are exercised and the amount paid by the spouse for the shares, and any amount paid by the spouse to acquire the options to purchase the shares, to the income for the year in which the options are exercised.

Disposal of shares

(2) If the spouse has disposed of the shares during a year, deduct from the income for that year the difference determined under subsection (1).

SOR/97-563, ss. 12 to 14; SOR/2000-337, ss. 8 to 11, 12(E); SOR/2001-292, s. 1.

Family Law Act

R.S.O. 1990, Chapter F.3

Amended by: 1992, c. 32, s. 12; 1993, c. 27, Sched.; 1997, c. 20; 1997, c. 25, Sched. E, s. 1; 1998, c. 26, s. 102; 1999, c. 6, s. 25; 2000, c. 4, s. 12; 2000, c. 33, s. 22; 2002, c. 17, Sched. F, Table; 2002, c. 24, Sched. B, ss. 25, 37; 2004, c. 31, Sched. 38, s. 2; 2005, c. 5, s. 27.

CONTENTS
PREAMBLE

PART I
FAMILY PROPERTY

PART II
MATRIMONIAL HOME

PART VI
AMENDMENTS TO THE COMMON LAW

GENERAL

Preamble

Whereas it is desirable to encourage and strengthen the role of the family; and whereas for that purpose it is necessary to recognize the equal position of spouses as individuals within marriage and to recognize marriage as a form of partnership; and whereas in support of such recognition it is necessary to provide in law for the orderly and equitable settlement of the affairs of the spouses upon the breakdown of the partnership, and to provide for other mutual obligations in family relationships, including the equitable sharing by parents of responsibility for their children;

Therefore, Her Majesty, by and with the advice and consent of the Legislative Assembly of the Province of Ontario, enacts as follows:

Definitions

1.(1) In this Act,

"child" includes a person whom a parent has demonstrated a settled intention to treat as a child of his or her family, except under an arrangement where the child is placed for valuable consideration in a foster home by a person having lawful custody; ("enfant")

"child support guidelines" means the guidelines established by the regulations made under subsections 69 (2) and (3); ("lignes directrices sur les aliments pour les enfants")

"cohabit" means to live together in a conjugal relationship, whether within or outside marriage; ("cohabiter")

"court" means the Ontario Court (Provincial Division), the Unified Family Court or the Ontario Court (General Division); ("tribunal")

"domestic contract" means a domestic contract as defined in Part IV (Domestic Contracts); ("contrat familial")

"parent" includes a person who has demonstrated a settled intention to treat a child as a child of his or her family, except under an arrangement where the child is placed for valuable consideration in a foster home by a person having lawful custody; ("père ou mère")

"paternity agreement" means a paternity agreement as defined in Part IV (Domestic Contracts); ("accord de paternité")

"spouse" means either of two persons who,
  (a) are married to each other, or
  (b) have together entered into a marriage that is voidable or void, in good faith on the part of a person relying on this clause to assert any right. ("conjoint") R.S.O. 1990, c. F.3, s. 1 (1); 1997, c. 20, s. 1; 1999, c. 6, s. 25 (1); 2005, c. 5, s. 27 (1, 2).

Polygamous marriages
  (2) In the definition of "spouse." a reference to marriage includes a marriage that is actually or potentially polygamous, if it was celebrated in a jurisdiction whose system of law recognizes it as valid. R.S.O. 1990, c. F.3, s. 1 (2).

Procedural and other miscellaneous matters
Staying application
  2. (1) If, in an application under this Act, it appears to the court that for the appropriate determination of the spouses' affairs it is necessary or desirable to have other matters determined first or simultaneously, the court may stay the application until another proceeding is brought or determined as the court considers appropriate. R.S.O. 1990, c. F.3, s. 2 (1).

All proceedings in one court
  (2) Except as this Act provides otherwise, no person who is a party to an application under this Act shall make another application under this Act to another court, but the court may order that the proceeding be transferred to a court having other jurisdiction where, in the first court's opinion, the other court is more appropriate to determine the matters in issue that should be determined at the same time. R.S.O. 1990, c. F.3, s. 2 (2).

Applications in Ontario Court (General Division)
  (3) In the Ontario Court (General Division), an application under this Act may be made by action or application. R.S.O. 1990, c. F.3, s. 2 (3).

Statement re removal of barriers to remarriage
  (4) A party to an application under section 7 (net family property), 10 (questions of title between spouses), 33 (support), 34 (powers of court) or 37 (variation) may serve on the other party and file with the court a statement, verified by oath or statutory declaration, indicating that,
  (a) the author of the statement has removed all barriers that are within his or her control and that would prevent the other spouse's remarriage within that spouse's faith; and
  (b) the other party has not done so, despite a request. R.S.O. 1990, c. F.3, s. 2 (4).

Idem
  (5) Within ten days after service of the statement, or within such longer period as the court allows, the party served with a statement under subsection (4) shall serve on the other party and file with the court a statement, verified by oath or statutory declaration, indicating that the author

of the statement has removed all barriers that are within his or her control and that would prevent the other spouse's remarriage within that spouse's faith. R.S.O. 1990, c. F.3, s. 2 (5).

Dismissal, etc.

(6) When a party fails to comply with subsection (5),

(a) if the party is an applicant, the proceeding may be dismissed;

(b) if the party is a respondent, the defence may be struck out. R.S.O. 1990, c. F.3, s. 2 (6).

Exception

(7) Subsections (5) and (6) do not apply to a party who does not claim costs or other relief in the proceeding. R.S.O. 1990, c. F.3, s. 2 (7).

Extension of times

(8) The court may, on motion, extend a time prescribed by this Act if it is satisfied that,

(a) there are apparent grounds for relief;

(b) relief is unavailable because of delay that has been incurred in good faith; and

(c) no person will suffer substantial prejudice by reason of the delay. R.S.O. 1990, c. F.3, s. 2 (8).

Incorporation of contract in order

(9) A provision of a domestic contract in respect of a matter that is dealt with in this Act may be incorporated in an order made under this Act. R.S.O. 1990, c. F.3, s. 2 (9).

Act subject to contracts

(10) A domestic contract dealing with a matter that is also dealt with in this Act prevails unless this Act provides otherwise. R.S.O. 1990, c. F.3, s. 2 (10).

Registration of orders

(11) An order made under this Act that affects real property does not affect the acquisition of an interest in the real property by a person acting in good faith without notice of the order, unless the order is registered in the proper land registry office. R.S.O. 1990, c. F.3, s. 2 (11).

Mediation

3. (1) In an application under this Act, the court may, on motion, appoint a person whom the parties have selected to mediate any matter that the court specifies. R.S.O. 1990, c. F.3, s. 3 (1).

Consent to act

(2) The court shall appoint only a person who,

(a) has consented to act as mediator; and

(b) has agreed to file a report with the court within the period of time specified by the court. R.S.O. 1990, c. F.3, s. 3 (2).

Duty of mediator

(3) The mediator shall confer with the parties, and with the children if the mediator considers it appropriate to do so, and shall endeavour to obtain an agreement between the parties. R.S.O. 1990, c. F.3, s. 3 (3).

Full or limited report

(4) Before entering into mediation, the parties shall decide whether,

(a) the mediator is to file a full report on the mediation, including anything that he or she considers relevant; or

(b) the mediator is to file a limited report that sets out only the agreement reached by the parties or states only that the parties did not reach agreement. R.S.O. 1990, c. F.3, s. 3 (4).

Filing and copies of report

(5) The mediator shall file with the clerk or registrar of the court a full or limited report, as the parties have decided, and shall give a copy to each of the parties. R.S.O. 1990, c. F.3, s. 3 (5).

Admissions, etc., in the course of mediation

(6) If the parties have decided that the mediator is to file a limited report, no evidence of anything said or of any admission or communication made in the course of the mediation is admissible in any proceeding, except with the consent of all parties to the proceeding in which the mediator was appointed. R.S.O. 1990, c. F.3, s. 3 (6).

Fees and expenses

(7) The court shall require the parties to pay the mediator's fees and expenses and shall specify in the order the proportions or amounts of the fees and expenses that each party is required to pay. R.S.O. 1990, c. F.3, s. 3 (7).

Idem, serious financial hardship

(8) The court may require one party to pay all the mediator's fees and expenses if the court is satisfied that payment would cause the other party or parties serious financial hardship. R.S.O. 1990, c. F.3, s. 3 (8).

PART I
FAMILY PROPERTY

Definitions

4. (1) In this Part,

"court" means a court as defined in subsection 1 (1), but does not include the Ontario Court (Provincial Division); ("tribunal")

"matrimonial home" means a matrimonial home under section 18 and includes property that is a matrimonial home under that section at the valuation date; ("foyer conjugal")

"net family property" means the value of all the property, except property described in subsection (2), that a spouse owns on the valuation date, after deducting,

(a) the spouse's debts and other liabilities, and

(b) the value of property, other than a matrimonial home, that the spouse owned on the date of the marriage, after deducting the spouse's debts and other liabilities, calculated as of the date of the marriage; ("biens familiaux nets")

"property" means any interest, present or future, vested or contingent, in real or personal property and includes,

(a) property over which a spouse has, alone or in conjunction with another person, a power of appointment exercisable in favour of himself or herself,

(b) property disposed of by a spouse but over which the spouse has, alone or in conjunction with another person, a power to revoke the disposition or a power to consume or dispose of the property, and

(c) in the case of a spouse's rights under a pension plan that have vested, the spouse's interest in the plan including contributions made by other persons; ("bien")

"valuation date" means the earliest of the following dates:

1 The date the spouses separate and there is no reasonable prospect that they will resume cohabitation.

2. The date a divorce is granted.

3. The date the marriage is declared a nullity.

4 The date one of the spouses commences an application based on subsection 5 (3) (improvident depletion) that is subsequently granted.

5. The date before the date on which one of the spouses dies leaving the other spouse surviving. ("date d'évaluation") R.S.O. 1990, c. F.3, s. 4 (1).

Excluded property

(2) The value of the following property that a spouse owns on the valuation date does not form part of the spouse's net family property:

1. Property, other than a matrimonial home, that was acquired by gift or inheritance from a third person after the date of the marriage.

2. Income from property referred to in paragraph 1, if the donor or testator has expressly stated that it is to be excluded from the spouse's net family property.

3. Damages or a right to damages for personal injuries, nervous shock, mental distress or loss of guidance, care and companionship, or the part of a settlement that represents those damages.

4. Proceeds or a right to proceeds of a policy of life insurance, as defined in the *Insurance Act*, that are payable on the death of the life insured.

Note: On the day the Statutes of Ontario, 2002, chapter 18, Schedule H, subsection 4 (1) comes into force, paragraph 4 is amended by the Statutes of Ontario, 2004, chapter 31, Schedule 38, subsection 2 (1) by striking out "life insurance, as defined in the *Insurance Act*" and substituting "life insurance, as defined under the *Insurance Act*." See: 2004, c. 31, Sched. 38, ss. 2 (1), 4 (2).

5. Property, other than a matrimonial home, into which property referred to in paragraphs 1 to 4 can be traced.

6. Property that the spouses have agreed by a domestic contract is not to be included in the spouse's net family property. R.S.O. 1990, c. F.3, s. 4 (2).

Onus of proof re deductions and exclusions

(3) The onus of proving a deduction under the definition of "net family property" or an exclusion under subsection (2) is on the person claiming it. R.S.O. 1990, c. F.3, s. 4 (3).

Close of business

(4) When this section requires that a value be calculated as of a given date, it shall be calculated as of close of business on that date. R.S.O. 1990, c. F.3, s. 4 (4).

Net family property not to be less than zero

(5) If a spouse's net family property as calculated under subsections (1), (2) and (4) is less than zero, it shall be deemed to be equal to zero. R.S.O. 1990, c. F.3, s. 4 (5).

Equalization of net family properties
Divorce, etc.

5. (1) When a divorce is granted or a marriage is declared a nullity, or when the spouses are separated and there is no reasonable prospect that they will resume cohabitation, the spouse whose net family property is the lesser of the two net family properties is entitled to one-half the difference between them. R.S.O. 1990, c. F.3, s. 5 (1).

Death of spouse

(2) When a spouse dies, if the net family property of the deceased spouse exceeds the net family property of the surviving spouse, the surviving spouse is entitled to one-half the difference between them. R.S.O. 1990, c. F.3, s. 5 (2).

Improvident depletion of spouse's net family property

(3) When spouses are cohabiting, if there is a serious danger that one spouse may improvidently deplete his or her net family property, the other spouse may on an application under section 7 have the difference between the net family properties divided as if the spouses were separated and there were no reasonable prospect that they would resume cohabitation. R.S.O. 1990, c. F.3, s. 5 (3).

No further division

(4) After the court has made an order for division based on subsection (3), neither spouse may make a further application under section 7 in respect of their marriage. R.S.O. 1990, c. F.3, s. 5 (4).

Idem

(5) Subsection (4) applies even though the spouses continue to cohabit, unless a domestic contract between the spouses provides otherwise. R.S.O. 1990, c. F.3, s. 5 (5).

Variation of share

(6) The court may award a spouse an amount that is more or less than half the difference between the net family properties if the court is of the opinion that equalizing the net family properties would be unconscionable, having regard to,

(a) a spouse's failure to disclose to the other spouse debts or other liabilities existing at the date of the marriage;

(b) the fact that debts or other liabilities claimed in reduction of a spouse's net family property were incurred recklessly or in bad faith;

(c) the part of a spouse's net family property that consists of gifts made by the other spouse;

(d) a spouse's intentional or reckless depletion of his or her net family property;

(e) the fact that the amount a spouse would otherwise receive under subsection (1), (2) or (3) is disproportionately large in relation to a period of cohabitation that is less than five years;

(f) the fact that one spouse has incurred a disproportionately larger amount of debts or other liabilities than the other spouse for the support of the family;

(g) a written agreement between the spouses that is not a domestic contract; or

(h) any other circumstance relating to the acquisition, disposition, preservation, maintenance or improvement of property. R.S.O. 1990, c. F.3, s. 5 (6).

Purpose

(7) The purpose of this section is to recognize that child care, household management and financial provision are the joint responsibilities of the spouses and that inherent in the marital relationship there is equal contribution, whether financial or otherwise, by the spouses to the assumption of these responsibilities, entitling each spouse to the equalization of the net family properties, subject only to the equitable considerations set out in subsection (6). R.S.O. 1990, c. F.3, s. 5 (7).

Election

Spouse's will

6. (1) When a spouse dies leaving a will, the surviving spouse shall elect to take under the will or to receive the entitlement under section 5. R.S.O. 1990, c. F.3, s. 6 (1).

Spouse's intestacy

(2) When a spouse dies intestate, the surviving spouse shall elect to receive the entitlement under Part II of the *Succession Law Reform Act* or to receive the entitlement under section 5. R.S.O. 1990, c. F.3, s. 6 (2).

Spouse's partial intestacy

(3) When a spouse dies testate as to some property and intestate as to other property, the surviving spouse shall elect to take under the will and to receive the entitlement under Part II of the *Succession Law Reform Act*, or to receive the entitlement under section 5. R.S.O. 1990, c. F.3, s. 6 (3).

Property outside estate

(4) A surviving spouse who elects to take under the will or to receive the entitlement under Part II of the *Succession Law Reform Act*, or both in the case of a partial intestacy, shall also receive the other property to which he or she is entitled because of the first spouse's death. R.S.O. 1990, c. F.3, s. 6 (4).

Gifts by will

(5) The surviving spouse shall receive the gifts made to him or her in the deceased spouse's will in addition to the entitlement under section 5 if the will expressly provides for that result. R.S.O. 1990, c. F.3, s. 6 (5).

Insurance, etc.

(6) Where a surviving spouse,

    (a)   is the beneficiary,

        (i) of a policy of life insurance, as defined in the *Insurance Act*, that was taken out on the life of the deceased spouse and owned by the deceased spouse or was taken out on the lives of a group of which he or she was a member, or

Note: On the day the Statutes of Ontario, 2002, chapter 18, Schedule H, subsection 4 (1) comes into force, subclause (i) is amended by the Statutes of Ontario, 2004, chapter 31, Schedule 38, subsection 2 (2) by striking out "life insurance, as defined in the *Insurance Act*" and substituting "life insurance, as defined under the *Insurance Act*." See: 2004, c. 31, Sched. 38, ss. 2 (2), 4 (2).

        (ii) of a lump sum payment provided under a pension or similar plan on the death of the deceased spouse; and

    (b)   elects or has elected to receive the entitlement under section 5,

the payment under the policy or plan shall be credited against the surviving spouse's entitlement under section 5, unless a written designation by the deceased spouse provides that the surviving spouse shall receive payment under the policy or plan in addition to the entitlement under section 5. R.S.O. 1990, c. F.3, s. 6 (6).

Idem

(7) If a surviving spouse,

    (a)   elects or has elected to receive the entitlement under section 5; and

    (b)   receives payment under a life insurance policy or a lump sum payment provided under a pension or similar plan that is in excess of the entitlement under section 5,

and there is no written designation by the deceased spouse described in subsection (6), the deceased spouse's personal representative may recover the excess amount from the surviving spouse. R.S.O. 1990, c. F.3, s. 6 (7).

Effect of election to receive entitlement under s. 5

(8) When a surviving spouse elects to receive the entitlement under section 5, the gifts made to him or her in the deceased spouse's will are revoked and the will shall be interpreted as if the surviving spouse had died before the other, unless the will expressly provides that the gifts are in addition to the entitlement under section 5. R.S.O. 1990, c. F.3, s. 6 (8).

Idem

(9) When a surviving spouse elects to receive the entitlement under section 5, the spouse shall be deemed to have disclaimed the entitlement under Part II of the *Succession Law Reform Act*. R.S.O. 1990, c. F.3, s. 6 (9).

Manner of making election

(10) The surviving spouse's election shall be in the form prescribed by the regulations made under this Act and shall be filed in the office of the Estate Registrar for Ontario within six months after the first spouse's death. R.S.O. 1990, c. F.3, s. 6 (10).

Deemed election

(11) If the surviving spouse does not file the election within that time, he or she shall be deemed to have elected to take under the will or to receive the entitlement under the *Succession Law Reform Act*, or both, as the case may be, unless the court, on application, orders otherwise. R.S.O. 1990, c. F.3, s. 6 (11).

Priority of spouse's entitlement

(12) The spouse's entitlement under section 5 has priority over,

(a) the gifts made in the deceased spouse's will, if any, subject to subsection (13);

(b) a person's right to a share of the estate under Part II (Intestate Succession) of the *Succession Law Reform Act*;

(c) an order made against the estate under Part V (Support of Dependants) of the *Succession Law Reform Act*, except an order in favour of a child of the deceased spouse. R.S.O. 1990, c. F.3, s. 6 (12).

Exception

(13) The spouse's entitlement under section 5 does not have priority over a gift by will made in accordance with a contract that the deceased spouse entered into in good faith and for valuable consideration, except to the extent that the value of the gift, in the court's opinion, exceeds the consideration. R.S.O. 1990, c. F.3, s. 6 (13).

Distribution within six months of death restricted

(14) No distribution shall be made in the administration of a deceased spouse's estate within six months of the spouse's death, unless,

(a) the surviving spouse gives written consent to the distribution; or

(b) the court authorizes the distribution. R.S.O. 1990, c. F.3, s. 6 (14).

Idem, notice of application

(15) No distribution shall be made in the administration of a deceased spouse's death after the personal representative has received notice of an application under this Part, unless,

    (a) the applicant gives written consent to the distribution; or

    (b) the court authorizes the distribution. R.S.O. 1990, c. F.3, s. 6 (15).

Extension of limitation period

(16) If the court extends the time for a spouse's application based on subsection 5 (2), any property of the deceased spouse that is distributed before the date of the order and without notice of the application shall not be brought into the calculation of the deceased spouse's net family property. R.S.O. 1990, c. F.3, s. 6 (16).

Exception

(17) Subsections (14) and (15) do not prohibit reasonable advances to dependants of the deceased spouse for their support. R.S.O. 1990, c. F.3, s. 6 (17).

Definition

(18) In subsection (17),

"dependant" has the same meaning as in Part V of the Succession Law Reform Act. R.S.O. 1990, c. F.3, s. 6 (18).

Liability of personal representative

(19) If the personal representative makes a distribution that contravenes subsection (14) or (15), the court makes an order against the estate under this Part and the undistributed portion of the estate is not sufficient to satisfy the order, the personal representative is personally liable to the applicant for the amount that was distributed or the amount that is required to satisfy the order, whichever is less. R.S.O. 1990, c. F.3, s. 6 (19).

Order suspending administration

(20) On motion by the surviving spouse, the court may make an order suspending the administration of the deceased spouse's estate for the time and to the extent that the court decides. R.S.O. 1990, c. F.3, s. 6 (20).

Application to court

7. (1) The court may, on the application of a spouse, former spouse or deceased spouse's personal representative, determine any matter respecting the spouses' entitlement under section 5. R.S.O. 1990, c. F.3, s. 7 (1).

Personal action; estates

(2) Entitlement under subsections 5 (1), (2) and (3) is personal as between the spouses but,

    (a) an application based on subsection 5 (1) or (3) and commenced before a spouse's death may be continued by or against the deceased spouse's estate; and

(b) an application based on subsection 5 (2) may be made by or against a deceased spouse's estate. R.S.O. 1990, c. F.3, s. 7 (2).

Limitation

(3) An application based on subsection 5 (1) or (2) shall not be brought after the earliest of,

(a) two years after the day the marriage is terminated by divorce or judgment of nullity;

(b) six years after the day the spouses separate and there is no reasonable prospect that they will resume cohabitation;

(c) six months after the first spouse's death. R.S.O. 1990, c. F.3, s. 7 (3).

Statement of property

8. In an application under section 7, each party shall serve on the other and file with the court, in the manner and form prescribed by the rules of the court, a statement verified by oath or statutory declaration disclosing particulars of,

(a) the party's property and debts and other liabilities,

(i) as of the date of the marriage,

(ii) as of the valuation date, and

(iii) as of the date of the statement;

(b) the deductions that the party claims under the definition of "net family property";

(c) the exclusions that the party claims under subsection 4 (2); and

(d) all property that the party disposed of during the two years immediately preceding the making of the statement, or during the marriage, whichever period is shorter. R.S.O. 1990, c. F.3, s. 8.

Powers of court

9. (1) In an application under section 7, the court may order,

(a) that one spouse pay to the other spouse the amount to which the court finds that spouse to be entitled under this Part;

(b) that security, including a charge on property, be given for the performance of an obligation imposed by the order;

(c) that, if necessary to avoid hardship, an amount referred to in clause (a) be paid in instalments during a period not exceeding ten years or that payment of all or part of the amount be delayed for a period not exceeding ten years; and

(d) that, if appropriate to satisfy an obligation imposed by the order,

(i) property be transferred to or in trust for or vested in a spouse, whether absolutely, for life or for a term of years, or

(ii) any property be partitioned or sold. R.S.O. 1990, c. F.3, s. 9 (1).

Financial information, inspections

(2) The court may, at the time of making an order for instalment or delayed payments or on motion at a later time, order that the spouse who has the obligation to make payments shall,

(a) furnish the other spouse with specified financial information, which may include periodic financial statements; and

(b) permit inspections of specified property of the spouse by or on behalf of the other spouse, as the court directs. R.S.O. 1990, c. F.3, s. 9 (2).

Variation

(3) If the court is satisfied that there has been a material change in the circumstances of the spouse who has the obligation to make instalment or delayed payments, the court may, on motion, vary the order, but shall not vary the amount to which the court found the spouse to be entitled under this Part. R.S.O. 1990, c. F.3, s. 9 (3).

Ten-year period

(4) Subsections (3) and 2 (8) (extension of times) do not permit the postponement of payment beyond the ten-year period mentioned in clause (1) (c). R.S.O. 1990, c. F.3, s. 9 (4).

Determination of questions of title between spouses

10. (1) A person may apply to the court for the determination of a question between that person and his or her spouse or former spouse as to the ownership or right to possession of particular property, other than a question arising out of an equalization of net family properties under section 5, and the court may,

(a) declare the ownership or right to possession;

(b) if the property has been disposed of, order payment in compensation for the interest of either party;

(c) order that the property be partitioned or sold for the purpose of realizing the interests in it; and

(d) order that either or both spouses give security, including a charge on property, for the performance of an obligation imposed by the order,

and may make ancillary orders or give ancillary directions. R.S.O. 1990, c. F.3, s. 10 (1).

Estates

(2) An application based on subsection (1) may be made by or continued against the estate of a deceased spouse. R.S.O. 1990, c. F.3, s. 10 (2).

Operating business or farm

11. (1) An order made under section 9 or 10 shall not be made so as to require or result in the sale of an operating business or farm or so as to seriously impair its operation, unless there is no reasonable alternative method of satisfying the award. R.S.O. 1990, c. F.3, s. 11 (1).

Idem

(2) To comply with subsection (1), the court may,

(a) order that one spouse pay to the other a share of the profits from the business or farm; and

(b) if the business or farm is incorporated, order that one spouse transfer or have the corporation issue to the other shares in the corporation. R.S.O. 1990, c. F.3, s. 11 (2).

Orders for preservation

12. In an application under section 7 or 10, if the court considers it necessary for the protection of the other spouse's interests under this Part, the court may make an interim or final order,

(a) restraining the depletion of a spouse's property; and

(b) for the possession, delivering up, safekeeping and preservation of the property. R.S.O. 1990, c. F.3, s. 12.

Variation and realization of security

13. If the court has ordered security or charged a property with security for the performance of an obligation under this Part, the court may, on motion,

(a) vary or discharge the order; or

(b) on notice to all persons having an interest in the property, direct its sale for the purpose of realizing the security or charge. R.S.O. 1990, c. F.3, s. 13.

Presumptions

14. The rule of law applying a presumption of a resulting trust shall be applied in questions of the ownership of property between spouses, as if they were not married, except that,

(a) the fact that property is held in the name of spouses as joint tenants is proof, in the absence of evidence to the contrary, that the spouses are intended to own the property as joint tenants; and

(b) money on deposit in the name of both spouses shall be deemed to be in the name of the spouses as joint tenants for the purposes of clause (a). R.S.O. 1990, c. F.3, s. 14; 2005, c. 5, s. 27 (3).

Conflict of laws

15. The property rights of spouses arising out of the marital relationship are governed by the internal law of the place where both spouses had their last common habitual residence or, if there is no place where the spouses had a common habitual residence, by the law of Ontario. R.S.O. 1990, c. F.3, s. 15.

Application of Part

16. (1) This Part applies to property owned by spouses,

(a) whether they were married before or after the 1st day of March, 1986; and

(b) whether the property was acquired before or after that day. R.S.O. 1990, c. F.3, s. 16 (1).

Application of s. 14

(2) Section 14 applies whether the event giving rise to the presumption occurred before or after the 1st day of March, 1986. R.S.O. 1990, c. F.3, s. 16 (2).

PART II
MATRIMONIAL HOME

Definitions

17. In this Part,

"court" means a court as defined in subsection 1 (1) but does not include the Ontario Court (Provincial Division); ("tribunal")

"property" means real or personal property. ("bien") R.S.O. 1990, c. F.3, s. 17.

Matrimonial home

18. (1) Every property in which a person has an interest and that is or, if the spouses have separated, was at the time of separation ordinarily occupied by the person and his or her spouse as their family residence is their matrimonial home. R.S.O. 1990, c. F.3, s. 18 (1).

Ownership of shares

(2) The ownership of a share or shares, or of an interest in a share or shares, of a corporation entitling the owner to occupy a housing unit owned by the corporation shall be deemed to be an interest in the unit for the purposes of subsection (1). R.S.O. 1990, c. F.3, s. 18 (2).

Residence on farmland, etc.

(3) If property that includes a matrimonial home is normally used for a purpose other than residential, the matrimonial home is only the part of the property that may reasonably be regarded as necessary to the use and enjoyment of the residence. R.S.O. 1990, c. F.3, s. 18 (3).

Possession of matrimonial home

19. (1) Both spouses have an equal right to possession of a matrimonial home. R.S.O. 1990, c. F.3, s. 19 (1).

Idem

(2) When only one of the spouses has an interest in a matrimonial home, the other spouse's right of possession,

(a) is personal as against the first spouse; and

(b) ends when they cease to be spouses, unless a separation agreement or court order provides otherwise. R.S.O. 1990, c. F.3, s. 19 (2).

Designation of matrimonial home

20. (1) One or both spouses may designate property owned by one or both of them as a matrimonial home, in the form prescribed by the regulations made under this Act. R.S.O. 1990, c. F.3, s. 20 (1).

Contiguous property

(2) The designation may include property that is described in the designation and is contiguous to the matrimonial home. R.S.O. 1990, c. F.3, s. 20 (2).

Registration

(3) The designation may be registered in the proper land registry office. R.S.O. 1990, c. F.3, s. 20 (3).

Effect of designation by both spouses

(4) On the registration of a designation made by both spouses, any other property that is a matrimonial home under section 18 but is not designated by both spouses ceases to be a matrimonial home. R.S.O. 1990, c. F.3, s. 20 (4).

Effect of designation by one spouse

(5) On the registration of a designation made by one spouse only, any other property that is a matrimonial home under section 18 remains a matrimonial home. R.S.O. 1990, c. F.3, s. 20 (5).

Cancellation of designation

(6) The designation of a matrimonial home is cancelled, and the property ceases to be a matrimonial home, on the registration or deposit of,

(a) a cancellation, executed by the person or persons who made the original designation, in the form prescribed by the regulations made under this Act;

(b) a decree absolute of divorce or judgment of nullity;

(c) an order under clause 23 (e) cancelling the designation; or

(d) proof of death of one of the spouse. R.S.O. 1990, c. F.3, s. 20 (6).

Revival of other matrimonial homes

(7) When a designation of a matrimonial home made by both spouses is cancelled, section 18 applies again in respect of other property that is a matrimonial home. R.S.O. 1990, c. F.3, s. 20 (7).

Alienation of matrimonial home

21. (1) No spouse shall dispose of or encumber an interest in a matrimonial home unless,

(a) the other spouse joins in the instrument or consents to the transaction;

(b) the other spouse has released all rights under this Part by a separation agreement;

(c)   a court order has authorized the transaction or has released the property from the application of this Part; or

(d)   the property is not designated by both spouses as a matrimonial home and a designation of another property as a matrimonial home, made by both spouses, is registered and not cancelled. R.S.O. 1990, c. F.3, s. 21 (1).

Setting aside transaction

(2)   If a spouse disposes of or encumbers an interest in a matrimonial home in contravention of subsection (1), the transaction may be set aside on an application under section 23, unless the person holding the interest or encumbrance at the time of the application acquired it for value, in good faith and without notice, at the time of acquiring it or making an agreement to acquire it, that the property was a matrimonial home. R.S.O. 1990, c. F.3, s. 21 (2).

Proof that property not a matrimonial home

(3)   For the purpose of subsection (2), a statement by the person making the disposition or encumbrance,

(a)   verifying that he or she is not, or was not, a spouse at the time of the disposition or encumbrance;

(b)   verifying that the person is a spouse who is not separated from his or her spouse and that the property is not ordinarily occupied by the spouses as their family residence;

(c)   verifying that the person is a spouse who is separated from his or her spouse and that the property was not ordinarily occupied by the spouses, at the time of their separation, as their family residence;

(d)   where the property is not designated by both spouses as a matrimonial home, verifying that a designation of another property as a matrimonial home, made by both spouses, is registered and not cancelled; or

(e)   verifying that the other spouse has released all rights under this Part by a separation agreement,

shall, unless the person to whom the disposition or encumbrance is made had notice to the contrary, be deemed to be sufficient proof that the property is not a matrimonial home. R.S.O. 1990, c. F.3, s. 21 (3).

Idem, attorney's personal knowledge

(4)   The statement shall be deemed to be sufficient proof that the property is not a matrimonial home if it is made by the attorney of the person making the disposition or encumbrance, on the basis of the attorney's personal knowledge. R.S.O. 1990, c. F.3, s. 21 (4).

Liens arising by operation of law

(5)   This section does not apply to the acquisition of an interest in property by operation of law or to the acquisition of a lien under section 48 of the Legal Aid Services Act, 1998. R.S.O. 1990, c. F.3, s. 21 (5); 1998, c. 26, s. 102.

Right of redemption and to notice

22. (1) When a person proceeds to realize upon a lien, encumbrance or execution or exercises a forfeiture against property that is a matrimonial home, the spouse who has a right of possession under section 19 has the same right of redemption or relief against forfeiture as the other spouse and is entitled to the same notice respecting the claim and its enforcement or realization. R.S.O. 1990, c. F.3, s. 22 (1).

Service of notice

(2) A notice to which a spouse is entitled under subsection (1) shall be deemed to be sufficiently given if served or given personally or by registered mail addressed to the spouse at his or her usual or last known address or, if none, the address of the matrimonial home, and, if notice is served or given by mail, the service shall be deemed to have been made on the fifth day after the day of mailing. R.S.O. 1990, c. F.3, s. 22 (2).

Idem: power of sale

(3) When a person exercises a power of sale against property that is a matrimonial home, sections 33 and 34 of the *Mortgages Act* apply and subsection (2) does not apply. R.S.O. 1990, c. F.3, s. 22 (3); 1993, c. 27, Sched.

Payments by spouse

(4) If a spouse makes a payment in exercise of the right conferred by subsection (1), the payment shall be applied in satisfaction of the claim giving rise to the lien, encumbrance, execution or forfeiture. R.S.O. 1990, c. F.3, s. 22 (4).

Realization may continue in spouse's absence

(5) Despite any other Act, when a person who proceeds to realize upon a lien, encumbrance or execution or exercises a forfeiture does not have sufficient particulars of a spouse for the purpose and there is no response to a notice given under subsection (2) or under section 33 of the *Mortgages Act*, the realization or exercise of forfeiture may continue in the absence and without regard to the interest of the spouse and the spouse's rights under this section end on the completion of the realization or forfeiture. R.S.O. 1990, c. F.3, s. 22 (5); 1993, c. 27, Sched.

Powers of court respecting alienation

23. The court may, on the application of a spouse or person having an interest in property, by order,

(a) determine whether or not the property is a matrimonial home and, if so, its extent;

(b) authorize the disposition or encumbrance of the matrimonial home if the court finds that the spouse whose consent is required,

(i) cannot be found or is not available,

(ii) is not capable of giving or withholding consent, or

(iii) is unreasonably withholding consent,

subject to any conditions, including provision of other comparable accommodation or payment in place of it, that the court considers appropriate;

(c) dispense with a notice required to be given under section 22;

(d) direct the setting aside of a transaction disposing of or encumbering an interest in the matrimonial home contrary to subsection 21 (1) and the revesting of the interest or any part of it on the conditions that the court considers appropriate; and

(e) cancel a designation made under section 20 if the property is not a matrimonial home. R.S.O. 1990, c. F.3, s. 23.

Order for possession of matrimonial home

24. (1) Regardless of the ownership of a matrimonial home and its contents, and despite section 19 (spouse's right of possession), the court may on application, by order,

(a) provide for the delivering up, safekeeping and preservation of the matrimonial home and its contents;

(b) direct that one spouse be given exclusive possession of the matrimonial home or part of it for the period that the court directs and release other property that is a matrimonial home from the application of this Part;

(c) direct a spouse to whom exclusive possession of the matrimonial home is given to make periodic payments to the other spouse;

(d) direct that the contents of the matrimonial home, or any part of them,

(i) remain in the home for the use of the spouse given possession, or

(ii) be removed from the home for the use of a spouse or child;

(e) order a spouse to pay for all or part of the repair and maintenance of the matrimonial home and of other liabilities arising in respect of it, or to make periodic payments to the other spouse for those purposes;

(f) authorize the disposition or encumbrance of a spouse's interest in the matrimonial home, subject to the other spouse's right of exclusive possession as ordered; and

(g) where a false statement is made under subsection 21 (3), direct,

(i) the person who made the false statement, or

(ii) a person who knew at the time he or she acquired an interest in the property that the statement was false and afterwards conveyed the interest,

to substitute other real property for the matrimonial home, or direct the person to set aside money or security to stand in place of it, subject to any conditions that the court considers appropriate. R.S.O. 1990, c. F.3, s. 24 (1).

Temporary or interim order

(2) The court may, on motion, make a temporary or interim order under clause (1) (a), (b), (c), (d) or (e). R.S.O. 1990, c. F.3, s. 24 (2).

Order for exclusive possession: criteria

(3) In determining whether to make an order for exclusive possession, the court shall consider,

(a) the best interests of the children affected;

(b) any existing orders under Part I (Family Property) and any existing support orders;

(c) the financial position of both spouses;

(d) any written agreement between the parties;

(e) the availability of other suitable and affordable accommodation; and

(f) any violence committed by a spouse against the other spouse or the children. R.S.O. 1990, c. F.3, s. 24 (3).

Best interests of child

(4) In determining the best interests of a child, the court shall consider,

(a) the possible disruptive effects on the child of a move to other accommodation; and

(b) the child's views and preferences, if they can reasonably be ascertained. R.S.O. 1990, c. F.3, s. 24 (4).

Offence

(5) A person who contravenes an order for exclusive possession is guilty of an offence and upon conviction is liable,

(a) in the case of a first offence, to a fine of not more than $5,000 or to imprisonment for a term of not more than three months, or to both; and

(b) in the case of a second or subsequent offence, to a fine of not more than $10,000 or to imprisonment for a term of not more than two years, or to both. R.S.O. 1990, c. F.3, s. 24 (5).

Arrest without warrant

(6) A police officer may arrest without warrant a person the police officer believes on reasonable and probable grounds to have contravened an order for exclusive possession. R.S.O. 1990, c. F.3, s. 24 (6).

Existing orders

(7) Subsections (5) and (6) also apply in respect of contraventions, committed on or after the 1st day of March, 1986, of orders for exclusive possession made under Part III of the *Family Law Reform Act*, being chapter 152 of the Revised Statutes of Ontario, 1980. R.S.O. 1990, c. F.3, s. 24 (7).

Variation
Possessory order

25. (1) On the application of a person named in an order made under clause 24 (1) (a), (b), (c), (d) or (e) or his or her personal representative, if the court is satisfied that there has been a material change in circumstances, the court may discharge, vary or suspend the order. R.S.O. 1990, c. F.3, s. 25 (1).

Conditions

(2) On the motion of a person who is subject to conditions imposed in an order made under clause 23 (b) or (d) or 24 (1) (g), or his or her personal representative, if the court is satisfied that the conditions are no longer appropriate, the court may discharge, vary or suspend them. R.S.O. 1990, c. F.3, s. 25 (2).

Existing orders

(3) Subsections (1) and (2) also apply to orders made under the corresponding provisions of Part III of the *Family Law Reform Act*, being chapter 152 of the Revised Statutes of Ontario, 1980. R.S.O. 1990, c. F.3, s. 25 (3).

Spouse without interest in matrimonial home
Joint tenancy with third person

26. (1) If a spouse dies owning an interest in a matrimonial home as a joint tenant with a third person and not with the other spouse, the joint tenancy shall be deemed to have been severed immediately before the time of death. R.S.O. 1990, c. F.3, s. 26 (1).

Sixty-day period after spouse's death

(2) Despite clauses 19 (2) (a) and (b) (termination of spouse's right of possession), a spouse who has no interest in a matrimonial home but is occupying it at the time of the other spouse's death, whether under an order for exclusive possession or otherwise, is entitled to retain possession against the spouse's estate, rent free, for sixty days after the spouse's death. R.S.O. 1990, c. F.3, s. 26 (2).

Registration of order

27. Orders made under this Part or under Part III of the *Family Law Reform Act*, being chapter 152 of the Revised Statutes of Ontario, 1980 are registrable against land under the *Registry Act* and the *Land Titles Act*. R.S.O. 1990, c. F.3, s. 27.

Application of Part

28. (1) This Part applies to matrimonial homes that are situated in Ontario. R.S.O. 1990, c. F.3, s. 28 (1).

Idem

(2) This Part applies,

(a) whether the spouses were married before or after the 1st day of March, 1986; and

(b) whether the matrimonial home was acquired before or after that day. R.S.O. 1990, c. F.3, s. 28 (2).

PART III
SUPPORT OBLIGATIONS

Definitions

29. In this Part,

"dependant" means a person to whom another has an obligation to provide support under this Part; ("personne à charge")

"spouse" means a spouse as defined in subsection 1 (1), and in addition includes either of two persons who are not married to each other and have cohabited,

(a) continuously for a period of not less than three years, or

(b) in a relationship of some permanence, if they are the natural or adoptive parents of a child. ("conjoint") R.S.O. 1990, c. F.3, s. 29; 1999, c. 6, s. 25 (2); 2005, c. 5, s. 27 (4-6).

Obligation of spouses for support

30. Every spouse has an obligation to provide support for himself or herself and for the other spouse, in accordance with need, to the extent that he or she is capable of doing so. R.S.O. 1990, c. F.3, s. 30; 1999, c. 6, s. 25 (3); 2005, c. 5, s. 27 (7).

Obligation of parent to support child

31. (1) Every parent has an obligation to provide support for his or her unmarried child who is a minor or is enrolled in a full time program of education, to the extent that the parent is capable of doing so. R.S.O. 1990, c. F.3, s. 31 (1); 1997, c. 20, s. 2.

Idem

(2) The obligation under subsection (1) does not extend to a child who is sixteen years of age or older and has withdrawn from parental control. R.S.O. 1990, c. F.3, s. 31 (2).

Obligation of child to support parent

32. Every child who is not a minor has an obligation to provide support, in accordance with need, for his or her parent who has cared for or provided support for the child, to the extent that the child is capable of doing so. R.S.O. 1990, c. F.3, s. 32.

Order for support

33. (1) A court may, on application, order a person to provide support for his or her dependants and determine the amount of support. R.S.O. 1990, c. F.3, s. 33 (1).

Applicants

(2) An application for an order for the support of a dependant may be made by the dependant or the dependant's parent. R.S.O. 1990, c. F.3, s. 33 (2).

Same

(2.1) The *Limitations Act, 2002* applies to an application made by the dependant's parent or by an agency referred to in subsection (3) as if it were made by the dependant himself or herself. 2002, c. 24, Sched. B, s. 37.

Same

(3) An application for an order for the support of a dependant who is the respondent's spouse or child may also be made by one of the following agencies,

(a) the Ministry of Community and Social Services in the name of the Minister;

(b) a municipality, excluding a lower-tier municipality in a regional municipality;

(c) a district social services administration board under the *District Social Services Administration Boards Act;*

(d) a band approved under section 15 of the *General Welfare Assistance Act;* or

(e) a delivery agent under the *Ontario Works Act, 1997,*

if the agency is providing or has provided a benefit under the *Family Benefits Act,* assistance under the *General Welfare Assistance Act* or the *Ontario Works Act, 1997* or income support under the *Ontario Disability Support Program Act, 1997* in respect of the dependant's support, or if an application for such a benefit or assistance has been made to the agency by or on behalf of the dependant. 1997, c. 25, Sched. E, s. 1; 1999, c. 6, s. 25 (4); 2002, c. 17, Sched. F, Table; 2005, c. 5, s. 27 (8).

Setting aside domestic contract

(4) The court may set aside a provision for support or a waiver of the right to support in a domestic contract or paternity agreement and may determine and order support in an application under subsection (1) although the contract or agreement contains an express provision excluding the application of this section,

(a) if the provision for support or the waiver of the right to support results in unconscionable circumstances;

(b) if the provision for support is in favour of or the waiver is by or on behalf of a dependant who qualifies for an allowance for support out of public money; or

(c) if there is default in the payment of support under the contract or agreement at the time the application is made. R.S.O. 1990, c. F.3, s. 33 (4).

Adding party
(5) In an application the court may, on a respondent's motion, add as a party another person who may have an obligation to provide support to the same dependant. R.S.O. 1990, c. F.3, s. 33 (5).

Idem
(6) In an action in the Ontario Court (General Division), the defendant may add as a third party another person who may have an obligation to provide support to the same dependant. R.S.O. 1990, c. F.3, s. 33 (6).

Purposes of order for support of child
(7) An order for the support of a child should,
(a) recognize that each parent has an obligation to provide support for the child;
(b) apportion the obligation according to the child support guidelines. R.S.O. 1990, c. F.3, s. 33 (7); 1997, c. 20, s. 3 (1).

Purposes of order for support of spouse
(8) An order for the support of a spouse should,
(a) recognize the spouse's contribution to the relationship and the economic consequences of the relationship for the spouse;
(b) share the economic burden of child support equitably;
(c) make fair provision to assist the spouse to become able to contribute to his or her own support; and
(d) relieve financial hardship, if this has not been done by orders under Parts I (Family Property) and II (Matrimonial Home). R.S.O. 1990, c. F.3, s. 33 (8); 1999, c. 6, s. 25 (5); 2005, c. 5, s. 27 (9).

Determination of amount for support of spouses, parents
(9) In determining the amount and duration, if any, of support for a spouse or parent in relation to need, the court shall consider all the circumstances of the parties, including,
(a) the dependant's and respondent's current assets and means;
(b) the assets and means that the dependant and respondent are likely to have in the future;
(c) the dependant's capacity to contribute to his or her own support;
(d) the respondent's capacity to provide support;
(e) the dependant's and respondent's age and physical and mental health;
(f) the dependant's needs, in determining which the court shall have regard to the accustomed standard of living while the parties resided together;
(g) the measures available for the dependant to become able to provide for his or her own support and the length of time and cost involved to enable the dependant to take those measures;
(h) any legal obligation of the respondent or dependant to provide support for another person;
(i) the desirability of the dependant or respondent remaining at

home to care for a child;

(j) a contribution by the dependant to the realization of the respondent's career potential;

(k) Repealed: 1997, c. 20, s. 3 (3).

(l) if the dependant is a spouse,

(i) the length of time the dependant and respondent cohabited,

(ii) the effect on the spouse's earning capacity of the responsibilities assumed during cohabitation,

(iii) whether the spouse has undertaken the care of a child who is of the age of eighteen years or over and unable by reason of illness, disability or other cause to withdraw from the charge of his or her parents,

(iv) whether the spouse has undertaken to assist in the continuation of a program of education for a child eighteen years of age or over who is unable for that reason to withdraw from the charge of his or her parents,

(v) any housekeeping, child care or other domestic service performed by the spouse for the family, as if the spouse were devoting the time spent in performing that service in remunerative employment and were contributing the earnings to the family's support,

(v.1) Repealed: 2005, c. 5, s. 27 (12).

(vi) the effect on the spouse's earnings and career development of the responsibility of caring for a child; and

(m) any other legal right of the dependant to support, other than out of public money. R.S.O. 1990, c. F.3, s. 33 (9); 1997, c. 20, s. 3 (2, 3); 1999, c. 6, s. 25 (6-9); 2005, c. 5, s. 27 (10-13).

Conduct

(10) The obligation to provide support for a spouse exists without regard to the conduct of either spouse, but the court may in determining the amount of support have regard to a course of conduct that is so unconscionable as to constitute an obvious and gross repudiation of the relationship. R.S.O. 1990, c. F.3, s. 33 (10); 1999, c. 6, s. 25 (10); 2005, c. 5, s. 27 (14).

Application of child support guidelines

(11) A court making an order for the support of a child shall do so in accordance with the child support guidelines. 1997, c. 20, s. 3 (4).

Exception: special provisions

(12) Despite subsection (11), a court may award an amount that is different from the amount that would be determined in accordance with the child support guidelines if the court is satisfied,

(a) that special provisions in an order or a written agreement respecting the financial obligations of the parents, or the division or transfer of their property, directly or indirectly benefit a child, or that special provisions have otherwise been made for the benefit of a child; and

(b)   that the application of the child support guidelines would result in an amount of child support that is inequitable given those special provisions. 1997, c. 20, s. 3 (4).

Reasons

(13) Where the court awards, under subsection (12), an amount that is different from the amount that would be determined in accordance with the child support guidelines, the court shall record its reasons for doing so. 1997, c. 20, s. 3 (4).

Exception: consent orders

(14) Despite subsection (11), a court may award an amount that is different from the amount that would be determined in accordance with the child support guidelines on the consent of both parents if the court is satisfied that,

(a)   reasonable arrangements have been made for the support of the child to whom the order relates; and

(b)   where support for the child is payable out of public money, the arrangements do not provide for an amount less than the amount that would be determined in accordance with the child support guidelines. 1997, c. 20, s. 3 (4).

Reasonable arrangements

(15) For the purposes of clause (14) (a), in determining whether reasonable arrangements have been made for the support of a child,

(a)   the court shall have regard to the child support guidelines; and

(b)   the court shall not consider the arrangements to be unreasonable solely because the amount of support agreed to is not the same as the amount that would otherwise have been determined in accordance with the child support guidelines. 1997, c. 20, s. 3 (4).

Powers of court

34. (1) In an application under section 33, the court may make an interim or final order,

(a)   requiring that an amount be paid periodically, whether annually or otherwise and whether for an indefinite or limited period, or until the happening of a specified event;

(b)   requiring that a lump sum be paid or held in trust;

(c)   requiring that property be transferred to or in trust for or vested in the dependant, whether absolutely, for life or for a term of years;

(d)   respecting any matter authorized to be ordered under clause 24 (1) (a), (b), (c), (d) or (e) (matrimonial home);

(e)   requiring that some or all of the money payable under the order be paid into court or to another appropriate person or agency for the dependant's benefit;

(f) requiring that support be paid in respect of any period before the date of the order;

(g) requiring payment to an agency referred to in subsection 33 (3) of an amount in reimbursement for a benefit or assistance referred to in that subsection, including a benefit or assistance provided before the date of the order;

(h) requiring payment of expenses in respect of a child's prenatal care and birth;

(i) requiring that a spouse who has a policy of life insurance as defined in the *Insurance Act* designate the other spouse or a child as the beneficiary irrevocably;

Note: On the day the Statutes of Ontario, 2002, chapter 18, Schedule H, subsection 4 (1) comes into force, clause (i) is amended by the Statutes of Ontario, 2004, chapter 31, Schedule 38, subsection 2 (3) by striking out "life insurance as defined in the *Insurance Act*" and substituting "life insurance as defined under the *Insurance Act*." See: 2004, c. 31, Sched. 38, ss. 2 (3), 4 (2).

(j) requiring that a spouse who has an interest in a pension plan or other benefit plan designate the other spouse or a child as beneficiary under the plan and not change that designation; and

(k) requiring the securing of payment under the order, by a charge on property or otherwise. R.S.O. 1990, c. F.3, s. 34 (1); 1999, c. 6, s. 25 (11); 2005, c. 5, s. 27 (15).

Limitation on jurisdiction of Ontario Court (Provincial Division)

(2) The Ontario Court (Provincial Division) shall not make an order under clause (1) (b), (c), (i), (j) or (k) except for the provision of necessities or to prevent the dependant from becoming or continuing to be a public charge, and shall not make an order under clause (d). R.S.O. 1990, c. F.3, s. 34 (2).

Assignment of support

(3) An order for support may be assigned to an agency referred to in subsection 33 (3). R.S.O. 1990, c. F.3, s. 34 (3).

Same

(3.1) An agency referred to in subsection 33 (3) to whom an order for support is assigned is entitled to the payments due under the order and has the same right to be notified of and to participate in proceedings under this Act to vary, rescind, suspend or enforce the order as the person who would otherwise be entitled to the payments. 1997, c. 20, s. 4 (1).

Support order binds estate

(4) An order for support binds the estate of the person having the support obligation unless the order provides otherwise. R.S.O. 1990, c. F.3, s. 34 (4).

Indexing of support payments

(5) In an order made under clause (1) (a), other than an order for the support of a child, the court may provide that the amount payable shall be increased annually on the order's anniversary date by the indexing factor, as defined in subsection (6), for November of the previous year. R.S.O. 1990, c. F.3, s. 34 (5); 1997, c. 20, s. 4 (2).

Definition

(6) The indexing factor for a given month is the percentage change in the Consumer Price Index for Canada for prices of all items since the same month of the previous year, as published by Statistics Canada. R.S.O. 1990, c. F.3, s. 34 (6).

Domestic contract, etc., may be filed with court

35. (1) A person who is a party to a domestic contract or paternity agreement may file the contract or agreement with the clerk of the Ontario Court (Provincial Division) or of the Unified Family Court together with the person's affidavit stating that the contract or agreement is in effect and has not been set aside or varied by a court or agreement. R.S.O. 1990, c. F.3, s. 35 (1).

Effect of filing

(2) A provision for support or maintenance contained in a contract or agreement that is filed in this manner,

(a) may be enforced;

(b) may be varied under section 37; and

(c) except in the case of a provision for the support of a child, may be increased under section 38,

as if it were an order of the court where it is filed. 1997, c. 20, s. 5.

Setting aside available

(3) Subsection 33 (4) (setting aside in unconscionable circumstances, etc.) applies to a contract or agreement that is filed in this manner. R.S.O. 1990, c. F.3, s. 35 (3).

Enforcement available despite waiver

(4) Subsection (1) and clause (2) (a) apply despite an agreement to the contrary. R.S.O. 1990, c. F.3, s. 35 (4).

Existing contracts, etc.

(5) Subsections (1) and (2) also apply to contracts and agreements made before the 1st day of March, 1986. R.S.O. 1990, c. F.3, s. 35 (5).

Existing arrears

(6) Clause (2) (a) also applies to arrears accrued before the 1st day of March, 1986. R.S.O. 1990, c. F.3, s. 35 (6).

Effect of divorce proceeding

36. (1) When a divorce proceeding is commenced under the *Divorce Act* (Canada), an application for support under this Part that has not been adjudicated is stayed, unless the court orders otherwise. R.S.O. 1990, c. F.3, s. 36 (1).

Arrears may be included in order

(2) The court that deals with a divorce proceeding under the *Divorce Act* (Canada) may determine the amount of arrears owing under an order for support made under this Part and make an order respecting that amount at the same time as it makes an order under the *Divorce Act* (Canada). R.S.O. 1990, c. F.3, s. 36 (2).

Idem

(3) If a marriage is terminated by divorce or judgment of nullity and the question of support is not adjudicated in the divorce or nullity proceedings, an order for support made under this Part continues in force according to its terms. R.S.O. 1990, c. F.3, s. 36 (3).

Application for variation

37. (1) An application to the court for variation of an order made or confirmed under this Part may be made by,

(a) a dependant or respondent named in the order;

(b) a parent of a dependant referred to in clause (a);

(c) the personal representative of a respondent referred to in clause (a); or

(d) an agency referred to in subsection 33 (3). 1997, c. 20, s. 6.

Powers of court: spouse and parent support

(2) In the case of an order for support of a spouse or parent, if the court is satisfied that there has been a material change in the dependant's or respondent's circumstances or that evidence not available on the previous hearing has become available, the court may,

(a) discharge, vary or suspend a term of the order, prospectively or retroactively;

(b) relieve the respondent from the payment of part or all of the arrears or any interest due on them; and

(c) make any other order under section 34 that the court considers appropriate in the circumstances referred to in section 33. 1997, c. 20, s. 6; 1999, c. 6, s. 25 (12); 2005, c. 5, s. 27 (16).

Powers of court: child support

(2.1) In the case of an order for support of a child, if the court is satisfied that there has been a change in circumstances within the meaning of the child support guidelines or that evidence not available on the previous hearing has become available, the court may,

(a) discharge, vary or suspend a term of the order, prospectively or retroactively;

(b) relieve the respondent from the payment of part or all of the arrears or any interest due on them; and

(c) make any other order for the support of a child that the court could make on an application under section 33. 1997, c. 20, s. 6.

Application of child support guidelines

(2.2) A court making an order under subsection (2.1) shall do so in accordance with the child support guidelines. 1997, c. 20, s. 6.

Exception: special provisions

(2.3) Despite subsection (2.2), a court may award an amount that is different from the amount that would be determined in accordance with the child support guidelines if the court is satisfied,

(a) that special provisions in an order or a written agreement respecting the financial obligations of the parents, or the division or transfer of their property, directly or indirectly benefit a child, or that special provisions have otherwise been made for the benefit of a child; and

(b) that the application of the child support guidelines would result in an amount of child support that is inequitable given those special provisions. 1997, c. 20, s. 6.

Reasons

(2.4) Where the court awards, under subsection (2.3), an amount that is different from the amount that would be determined in accordance with the child support guidelines, the court shall record its reasons for doing so. 1997, c. 20, s. 6.

Exception: consent orders

(2.5) Despite subsection (2.2), a court may award an amount that is different from the amount that would be determined in accordance with the child support guidelines on the consent of both parents if the court is satisfied that,

(a) reasonable arrangements have been made for the support of the child to whom the order relates; and

(b) where support for the child is payable out of public money, the arrangements do not provide for an amount less than the amount that would be determined in accordance with the child support guidelines. 1997, c. 20, s. 6.

Reasonable arrangements

(2.6) For the purposes of clause (2.5) (a), in determining whether reasonable arrangements have been made for the support of a child,

(a) the court shall have regard to the child support guidelines; and

(b) the court shall not consider the arrangements to be unreasonable solely because the amount of support agreed to is not the same as the amount that would otherwise have been determined in accordance with the child support guidelines. 1997, c. 20, s. 6.

Limitation on applications for variation

(3) No application for variation shall be made within six months after the making of the order for support or the disposition of another application for variation in respect of the same order, except by leave of the court. R.S.O. 1990, c. F.3, s. 37 (3).

Indexing existing orders
Non-application to orders for child support

38. (1) This section does not apply to an order for the support of a child. 1997, c. 20, s. 7.

Application to have existing order indexed

(2) If an order made or confirmed under this Part is not indexed under subsection 34 (5), the dependant, or an agency referred to in subsection 33 (3), may apply to the court to have the order indexed in accordance with subsection 34 (5). R.S.O. 1990, c. F.3, s. 38 (1); 1997, c. 20, s. 7.

Power of court

(3) The court shall, unless the respondent shows that his or her income, assets and means have not increased sufficiently to permit the increase, order that the amount payable be increased by the indexing factor, as defined in subsection 34 (6), for November of the year before the year in which the application is made and be increased in the same way annually thereafter on the anniversary date of the order under this section. R.S.O. 1990, c. F.3, s. 38 (2); 1997, c. 20, s. 7.

Priority to child support

38.1 (1) Where a court is considering an application for the support of a child and an application for the support of a spouse, the court shall give priority to the support of the child in determining the applications. 1997, c. 20, s. 8; 1999, c. 6, s. 25 (13); 2005, c. 5, s. 27 (17).

Reasons

(2) Where as a result of giving priority to the support of a child, the court is unable to make an order for the support of a spouse or the court makes an order for the support of a spouse in an amount less than it otherwise would have, the court shall record its reasons for doing so. 1997, c. 20, s. 8; 1999, c. 6, s. 25 (14); 2005, c. 5, s. 27 (18).

Consequences of reduction or termination of child support

(3) Where as a result of giving priority to the support of a child, an order for the support of a spouse is not made or the amount of the order for the support of a spouse is less than it otherwise would have been, any material reduction or termination of the support for the child constitutes a material change of circumstances for the purposes of an application for the support of the spouse or for variation of an order for the support of the spouse. 1997, c. 20, s. 8; 1999, c. 6, s. 25 (15); 2005, c. 5, s. 27 (19).

(4) Repealed: 2002, c. 24, Sched. B, s. 25.

Existing orders

39. (1) Sections 36 to 38 also apply to orders for maintenance or alimony made before the 31st day of March, 1978 or in proceedings commenced before the 31st day of March, 1978 and to orders for support made under Part II of the *Family Law Reform Act*, being chapter 152 of the Revised Statutes of Ontario, 1980. R.S.O. 1990, c. F.3, s. 39.

Combined support orders

(2) Where an application is made under section 37 to vary an order that provides a single amount of money for the combined support of one or more children and a spouse, the court shall rescind the order and treat the application as an application for an order for the support of a child and an application for an order for the support of a spouse. 1997, c. 20, s. 9; 1999, c. 6, s. 25 (17); 2005, c. 5, s. 27 (20).

Existing proceedings

(3) Where an application for the support of a child, including an application under section 37 to vary an order for the support of a child, is made before the day the *Uniform Federal and Provincial Child Support Guidelines Act, 1997* comes into force and the court has not considered any evidence in the application, other than in respect of an interim order, before that day, the proceeding shall be deemed to be an application under the *Family Law Act* as amended by the *Uniform Federal and Provincial Child Support Guidelines Act, 1997*, subject to such directions as the court considers appropriate. 1997, c. 20, s. 9.

Restraining orders

40. The court may, on application, make an interim or final order restraining the depletion of a spouse's property that would impair or defeat a claim under this Part. R.S.O. 1990, c. F.3, s. 40; 1999, c. 6, s. 25 (18); 2005, c. 5, s. 27 (21).

Financial statement

41. In an application under section 33 or 37, each party shall serve on the other and file with the court a financial statement verified by oath or statutory declaration in the manner and form prescribed by the rules of the court. R.S.O. 1990, c. F.3, s. 41.

Obtaining information
Order for return by employer

42. (1) In an application under section 33 or 37, the court may order the employer of a party to the application to make a written return to the court showing the party's wages or other remuneration during the preceding twelve months. R.S.O. 1990, c. F.3, s. 42 (1).

Return as evidence

(2) A return purporting to be signed by the employer may be received in evidence as proof, in the absence of evidence to the contrary, of its contents. R.S.O. 1990, c. F.3, s. 42 (2).

Order for access to information

(3) The court may, on motion, make an order under subsection (4) if it appears to the court that, in order to make an application under section 33 or 37, the moving party needs to learn or confirm the proposed respondent's whereabouts. R.S.O. 1990, c. F.3, s. 42 (3).

Idem

(4) The order shall require the person or public body to whom it is directed to provide the court or the moving party with any information that is shown on a record in the person's or public body's possession or control and that indicates the proposed respondent's place of employment, address or location. R.S.O. 1990, c. F.3, s. 42 (4).

Crown bound

(5) This section binds the Crown in right of Ontario. R.S.O. 1990, c. F.3, s. 42 (5).

Arrest of absconding debtor

43. (1) If an application is made under section 33 or 37 and the court is satisfied that the respondent is about to leave Ontario and that there are reasonable grounds for believing that the respondent intends to evade his or her responsibilities under this Act, the court may issue a warrant for the respondent's arrest for the purpose of bringing him or her before the court. R.S.O. 1990, c. F.3, s. 43 (1).

Bail

(2) Section 150 (interim release by justice of the peace) of the *Provincial Offences Act* applies with necessary modifications to an arrest under the warrant. R.S.O. 1990, c. F.3, s. 43 (2).

Provisional orders

44. (1) In an application under section 33 or 37 in the Ontario Court (Provincial Division) or the Unified Family Court, the court shall proceed under this section, whether or not the respondent in the application files a financial statement, if,

(a) the respondent fails to appear;

(b) it appears to the court that the respondent resides in a locality in Ontario that is more than 150 kilometres away from the place where the court sits; and

(c) the court is of the opinion, in the circumstances of the case, that the issues can be adequately determined by proceeding under this section. R.S.O. 1990, c. F.3, s. 44 (1).

Idem

(2) If the court determines that it would be proper to make a final order, were it not for the respondent's failure to appear, the court shall make an order for support that is provisional only and has no effect until it is confirmed by the Ontario Court (Provincial Division) or the Unified Family Court sitting nearest the place where the respondent resides. R.S.O. 1990, c. F.3, s. 44 (2).

Transmission for hearing

(3) The court that makes a provisional order shall send to the court in the locality in which the respondent resides copies of such documents

and records, certified in such manner, as are prescribed by the rules of the court. R.S.O. 1990, c. F.3, s. 44 (3).

Show cause

(4) The court to which the documents and records are sent shall cause them to be served upon the respondent, together with a notice to file with the court the financial statement required by section 41, and to appear and show cause why the provisional order should not be confirmed. R.S.O. 1990, c. F.3, s. 44 (4).

Confirmation of order

(5) At the hearing, the respondent may raise any defence that might have been raised in the original proceeding, but if the respondent fails to satisfy the court that the order ought not to be confirmed, the court may confirm the order without variation or with the variation that the court considers proper having regard to all the evidence. R.S.O. 1990, c. F.3, s. 44 (5).

Adjournment for further evidence

(6) If the respondent appears before the court and satisfies the court that for the purpose of a defence or for the taking of further evidence or otherwise it is necessary to remit the case to the court where the applicant resides, the court may remit the case and adjourn the proceeding for that purpose. R.S.O. 1990, c. F.3, s. 44 (6).

Where order not confirmed

(7) If the respondent appears before the court and the court, having regard to all the evidence, is of the opinion that the order ought not to be confirmed, the court shall remit the case to the court sitting where the order was made with a statement of the reasons for doing so, and the court sitting where the order was made shall dispose of the application in accordance with the statement. R.S.O. 1990, c. F.3, s. 44 (7).

Certificates as evidence

(8) A certificate certifying copies of documents or records for the purpose of this section and purporting to be signed by the clerk of the court is, without proof of the clerk's office or signature, admissible in evidence in a court to which it is transmitted under this section as proof, in the absence of evidence to the contrary, of the copy's authenticity. R.S.O. 1990, c. F.3, s. 44 (8).

Right of appeal

(9) No appeal lies from a provisional order made under this section, but a person bound by an order confirmed under this section has the same right of appeal as he or she would have had if the order had been made under section 34. R.S.O. 1990, c. F.3, s. 44 (9).

Necessities of life
Pledging credit of spouse

45. (1) During cohabitation, a spouse has authority to render himself or herself and his or her spouse jointly and severally liable to a third party for necessities of life, unless the spouse has notified the third party that he or she has withdrawn the authority. R.S.O. 1990, c. F.3, s. 45 (1); 1999, c. 6, s. 25 (19); 2005, c. 5, s. 27 (22).

Liability for necessities of minor

(2) If a person is entitled to recover against a minor in respect of the provision of necessities for the minor, every parent who has an obligation to support the minor is liable for them jointly and severally with the minor. R.S.O. 1990, c. F.3, s. 45 (2).

Recovery between persons jointly liable

(3) If persons are jointly and severally liable under this section, their liability to each other shall be determined in accordance with their obligation to provide support. R.S.O. 1990, c. F.3, s. 45 (3).

Common law supplanted

(4) This section applies in place of the rules of common law by which a wife may pledge her husband's credit. R.S.O. 1990, c. F.3, s. 45 (4).

Order restraining harassment

46. (1) On application, a court may make an interim or final order restraining the applicant's spouse or former spouse from molesting, annoying or harassing the applicant or children in the applicant's lawful custody, or from communicating with the applicant or children, except as the order provides, and may require the applicant's spouse or former spouse to enter into the recognizance that the court considers appropriate. R.S.O. 1990, c. F.3, s. 46 (1); 1999, c. 6, s. 25 (20); 2005, c. 5, s. 27 (23).

Offence

(2) A person who contravenes a restraining order is guilty of an offence and upon conviction is liable,

> (a) in the case of a first offence, to a fine of not more than $5,000 or to imprisonment for a term of not more than three months, or to both; and
>
> (b) in the case of a second or subsequent offence, to a fine of not more than $10,000 or to imprisonment for a term of not more than two years, or to both. R.S.O. 1990, c. F.3, s. 46 (2).

Note: On a day to be named by proclamation of the Lieutenant Governor, subsection (2) is repealed by the Statutes of Ontario, 2000, chapter 33, subsection 22 (1). See: 2000, c. 33, ss. 22 (1), 23.

Note: Despite the repeal of subsection (2), any prosecution begun under that subsection before its repeal shall continue as if it were still in force. See: 2000, c. 33, s. 22 (3).

Arrest without warrant

(3) A police officer may arrest without warrant a person the police officer believes on reasonable and probable grounds to have contravened a restraining order. R.S.O. 1990, c. F.3, s. 46 (3).

Existing orders

(4) Subsections (2) and (3) also apply in respect of contraventions, committed, on or after the 1st day of March, 1986, of restraining orders made under Part II of the *Family Law Reform Act*, being chapter 152 of the Revised Statutes of Ontario, 1980. R.S.O. 1990, c. F.3, s. 46 (4).

Note: On a day to be named by proclamation of the Lieutenant Governor, section 46 is repealed by the Statutes of Ontario, 2000, chapter 33, subsection 22 (2). See: 2000, c. 33, ss. 22 (2), 23.

Note: Despite the repeal of section 46, any proceeding begun under that section before its repeal shall continue as if section 46 were still in force, and any order made under section 46, after its repeal, remains in force until it terminates by its own terms or is rescinded or terminated by a court. See: 2000, c. 33, s. 22 (4).

Application for custody

47. The court may direct that an application for support stand over until an application for custody under the *Children's Law Reform Act* has been determined. R.S.O. 1990, c. F.3, s. 47.

Appeal from Ontario Court (Provincial Division)

48. An appeal lies from an order of the Ontario Court (Provincial Division) under this Part to the Ontario Court (General Division). R.S.O. 1990, c. F.3, s. 48.

Contempt of orders of Ontario Court (Provincial Division)

49. (1) In addition to its powers in respect of contempt, the Ontario Court (Provincial Division) may punish by fine or imprisonment, or by both, any wilful contempt of or resistance to its process, rules or orders under this Act, but the fine shall not exceed $5,000 nor shall the imprisonment exceed ninety days. R.S.O. 1990, c. F.3, s. 49 (1).

Conditions of imprisonment

(2) An order for imprisonment under subsection (1) may be conditional upon default in the performance of a condition set out in the order and may provide for the imprisonment to be served intermittently. R.S.O. 1990, c. F.3, s. 49 (2).

50. Repealed: 2002, c. 24, Sched. B, s. 25.

PART IV
DOMESTIC CONTRACTS

Definitions
51. In this Part,

"cohabitation agreement" means an agreement entered into under section 53; ("accord de cohabitation")

"domestic contract" means a marriage contract, separation agreement or cohabitation agreement; ("contrat familial")

"marriage contract" means an agreement entered into under section 52; ("contrat de mariage")

"paternity agreement" means an agreement entered into under section 59; ("accord de paternité")

"separation agreement" means an agreement entered into under section 54. ("accord de séparation") R.S.O. 1990, c. F.3, s. 51.

Marriage contracts
52. (1) Two persons who are married to each other or intend to marry may enter into an agreement in which they agree on their respective rights and obligations under the marriage or on separation, on the annulment or dissolution of the marriage or on death, including,

(a) ownership in or division of property;

(b) support obligations;

(c) the right to direct the education and moral training of their children, but not the right to custody of or access to their children; and

(d) any other matter in the settlement of their affairs. R.S.O. 1990, c. F.3, s. 52 (1); 2005, c. 5, s. 27 (25).

Rights re matrimonial home excepted
(2) A provision in a marriage contract purporting to limit a spouse's rights under Part II (Matrimonial Home) is unenforceable. R.S.O. 1990, c. F.3, s. 52 (2).

Cohabitation agreements
53. (1) Two persons who are cohabiting or intend to cohabit and who are not married to each other may enter into an agreement in which they agree on their respective rights and obligations during cohabitation, or on ceasing to cohabit or on death, including,

(a) ownership in or division of property;

(b) support obligations;

(c) the right to direct the education and moral training of their children, but not the right to custody of or access to their children; and

(d) any other matter in the settlement of their affairs. R.S.O. 1990, c. F.3, s. 53 (1); 1999, c. 6, s. 25 (23); 2005, c. 5, s. 27 (26).

Effect of marriage on agreement

(2) If the parties to a cohabitation agreement marry each other, the agreement shall be deemed to be a marriage contract. R.S.O. 1990, c. F.3, s. 53 (2).

Separation agreements

54. Two persons who cohabited and are living separate and apart may enter into an agreement in which they agree on their respective rights and obligations, including,

(a) ownership in or division of property;

(b) support obligations;

(c) the right to direct the education and moral training of their children;

(d) the right to custody of and access to their children; and

(e) any other matter in the settlement of their affairs. R.S.O. 1990, c. F.3, s. 54; 1999, c. 6, s. 25 (24); 2005, c. 5, s. 27 (27).

Form and capacity
Form of contract

55. (1) A domestic contract and an agreement to amend or rescind a domestic contract are unenforceable unless made in writing, signed by the parties and witnessed. R.S.O. 1990, c. F.3, s. 55 (1).

Capacity of minor

(2) A minor has capacity to enter into a domestic contract, subject to the approval of the court, which may be given before or after the minor enters into the contract. R.S.O. 1990, c. F.3, s. 55 (2).

Guardian of property

(3) If a mentally incapable person has a guardian of property other than his or her own spouse, the guardian may enter into a domestic contract or give any waiver or consent under this Act on the person's behalf, subject to the approval of the court, given in advance. 1992, c. 32, s. 12.

P.G.T.

(4) In all other cases of mental incapacity, the Public Guardian and Trustee has power to act on the person's behalf in accordance with subsection (3). 1992, c. 32, s. 12.

Provisions that may be set aside or disregarded
Contracts subject to best interests of child

56. (1) In the determination of a matter respecting the education, moral training or custody of or access to a child, the court may disregard any provision of a domestic contract pertaining to the matter where, in the opinion of the court, to do so is in the best interests of the child. R.S.O. 1990, c. F.3, s. 56 (1); 1997, c. 20, s. 10 (1).

Contracts subject to child support guidelines

(1.1) In the determination of a matter respecting the support of a child, the court may disregard any provision of a domestic contract or paternity agreement pertaining to the matter where the provision is unreasonable having regard to the child support guidelines, as well as to any other provision relating to support of the child in the contract or agreement. 1997, c. 20, s. 10 (2).

Clauses requiring chastity

(2) A provision in a domestic contract to take effect on separation whereby any right of a party is dependent upon remaining chaste is unenforceable, but this subsection shall not be construed to affect a contingency upon marriage or cohabitation with another. R.S.O. 1990, c. F.3, s. 56 (2).

Idem

(3) A provision in a domestic contract made before the 1st day of March, 1986 whereby any right of a party is dependent upon remaining chaste shall be given effect as a contingency upon marriage or cohabitation with another. R.S.O. 1990, c. F.3, s. 56 (3).

Setting aside domestic contract

(4) A court may, on application, set aside a domestic contract or a provision in it,

   (a)   if a party failed to disclose to the other significant assets, or significant debts or other liabilities, existing when the domestic contract was made;

   (b)   if a party did not understand the nature or consequences of the domestic contract; or

   (c)   otherwise in accordance with the law of contract. R.S.O. 1990, c. F.3, s. 56 (4).

Barriers to remarriage

(5) The court may, on application, set aside all or part of a separation agreement or settlement, if the court is satisfied that the removal by one spouse of barriers that would prevent the other spouse's remarriage within that spouse's faith was a consideration in the making of the agreement or settlement. R.S.O. 1990, c. F.3, s. 56 (5).

Idem

(6) Subsection (5) also applies to consent orders, releases, notices of discontinuance and abandonment and other written or oral arrangements. R.S.O. 1990, c. F.3, s. 56 (6).

Application of subss. (4, 5, 6)

(7) Subsections (4), (5) and (6) apply despite any agreement to the contrary. R.S.O. 1990, c. F.3, s. 56 (7).

Rights of donors of gifts

57. If a domestic contract provides that specific gifts made to one or both parties may not be disposed of or encumbered without the consent of the donor, the donor shall be deemed to be a party to the contract for the purpose of enforcement or amendment of the provision. R.S.O. 1990, c. F.3, s. 57.

Contracts made outside Ontario

58. The manner and formalities of making a domestic contract and its essential validity and effect are governed by the proper law of the contract, except that,

(a) a contract of which the proper law is that of a jurisdiction other than Ontario is also valid and enforceable in Ontario if entered into in accordance with Ontario's internal law;

(b) subsection 33 (4) (setting aside provision for support or waiver) and section 56 apply in Ontario to contracts for which the proper law is that of a jurisdiction other than Ontario; and

(c) a provision in a marriage contract or cohabitation agreement respecting the right to custody of or access to children is not enforceable in Ontario. R.S.O. 1990, c. F.3, s. 58.

Paternity agreements

59. (1) If a man and a woman who are not spouses enter into an agreement for,

(a) the payment of the expenses of a child's prenatal care and birth;

(b) support of a child; or

(c) funeral expenses of the child or mother,

on the application of a party, or a children's aid society, to the Ontario Court (Provincial Division) or the Unified Family Court, the court may incorporate the agreement in an order, and Part III (Support Obligations) applies to the order in the same manner as if it were an order made under that Part. R.S.O. 1990, c. F.3, s. 59 (1).

Child support guidelines

(1.1) A court shall not incorporate an agreement for the support of a child in an order under subsection (1) unless the court is satisfied that the agreement is reasonable having regard to the child support guidelines, as well as to any other provision relating to support of the child in the agreement. 1997, c. 20, s. 11.

Absconding respondent

(2) If an application is made under subsection (1) and a judge of the court is satisfied that the respondent is about to leave Ontario and that there are reasonable grounds to believe that the respondent intends to evade his or her responsibilities under the agreement, the judge may issue a warrant in the form prescribed by the rules of the court for the respondent's arrest. R.S.O. 1990, c. F.3, s. 59 (2).

Bail

(3) Section 150 (interim release by justice of the peace) of the *Provincial Offences Act* applies with necessary modifications to an arrest under the warrant. R.S.O. 1990, c. F.3, s. 59 (3).

Capacity of minor

(4) A minor has capacity to enter into an agreement under subsection (1) that is approved by the court, whether the approval is given before or after the minor enters into the agreement. R.S.O. 1990, c. F.3, s. 59 (4).

Application to existing agreements

(5) This section applies to paternity agreements that were made before the 1st day of March, 1986. R.S.O. 1990, c. F.3, s. 59 (5).

Application of Act to existing contracts

60. (1) A domestic contract validly made before the 1st day of March, 1986 shall be deemed to be a domestic contract for the purposes of this Act. R.S.O. 1990, c. F.3, s. 60 (1).

Contracts entered into before the 1st day of March, 1986

(2) If a domestic contract was entered into before the 1st day of March, 1986 and the contract or any part would have been valid if entered into on or after that day, the contract or part is not invalid for the reason only that it was entered into before that day. R.S.O. 1990, c. F.3, s. 60 (2).

Idem

(3) If property is transferred, under an agreement or understanding reached before the 31st day of March, 1978, between spouses who are living separate and apart, the transfer is effective as if made under a domestic contract. R.S.O. 1990, c. F.3, s. 60 (3).

PART V
DEPENDANTS' CLAIM FOR DAMAGES

Right of dependants to sue in tort

61. (1) If a person is injured or killed by the fault or neglect of another under circumstances where the person is entitled to recover damages, or would have been entitled if not killed, the spouse, as defined in Part III (Support Obligations), children, grandchildren, parents, grandparents, brothers and sisters of the person are entitled to recover their pecuniary loss resulting from the injury or death from the person from whom the person injured or killed is entitled to recover or would have been entitled if not killed, and to maintain an action for the purpose in a court of competent jurisdiction. R.S.O. 1990, c. F.3, s. 61 (1); 1999, c. 6, s. 25 (25); 2005, c. 5, s. 27 (28).

Damages in case of injury

(2) The damages recoverable in a claim under subsection (1) may include,

(a) actual expenses reasonably incurred for the benefit of the person injured or killed;

(b) actual funeral expenses reasonably incurred;

(c) a reasonable allowance for travel expenses actually incurred in visiting the person during his or her treatment or recovery;

(d) where, as a result of the injury, the claimant provides nursing, housekeeping or other services for the person, a reasonable allowance for loss of income or the value of the services; and

(e) an amount to compensate for the loss of guidance, care and companionship that the claimant might reasonably have expected to receive from the person if the injury or death had not occurred. R.S.O. 1990, c. F.3, s. 61 (2).

Contributory negligence

(3) In an action under subsection (1), the right to damages is subject to any apportionment of damages due to contributory fault or neglect of the person who was injured or killed. R.S.O. 1990, c. F.3, s. 61 (3).

(4) Repealed: 2002, c. 24, Sched. B, s. 25.

Offer to settle for global sum

62. (1) The defendant may make an offer to settle for one sum of money as compensation for his or her fault or neglect to all plaintiffs, without specifying the shares into which it is to be divided. R.S.O. 1990, c. F.3, s. 62 (1).

Apportionment

(2) If the offer is accepted and the compensation has not been otherwise apportioned, the court may, on motion, apportion it among the plaintiffs. R.S.O. 1990, c. F.3, s. 62 (2).

Payment before apportionment

(3) The court may direct payment from the fund before apportionment. R.S.O. 1990, c. F.3, s. 62 (3).

Payment may be postponed

(4) The court may postpone the distribution of money to which minors are entitled. R.S.O. 1990, c. F.3, s. 62 (4).

Assessment of damages, insurance

63. In assessing damages in an action brought under this Part, the court shall not take into account any sum paid or payable as a result of the death or injury under a contract of insurance. R.S.O. 1990, c. F.3, s. 63.

PART VI
AMENDMENTS TO THE COMMON LAW

Unity of legal personality abolished

64. (1) For all purposes of the law of Ontario, a married person has a legal personality that is independent, separate and distinct from that of his or her spouse. R.S.O. 1990, c. F.3, s. 64 (1).

Capacity of married person

(2) A married person has and shall be accorded legal capacity for all purposes and in all respects as if he or she were an unmarried person and, in particular, has the same right of action in tort against his or her spouse as if they were not married. R.S.O. 1990, c. F.3, s. 64 (2).

Purpose of subss. (1, 2)

(3) The purpose of subsections (1) and (2) is to make the same law apply, and apply equally, to married men and married women and to remove any difference in it resulting from any common law rule or doctrine. R.S.O. 1990, c. F.3, s. 64 (3).

Actions between parent and child

65. No person is disentitled from bringing an action or other proceeding against another for the reason only that they are parent and child. R.S.O. 1990,c. F.3, s. 65.

Recovery for prenatal injuries

66. No person is disentitled from recovering damages in respect of injuries for the reason only that the injuries were incurred before his or her birth. R.S.O. 1990, c. F.3, s. 66.

Domicile of minor

67. The domicile of a person who is a minor is,

(a)   if the minor habitually resides with both parents and the parents have a common domicile, that domicile;

(b)   if the minor habitually resides with one parent only, that parent's domicile;

(c)   if the minor resides with another person who has lawful custody of him or her, that person's domicile; or

(d)   if the minor's domicile cannot be determined under clause (a), (b) or (c), the jurisdiction with which the minor has the closest connection. R.S.O. 1990, c. F.3, s. 67.

68. Repealed: 2000, c. 4, s. 12.

General
Regulations

69. (1) The Lieutenant Governor in Council may make regulations respecting any matter referred to as prescribed by the regulations. R.S.O. 1990, c. F.3, s. 69.

Same

(2) The Lieutenant Governor in Council may make regulations establishing,

(a)   guidelines respecting the making of orders for child support under this Act; and
(b)   guidelines that may be designated under subsection 2 (5) of the *Divorce Act* (Canada). 1997, c. 20, s. 12.

Same
(3) Without limiting the generality of subsection (2), guidelines may be established under subsection (2),
(a)   respecting the way in which the amount of an order for child support is to be determined;
(b)   respecting the circumstances in which discretion may be exercised in the making of an order for child support;
(c)   respecting the circumstances that give rise to the making of a variation order in respect of an order for the support of a child;
(d)   respecting the determination of income for the purposes of the application of the guidelines;
(e)   authorizing a court to impute income for the purposes of the application of the guidelines;
(f)   respecting the production of income information and providing for sanctions when that information is not provided. 1997, c. 20, s. 12.

Transition
Application of ss. 5-8
70. (1) Sections 5 to 8 apply unless,
(a)   an application under section 4 of the *Family Law Reform Act*, being chapter 152 of the Revised Statutes of Ontario, 1980 was adjudicated or settled before the 4th day of June, 1985; or
(b)   the first spouse's death occurred before the 1st day of March, 1986. R.S.O. 1990, c. F.3, s. 70 (1).

Application of Part II
(2) Part II (Matrimonial Home) applies unless a proceeding under Part III of the *Family Law Reform Act*, being chapter 152 of the Revised Statutes of Ontario, 1980 to determine the rights between spouses in respect of the property concerned was adjudicated or settled before the 4th day of June, 1985. R.S.O. 1990, c. F.3, s. 70 (2).

Interpretation of existing contracts
(3) A separation agreement or marriage contract that was validly made before the 1st day of March, 1986 and that excludes a spouse's property from the application of sections 4 and 8 of the *Family Law Reform Act*, being chapter 152 of the Revised Statutes of Ontario, 1980,
(a)   shall be deemed to exclude that property from the application of section 5 of this Act; and
(b)   shall be read with necessary modifications. R.S.O. 1990, c. F.3, s. 70 (3).

Family Responsibility and Support Arrears Enforcement Act, 1996
S.O. 1996, CHAPTER 31

Amended by: 1996, c. 31, s. 64; 1997, c. 25, Sched. E, s. 2; 1999, c. 6, s. 26; 1999, c. 12, Sched. B, s. 8; 2001, c. 9, Sched. C, s. 1; 2002, c. 8, Sched. I, s. 11; 2002, c. 13, s. 57; 2002, c. 17, Sched. F, Table; 2005, c. 5, s. 28; 2005, c. 16, ss. 1-40.

CONTENTS

Part I
INTERPRETATION

Interpretation
Definitions
1. (1) In this Act,

"Director" means the Director of the Family Responsibility Office; ("directeur")

"income source" means an individual, corporation or other entity that owes or makes any payment, whether periodically or in a lump sum, to or on behalf of a payor of,

(a) wages, wage supplements or salary, or draws or advances on them,

(b) a commission, bonus, piece-work allowance or similar payment,

(c) a payment made under a contract for service,

(d) a benefit under an accident, disability or sickness plan,

(e) a disability, retirement or other pension,

(f) an annuity,

(g) vacation pay, termination pay and severance pay,

(h) an employee loan,

(i) a shareholder loan or dividends on shares, if the corporation that issued the shares is effectively controlled by the payor or the payor and the payor's parent, spouse, child or other relative or a body corporate which the payor and his or her parent, spouse, child or other relative effectively control, directly or indirectly,

(j) refunds under the *Income Tax Act* (Canada),

(k) lump sum payments under the *Family Orders and Agreements Enforcement Assistance Act* (Canada),

(l) income of a type described in the regulations; ("source de revenu")

"payor" means a person who is required to pay support under a support order; ("payeur")

"provisional order" means an order that has no effect until it is confirmed by another court and includes orders made under subsection 18 (2) of the *Divorce Act* (Canada), sections 7 and 30 of the *Interjurisdictional Support Orders Act*, 2002 and section 44 of the *Family Law Act*; ("ordonnance conditionnelle")

"recipient" means a person entitled to support under a support order or the parent, other than the payor, of a child entitled to support under a support order; ("bénéficiaire")

"reciprocating jurisdiction" has the same meaning as in the *Interjurisdictional Support Orders Act, 2002*; ("autorité pratiquant la réciprocité")

"regulations" means the regulations made under this Act; ("règlements")

"spouse" means,

(a) a spouse as defined in section 1 of the *Family Law Act*, or

(b) either of two persons who live together in a conjugal relationship outside marriage; ("conjoint")

"support deduction order" means a support deduction order made or deemed to have been made under this Act or its predecessor; ("ordonnance de retenue des aliments")

"support order" means a provision in an order made in or outside

Ontario and enforceable in Ontario for the payment of money as support or maintenance, and includes a provision for,

(a)   the payment of an amount periodically, whether annually or otherwise and whether for an indefinite or limited period, or until the happening of a specified event,

(b)   a lump sum to be paid or held in trust,

(c)   payment of support or maintenance in respect of a period before the date of the order,

(d)   payment to an agency of an amount in reimbursement for a benefit or assistance provided to a party under a statute, including a benefit or assistance provided before the date of the order,

(e)   payment of expenses in respect of a child's prenatal care and birth,

(e.1)   payment of expenses in respect of DNA testing to establish parentage,

(f)   the irrevocable designation, by a spouse who has a policy of life insurance or an interest in a benefit plan, of the other spouse or a child as the beneficiary, or

(g)   interest or the payment of legal fees or other expenses arising in relation to support or maintenance,

and includes such a provision in a domestic contract or paternity agreement that is enforceable under section 35 of the *Family Law Act*. ("ordonnance alimentaire") 1996, c. 31, s. 1 (1); 1999, c. 6, s. 26; 2002, c. 13, s. 57 (1); 2005, c. 5, s. 28; 2005, c. 16, s. 1.

Interpretation – income source

(2) An individual, corporation or other entity continues to be an income source despite temporary interruptions in the payments owed to a payor. 1996, c. 31, s. 1 (2).

Same – related orders

(3) A support deduction order is related to the support order on which it is based and a support order is related to the support deduction order that is based on it. 1996, c. 31, s. 1 (3).

Part II
Director of the Family Responsibility Office

Director of Family Responsibility Office

2. There shall be a Director of the Family Responsibility Office who shall be appointed by the Lieutenant Governor in Council. 1996, c. 31, s. 2.

Enforcement officers

3. (1) The Director may appoint employees of the Director's office as enforcement officers for the purposes of this Act. 1996, c. 31, s. 3 (1).

Powers

(2) An enforcement officer may act for the Director and in his or her name. 1996, c. 31, s. 3 (2).

Assignment of Director's powers, etc.

4. (1) The Attorney General may, subject to the approval of the Lieutenant Governor in Council, assign to any person, agency or body, or class thereof, any of the powers, duties or functions of the Director under this Act, subject to the limitations, conditions and requirements set out in the assignment. 1996, c. 31, s. 4 (1).

Same

(2) An assignment may include powers, duties or functions that are not purely administrative in nature, including statutory powers of decision and discretionary powers given to the Director under this Act, and may provide that an assignee may be a party in any action or proceeding instead of the Director. 1996, c. 31, s. 4 (2).

Fees, etc.

(3) An assignment may, subject to any regulation made under clause 63 (1), set out the fees, costs, disbursements, surcharges and other charges that the assignee may charge to the payor, or a method for determining them, how and when they may be collected, and may exempt the assignee from clause 22 (a) of the *Collection Agencies Act*. 1996, c. 31, s. 4 (3).

Same

(4) An assignee may charge fees, costs, disbursements, surcharges and other charges as set out in the assignment and such fees, costs, disbursements, surcharges and other charges may,

(a) be in respect of services for which the Director may not charge anything;

(b) be higher than a fee, cost, disbursement, surcharge or other charge that the Director is permitted to charge for the same service; and

(c) be applied in a manner other than that provided in section 57. 1996, c. 31, s. 4 (4).

Same

(5) Any fees, costs, disbursements, surcharges or other charges charged by an assignee must be charged to the payor and may be added to the amount of arrears owing by the payor and may be collected in like manner as arrears. 1996, c. 31, s. 4 (5).

Interest

(6) For the purposes of subsections (3), (4) and (5), "other charges" includes interest at a rate prescribed by regulation. 1996, c. 31, s. 4 (6).

Use of information restricted

(7) An assignee shall not use or disclose the information it has collected in carrying out any power, duty or function assigned to the assignee under subsection (1) except for the purposes of this Act. 1996, c. 31, s. 4 (7).

Duty of Director

5. (1) It is the duty of the Director to enforce support orders where the support order and the related support deduction order, if any, are filed in the Director's office and to pay the amounts collected to the person to whom they are owed. 1996, c. 31, s. 5 (1).

Transition

(2) Subject to subsection (4), a support order or support deduction order that is filed in the office of the Director of the Family Support Plan immediately before the day this section comes into force shall be deemed to be filed in the Director's office on the day this section comes into force. 1996, c. 31, s. 5 (2).

Same

(3) If a support deduction order is filed in the office of the Director of the Family Support Plan immediately before the day this section comes into force and the related support order was never filed in his or her office before that day, it is the duty of the Director to enforce the support deduction order so long as it is filed in the Director's office. 1996, c. 31, s. 5 (3).

Same

(4) If a support deduction order is filed in the office of the Director of the Family Support Plan immediately before the day this section comes into force and the related support order was withdrawn from his or her office before that day, either when the support order was made or later, the support deduction order shall be deemed to be withdrawn from the Director's office on the day this section comes into force. 1996, c. 31, s. 5 (4).

Powers

6. (1) The Director shall carry out his or her duties in the manner, if any, that appears practical to the Director and, for the purpose, may commence and conduct a proceeding and take any steps in the Director's name for the benefit of recipients, including,

(a) enforcing support deduction orders that are filed in the Director's office, as provided by this Act;

(b) employing any other enforcement mechanisms expressly provided for in this Act;

(c) employing any other enforcement mechanisms not expressly provided for in this Act. 1996, c. 31, s. 6 (1).

Transition

(2) The Director may enforce the payment of arrears of support under a support order although they were incurred before the order was filed in the Director's office or before July 2, 1987. 1996, c. 31, s. 6 (2).

Same

(3) The Director may enforce the payment of the arrears of support owed on the day this section comes into force under an order that,

(a) is not a support order as defined in subsection 1 (1) but was a support order within the meaning of the *Family Support Plan Act*, as it read immediately before its repeal by this Act; and

(b) is filed in the office of the Director of the Family Support Plan immediately before such repeal. 1996, c. 31, s. 6 (3).

Same

(4) For the purpose of subsection (3), an order described in that subsection shall be deemed to be a support order as defined in subsection 1 (1). 1996, c. 31, s. 6 (4).

Note: Subsection (5) comes into force on a day to be named by proclamation of the Lieutenant Governor. See: 1996, c. 31, s. 74.

Same

(5) The Director shall not enforce custody orders made by a Canadian court, even if they were filed with the Director before this section comes into force. 1996, c. 31, s. 6 (5).

Enforcement alternatives

(6) Enforcement of a support order or support deduction order by one means does not prevent enforcement by other means at the same time or different times. 1996, c. 31, s. 6 (6).

Enforcement by Director exclusive

(7) Subject to section 4, no person other than the Director shall enforce a support order that is filed in the Director's office. 1996, c. 31, s. 6 (7).

Same

(8) Subject to section 4, no person other than the Director shall enforce a support deduction order, whether the order is filed in the Director's office or not. 1996, c. 31, s. 6 (8).

Director may refuse to enforce

7. (1) Despite section 5, the Director may at any time refuse to enforce a support order or support deduction order that is filed in the Director's office if, in his or her opinion,

(a) the amount of the support is nominal;

(b) the amount of the support cannot be determined from the face of the order because it is expressed as a percentage of the payor's income or it is dependent on another variable that does not appear on the order;

(c) the meaning of the order is unclear or ambiguous;

(d) the recipient has not complied with reasonable requests to provide the Director with accurate or sufficient information as may be needed in order to enforce the order or respecting the amount of arrears owed under the order;

(e) the whereabouts of the recipient cannot be determined after reasonable efforts have been made;

(f) the payor is in prison serving a sentence of five years or longer and has no assets or income available to satisfy the support order and any arrears under the order;

(g) the payor is receiving benefits under the *Family Benefits Act*, assistance under the *General Welfare Assistance Act* or the *Ontario Works Act, 1997* or income support under the *Ontario Disability Support Program Act, 1997* and has no assets or income available to satisfy the support order and any arrears under the order;

(h) the recipient repeatedly accepts payment of support directly from the payor;

(i) the recipient consents to a limitation of enforcement of the support order by the Director;

(j) enforcement of the support order has been stayed by a court; or

(k) enforcement of the order is otherwise unreasonable or impractical. 1996, c. 31, s. 7 (1); 1997, c. 25, Sched. E, s. 2 (1).

Policies and procedures

(2) The Attorney General may establish policies and procedures respecting subsection (1) and the Director shall consider them in exercising his or her discretion under that subsection. 1996, c. 31, s. 7 (2).

Order deemed withdrawn

(3) If the Director refuses to enforce an order under subsection (1), the Director shall notify the payor and the recipient and the support order and the related support deduction order, if any, shall be deemed to be withdrawn from the Director's office on the date set out in the notice. 1996, c. 31, s. 7 (3).

Cost of living clauses

(4) The Director shall not enforce a cost of living clause in a support order or support deduction order made in Ontario unless it is calculated in accordance with subsection 34 (5) of the *Family Law Act* or in a manner prescribed by regulation. 1996, c. 31, s. 7 (4).

Same

(5) The Director shall not enforce a cost of living clause in a support order or a support deduction order if the support order was made outside Ontario unless it is calculated in a manner that the Director considers similar to that provided in subsection 34 (5) of the *Family Law Act* or in a manner prescribed by regulation. 1996, c. 31, s. 7 (5).

Same

(6) Where the cost of living clause in an order is not calculated in accordance with subsection 34 (5) of the *Family Law Act* or in a manner prescribed by regulation or, if the order was made outside Ontario, in a manner that the Director considers similar, the Director shall, subject to

subsection (1), enforce the order as if it contained no cost of living clause. 1996, c. 31, s. 7 (6).

Transition

(7) Despite subsections (5) and (6), if an order contains a cost of living clause that is not calculated in accordance with subsection 34 (5) of the *Family Law Act* or in a manner prescribed by regulation or, if the order was made outside Ontario, in a manner that the Director considers similar, which became effective before this section came into force,

(a) the Director shall continue to enforce the order and the cost of living clause at the same amount at which the Director of the Family Support Plan was enforcing them immediately before this section came into force; and

(b) the Director shall not make any further adjustments under the cost of living clause after this section comes into force. 1996, c. 31, s. 7 (7).

Same

(8) This section applies even if the order was filed in the Director's office before this section comes into force. 1996, c. 31, s. 7 (8).

Note: On a day to be named by proclamation of the Lieutenant Governor, the Act is amended by the Statutes of Ontario, 2005, chapter 16, section 2 by adding the following section:

Interest

7.1 (1) If the recipient under a support order is entitled to interest on arrears, the Director may add interest to the arrears and collect the interest in the same manner as the arrears. 2005, c. 16, s. 2.

Rate of interest and manner of calculation

(2) Interest added and collected under subsection (1) shall be calculated,

(a) by the Director, at the rate and in the manner prescribed by the regulations; or

(b) by the recipient, at the rate and in the manner required by the support order. 2005, c. 16, s. 2.

When interest begins to accrue

(3) Interest added and collected under subsection (1) begins to accrue on the latest of the following:

1. The date the support becomes payable.

2. The date the arrears become payable.

3. The date the support order or support deduction order is filed with the Director.

4. The day section 2 of the *Family Responsibility and Support Arrears Enforcement Amendment Act, 2005* comes into force. 2005, c. 16, s. 2.

Exception

(4) No interest is payable on support that is paid within 30 days after the day on which it becomes payable. 2005, c. 16, s. 2.

Non-application of *Courts of Justice Act*, s. 129

(5) Section 129 of the *Courts of Justice Act* does not apply to interest calculated by the Director under clause (2) (a). 2005, c. 16, s. 2.

See: 2005, c. 16, ss. 2, 42 (2).

Director to cease enforcement

8. (1) The Director shall cease enforcement of a support obligation provided for in a support order or support deduction order filed in the Director's office if the support obligation has terminated; however, if the support order has been assigned to an agency described in subsection 33 (3) of the *Family Law Act*, the Director shall not cease enforcement of the support obligation without the agency's consent. 1996, c. 31, s. 8 (1).

Same

(2) The Director shall not enforce a support order or support deduction order against the estate of a payor after he or she is notified, in accordance with the regulations, of the payor's death. 1996, c. 31, s. 8 (2).

Date of termination

(3) For the purpose of subsection (1), the termination of a support obligation shall be determined in one of the following ways:

1. If the parties to the support order or support deduction order agree in the manner prescribed by the regulations that the support obligation has terminated.

2. If the support obligation is stated in the support order or support deduction order to terminate on a set calendar date.

3. If a court orders that the obligation has terminated. 1996, c. 31, s. 8 (3).

Notice to Director

(4) Each of the parties to a support order, if the support order or related support deduction order is filed in the Director's office, shall give to the Director notice of the termination of a support obligation under the order, in the manner and at such time as may be prescribed by the regulations. 1996, c. 31, s. 8 (4).

Disputes

(5) If the parties to the order do not agree or if the agency referred to in subsection (1) does not consent, the court that made the support order shall, on the motion of a party to the order or of the agency, decide if the support obligation has terminated and shall make an order to that effect. 1996, c. 31, s. 8 (5).

Same

(6) If the support order was not made by a court, the order described in subsection (5) shall be made by the Ontario Court (Provincial Division) or the Family Court. 1996, c. 31, s. 8 (6).

Order to repay

(7) A court that finds that a support obligation has terminated may order repayment in whole or in part from a person who received support after the obligation was terminated if the court is of the opinion that the person ought to have notified the Director that the support obligation had terminated. 1996, c. 31, s. 8 (7).

Same

(8) In determining whether to make an order under subsection (7), the court shall consider the circumstances of each of the parties to the support order. 1996, c. 31, s. 8 (8).

Continued enforcement

(9) The Director shall continue to enforce the support obligation until he or she receives a copy of the court's order terminating the support obligation. 1996, c. 31, s. 8 (9).

Same

(10) Despite the termination of a support obligation, the Director shall continue to enforce the support obligation in respect of any arrears which have accrued. 1996, c. 31, s. 8 (10).

Director not a party

(11) The Director is not a party to any proceeding to determine the entitlement of any person to support under a support order or to a motion to decide whether a support obligation has terminated. 1996, c. 31, s. 8 (11).

Note: On a day to be named by proclamation of the Lieutenant Governor, section 8 is repealed by the Statutes of Ontario, 2005, chapter 16, section 3 and the following substituted:
Director to cease enforcement

Termination of support obligation

8. (1) The Director shall cease enforcement of a support obligation provided for in a support order or support deduction order filed in the Director's office if the support obligation has terminated. 2005, c. 16, s. 3.

Agency's consent required

(2) Despite subsection (1), if the support order has been assigned to an agency described in subsection 33 (3) of the *Family Law Act*, the Director shall not cease enforcement without the agency's consent. 2005, c. 16, s. 3.

Payor's death

(3) The Director shall not enforce a support order or support deduction order against the estate of a payor after he or she is notified, in accordance with the regulations, of the payor's death. 2005, c. 16, s. 3.

How termination is determined

(4) For the purpose of subsection (1), a support obligation is terminated if,

(a)   the parties to the support order or support deduction order agree, in the manner prescribed by the regulations, that the support obligation has terminated;

(b)   the support order or support deduction order states that the support obligation terminates on a set calendar date, and that date arrives; or

(c)   a court orders that the obligation has terminated. 2005, c. 16, s. 3.

Notice to Director

(5) If a support order or related support deduction order is filed in the Director's office, each party to the support order shall give the Director notice of the termination of a support obligation under the order, in the manner and at the time prescribed by the regulations. 2005, c. 16, s. 3.

Disputes

(6) If the parties to the support order do not agree or if the agency referred to in subsection (2) does not consent, the court that made the support order shall, on the motion of a party to the support order or of the agency,

(a)   decide whether the support obligation has terminated; and

(b)   make an order to that effect. 2005, c. 16, s. 3.

Same

(7) If the support order was not made by a court, the order described in subsection (6) shall be made by the Ontario Court of Justice or the Family Court. 2005, c. 16, s. 3.

Same

(8) If an issue as to whether the support obligation has terminated arises within an application between the parties, it is not necessary to make a separate motion under subsection (6). 2005, c. 16, s. 3.

Order to repay

(9) A court that finds that a support obligation has terminated may order repayment in whole or in part from a person who received support after the obligation was terminated if the court is of the opinion that the person ought to have notified the Director that the support obligation had terminated. 2005, c. 16, s. 3.

Same

(10) In determining whether to make an order under subsection (9), the court shall consider the circumstances of each of the parties to the support order. 2005, c. 16, s. 3.

Role of Director

(11) An order under subsection (9) is not a support order and shall not be enforced by the Director. 2005, c. 16, s. 3.

Continued enforcement

(12) The Director shall continue to enforce the support obligation until he or she receives a copy of the court's order terminating the support obligation. 2005, c. 16, s. 3.

Same

(13) Despite the termination of a support obligation, the Director shall continue to enforce the support obligation in respect of any arrears that have accrued. 2005, c. 16, s. 3.

Director not a party

(14) The Director is not a party to,

(a) a proceeding to determine a person's entitlement to support under a support order; or

(b) a motion to decide whether a support obligation has terminated. 2005, c. 16, s. 3.

Director's discretion

8.1 (1) Despite section 5, the Director has discretion to discontinue enforcement of a support order or support deduction order that is filed in the Director's office if,

(a) the payor notifies the Director that the support obligation has terminated;

(b) the Director serves on the recipient a request to confirm or deny that the support obligation has terminated; and

(c) the recipient does not respond in writing within 20 days after being served. 2005, c. 16, s. 3.

Reinstatement

(2) If, after enforcement has been discontinued in accordance with subsection (1), the Director receives a written notice from the recipient denying that the support obligation has terminated, the Director may resume enforcement. 2005, c. 16, s. 3.

Discretion to enforce for lesser amount if child's entitlement ceases

8.2 (1) If the conditions set out in subsection (2) are satisfied with respect to a support order or support deduction order, the Director may exercise discretion to enforce a lesser amount of support in accordance with the table set out in the applicable child support guidelines. 2005, c. 16, s. 3.

Conditions

(2) The conditions referred to in subsection (1) are:

1. The order was made in accordance with the table set out in the applicable child support guidelines.

2. It has been agreed under clause 8 (4) (a) that the support obligation under the order has terminated with respect to a child.

3. The support obligation under the order still continues with respect to another child.
4. The order states,
   i. the number of children, and
   ii. the total amount of support determined in accordance with the table. 2005, c. 16, s. 3.

See: 2005, c. 16, ss. 3, 42 (2).

Part III
Support Orders and Support Deduction Orders — Making and Filing

Contents of support order
9. (1) Every support order made by an Ontario court, other than a provisional order, shall state in its operative part that unless the order is withdrawn from the Director's office, it shall be enforced by the Director and that amounts owing under the order shall be paid to the Director, who shall pay them to the person to whom they are owed. 1996, c. 31, s. 9 (1).

Court may require that order may not be withdrawn
(2) If the court considers it appropriate to do so, it may state in the operative part of the order, instead of the wording prescribed by subsection (1), that the order and the related support deduction order shall be enforced by the Director and that they cannot be withdrawn from the Director's office. 1996, c. 31, s. 9 (2).

Director retains discretion to not enforce orders
(3) Section 7 applies to every support order worded as provided in subsection (1) or (2), whether the order was made before or after this section comes into force and despite the wording of an order made under subsection (2). 1996, c. 31, s. 9 (3).

Support deduction orders to be made
10. (1) An Ontario court that makes a support order, as defined in subsection 1 (1), shall also make a support deduction order. 1996, c. 31, s. 10 (1).

New orders to be made
(2) When a support order is changed and the changed order is a support order as defined in subsection 1 (1), the court shall also make a support deduction order to reflect the change. 2005, c. 16, s. 4.

Transition
(3) When a support order, within the meaning of the *Family Support Plan Act* as it read immediately before its repeal by this Act, is changed and the changed order is a support order as defined in subsection 1 (1), the court shall also make a support deduction order to reflect the change. 2005, c. 16, s. 4.

Order mandatory

(4) A support deduction order shall be made even though the court cannot identify an income source in respect of the payor at the time the support order is made. 1996, c. 31, s. 10 (4).

Exception

(5) A support deduction order shall not be made in respect of a provisional order. 1996, c. 31, s. 10 (5).

Form of support deduction order

11. (1) A support deduction order shall be in the form prescribed by the regulations. 1996, c. 31, s. 11 (1).

Information re payor, income source

(2) Before making a support deduction order, the court shall make such inquiries of the parties as it considers necessary to determine the names and addresses of each income source of the payor and the amounts paid to the payor by each income source and shall make such other inquiries to obtain information as may be prescribed by the regulations. 1996, c. 31, s. 11 (2).

Same

(3) If the support order is sought on consent or by way of motion for judgment or if the making of the support order is uncontested, the parties shall give the court the particulars described in subsection (2) and such other information as may be prescribed by the regulations. 1996, c. 31, s. 11 (3).

Completion of form, etc.

(4) The support deduction order shall be completed and signed by the court, or by the clerk or registrar of the court, at the time the support order is made and shall be entered in the court records promptly after it is signed, even if the support order may not have been settled or signed at that time. 1996, c. 31, s. 11 (4).

Court to file orders

12. (1) The clerk or registrar of the court that makes a support order shall file it with the Director's office promptly after it is signed. 1996, c. 31, s. 12 (1).

Support deduction orders

(2) The clerk or registrar of the court that makes a support deduction order shall file it with the Director's office promptly after it is signed, even if the related support order may not have been settled or signed at the time. 1996, c. 31, s. 12 (2).

Orders of other jurisdictions

13. (1) When a support order made by a court outside Ontario is registered under subsection 19 (1) of the *Interjurisdictional Support Orders*

Act, 2002, the clerk who registers the order shall promptly file it with the Director's office, unless the order is accompanied by a notice signed by the person seeking enforcement stating that he or she does not want the order enforced by the Director. 2002, c. 13, s. 57 (2).

Same – *Divorce Act* (Canada) orders

(2) A support order made by a court outside Ontario under the *Divorce Act* (Canada) may be filed in the Director's office by the recipient under the order and, for the purpose of subsection 20 (3) of the *Divorce Act* (Canada), the order becomes enforceable by the Director upon its filing in the Director's office without it having been registered in a court in Ontario. 1996, c. 31, s. 13 (2).

Orders filed by Minister, etc.

14. (1) If a recipient has applied and is eligible for, or has received, a benefit under the *Family Benefits Act* or assistance under the *General Welfare Assistance Act* or the *Ontario Works Act, 1997* or income support under the *Ontario Disability Support Program Act, 1997,* a support order may be filed in the Director's office, whether or not the payor and recipient have given a notice to withdraw under subsection 16 (1.1), by the following:

1. The Ministry of Community and Social Services in the name of the Minister.

2. A municipality, excluding a lower-tier municipality in a regional municipality.

3. A district social services administration board under the *District Social Services Administration Boards Act.*

4. A band approved under section 15 of the *General Welfare Assistance Act.*

5. A delivery agent under the *Ontario Works Act, 1997.* 1997, c. 25, Sched. E, s. 2 (2); 2002, c. 17, Sched. F, Table; 2005, c. 16, s. 5 (1).

Same, reciprocating jurisdiction

(1.1) If a recipient has applied and is eligible for, or has received, social assistance benefits in a reciprocating jurisdiction, or if a support order has been assigned to a social assistance provider in a reciprocating jurisdiction, the support order may be filed in the Director's office by the social assistance provider in the reciprocating jurisdiction, whether or not the payor and recipient have given a notice to withdraw under subsection 16 (1.1). 2005, c. 16, s. 5 (2).

Same

(2) If a support order is filed under subsection (1) or (1.1), the related support deduction order, if any, shall be deemed to be filed in the Director's office at the same time. 1997, c. 25, Sched. E, s. 2 (2); 2005, c. 16, s. 5 (3).

Payors, recipients may file support orders

15. Subject to sections 12, 13 and 14, a support order may be filed in the Director's office only by the payor or recipient under the order. 1996, c. 31, s. 15.

Withdrawal of orders

16. (1) A support order or support deduction order filed in the office of the Director may be withdrawn at any time, as described in subsection (1.1), unless the support order states that it and the related support deduction order cannot be withdrawn from the Director's office. 2005, c. 16, s. 6.

Method

(1.1) Withdrawal is effected by a written notice signed by,

(a) the recipient and the payor, if the payor is in compliance as defined in the regulations; or

(b) the recipient, if the payor is not in compliance as defined in the regulations. 2005, c. 16, s. 6.

Consent of agency filing order

(2) A support order and related support deduction order, if any, that have been assigned to an agency referred to in subsection 14 (1) may not be withdrawn under subsection (1) except by the agency or with the consent of the agency so long as the orders are under assignment. 1997, c. 25, Sched. E, s. 2 (3).

Effect of withdrawal

(3) The Director shall cease enforcement of an order upon its withdrawal from the Director's office. 1996, c. 31, s. 16 (3).

Same

(4) If there are arrears owing to an agency referred to in subsection 14 (1) from a past assignment, the Director may continue to enforce the support order and related support deduction order, if any, to collect the arrears owed to the agency, even if the payor and recipient have withdrawn the orders under this section. 1997, c. 25, Sched. E, s. 2 (4).

Support and support deduction order must be withdrawn together

(5) A support order cannot be withdrawn under subsection (1) unless the related support deduction order, if any, is also withdrawn and a support deduction order cannot be withdrawn under subsection (1) unless the related support order, if any, is also withdrawn. 1996, c. 31, s. 16 (5).

Filing after withdrawal

(6) A support order or support deduction order that has been withdrawn under subsection (1) or that has been deemed to have been withdrawn under subsection 7 (3) may be filed in the office of the Director at any time by a written notice signed by either the payor or the recipient. 2001, c. 9, Sched. C, s. 1.

Effect

(7) Filing under subsection (6) has the same effect for all purposes, including the purposes of subsection 6 (2), as filing under sections 12 to 15. 2001, c. 9, Sched. C, s. 1.

Application

(7.1) Subsection (7) applies whether the order was filed under subsection (6) before or after the day the *Government Efficiency Act, 2001* receives Royal Assent. 2001, c. 9, Sched. C, s. 1.

Support and support deduction orders, filing together after withdrawal

(7.2) A support order cannot be filed under subsection (6) unless the related support deduction order, if any, is also filed and a support deduction order cannot be filed under subsection (6) unless the related support order is also filed. 2001, c. 9, Sched. C, s. 1.

Transition

(8) Despite subsection 6 (4), subsection (7) does not apply to an order that is not a support order as defined in subsection 1 (1), but was a support order within the meaning of the *Family Support Plan Act*, as it read immediately before its repeal by this Act, and was filed in the office of the Director of the Family Support Plan immediately before this section came into force. 1996, c. 31, s. 16 (8).

Notice of filings and withdrawals

17. The Director shall give notice of the filing or withdrawal of a support order or support deduction order to all the parties to the order, and at the request of any agency referred to in subsection 14 (1), to the agency. 1997, c. 25, Sched. E, s. 2 (5).

Duty to advise re unfiled support orders

18. Where a support deduction order that was made before this section came into force is filed in the Director's office but the related support order was never filed in the Director's office, the recipient shall inform the Director in writing of,

(a) the amount of money received on account of the support order other than by means of the support deduction order; and

(b) any changes in the amount to be paid under the support order. 1996, c. 31, s. 18; 2005, c. 16, s. 7.

Updating contact information

19. (1) A payor or recipient under a support order or support deduction order that is filed in the Director's office shall, within 10 days after any change in information listed in subsection (2), advise the Director of the details. 2005, c. 16, s. 8.

Same

(2) Subsection (1) applies with respect to,

(a) the payor's or recipient's home address, and the mailing address if different from the home address;

(b) all telephone numbers of the payor or recipient; and

(c)   other contact information, such as the payor's or recipient's work address, fax number or e-mail address, if the payor or recipient has previously provided that contact information to the Director. 2005, c. 16, s. 8.

Part IV
Support Deduction Orders — Enforcement

Director to enforce support deduction orders

20. (1) The Director shall enforce a support deduction order that is filed in the Director's office, subject to section 7, to any change made to the support deduction order and to any alternative payment order made under section 28, until the related support order is terminated and there are no arrears owing or until the support order and support deduction order are withdrawn. 2005, c. 16, s. 9.

Notice of support deduction order to income sources

(2) The Director may serve a notice of a support deduction order to each income source from whom the Director is seeking payment, and may serve new notices when the amount to be paid under a support order changes or arrears are owing. 1996, c. 31, s. 20 (2).

Contents of notice

(3) The notice shall set out the amount of support owed by the payor under the support order and may also set out any amount in arrears under the support order and the amount required to be paid by the income source to the Director. 1996, c. 31, s. 20 (3).

Notice to payor

(4) The Director shall send to the payor a copy of every notice sent under subsection (2). 1996, c. 31, s. 20 (4).

Notice deemed garnishment for *Family Orders and Agreements Enforcement Assistance Act* (Canada)

(5) A notice of a support deduction order shall be deemed to be a notice of garnishment made under provincial garnishment law for the purposes of the *Family Orders and Agreements Enforcement Assistance Act* (Canada). 1996, c. 31, s. 20 (5).

Support deduction order not affected by stay of enforcement of support order

(6) The operation or enforcement of a support deduction order is not affected by an order staying the enforcement of the related support order unless the support order is also stayed. 1996, c. 31, s. 20 (6).

Support deduction order deemed to be made

21. (1) A support deduction order shall be deemed to have been made in respect of a support order described in subsection (8) if,

(a) the recipient requests that the Director enforce the support order under this Part and the Director considers it practical to do so; or

(b) the Director considers it advisable to enforce the support order under this Part. 1996, c. 31, s. 21 (1).

Notice to payor

(2) The Director shall give notice to the payor of the Director's intention to enforce the support order under this Part. 1996, c. 31, s. 21 (2).

When and by what court deemed order is made

(3) The support deduction order shall, 30 days after the notice is served on the payor, be deemed to have been made by the court that made the support order or,

(a) if the support order was made under the *Divorce Act* (Canada) by a court outside Ontario, by the Superior Court of Justice or, where applicable, the Family Court;

(b) if the support order (other than an order under the *Divorce Act* (Canada)) was made by a court outside Ontario, by a court in Ontario that is the same level as the court that has the jurisdiction to make the order enforceable in Ontario;

(c) if the support order is a domestic contract or paternity agreement, by the Ontario Court of Justice or the Family Court. 1996, c. 31, s. 21 (3); 2005, c. 16, s. 10 (1, 2).

Alternative payment order

(4) The payor may, within 30 days after being served with the notice under subsection (2), make a motion for an alternative payment order under section 28, in the court that is deemed to have made the support deduction order. 2005, c. 16, s. 10 (3).

Delay of effective date

(5) If a motion is made under subsection (4), a deemed support deduction order does not come into force until the motion is determined. 1996, c. 31, s. 21 (5); 2005, c. 16, s. 10 (4).

Withdrawal of support deduction order

(6) Section 16 applies to a deemed support deduction order. 1996, c. 31, s. 21 (6).

No form required

(7) Subsection 11 (1) does not apply to a deemed support deduction order. 1996, c. 31, s. 21 (7).

Application of this section

(8) This section applies only to support orders filed in the Director's office that are,

(a) support orders made by an Ontario court before March 1, 1992;

(b) domestic contracts or paternity agreements that are enforceable under section 35 of the *Family Law Act*;

(c) support orders made by a court outside Ontario that are enforceable in Ontario. 1996, c. 31, s. 21 (8).

Duty of income source

22. (1) An income source that receives notice of a support deduction order, whether or not the income source is named in the order, shall, subject to section 23, deduct from the money the income source owes to the payor the amount of the support owed by the payor, or such other amount that is set out in the notice, and shall pay that amount to the Director. 1996, c. 31, s. 22 (1).

First payment

(2) The income source shall begin making payments to the Director not later than the day the first payment is to be paid to the payor that falls at least 14 days after the day on which the income source is served with the notice. 1996, c. 31, s. 22 (2).

Electronic payment

(2.1) The income source may make the payments by a prescribed method of electronic transmission. 2005, c. 16, s. 11.

Payor's duty to pay

(3) Until an income source begins deducting support payments in respect of a support deduction order or if payments by an income source are interrupted or terminated, the payor shall pay the amounts owing under the support order to the Director, if the support order is filed in the Director's office, or to the recipient, if the support order is not filed in the Director's office. 1996, c. 31, s. 22 (3).

Maximum deduction by income source

23. (1) The total amount deducted by an income source and paid to the Director under a support deduction order shall not exceed 50 per cent of the net amount owed by the income source to the payor. 1996, c. 31, s. 23 (1).

Note: Subsection (2) comes into force on a day to be named by proclamation of the Lieutenant Governor. See: 1996, c. 31, s. 74.

Deduction must equal ongoing support

(2) Despite subsection (1), the total amount deducted by an income source and paid to the Director under a support deduction order made or deemed to have been made after this section comes into force shall not be less than the amount of ongoing support specified in the support order, even if that amount is greater than 50 per cent of the net income owed by the income source to the payor, unless the court orders otherwise when it makes the support order. 1996, c. 31, s. 23 (2).

Exception for certain federal payments

(3) Despite subsection (1), up to 100 per cent of a payor's income tax refund or other lump sum payment that is attachable under the *Family Orders and Agreements Enforcement Assistance Act* (Canada) may be deducted and paid to the Director under a support deduction order. 1996, c. 31, s. 23 (3).

Note: Subsection (4) comes into force on a day to be named by proclamation of the Lieutenant Governor. See: 1996, c. 31, s. 74.

Transition

(4) The Director may, on notice to the payor, bring a motion to the court that made or is deemed to have made a support deduction order before this section comes into force, to increase the amount required to be deducted and paid to the Director up to the amount of the ongoing support specified in the support order, even if that amount is greater than 50 per cent of the net income owed by the income source to the payor. 1996, c. 31, s. 23 (4).

Note: On a day to be named by proclamation of the Lieutenant Governor, subsection (4) is amended by the Statutes of Ontario, 2005, chapter 16, section 12 by striking out "bring" and substituting "make." See: 2005, c. 16, ss. 12, 42 (2).

Interpretation – net amount

(5) For the purposes of this section,

"net amount" means the total amount owed by the income source to the payor at the time payment is to be made to the Director, less the total of the following deductions:

1. Income Tax.
2. Canada Pension Plan.
3. Employment Insurance.
4. Union dues.
5. Such other deductions as may be prescribed by the regulations. 1996, c. 31, s. 23 (5).

Same

(6) Despite any other provision of this Act, no deduction shall be made under a support deduction order in respect of amounts owing to a payor as reimbursement for expenses covered by a medical, health, dental or hospital insurance contract or plan. 1996, c. 31, s. 23 (6).

Crown bound by support deduction order

24. (1) A support deduction order is effective against the Crown only in respect of amounts payable on behalf of the administrative unit served with notice of the support deduction order to the payor named in the notice. 1996, c. 31, s. 24 (1).

Social assistance benefits

(2) Despite subsection (1), no amounts shall be deducted from any amount payable to a payor as a benefit under the *Family Benefits Act* or as assistance under the *General Welfare Assistance Act* or the *Ontario Works Act, 1997* or as income support under the *Ontario Disability Support Program Act, 1997*, in order to comply with a support deduction order unless authorized under the *Ontario Works Act, 1997* or the *Ontario Disability Support Program Act, 1997*. 1997, c. 25, Sched. E, s. 2 (6).

Definition

(3) In subsection (1),

"administrative unit" means a ministry of the Government of Ontario, a Crown agency within the meaning of the *Crown Agency Act* or the Office of the Assembly. 1996, c. 31, s. 24 (3).

Duty to inform re payment interruption

25. (1) Within 10 days after the termination or beginning of an interruption of payments by an income source to a payor, both the income source and the payor shall give written notice of the termination or interruption to the Director, together with such other information as may be required by the regulations. 1996, c. 31, s. 25 (1).

Same

(2) If notice has been or should have been given under subsection (1),

(a) the payor and the income source, within 10 days after the resumption of payments that have been interrupted, shall give written notice to the Director of the resumption;

(b) the payor, within 10 days of beginning employment with another income source or of becoming entitled to payments from another income source, shall give written notice to the Director of the new employment or entitlement and of the name and address of the income source. 1996, c. 31, s. 25 (2).

Disputes re income source

26. (1) If an individual, corporation or other entity served with notice of a support deduction order is not an income source of the payor named in the notice, the individual, corporation or other entity shall give written notice in the prescribed form of that fact to the Director within 10 days after the service of the notice. 1996, c. 31, s. 26 (1).

Same

(2) The Director or an individual, corporation or other entity who has notified the Director under subsection (1) may, on notice to each other, make a motion to the court that made or is deemed to have made the support deduction order to determine whether the individual, corporation or other entity is an income source. 1996, c. 31, s. 26 (2); 2005, c. 16, s. 13 (1).

Same

(3) The Director or an income source may, on notice to each other, make a motion to the court that made or is deemed to have made the support deduction order to determine,

(a) whether the income source has failed to comply with the order; or

(b) whether the amount the income source is deducting and paying to the Director under the order is correct. 1996, c. 31, s. 26 (3); 2005, c. 16, s. 13 (2).

Determination by court

(4) In a motion under subsection (2) or (3), the court shall determine the issue in a summary manner and make such order as it considers appropriate in the circumstances. 1996, c. 31, s. 26 (4).

Limitation

(5) A motion shall not be made under subsection (2) by an individual (other than the Director), corporation or other entity until at least 14 days after the individual, corporation or other entity gave written notice to the Director as required by subsection (1). 1996, c. 31, s. 26 (5); 2005, c. 16, s. 13 (3).

Same

(6) A motion shall not be made by an income source under subsection (3) unless the income source has given written particulars of the proposed motion to the Director at least 14 days before serving the Director with notice of the motion. 1996, c. 31, s. 26 (6); 2005, c. 16, s. 13 (4).

Liability

(7) An income source is liable to pay to the Director any amount that it failed without proper reason to deduct and pay to the Director after receiving notice of a support deduction order and, in a motion under subsection (3), the court may order the income source to pay the amount that it ought to have deducted and paid to the Director. 1996, c. 31, s. 26 (7).

Other enforcement

(8) In addition to any other method available to enforce an order in a civil proceeding, any order made under subsection (4) or (7) may be enforced under this Act in the same manner and with the same remedies as a support order. 1996, c. 31, s. 26 (8).

Disputes, etc., by payor

27. (1) A payor, on motion in the court that made or is deemed to have made the support deduction order,

(a) may dispute the amount being deducted by an income source under a support deduction order if he or she is of the opinion that because of a mistake of fact more is being deducted than is required under this Act;

(b) may dispute whether he or she has defaulted in paying support after an alternative payment order has been made under section 28;

(c) may seek relief regarding the amount that is being deducted by an income source under a support deduction order for arrears under a support order. 1996, c. 31, s. 27 (1); 2005, c. 16, s. 14 (1).

Motion to increase deductions for arrears

(2) If an order has been made on a motion under clause (1) (c), the Director may, on motion in the court that made the order, request that the amount to be deducted by an income source be increased if there has been an improvement in the payor's financial circumstances. 1996, c. 31, s. 27 (2).

Dispute over entitlement

(3) On a motion under subsection (1) or (2), the payor shall not dispute the entitlement of a person to support under a support order. 1996, c. 31, s. 27 (3).

Necessary party

(4) The Director is a necessary party to a motion under subsection (1) and the payor is a necessary party to a motion under subsection (2). 1996, c. 31, s. 27 (4).

Determination by court

(5) The court shall determine the issue in a motion under subsection (1) or (2) in a summary manner and make such order as it considers appropriate in the circumstances. 1996, c. 31, s. 27 (5).

Same

(6) On a motion under clause (1) (c), the payor shall be presumed to have the ability to pay the amount being deducted for arrears and the court may change the amount being deducted only if it is satisfied that the payor is unable for valid reasons to pay that amount, but this does not affect the accruing of arrears. 1996, c. 31, s. 27 (6); 2005, c. 16, s. 14 (2).

Change of support deduction order

(7) A court shall not change the amount to be paid under a support deduction order except under subsection (5) or 23 (4) or if the related support order is changed. 1996, c. 31, s. 27 (7); 2005, c. 16, s. 14 (3).

Alternative payment order

28. (1) A court that makes a support deduction order may make an order requiring the payor to make payments directly to the Director, at the same time as it makes the support deduction order, or subsequently on motion. 2005, c. 16, s. 15.

Same

(2) A court that is deemed to have made a support deduction order may, on a motion made under subsection 21 (4), make an order requiring the payor to make payments directly to the Director. 2005, c. 16, s. 15.

Effect on support order and support deduction order

(3) An alternative payment order made under subsection (1) or (2) suspends the support deduction order, but it does not affect the payor's obligations under the support order nor does it affect any other means of enforcing the support order. 2005, c. 16, s. 15.

Criteria

(4) The court may make an alternative payment order under subsection (1) or (2) only if,

(a) it finds that it would be unconscionable, having regard to all of the circumstances, to require the payor to make support payments by means of a support deduction order; or

(b) the parties to the support order agree that they do not want support payments collected by means of a support deduction order and the court requires the payor to post such security as it considers adequate and in accordance with the regulations. 2005, c. 16, s. 15.

Agency's consent required

(5) If the support order has been assigned to an agency described in subsection 33 (3) of the *Family Law Act* or if there are arrears owing to the agency from a past assignment, the court shall not make an alternative payment order in the circumstances described in clause (4) (b) without the agency's consent. 2005, c. 16, s. 15.

Unconscionable, determination

(6) The following shall not be considered by a court in determining whether it would be unconscionable to require a payor to make support payments by means of a support deduction order:

1. The fact that the payor has demonstrated a good payment history in respect of his or her debts, including support obligations.

2. The fact that the payor has had no opportunity to demonstrate voluntary compliance in respect of support obligations.

3. The fact that the parties have agreed to the making of an alternative payment order.

4. The fact that there are grounds upon which a court might find that the amount payable under the support order should be changed. 2005, c. 16, s. 15.

Security

(7) For the purposes of clause (4) (b), security shall be in a minimum amount equal to the support payable for four months and the security shall be in money or in such other form as may be prescribed in the regulations. 2005, c. 16, s. 15.

When Director is a party

(8) The Director is not a party to a motion made to obtain an alternative payment order, but if the motion relates to a support deduction order deemed to have been made under section 21, the Director,

    (a) shall also be served with notice of the motion; and

    (b) may be added as a party. 2005, c. 16, s. 15.

When agency is a party

(9) If the support order was filed in the Director's office by an agency under subsection 14 (1), or has been assigned to an agency referred to in that subsection, the agency,

    (a) shall also be served with notice of the motion; and

    (b) may be added as a party. 2005, c. 16, s. 15.

Completion of form, etc.

(10) An alternative payment order shall be completed and signed by the court or by the clerk or registrar of the court at the time it is made and

shall be entered in the court records promptly after it is signed. 2005, c. 16, s. 15.

Prompt filing

(11) The clerk or registrar of the court that makes an alternative payment order shall file it in the Director's office promptly after it is made. 2005, c. 16, s. 15.

Form and effective date

(12) An alternative payment order shall be in the form prescribed by the regulations and takes effect only when it is filed in the Director's office and every income source affected by the alternative payment order has received notice of it and of its effect on the support deduction order. 2005, c. 16, s. 15.

Termination of alternative payment order

(13) An alternative payment order is automatically terminated if the payor fails to post security of the type or within the time period set out in the alternative payment order or if the payor fails to comply with the support order. 2005, c. 16, s. 15.

Effect of termination

(14) When an alternative payment order is terminated under subsection (13), the support deduction order is reinstated and the Director may immediately realize on any security that was posted. 2005, c. 16, s. 15.

Effect of withdrawing support order and support deduction order

(15) If the support order and the related support deduction order are withdrawn from the Director's office while an alternative payment order is in effect, the alternative payment order is terminated and the Director shall repay to the payor any security that was posted. 2005, c. 16, s. 15.

Effect of changing support order or support deduction order

(16) If the support order or the related support deduction order is changed while an alternative payment order is in effect, the alternative payment order is terminated and the Director shall repay to the payor any security that was posted. 2005, c. 16, s. 15.

Transition

(17) A suspension order made under this section as it read on the day before section 15 of the *Family Responsibility and Support Arrears Enforcement Amendment Act, 2005* came into force has the same effect as an alternative payment order, and this Act applies to the suspension order as if it were an alternative payment order. 2005, c. 16, s. 15.

Income source to keep information confidential

29. Information about a payor obtained as a result of the application of this Part by an income source or an individual, corporation or other entity believed to be an income source shall not be disclosed by the income source or the individual, corporation or other entity, as the case may be, or any director, officer, employee or agent thereof, except for the purposes of complying with a support deduction order or this Act. 1996, c. 31, s. 29.

Priority of support deduction orders

30. (1) Despite any other Act, a support deduction order has the same priority over other judgment debts as a support order has under the *Creditors' Relief Act* and all support orders and support deduction orders rank equally with each other. 1996, c. 31, s. 30 (1).

Same

(2) If an income source is required to make payments to the Director under a support deduction order and the income source receives a garnishment notice related to the same support obligation, the income source shall make full payment under the support deduction order and the garnishment shall be of no effect until the income source has received notice from the Director that an alternative payment order has been made or that the support deduction order is terminated or withdrawn from the Director's office. 2005, c. 16, s. 16.

Anti-avoidance

31. An agreement by the parties to a support order to change enforcement of a support deduction order that is filed in the Director's office and any agreement or arrangement to avoid or prevent enforcement of a support deduction order that is filed in the Director's office are of no effect. 1996, c. 31, s. 31; 2005, c. 16, s. 17.

Conflict with other Acts

32. A support deduction order may be enforced despite any provision in any other Act protecting any payment owed by an income source to a payor from attachment or other process for the enforcement of a judgment debt. 1996, c. 31, s. 32.

Part V
Suspension of Drivers' Licences

Definition, Part V

33. In this Part,
"driver's licence" has the same meaning as in subsection 1 (1) of the *Highway Traffic Act*. 1996, c. 31, s. 33.

First notice

34. When a support order that is filed in the Director's office is in default, the Director may serve a first notice on the payor, informing the payor that his or her driver's licence may be suspended unless, within 30 days after the day the first notice is served,

(a) the payor makes an arrangement satisfactory to the Director for complying with the support order and for paying the arrears owing under the support order;

(b) the payor obtains an order to refrain under subsection 35 (1) and files the order in the Director's office; or

(c) the payor pays all arrears owing under the support order. 1996, c. 31, s. 34.

Order to refrain

35. (1) A payor who receives a first notice and makes a motion to change the support order may also, on notice to the Director, make a motion for an order that the Director refrain from directing the suspension of the payor's driver's licence under subsection 37 (1), on the terms that the court considers just, which may include payment terms. 2005, c. 16, s. 18.

Interjurisdictional Support Orders Act, 2002

(2) For the purposes of this section, submitting a support variation application to the designated authority in Ontario under the *Interjurisdictional Support Orders Act, 2002* has the same effect as making a motion to change a support order. 2005, c. 16, s. 18.

Effect on arrears

(3) Payment terms that are included in an order to refrain do not affect the accruing of arrears, nor do they affect any other means of enforcing the support order. 2005, c. 16, s. 18.

Exceptions

(4) Despite subsection (1), a motion for an order to refrain may be made,

(a) before making a motion to change the support order, on the undertaking of the payor or the payor's lawyer to obtain, within 20 days after the date of the order to refrain, a court date for the motion to change the support order; or

(b) without making a motion to change the support order, if the payor has started an appeal of the support order and the appeal has not been determined. 2005, c. 16, s. 18.

Court with jurisdiction to change support order

(5) A motion for an order to refrain shall be made in the court that has jurisdiction to change the support order. 2005, c. 16, s. 18.

Same

(6) The court that has jurisdiction to change a support order is,

(a) in the case of a support order that was made in Ontario,

(i) the court that made the support order, unless subclause (ii) applies,

(ii) if the support order is a provision in a domestic contract or paternity agreement, the Ontario Court of Justice or the Family Court; and

(b) in the case of a support order that was made outside Ontario,

(i) if the support order was made under the *Divorce Act* (Canada), the Superior Court of Justice or the Family Court,

(ii) if the support order is registered under the *Interjurisdictional Support Orders Act, 2002*, the court in Ontario that has jurisdiction under that Act to vary the support order. 2005, c. 16, s. 18.

Financial statement and proof of income

(7) A payor who makes a motion for an order to refrain shall serve and file,

(a) a financial statement, in the form prescribed by the regulations or in the form prescribed by the rules of court; and

(b) such proof of income as may be prescribed by the regulations. 2005, c. 16, s. 18.

Exception, undertaking

(8) Despite clause (7) (b), if the payor is unable to serve and file the proof of income before the motion is heard, the court may make the order to refrain subject to the undertaking of the payor or the payor's lawyer to serve and file the proof of income within 20 days. 2005, c. 16, s. 18.

Court may change or terminate order to refrain

(9) When an undertaking is made under subsection (8), the court may change or terminate the order to refrain, without proof of a material change in circumstances, on motion by the Director, if,

(a) the 20-day period has expired and the proof of income has not been served and filed; or

(b) the proof of income has been served and filed and the court is satisfied that a different order would have been made if the proof of income had been available when the motion for the order to refrain was heard. 2005, c. 16, s. 18.

Time limits and changing order to refrain

(10) A court shall not make an order to refrain after the 30-day period referred to in the first notice, but an order to refrain may be changed, on motion by the payor or the Director, at any time before the motion to change support is determined if there is a material change in the payor's circumstances. 2005, c. 16, s. 18.

Same

(11) A court may make an order to refrain only within the 30-day period referred to in the first notice and may make only one order to refrain in respect of any first notice. 2005, c. 16, s. 18.

Same

(12) For greater certainty, the 30-day period referred to in the first notice can not be extended for the purposes of subsections (10) and (11). 2005, c. 16, s. 18.

Same

(13) For greater certainty, if the 30-day period referred to in the first notice expires on a day when court offices are closed, the last day for making an order to refrain is the last day on which court offices are open before the 30-day period expires. 2005, c. 16, s. 18.

Order re arrears

(14) When a court that has determined a motion for an order to refrain also determines the related motion to change support, the court,

(a) shall state the amount of the arrears owing, after any change to the support order; and

(b) may make an order respecting payment of the arrears. 2005, c. 16, s. 18.

Same

(15) For the purpose of clause (14) (b), the court may make any order that may be made under clause 41 (10) (a), (b), (c), (e), (h) or (i) or subsection 41 (19) and, in the case of an order provided by clause 41 (10) (h) or (i), imprisonment does not discharge arrears under the support order. 2005, c. 16, s. 18.

When Director is a party

(16) The Director is not a party to a motion to change a support order referred to in subsection (1), but the Director and the payor are the only parties to a motion under subsection (1) for an order to refrain. 2005, c. 16, s. 18.

Filing with Director's office

(17) The court shall file a copy of the order in the Director's office promptly after the order is signed. 2005, c. 16, s. 18.

Form and effective date

(18) An order to refrain shall be in the form prescribed by the regulations and takes effect only when it is filed in the Director's office. 2005, c. 16, s. 18.

Duration of order

(19) An order to refrain terminates on the earliest of,

(a) the day the order to refrain is terminated under subsection (9);

(b) the day the motion to change or the appeal is determined;

(c) the day the support order is withdrawn from the Director's office; and

(d) the day that is six months after the order to refrain is made. 2005, c. 16, s. 18.

Exception

(20) Despite subsection (19), an order to refrain made before the making of a motion to change the support order is automatically terminated if the payor does not, within 20 days after the date of the order to refrain, obtain a court date for the motion to change the support order. 2005, c. 16, s. 18.

Extension of order

(21) The court that made an order to refrain may, on a motion made by the payor with notice to the Director, extend the order for one further period of,

(a) three months, unless clause (b) applies; or

(b) six months, if the motion to change is being dealt with under section 44 of the *Family Law Act*, sections 18 and 19 of the *Divorce Act* (Canada) or the *Interjurisdictional Support Orders Act, 2002.* 2005, c. 16, s. 18.

Time for extending order

(22) An extending order under subsection (21) shall not be made after the order to refrain has terminated. 2005, c. 16, s. 18.

Same

(23) For greater certainty, if the order to refrain terminates on a day when court offices are closed, the last day for making an extending order is the last day on which court offices are open before the order terminates. 2005, c. 16, s. 18.

Application of order

(24) An order to refrain is applicable only to the notice in respect of which the motion for an order to refrain was made under subsection (1). 2005, c. 16, s. 18.

Final notice

36. (1) The Director may serve a final notice on the payor if, at any time in the 24 months after the payor made an arrangement under clause 34 (a) or obtained an order under subsection 35 (1) or clause 35 (14) (b), the payor fails to comply with,

(a) the terms of the arrangement made with the Director in response to the first notice;

(b) the terms of an order to refrain under subsection 35 (1); or

(c) the terms of the changed support order and an order respecting payment of arrears under clause 35 (14) (b). 1996, c. 31, s. 36 (1); 2005, c. 16, s. 19.

Contents

(2) The final notice shall inform the payor that his or her driver's licence may be suspended,

(a) unless, within 15 days after the day the final notice is served,

(i) the payor complies with clause (1) (a), (b) or (c), or

(ii) the payor pays all arrears owing under the support order; or

(b) if, within 24 months after the payor makes an arrangement under clause (1) (a) or obtains an order under subsection 35 (1) or clause 35 (14) (b), the payor fails to comply with the arrangement or order. 1996, c. 31, s. 36 (2); 2005, c. 16, s. 19 (2).

Interpretation: arrangement in response to notice

(3) For the purposes of this section, an arrangement is made in response to a first notice if it is made within the time referred to in the first notice. 1996, c. 31, s. 36 (3).

Same

(4) An arrangement that is made in response to a first notice and is then amended by agreement in writing remains an arrangement made in response to the first notice. 1996, c. 31, s. 36 (4).

Direction to suspend
After first notice

37. (1) The Director may direct the Registrar of Motor Vehicles to suspend a payor's driver's licence if, within the 30-day period referred to in the first notice, the payor does not,

(a) make an arrangement satisfactory to the Director for complying with the support order;

(b) obtain an order to refrain under subsection 35 (1) and file the order in the Director's office; or

(c) pay all arrears owing under the support order. 1996, c. 31, s. 37 (1).

After final notice

(2) The Director may direct the Registrar of Motor Vehicles to suspend a payor's driver's licence if, within the 15-day period referred to in the final notice or at any time in the 24-month period referred to in the final notice, the payor does not,

(a) comply with clause 36 (1) (a), (b) or (c); or

(b) pay all arrears owing under the support order. 1996, c. 31, s. 37 (2); 2005, c. 16, s. 20.

Form of direction

(3) A direction under this section shall be in a form approved by the Director and the Registrar of Motor Vehicles. 1996, c. 31, s. 37 (3).

Direction to reinstate

38. (1) The Director shall direct the Registrar of Motor Vehicles to reinstate a driver's licence suspended as a result of a direction under section 37 if,

(a)   the payor pays all the arrears owing under the support order;

(b)   the payor is complying with the terms of the arrangement made with the Director in response to the first notice;

(c)   the payor is complying with the terms of an order to refrain that has not expired;

(d)   the support order has been changed and the payor is complying with the terms of the changed support order, including the terms of any order under clause 35 (14) (b) that relates to the support order;

(d.1)   the payor makes an arrangement satisfactory to the Director for complying with the support order and for paying the arrears owing under the support order; or

(e)   the support order is withdrawn under section 16. 1996, c. 31, s. 38 (1); 2005, c. 16, s. 21 (1).

Notice revived if payor breaches arrangement or order

(2) If the Director directs the Registrar of Motor Vehicles to reinstate a driver's licence under clause (1) (b), (c) or (d) and the payor subsequently defaults within 24 months from the date of reinstatement or if the payor subsequently defaults within 24 months after the payor entered into an

arrangement under clause 34 (a) or obtained an order under clause 35 (14) (b), the Director may proceed to act in accordance with the most recent notice that was served on the payor under this Part. 1996, c. 31, s. 38 (2); 2005, c. 16, s. 21 (2).

More than one order in default

(3) If the payor is in default on one or more other support orders, the Director shall not direct the Registrar of Motor Vehicles to reinstate the driver's licence unless,

(a) all arrears under all the support orders are paid;

(b) an arrangement or arrangements have been made, on terms satisfactory to the Director, to pay all arrears under all the support orders, and the payor is in compliance with the arrangement or arrangements; or

(c) all arrears under all the support orders are the subject of a court order or orders for payment and the payor is in compliance with the court order or orders. 2005, c. 16, s. 21 (3).

Discretion to reinstate

(4) The Director may direct the Registrar of Motor Vehicles to reinstate a driver's licence suspended as a result of a direction under section 37 if, in the opinion of the Director, it would be unconscionable not to do so. 1996, c. 31, s. 38 (4); 2005, c. 16, s. 21 (4).

Form of direction

(5) A direction under this section shall be in a form approved by the Director and the Registrar of Motor Vehicles. 1996, c. 31, s. 38 (5).

Anti-avoidance

39. An agreement by the parties to a support order to avoid or prevent its enforcement under this Part is of no effect. 1996, c. 31, s. 39.

Note: On a day to be named by proclamation of the Lieutenant Governor, Part V is repealed by section 64 and the following substituted:

Part V
Suspension of Drivers' Licences and Vehicle Permits

Definitions, Part V

33. In this Part,

"driver's licence" has the same meaning as in subsection 1 (1) of the *Highway Traffic Act*; ("permis de conduire")

"permit" means a permit, or a portion of a permit, issued exclusively in the name of an individual under subsection 7 (7) of the *Highway Traffic Act*, but does not include a permit issued in respect of a commercial motor vehicle, as defined in subsection 16 (1) of that Act, or in respect of a trailer. ("certificat d'immatriculation") 1996, c. 31, s. 64.

First notice

34. When a support order that is filed in the Director's office is in default, the Director may serve a first notice on the payor, informing the payor that his or her driver's licence and permit may be suspended and his or her permit may not be validated and he or she may be refused issuance of a new permit unless, within 30 days after the day the first notice is served,

(a)   the payor makes an arrangement satisfactory to the Director for complying with the support order and for paying the arrears owing under the support order;

(b)   the payor obtains an order to refrain under subsection 35 (1) and files the order in the Director's office; or

(c)   the payor pays all arrears owing under the support order. 1996, c. 31, s. 64.

Order to refrain

35. (1) A payor who receives a first notice may, on notice to the Director, in an application to vary the support order, make a motion for an order that the Director refrain from making a direction under subsection 37 (1) on the terms that the court considers just. 1996, c. 31, s. 64.

Exception

(2) Despite subsection (1), a motion for an order that the Director refrain from directing the suspension of the payor's driver's licence may be made before the commencement of an application to vary the support order on the undertaking of the payor or the payor's solicitor to commence the proceeding forthwith. 1996, c. 31, s. 64.

Time limits and variation

(3) A court shall not make an order to refrain after the 30-day period referred to in the first notice, but an order to refrain may be varied, on motion by the payor or the Director, at any time before the application to vary support is determined if there is a material change in the payor's circumstances. 1996, c. 31, s. 64.

Same

(4) A court may make an order to refrain only within the 30-day period referred to in the first notice and may make only one order to refrain in respect of any first notice. 1996, c. 31, s. 64.

Order re arrears

(5) When determining the variation application, a court that makes an order to refrain,

(a)   shall state the amount of the arrears owing, after any variation; and

(b)   may make an order respecting payment of the arrears. 1996, c. 31, s. 64.

Same

(6) For the purpose of clause (5) (b), the court may make any order that may be made under clause 41 (9) (a), (b), (c), (d), (g) or (h) or

subsection 41 (16) and, in the case of an order provided for in clause 41 (9) (g) or (h), imprisonment does not discharge arrears under the support order. 1996, c. 31, s. 64.

When Director is a party

(7) The Director is not a party to an application to vary a support order referred to in subsection (1), but the Director and the payor are the only parties to a motion under subsection (1) for an order to refrain. 1996, c. 31, s. 64.

Filing with Director's office

(8) The court shall file a copy of the order in the Director's office promptly after the order is signed. 1996, c. 31, s. 64.

Form and effective date

(9) An order to refrain shall be in the form prescribed by the regulations and takes effect only when it is filed in the Director's office. 1996, c. 31, s. 64.

Duration of order

(10) An order to refrain terminates on the earliest of the day the application to vary is determined, the day the support order is withdrawn from the Director's office and the day that is six months after the order to refrain is made. 1996, c. 31, s. 64.

Exception

(11) Despite subsection (10), an order to refrain made before the commencement of an application to vary the support order is automatically terminated if the payor does not commence the application within 20 days of the date of the order to refrain. 1996, c. 31, s. 64.

Extension of order

(12) The court that makes an order to refrain may, on a motion by the payor before the order terminates and with notice to the Director, extend the order for one further period of three months. 1996, c. 31, s. 64.

Application of order

(13) An order to refrain is applicable only to the notice in respect of which the motion was made under subsection (1). 1996, c. 31, s. 64.

Note: On a day to be named by proclamation of the Lieutenant Governor, section 35, as set out in the Statutes of Ontario, 1996, chapter 31, section 64, is repealed by the Statutes of Ontario, 2005, chapter 16, section 37 and the following substituted:

Order to refrain

35. (1) A payor who receives a first notice and makes a motion to change the support order may also, on notice to the Director, make a motion for an order that the Director refrain from making a direction under subsection 37 (1), on the terms that the court considers just, which may include payment terms. 2005, c. 16, s. 37.

Interjurisdictional Support Orders Act, 2002

(2) For the purposes of this section, submitting a support variation application to the designated authority in Ontario under the *Interjurisdictional Support Orders Act, 2002* has the same effect as making a motion to change a support order. 2005, c. 16, s. 37.

Effect on arrears

(3) Payment terms that are included in an order to refrain do not affect the accruing of arrears, nor do they affect any other means of enforcing the support order. 2005, c. 16, s. 37.

Exceptions

(4) Despite subsection (1), a motion for an order to refrain may be made,

(a) before making a motion to change the support order, on the undertaking of the payor or the payor's lawyer to obtain, within 20 days after the date of the order to refrain, a court date for the motion to change the support order; or

(b) without making a motion to change the support order, if the payor has started an appeal of the support order and the appeal has not been determined. 2005, c. 16, s. 37.

Court with jurisdiction to change support order

(5) A motion for an order to refrain shall be made in the court that has jurisdiction to change the support order. 2005, c. 16, s. 37.

Same

(6) The court that has jurisdiction to change a support order is,

(a) in the case of a support order that was made in Ontario,

(i) the court that made the support order, unless subclause (ii) applies,

(ii) if the support order is a provision in a domestic contract or paternity agreement, the Ontario Court of Justice or the Family Court; and

(b) in the case of a support order that was made outside Ontario,

(i) if the support order was made under the *Divorce Act* (Canada), the Superior Court of Justice or the Family Court,

(ii) if the support order is registered under the *Interjurisdictional Support Orders Act, 2002*, the court in Ontario that has jurisdiction under that Act to vary the support order. 2005, c. 16, s. 37.

Financial statement and proof of income

(7) A payor who makes a motion for an order to refrain shall serve and file,

(a) a financial statement, in the form prescribed by the regulations or in the form prescribed by the rules of court; and

(b) such proof of income as may be prescribed by the regulations. 2005, c. 16, s. 37.

Exception, undertaking

(8) Despite clause (7) (b), if the payor is unable to serve and file the

proof of income before the motion is heard, the court may make the order to refrain subject to the undertaking of the payor or the payor's lawyer to serve and file the proof of income within 20 days. 2005, c. 16, s. 37.

Court may change or terminate order to refrain

(9) When an undertaking is made under subsection (8), the court may change or terminate the order to refrain, without proof of a material change in circumstances, on motion by the Director, if,

(a) the 20-day period has expired and the proof of income has not been served and filed; or

(b) the proof of income has been served and filed and the court is satisfied that a different order would have been made if the proof of income had been available when the motion for the order to refrain was heard. 2005, c. 16, s. 37.

Time limits and changing order to refrain

(10) A court shall not make an order to refrain after the 30-day period referred to in the first notice, but an order to refrain may be changed, on motion by the payor or the Director, at any time before the motion to change support is determined if there is a material change in the payor's circumstances. 2005, c. 16, s. 37.

Same

(11) A court may make an order to refrain only within the 30-day period referred to in the first notice and may make only one order to refrain in respect of any first notice. 2005, c. 16, s. 37.

Same

(12) For greater certainty, the 30-day period referred to in the first notice can not be extended for the purposes of subsections (10) and (11). 2005, c. 16, s. 37.

Same

(13) For greater certainty, if the 30-day period referred to in the first notice expires on a day when court offices are closed, the last day for making an order to refrain is the last day on which court offices are open before the 30-day period expires. 2005, c. 16, s. 37.

Order re arrears

(14) When a court that has determined a motion for an order to refrain also determines the related motion to change support, the court,

(a) shall state the amount of the arrears owing, after any change to the support order; and

(b) may make an order respecting payment of the arrears. 2005, c. 16, s. 37.

Same

(15) For the purpose of clause (14) (b), the court may make any order that may be made under clause 41 (10) (a), (b), (c), (e), (h) or (i) or subsection 41 (19) and, in the case of an order provided by clause 41 (10) (h) or (i), imprisonment does not discharge arrears under the support order. 2005, c. 16, s. 37.

When Director is a party

(16) The Director is not a party to a motion to change a support order referred to in subsection (1), but the Director and the payor are the only parties to a motion under subsection (1) for an order to refrain. 2005, c. 16, s. 37.

Filing with Director's office

(17) The court shall file a copy of the order in the Director's office promptly after the order is signed. 2005, c. 16, s. 37.

Form and effective date

(18) An order to refrain shall be in the form prescribed by the regulations and takes effect only when it is filed in the Director's office. 2005, c. 16, s. 37.

Duration of order

(19) An order to refrain terminates on the earliest of,

(a) the day the order to refrain is terminated under subsection (9);

(b) the day the motion to change or the appeal is determined;

(c) the day the support order is withdrawn from the Director's office; and

(d) the day that is six months after the order to refrain is made. 2005, c. 16, s. 37.

Exception

(20) Despite subsection (19), an order to refrain made before the making of a motion to change the support order is automatically terminated if the payor does not, within 20 days after the date of the order to refrain, obtain a court date for the motion to change the support order. 2005, c. 16, s. 37.

Extension of order

(21) The court that made an order to refrain may, on a motion made by the payor with notice to the Director, extend the order for one further period of,

(a) three months, unless clause (b) applies; or

(b) six months, if the motion to change is being dealt with under section 44 of the *Family Law Act*, sections 18 and 19 of the *Divorce Act* (Canada) or the *Interjurisdictional Support Orders Act, 2002*. 2005, c. 16, s. 37.

Time for extending order

(22) An extending order under subsection (21) shall not be made after the order to refrain has terminated. 2005, c. 16, s. 37.

Same

(23) For greater certainty, if the order to refrain terminates on a day when court offices are closed, the last day for making an extending order is the last day on which court offices are open before the order terminates. 2005, c. 16, s. 37.

Application of order

(24) An order to refrain is applicable only to the notice in respect of which the motion for an order to refrain was made under subsection (1).

2005, c. 16, s. 37.
See: 2005, c. 16, ss. 37, 42 (2).

Second notice

36. (1) The Director may serve a second notice on the payor if, at any time in the 24 months after the payor made an arrangement under clause 34 (a) or obtained an order under subsection 35 (1) or clause 35 (5) (b), the payor fails to comply with,

Note: On a day to be named by proclamation of the Lieutenant Governor, subsection (1) is amended by the Statutes of Ontario, 2005, chapter 16, subsection 38 (2) by striking out "second notice" and substituting in each case "final notice." See: 2005, c. 16, ss. 38 (2), 42 (2).

> (a)   the terms of the arrangement made with the Director in response to the first notice;
> (b)   the terms of an order to refrain under subsection 35 (1); or
> (c)   the terms of the varied support order and an order respecting payment of arrears under clause 35 (5) (b). 1996, c. 31, s. 64.

Note: On a day to be named by proclamation of the Lieutenant Governor, clause (c) is amended by the Statutes of Ontario, 2005, chapter 16, subsection 38 (1) by striking out "varied support order" and substituting "changed support order." See: 2005, c. 16, ss. 38 (1), 42 (2).

Note: On a day to be named by proclamation of the Lieutenant Governor, subsection (1) is amended by the Statutes of Ontario, 2005, chapter 16, subsection 38 (2) by striking out "clause 35 (5) (b)" wherever it appears and substituting in each case "clause 35 (14) (b)." See: 2005, c. 16, ss. 38 (2), 42 (2).

Contents

(2) The second notice shall inform the payor that his or her driver's licence and permit may be suspended, his or her permit may not be validated and he or she may be refused issuance of a new permit,

> (a)   unless, within 15 days after the day the second notice is served,
> > (i)   the payor complies with clause (1) (a), (b) or (c), or
> > (ii)   the payor pays all arrears owing under the support order; or
> (b)   if, within 24 months after the payor makes an arrangement under clause (1) (a) or obtains an order under subsection 35 (1) or clause 35 (5) (b), the payor fails to comply with the arrangement or order. 1996, c. 31, s. 64.

Note: On a day to be named by proclamation of the Lieutenant Governor, clause (b) is amended by the Statutes of Ontario, 2005, chapter 16, subsection 38 (2) by striking out "clause 35 (5) (b)" and substituting "clause 35 (14) (b)." See: 2005, c. 16, ss. 38 (2), 42 (2).

Note: On a day to be named by proclamation of the Lieutenant Governor, subsection (2) is amended by the Statutes of Ontario, 2005, chapter 16, subsection 38 (2) by striking out "second notice" wherever it appears and substituting in each case "final notice." See: 2005, c. 16, ss. 38 (2), 42 (2).

Interpretation: arrangement in response to notice

(3) For the purposes of this section, an arrangement is made in response to a first notice if it is made within the time referred to in the first notice. 1996, c. 31, s. 64.

Same

(4) An arrangement that is made in response to a first notice and is then amended by agreement in writing remains an arrangement made in response to the first notice. 1996, c. 31, s. 64.

Direction to suspend
After first notice

37. (1) The Director may direct the Registrar of Motor Vehicles to suspend a payor's driver's licence and permit or to refuse to validate his or her permit or to refuse to issue a new permit to the payor if, within the 30-day period referred to in the first notice, the payor does not,

    (a)   make an arrangement satisfactory to the Director for complying with the support order;

    (b)   obtain an order to refrain under subsection 35 (1) and file the order in the Director's office; or

    (c)   pay all arrears owing under the support order. 1996, c. 31, s. 64.

After second notice

(2) The Director may direct the Registrar of Motor Vehicles to suspend a payor's driver's licence and permit or to refuse to validate his or her permit or to refuse to issue a new permit to the payor if, within the 15-day period referred to in the second notice or at any time in the 24-month period referred to in the second notice, the payor does not,

    (a)   comply with clause 36 (1) (a), (b) or (c); or

    (b)   pay all arrears owing under the support order. 1996, c. 31, s. 64.

Note: On a day to be named by proclamation of the Lieutenant Governor, subsection (2) is amended by the Statutes of Ontario, 2005, chapter 16, subsection 39 by striking out "second notice" wherever it appears and substituting in each case "final notice." See: 2005, c. 16, ss. 39, 42 (2).

Form of direction
(3) A direction under this section shall be in a form approved by the Director and the Registrar of Motor Vehicles and may contain any one or more of the directions that the Director is permitted to make under this section. 1996, c. 31, s. 64.

Direction to reinstate
38. (1) The Director shall direct the Registrar of Motor Vehicles to reinstate a driver's licence and permit suspended as a result of a direction under section 37 and to rescind a direction under section 37 to refuse to validate a permit or to refuse to issue a new permit to the payor if,
    (a) the payor pays all the arrears owing under the support order;
    (b) the payor is complying with the terms of the arrangement made with the Director in response to the first notice;
    (c) the payor is complying with the terms of the support order as well as the terms of any order under section 35 or 41 that relates to the support order;

Note: On a day to be named by proclamation of the Lieutenant Governor, clause (c) is repealed by the Statutes of Ontario, 2005, chapter 16, subsection 40 (1) and the following substituted:
    (c) the payor is complying with the terms of an order to refrain that has not expired;
See: 2005, c. 16, ss. 40 (1), 42 (2).
    (d) the payor makes an arrangement satisfactory to the Director for complying with the support order;

Note: On a day to be named by proclamation of the Lieutenant Governor, clause (d) is repealed by the Statutes of Ontario, 2005, chapter 16, subsection 40 (1) and the following substituted:
    (d) the support order has been changed and the payor is complying with the terms of the changed support order, including the terms of any order under clause 35 (14) (b) that relates to the support order;
    (d.1) the payor makes an arrangement satisfactory to the Director for complying with the support order and for paying the arrears owing under the support order;
See: 2005, c. 16, ss. 40 (1), 42 (2).
    (e) the support order is withdrawn under section 16; or
    (f) in the case of a permit issued in respect of a vehicle that is registered as a security interest under the *Personal Property Security Act*, the secured party enforces on the security interest and requests that the Director direct the reinstatement of the permit for that purpose. 1996, c. 31, s. 64.

Notice revived if payor breaches arrangement or order
(2) If the Director directs the Registrar of Motor Vehicles under clause

(1) (b), (c) or (d) and the payor subsequently defaults within 24 months from the date of reinstatement or if the payor subsequently defaults within 24 months after the payor entered into an arrangement under clause 34 (a) or obtained an order under clause 35 (5) (b), the Director may proceed to act in accordance with the last notice that was served on the payor under this Part. 1996, c. 31, s. 64.

Note: On a day to be named by proclamation of the Lieutenant Governor, subsection (2) is amended by the Statutes of Ontario, 2005, chapter 16, subsection 40 (2) by striking out "clause 35 (5) (b)" and substituting "clause 35 (14) (b)" and by striking out "last notice" and substituting "most recent notice". See: 2005, c. 16, ss. 40 (2), 42 (2).

Where more than one order in default

(3) Where the payor is in default on one or more other support orders, the Director shall not direct the Registrar of Motor Vehicles to reinstate a driver's licence or permit or to validate a permit or issue a new permit unless all arrears under all the support orders are,

(a)   paid;

(b)   arranged to be paid on terms satisfactory to the Director and the payor is in compliance with such arrangement or arrangements; or

(c)   the subject of a court order or orders for payment and the payor is in compliance with such court order or orders. 1996, c. 31, s. 64.

Note: On a day to be named by proclamation of the Lieutenant Governor, subsection (3) is repealed by the Statutes of Ontario, 2005, chapter 16, subsection 40 (3) and the following substituted:

More than one order in default

(3)   If the payor is in default on one or more other support orders, the Director shall not direct the Registrar of Motor Vehicles to reinstate a driver's licence or permit or to validate a permit or issue a new permit unless,

(a)   all arrears under all the support orders are paid;

(b)   an arrangement or arrangements have been made, on terms satisfactory to the Director, to pay all arrears under all the support orders, and the payor is in compliance with the arrangement or arrangements; or

(c)   all arrears under all the support orders are the subject of a court order or orders for payment and the payor is in compliance with the court order or orders. 2005, c. 16, s. 40 (3).

See: 2005, c. 16, ss. 40 (3), 42 (2).

Discretion to reinstate

(4) The Director may direct the Registrar of Motor Vehicles to reinstate a driver's licence or permit suspended as a result of a direction under section 37 or tovalidate a permit or issue a new permit if the validation or issuance was refused as a result of a direction under section 37 if, in the opinion of the Director, it would be unconscionable not to do so. 1996, c. 31, s. 64.

Note: On a day to be named by proclamation of the Lieutenant Governor, the French version of subsection (4) is amended by the Statutes of Ontario, 2005, chapter 16, subsection 40 (4) by striking out "déraisonnable" and substituting "inadmissible". See: 2005, c. 16, ss. 40 (4), 42 (2).

Form of direction

(5) A direction under this section shall be in a form approved by the Director and the Registrar of Motor Vehicles and may contain one or more of the directions that the Director is permitted to make under this section. 1996, c. 31, s. 64.

Anti-avoidance

39. An agreement by the parties to a support order to avoid or prevent its enforcement under this Part is of no effect. 1996, c. 31, s. 64.

See: 1996, c. 31, ss. 64, 74.

Note: On a day to be named by proclamation of the Lieutenant Governor, the Act is amended by the Statutes of Ontario, 2005, chapter 16, section 22 by adding the following Part:

Part V.1
Suspension of Licences under fish and wildlife conservation Act, 1997

Definition, Part V.1

39.1 In this Part,

"licences," when used with respect to a payor, means any hunting and sport fishing licences that,

(a)   have been issued to the payor under the *Fish and Wildlife Conservation Act, 1997*, and

(b)   belong to a class that is prescribed by the regulations. 2005, c. 16, s. 22.

Suspension
Notice
39.2 (1) When a support order that is filed in the Director's office is in default, the Director may serve a notice on the payor, informing the payor that his or her licences may be suspended unless, within 30 days after the day the notice is served,

(a) the payor makes an arrangement satisfactory to the Director for complying with the support order and for paying the arrears owing under the support order; or

(b) the payor pays all arrears owing under the support order. 2005, c. 16, s. 22.

Request
(2) The Director may request that the Minister of Natural Resources suspend a payor's licences if, within the 30-day period referred to in the notice, the payor does not,

(a) make an arrangement satisfactory to the Director for complying with the support order; or

(b) pay all arrears owing under the support order. 2005, c. 16, s. 22.

Form
(3) A request under this section shall be in a form approved by the Director and the Minister of Natural Resources. 2005, c. 16, s. 22.

Reinstatement

Request
39.3 (1) The Director shall request that the Minister of Natural Resources reinstate a payor's licences that were suspended as a result of a request under section 39.2 if,

(a) the payor pays all the arrears owing under the support order;

(b) the payor is complying with the terms of the arrangement made with the Director in response to the notice;

(c) the support order has been changed and the payor is complying with the terms of the changed support order;

(d) the payor makes an arrangement satisfactory to the Director for complying with the support order and for paying the arrears owing under the support order; or

(e) the support order is withdrawn under section 16. 2005, c. 16, s. 22.

Notice revived if payor breaches arrangement or order
(2) If the Director requests that the Minister of Natural Resources reinstate a payor's licences under clause (1) (b), (c) or (d) and the payor subsequently defaults within 24 months from the date of reinstatement or if the payor subsequently defaults within 24 months after the payor entered into an arrangement under clause 39.2 (1) (a), the Director may again request that the Minister of Natural Resources suspend the payor's

licences in accordance with the notice served under section 39.2. 2005, c. 16, s. 22.

More than one order in default

(3) If the payor is in default on one or more other support orders, the Director shall not request that the Minister of Natural Resources reinstate the payor's licences unless,

(a) all arrears under all the support orders are paid;

(b) an arrangement or arrangements have been made, on terms satisfactory to the Director, to pay all arrears under all the support orders, and the payor is in compliance with the arrangement or arrangements; or

(c) all arrears under all the support orders are the subject of a court order or orders for payment and the payor is in compliance with the court order or orders. 2005, c. 16, s. 22.

Discretion to request reinstatement

(4) The Director may request that the Minister of Natural Resources reinstate a payor's licences that were suspended as a result of a request under section 39.2 if, in the opinion of the Director, it would be unconscionable not to do so. 2005, c. 16, s. 22.

Form

(5) A request under this section shall be in a form approved by the Director and the Minister of Natural Resources. 2005, c. 16, s. 22.

Anti-avoidance

39.4 An agreement by the parties to a support order to avoid or prevent its enforcement under this Part is of no effect. 2005, c. 16, s. 22.

See: 2005, c. 16, ss. 22, 42 (2).

Part VI
Other Enforcement Mechanisms

Financial statements

40. (1) The Director may request that a payor who is in default under a support order, where the support order or related support deduction order is filed in the Director's office, complete and deliver to the Director a financial statement in the form prescribed by the regulations together with such proof of income as may be required by the regulations. 1996, c. 31, s. 40 (1).

Same

(2) The payor shall deliver the completed financial statement to the Director within 15 days after he or she was served with the request to complete the form. 1996, c. 31, s. 40 (2).

Changes in information

(3) If a payor discovers that any information was incomplete or wrong at the time he or she completed the financial statement, he or she shall, within 10 days of the discovery, deliver the corrected information to the Director. 1996, c. 31, s. 40 (3).

Failure to comply

(4) The Ontario Court of Justice or the Family Court, on the motion of the Director, may order a payor to comply with a request under subsection (1) and subsections 41 (6) and (7) apply with necessary modifications. 1996, c. 31, s. 40 (4); 2005, c. 16, s. 23.

Limitation

(5) The Director may request a financial statement under this section once in any six-month period but this does not restrict the Director's right to obtain a financial statement under section 41. 1996, c. 31, s. 40 (5).

Default hearing

41. (1) When a support order that is filed in the Director's office is in default, the Director may prepare a statement of the arrears and, by notice served on the payor together with the statement of arrears, may require the payor to deliver to the Director a financial statement and such proof of income as may be required by the regulations and to appear before the court to explain the default. 2005, c. 16, s. 24.

Same

(2) When a support order that is not filed in the Director's office is in default, the recipient may file a request with the court, together with a statement of arrears, and, on such filing, the clerk of the court shall, by notice served on the payor together with the statement of arrears, require the payor to file a financial statement and appear before the court to explain the default. 2005, c. 16, s. 24.

Persons financially connected to payor

(3) The Director or the recipient may, at any time during a default hearing under subsection (1) or (2), request that the court make an order under subsection (4) or (5) or both. 2005, c. 16, s. 24.

Financial statement

(4) The court may, by order, require a person to file a financial statement and any other relevant documents with the court if the court is satisfied that the person is financially connected to the payor. 2005, c. 16, s. 24.

Adding party

(5) The court may, by order, add a person as a party to the hearing if the court,

    (a) has made or could make an order under subsection (4); and

    (b) is satisfied on considering all the circumstances, including the purpose and effect of the dealings between the person and the

payor and their benefit or expected benefit to the payor, that there is some evidence that the person has sheltered assets or income of the payor such that enforcement of the support order against the payor may be frustrated. 2005, c. 16, s. 24.

Form of statements

(6) A financial statement and statement of arrears required by subsection (2) shall be in the form prescribed by the rules of the court and a financial statement required by subsection (1) or (4) shall be in the form prescribed by the regulations. 2005, c. 16, s. 24.

Arrest of payor

(7) If the payor fails to file the financial statement or to appear as the notice under subsection (1) or (2) requires, the court may issue a warrant for the payor's arrest for the purpose of bringing him or her before the court. 2005, c. 16, s. 24.

Bail

(8) Section 150 (interim release by justice of the peace) of the *Provincial Offences Act* applies with necessary modifications to an arrest under the warrant. 2005, c. 16, s. 24.

Presumptions at hearing

(9) At the default hearing, unless the contrary is shown, the payor shall be presumed to have the ability to pay the arrears and to make subsequent payments under the order, and the statement of arrears prepared and served by the Director shall be presumed to be correct as to arrears accruing while the order is filed in the Director's office. 2005, c. 16, s. 24.

Powers of court

(10) The court may, unless it is satisfied that the payor is unable for valid reasons to pay the arrears or to make subsequent payments under the order, order that the payor,

(a) pay all or part of the arrears by such periodic payments as the court considers just, but an order for partial payment does not rescind any unpaid arrears;

(b) discharge the arrears in full by a specified date;

(c) comply with the order to the extent of the payor's ability to pay;

(d) make a motion to change the support order;

(e) provide security in such form as the court directs for the arrears and subsequent payment;

(f) report periodically to the court, the Director or a person specified in the order;

(g) provide to the court, the Director or a person specified in the order particulars of any future change of address or employment as soon as they occur;

(h) be imprisoned continuously or intermittently until the period specified in the order, which shall not be more than 180 days, has

expired, or until the arrears are paid, whichever is sooner; and
(i)   on default in any payment ordered under this subsection, be imprisoned continuously or intermittently until the period specified in the order, which shall not be more than 180 days, has expired, or until the payment is made, whichever is sooner. 2005, c. 16, s. 24.

No effect on accruing of arrears or other means of enforcement

(11) An order under subsection (10) does not affect the accruing of arrears, nor does it affect any other means of enforcing the support order. 2005, c. 16, s. 24.

Order against person financially connected to payor

(12) If the court is satisfied that a person who was made a party to the hearing under subsection (5) sheltered assets or income of the payor such that enforcement of the support order against the payor has been frustrated, the court may, having regard to all the circumstances, including the purpose and effect of the dealings and the benefit or expected benefit therefrom to the payor, make any order against the person that it may make against the payor under clauses (10) (a), (b), (c), (e), (f) and (g) and subsection (19), to the extent of the value of the sheltered assets or income and, for the purpose, in clause (10) (c), "payor's" shall be read as "person's". 2005, c. 16, s. 24.

Same

(13) Subsections (7) and (8) apply with necessary modifications to a person with respect to whom an order is made under subsection (4) or (5). 2005, c. 16, s. 24.

Temporary orders

(14) The court may make a temporary order against the payor, or a person who was made a party to the hearing under subsection (5), that includes any order that may be made under subsection (10) or (12), as the case may be. 2005, c. 16, s. 24.

Power to change order

(15) The court that made an order under subsection (10) or (12) may change the order on motion if there is a material change in the payor's or other person's circumstances, as the case may be. 2005, c. 16, s. 24.

Enforcement of order

(16) The Director may enforce an order against a person made under subsection (12), (14) or (15) in the same manner as he or she may enforce an order against the payor. 2005, c. 16, s. 24.

Imprisonment does not discharge arrears

(17) Imprisonment of a payor under clause (10) (h) or (i) does not discharge arrears under an order. 2005, c. 16, s. 24.

No early release

(18) Section 28 of the *Ministry of Correctional Services Act* does not apply to the imprisonment of a payor under clause (10) (h) or (i). 2005, c. 16, s. 24.

Realizing on security

(19) An order for security under clause (10) (e) or a subsequent order of the court may provide for the realization of the security by seizure, sale or other means, as the court directs. 2005, c. 16, s. 24.

Proof of service not necessary

(20) Proof of service of a support order or a changed support order is not necessary for the purpose of a default hearing. 2005, c. 16, s. 24.

Joinder of default and change hearings

(21) A default hearing under this section and a hearing on a motion to change the support order may be held together or separately. 2005, c. 16, s. 24.

Effect of change on default hearing

(22) If an order changing a support order is made while a default hearing under this section in relation to the support order is under way,

    (a)   the default hearing continues;

    (b)   it is not necessary to serve fresh documents under subsection (1) or (2); and

    (c)   the payment terms of the changed support order shall be incorporated into any subsequent order made under subsection (10). 2005, c. 16, s. 24.

Spouses compellable witnesses

(23) Spouses are competent and compellable witnesses against each other on a default hearing. 2005, c. 16, s. 24.

Records sealed

(24) A financial statement or other document filed under subsection (4) shall be sealed in the court file and shall not be disclosed except as permitted by the order or a subsequent order or as necessary to enforce an order made under subsection (12) or (14) against a person other than the payor. 2005, c. 16, s. 24.

Definition

(25) In this section,

"court" means the Ontario Court of Justice or the Family Court. 2005, c. 16, s. 24.

Registration against land

42. (1) A support order may be registered in the proper land registry office against the payor's land and on registration the obligation under the order becomes a charge on the property. 1996, c. 31, s. 42 (1).

Sale of property

(2) A charge created by subsection (1) may be enforced by sale of the property against which it is registered in the same manner as a sale to realize on a mortgage. 1996, c. 31, s. 42 (2).

Discharge or postponement of charge

(3) A court may order the discharge, in whole or in part, or the postponement, of a charge created by subsection (1), on such terms as to security or other matters as the court considers just. 1996, c. 31, s. 42 (3).

Notice

(4) An order under subsection (3) may be made only after notice to the Director, if the support order or a related support deduction order is filed with the Director's office for enforcement. 2005, c. 16, s. 25.

Registration under the *Personal Property Security Act*

43. (1) Arrears owing from time to time under a support order are, upon registration by the Director or the recipient with the registrar under the *Personal Property Security Act* of a notice claiming a lien and charge under this section, a lien and charge on any interest in all the personal property in Ontario owned or held at the time of registration or acquired afterwards by the payor. 1996, c. 31, s. 43 (1).

Amounts included and priority

(2) The lien and charge is in respect of the arrears owed by the payor under a support order at the time of registration of the notice and the arrears owed by the payor under the support order which accrue afterwards while the notice remains registered and, upon registration of a notice of lien and charge, the lien and charge has priority over,

(a) any perfected security interest registered after the notice is registered;

(b) any security interest perfected by possession after the notice is registered; and

(c) any encumbrance or other claim that is registered against or that otherwise arises and affects the payor's property after the notice is registered. 1996, c. 31, s. 43 (2).

Exception

(3) For the purpose of subsection (2), the notice of lien and charge does not have priority over a perfected purchase money security interest in collateral or its proceeds and shall be deemed to be a security interest perfected by registration for the purpose of the priority rules under section 28 of the *Personal Property Security Act*. 1996, c. 31, s. 43 (3).

Effective period

(4) The notice of lien and charge is effective from the time assigned to its registration by the registrar or branch registrar until its discharge or expiry. 1996, c. 31, s. 43 (4).

Secured party

(5) In addition to any other rights and remedies, if any arrears under a support order remain unpaid, the Director or recipient, as the case may be, has, in respect of the lien and charge,

(a) all the rights, remedies and duties of a secured party under sections 17, 59, 61, 62, 63 and 64, subsections 65 (4), (5), (6) and (7) and section 66 of the *Personal Property Security Act*;

(b) a security interest in the collateral for the purpose of clause 63 (4) (c) of that Act; and

(c) a security interest in the personal property for the purposes of sections 15 and 16 of the *Repair and Storage Liens Act*, if it is an article as defined in that Act. 1996, c. 31, s. 43 (5).

Registration of documents

(6) The notice of lien and charge shall be in the form of a financing statement as prescribed by regulation under the *Personal Property Security Act* and may be tendered for registration at a branch office as provided in Part IV of that Act. 1996, c. 31, s. 43 (6).

Errors in documents

(7) The notice of lien and charge is not invalidated nor its effect impaired by reason only of an error or omission in the notice or in its execution or registration, unless a reasonable person is likely to be materially misled by the error or omission. 1996, c. 31, s. 43 (7).

Bankruptcy and Insolvency Act (Canada) unaffected

(8) Subject to Crown rights provided under section 87 of the *Bankruptcy and Insolvency Act* (Canada), nothing in this section affects or purports to affect the rights and obligations of any person under that Act. 1996, c. 31, s. 43 (8).

Writs of seizure and sale – amending amounts owing

44. (1) If a writ of seizure and sale is filed with a sheriff in respect of a support order, the person who filed the writ may at any time file with the sheriff a statutory declaration specifying the amount currently owing under the order. 1996, c. 31, s. 44 (1).

Same

(2) When a statutory declaration is filed under subsection (1), the writ of seizure and sale shall be deemed to be amended to specify the amount owing in accordance with the statutory declaration. 1996, c. 31, s. 44 (2).

Notice from sheriff of opportunity to amend writ

(3) A sheriff who comes into possession of money to be paid out under a writ of seizure and sale in respect of a support order shall, not later than seven days after making the entry required by subsection 5 (1) of the *Creditors' Relief Act*, give notice to the person who filed the writ of the opportunity to file a statutory declaration under subsection (1). 1996, c. 31, s. 44 (3).

Same

(4) A sheriff who receives a request for information about the amount owing under a writ of seizure and sale in respect of a support order from a person seeking to have the writ removed from the sheriff's file shall promptly give notice to the person who filed the writ of the opportunity to file a statutory declaration under subsection (1). 1996, c. 31, s. 44 (4).

Removal of writ from sheriff's file

(5) A sheriff shall not remove a writ of seizure and sale in respect of a support order from his or her file unless,

(a) the writ has expired and has not been renewed;

(b) the sheriff receives written notice from the person who filed the writ to the effect that the writ should be withdrawn;

(c) notice is given under subsection (3) or (4), a statutory declaration is subsequently filed under subsection (1) and the writ, as deemed to be amended under subsection (2), has been fully satisfied; or

(d) notice is given under subsection (3) or (4), 10 days have elapsed since the notice was given, no statutory declaration has been filed under subsection (1) since the giving of the notice and the writ has been fully satisfied. 1996, c. 31, s. 44 (5).

Delivery of statutory declaration to land registrar

(6) If a copy of a writ of seizure and sale has been delivered by the sheriff to a land registrar under section 136 of the *Land Titles Act* and a statutory declaration is filed under subsection (1) in respect of the writ, the sheriff shall promptly deliver a copy of the statutory declaration to the land registrar and the amendment deemed to be made to the writ under subsection (2) does not bind land registered under the *Land Titles Act* until a copy of the statutory declaration has been received and recorded by the land registrar. 1996, c. 31, s. 44 (6).

Garnishment of joint accounts

45. (1) Upon being served on a financial institution, a notice of garnishment issued by the Director to enforce a support order against a payor attaches 50 per cent of the money credited to a deposit account held in the financial institution in the name of the payor together with one or more other persons as joint or joint and several deposit account holders, and the financial institution shall pay up to 50 per cent of the money credited to the deposit account to the Director in accordance with the notice of garnishment. 1996, c. 31, s. 45 (1).

Duties of financial institution

(2) The financial institution shall, within 10 days of being served with the notice of garnishment,

(a) pay the money to the Director and, at the same time, notify the Director if the account is held jointly or jointly and severally in the name of two or more persons; and

(b) notify the co-holders of the account who are not named in the notice of garnishment of the garnishment. 1996, c. 31, s. 45 (2).

Dispute by co-holder

(3) Within 30 days after the financial institution notified the Director under clause (2) (a), a co-holder of the deposit account may file a dispute to the garnishment in the Ontario Court of Justice or the Family Court

claiming ownership of all or part of the money that the financial institution paid to the Director. 1996, c. 31, s. 45 (3); 2005, c. 16, s. 26.

Director to hold money for 30 days

(4) If the financial institution notifies the Director under clause (2) (a), the Director shall not release the money received under subsection (1) until 30 days after the financial institution so notified the Director, and the Director may release the money after the 30 days unless a co-holder of the deposit account first serves on the Director a copy of the dispute to the garnishment that the co-holder filed under subsection (3). 1996, c. 31, s. 45 (4).

Determination by court

(5) In a hearing to determine the dispute to the garnishment, the money paid to the Director shall be presumed to be owned by the payor and the court shall order,

(a) that the garnishment be limited to the payor's interest in the money that was paid to the Director; and

(b) that all or part of the money that was paid to the Director be returned to the co-holder only if it is satisfied that the co-holder owns that money. 1996, c. 31, s. 45 (5).

Payment by Director

(6) Upon receipt of a copy of the court's order, the Director shall return to the co-holder any money determined by the court to belong to the co-holder and may release any remaining money, if any, to the recipient. 1996, c. 31, s. 45 (6).

Action by joint account co-holder against payor

(7) A co-holder may bring an action against the payor in a court of competent jurisdiction,

(a) to recover any money owned by the co-holder that was paid to the Director under subsection (1);

(b) to recover any interest that the co-holder would have earned on the money owned by the co-holder that was paid to the Director under subsection (1). 1996, c. 31, s. 45 (7).

Director and recipient are not parties

(8) The Director and the recipient are not parties to an action under subsection (7). 1996, c. 31, s. 45 (8).

Definition

(9) In this section,

"deposit account" includes a deposit as defined in the *Deposits Regulation Act* and a demand account, time account, savings account, passbook account, checking account, current account and other similar accounts in,

(a) a bank listed in Schedule I or II to the *Bank Act* (Canada),

(b) a loan corporation or trust corporation as defined in the *Loan and Trust Corporations Act*,

(c) a credit union as defined in the *Credit Unions and Caisses Populaires Act*, 1994, or

(d) a similar institution.

(e) Repealed: 2002, c. 8, Sched. I, s. 11.

1996, c. 31, s. 45 (9); 2002, c. 8, Sched. I, s. 11.

Garnishment of lottery prizes

46. (1) In this section,

"Corporation" means the Ontario Lottery Corporation; ("Société")

"lottery" means a lottery scheme, as defined in section 1 of the *Ontario Lottery Corporation Act*, that is conducted by the Corporation in Ontario and involves the issuance and sale of tickets; ("loterie")

"prize" means a prize in a lottery. ("prix") 1999, c. 12, Sched. B, s. 8.

Deduction of arrears from prize

(2) If a payor who owes arrears under a support order that is filed in the Director's office is entitled to a single monetary prize of $1,000 or more from the Corporation, the Corporation shall,

(a) deduct from the prize the amount of the arrears or the amount of the prize, whichever is less;

(b) pay the amount deducted to the Director; and

(c) pay any balance to the payor. 1999, c. 12, Sched. B, s. 8.

Non-monetary prize

(3) If a payor who owes arrears under a support order that is filed in the Director's office is entitled to a non-monetary prize from the Corporation that the Corporation values at $1,000 or more, the Corporation shall promptly disclose to the Director,

(a) any identifying information about the payor from the Corporation's records, including his or her name and address; and

(b) a complete description of the prize. 1999, c. 12, Sched. B, s. 8.

Exchange of information

(4) For the purposes of subsections (2) and (3),

(a) the Director shall disclose to the Corporation any identifying information about payors from the Director's records, including their names and addresses and the status and particulars of their support obligations; and

(b) the Corporation shall disclose to the Director any identifying information about prize winners from its records, including their names and addresses. 1999, c. 12, Sched. B, s. 8.

Defaulters reported to consumer reporting agencies

47. The Director may disclose to a consumer reporting agency registered under the *Consumer Reporting Act*,

(a) the name of a payor who is in default on a support order filed in the Director's office;

(b) the date of the support order;

(c) the amount and frequency of the payor's support obligation under the support order;

(d) the amount of the arrears owing under the support order at the

time of the disclosure; and
(e) such other information as may be prescribed. 1996, c. 31, s. 47.

Note: On a day to be named by proclamation of the Lieutenant Governor, section 47 is repealed by the Statutes of Ontario, 2005, chapter 16, section 27 and the following substituted:

Reporting default to consumer reporting agency
47. The Director may disclose the information set out in section 47.2 to a consumer reporting agency registered under the *Consumer Reporting Act*. 2005, c. 16, s. 27.

Reporting default to prescribed entity
47.1 (1) The Director may disclose the information set out in section 47.2 to a prescribed entity that is,
(a) a professional or occupational organization;
(b) the governing body of a self-governing or regulated profession; or
(c) an entity that is responsible for licensing or registering individuals for occupational purposes. 2005, c. 16, s. 27.

Presumption
(2) In the absence of evidence to the contrary, it shall be presumed that the amount disclosed with respect to arrears as described in clause 47.2 (d) is correct. 2005, c. 16, s. 27.

Information that may be disclosed
47.2 The information that may be disclosed under section 47 or 47.1 is,
(a) the name of a payor who is in default on a support order filed in the Director's office;
(b) the date of the support order;
(c) the amount and frequency of the payor's support obligation under the support order;
(d) the amount of the arrears owing under the support order at the time of the disclosure; and
(e) such other information as may be prescribed. 2005, c. 16, s. 27.

See: 2005, c. 16, ss. 27, 42 (2).

Restraining order
48. A court, including the Ontario Court of Justice, may make an order restraining the disposition or wasting of assets that may hinder or defeat the enforcement of a support order or support deduction order. 1996, c. 31, s. 48; 2005, c. 16, s. 28.

Arrest of absconding payor

49. (1) The Ontario Court of Justice or the Family Court may issue a warrant for a payor's arrest for the purpose of bringing him or her before the court if the court is satisfied that the payor is about to leave Ontario and that there are reasonable grounds for believing that the payor intends to evade his or her obligations under the support order. 1996, c. 31, s. 49 (1); 2005, c. 16, s. 29 (1).

Bail

(2) Section 150 (interim release by justice of the peace) of the *Provincial Offences Act* applies with necessary modifications to an arrest under the warrant. 1996, c. 31, s. 49 (2).

Powers of court

(3) When the payor is brought before the court, it may make any order provided for in subsection 41 (10). 1996, c. 31, s. 49 (3); 2005, c. 16, s. 29 (2).

Recognition of extra-provincial garnishments

50. (1) On the filing of a garnishment process that,

(a) is issued outside Ontario and is directed to a garnishee in Ontario;

(b) states that it is issued in respect of support or maintenance; and

(c) is written in or accompanied by a sworn or certified translation into English or French,

the clerk of the Ontario Court of Justice or Family Court shall issue a notice of garnishment to enforce the support or maintenance obligation. 1996, c. 31, s. 50 (1); 2005, c. 16, s. 30.

Foreign currencies

(2) If the garnishment process refers to an obligation in a foreign currency, section 44 of the *Interjurisdictional Support Orders Act, 2002* applies with necessary modifications. 1996, c. 31, s. 50 (2); 2002, c. 13, s. 57 (3).

Part VII
Offences and Penalties

Offences – payors, income sources, etc.

51. (1) A payor who knowingly contravenes or knowingly fails to comply with section 19 or subsection 25 (1) or (2) or 40 (2) or (3) is guilty of an offence and on conviction is liable to a fine of not more than $10,000. 1996, c. 31, s. 51 (1).

Income sources

(2) An income source who knowingly contravenes or knowingly fails to comply with subsection 22 (2) or 25 (1) or (2) or section 29 is guilty of an offence and on conviction is liable to a fine of not more than $10,000. 1996, c. 31, s. 51 (2).

Individuals, etc., believed to be an income source

(3) An individual, corporation or other entity that knowingly contravenes or knowingly fails to comply with subsection 26 (1) or section 29 is guilty of an offence and on conviction is liable to a fine of not more than $10,000. 1996, c. 31, s. 51 (3).

Offences – assignees

52. (1) An assignee under section 4 who knowingly contravenes or knowingly fails to comply with this Act or its regulations or the limitations, conditions or requirements set out in the assignment is guilty of an offence and on conviction is liable to a fine of not more than $10,000. 1996, c. 31, s. 52 (1).

Same – directors, officers, employees, agents

(2) A director, officer, employee or agent of an assignee who commits an offence described in subsection (1) on conviction is liable to a fine of not more than $10,000. 1996, c. 31, s. 52 (2).

Same – directors, officers

(3) A director or officer of an assignee is guilty of an offence if he or she,

(a) knowingly causes, authorizes, permits or participates in the commission of an offence described in subsection (1); or

(b) fails to take reasonable care to prevent the commission of an offence described in subsection (1). 1996, c. 31, s. 52 (3).

Penalty

(4) A person who is convicted of an offence under subsection (3) is liable to a fine of not more than $10,000. 1996, c. 31, s. 52 (4).

Contempt

53. (1) In addition to its powers in respect of contempt, a court, including the Ontario Court of Justice, may punish by fine or imprisonment, or by both, any wilful contempt of, or resistance to, its process, rules or orders under this Act, but the fine shall not exceed $10,000 nor shall the imprisonment exceed 90 days. 1996, c. 31, s. 53 (1); 2005, c. 16, s. 31.

Conditions of imprisonment

(2) An order for imprisonment under subsection (1) may be conditional upon default in the performance of a condition set out in the order and may provide for the imprisonment to be served intermittently. 1996, c. 31, s. 53 (2).

Part VIII
Miscellaneous

Director's access to information
Definitions
54. (1) In this section,
"enforcement-related information" means information that indicates any of the following about a payor:
1. employer or place of employment,
2. wages, salary or other income,
3. assets or liabilities,
4. home, work or mailing address, or location,
5. telephone number, fax number or e-mail address; ("renseignements liés à l'exécution")
"recipient information" means information that indicates any of the following about a recipient:
1. home, work or mailing address, or location,
2. telephone number, fax number or e-mail address. ("renseignements sur le bénéficiaire") 2005, c. 16, s. 32.

Power of Director
(2) The Director may, for the purpose of enforcing a support order or support deduction order filed in the Director's office or for the purpose of assisting an office or person in another jurisdiction performing similar functions to those performed by the Director,

(a) demand enforcement-related information or recipient information from any person, public body or other entity from a record in the possession or control of the person, public body or other entity;

(b) subject to subsections (4) and (5), have access to all records that may contain enforcement-related information or recipient information and that are in the possession or control of any ministry, agency, board or commission of the Government of Ontario in order to search for and obtain the information from the records;

(c) subject to subsections (4) and (5), enter into an agreement with any person, public body or other entity, including the Government of Canada, a Crown corporation, the government of another province or territory or any agency, board or commission of such government, to permit the Director to have access to records in the possession or control of the person, public body or other entity that may contain enforcement-related information or recipient information, in order to search for and obtain the information from the records; and

(d) disclose information obtained under clause (a), (b) or (c) to a person performing similar functions to those of the Director in another jurisdiction. 2005, c. 16, s. 32.

10-day period for response

(3) When the Director demands information under clause (2) (a), the person, public body or other entity shall provide the information within 10 days after being served with the demand. 2005, c. 16, s. 32.

Access to part of record

(4) Where the record referred to in clause (2) (b) or (c) is part of a larger record, the Director,

(a)   may have access to the part of the record that may contain enforcement-related information or recipient information; and

(b)   may have incidental access to any other information contained in that part of the record, but may not use or disclose that other information. 2005, c. 16, s. 32.

Restriction on access to health information

(5) Despite subsection (4), if a record described in clause (2) (b) or (c) contains health information, as defined in the regulations, the Director shall not have access to the health information but shall have access only to the part of the record that may contain enforcement-related information or recipient information. 2005, c. 16, s. 32.

Information confidential

(6) Information obtained under subsection (2) shall not be disclosed except,

(a)   to the extent necessary for the enforcement of the support order or support deduction order;

(b)   as provided in clause (2) (d); or

(c)   to a police officer who needs the information for a criminal investigation that is likely to assist the enforcement of the support order or support deduction order. 2005, c. 16, s. 32.

Court order for access to information

(7) A court may, on motion, make an order requiring any person, public body or other entity to provide the court or the person whom the court names with any enforcement-related information or recipient information that is shown on a record in the possession or control of the person, public body or other entity if it appears that,

(a)   the Director has been refused information after making a demand under clause (2) (a);

(b)   the Director has been refused access to a record under clause (2) (b); or

(c)   a person needs an order under this subsection for the enforcement of a support order that is not filed in the Director's office. 2005, c. 16, s. 32.

Court order re agreement

(8) A court may, on motion, make an order requiring any person, public body or other entity to enter into an agreement described in clause (2) (c) with the Director if it appears that the person, public body or other entity has unreasonably refused to enter into such an agreement. 2005, c. 16, s. 32.

Costs

(9) If the Director obtains an order under clause (7) (a) or (b) or under subsection (8), the court shall award the costs of the motion to the Director. 2005, c. 16, s. 32.

Information confidential

(10) Information obtained under an order under clause (7) (c) shall be sealed in the court file and shall not be disclosed except,

(a) as permitted by the order or a subsequent order;

(b) to the extent necessary for the enforcement of the support order or support deduction order;

(c) as provided in clause (2) (d); or

(d) to a police officer who needs the information for a criminal investigation that is likely to assist the enforcement of the support order or support deduction order. 2005, c. 16, s. 32.

Section governs

(11) This section applies despite any other Act or regulation and despite any common law rule of confidentiality. 2005, c. 16, s. 32.

Federal-provincial agreement

55. (1) The Attorney General may, on behalf of the Government of Ontario, enter into an agreement with the Government of Canada concerning the searching for and the release of information under Part I of the *Family Orders and Agreements Enforcement Assistance Act* (Canada). 1996, c. 31, s. 55 (1).

Information obtained from federal government

(2) The Director shall not disclose information obtained under the *Family Orders and Agreements Enforcement Assistance Act* (Canada) for the enforcement of a support order, except,

(a) to the extent necessary for the enforcement of the order; or

(b) as permitted by the *Freedom of Information and Protection of Privacy Act*. 1996, c. 31, s. 55 (2).

Payments pending court decisions

56. (1) The Director shall pay any money he or she receives in respect of a support order or a support deduction order to the recipient despite the commencement of any court proceeding in respect of the support obligation or its enforcement, in the absence of a court order to the contrary. 1996, c. 31, s. 56 (1).

Exception

(2) If a court orders the Director to hold any of the money received in respect of a support order or a support deduction order pending the disposition of the proceeding, the Director shall, upon receipt of a copy of the order, hold any money he or she receives to the extent required by the court. 1996, c. 31, s. 56 (2).

Application of payments

57. (1) Money paid to the Director on account of a support order or support deduction order shall be credited as prescribed by the regulations. 1996, c. 31, s. 57 (1).

Same

(2) Despite anything in this Act, the payor shall not be credited with making a payment until the money for that payment is received by the Director and if a payment is made but not honoured, the amount of the payment shall be added to the support arrears owed by the payor. 1996, c. 31, s. 57 (2).

Fees

58. (1) The Director shall not charge any fee to any person for his or her services except as provided by regulation. 1996, c. 31, s. 58 (1).

Enforcement of orders to collect fees, etc.

(2) The Director may continue to enforce a support order or support deduction order to collect an amount described in subsection (3), even if,

(a) the support order or support deduction order to which the amount relates has been withdrawn from the Director's office;

(b) there is no current support obligation, and there are no arrears, or any arrears are rescinded by a changed support order; or

(c) the support obligation has terminated and there are no arrears, or any arrears are rescinded by a changed support order. 2005, c. 16, s. 33.

Same

(3) Subsection (2) applies with respect to,

(a) fees;

(b) costs awarded to the Director by a court;

(c) any amount owed to the Director as reimbursement for money paid to a recipient; and

(d) any amount similar to the ones described in clauses (a), (b) and (c) that is owed to a support enforcement program in a reciprocating jurisdiction, if the support order to which the amount relates is registered in Ontario under the *Interjurisdictional Support Orders Act*, 2002. 2005, c. 16, s. 33.

Protection from personal liability

59. (1) No action or other proceeding for damages shall be instituted against the Director or any employee of the Director's office for any act done in good faith in the execution or intended execution of any duty or authority under this Act or for any alleged neglect or default in the execution in good faith of any duty or authority under this Act. 1996, c. 31, s. 59 (1).

Crown not relieved of liability

(2) Despite subsections 5 (2) and (4) of the *Proceedings Against the*

Crown Act, subsection (1) does not relieve the Crown of liability in respect of a tort committed by a person mentioned in subsection (1) to which it would otherwise be subject. 1996, c. 31, s. 59 (2).

Acting by lawyer
    60. Anything that this Act requires to be signed or done by a person, or that is referred to in this Act as signed or done by a person, may be signed or done by a lawyer acting on the person's behalf. 1996, c. 31, s. 60.

Disclosure of personal information
    61. (1) The Director shall collect, disclose and use personal information about an identifiable individual for the purpose of enforcing a support order or a support deduction order under this Act. 1996, c. 31, s. 61 (1).

Same
    (2) Any person, public body or other entity that is referred to in clause 54 (2) (a) shall disclose personal information about an identifiable individual to the Director for the purpose of section 54, within 10 days after being served with the Director's demand. 2005, c. 16, s. 34 (1).

Notice to individual not required
    (3) Subsection 39 (2) of the *Freedom of Information and Protection of Privacy Act* does not apply to the collection of personal information about an identifiable individual under this Act. 1996, c. 31, s. 61 (3).

Act prevails over confidentiality provisions
    (4) This Act prevails over a confidentiality provision in another Act that would, if not for this Act, prohibit the disclosure of information to the Director. 1996, c. 31, s. 61 (4).

Law enforcement
    (5) The Director shall be deemed to be engaged in law enforcement for the purposes of section 14 of the *Freedom of Information and Protection of Privacy Act* when collecting information, under section 54 or otherwise, for the purpose of enforcing a support order or support deduction order under this Act. 2005, c. 16, s. 34 (2).

Note: On a day to be named by proclamation of the Lieutenant Governor, the Act is amended by the Statutes of Ontario, 2005, chapter 16, section 35 by adding the following section:

Obtaining information about payor by means of Internet posting
Director's discretion
    61.1 (1) The Director may post a payor's name and other prescribed information relating to the payor on a website on the Internet if,

(a) the payor is in default under a support order;
(b) the support order or a related support deduction order is filed in the Director's office;
(c) the Director has been unsuccessful in locating the payor; and
(d) the prescribed conditions are satisfied. 2005, c. 16, s. 35.

Purpose of posting

(2) The sole purpose of posting information under subsection (1) is to assist the Director in locating the payor. 2005, c. 16, s. 35.

Confidentiality of information obtained as a result of posting

(3) Subsection 54 (6) applies, with necessary modifications, to any information obtained by the Director as a result of the posting. 2005, c. 16, s. 35. See: 2005, c. 16, ss. 35, 42 (2).

Act binds Crown

62. This Act binds the Crown. 1996, c. 31, s. 62.

Regulations

63. (1) The Lieutenant Governor in Council may make regulations,
(a) prescribing forms and providing for their use;
(b) prescribing types of income for the purposes of clause (l) of the definition of "income source" in subsection 1 (1);
(c) prescribing the manner of calculating a cost of living clause for the purposes of subsections 7 (4), (5), (6) and (7);
(d) prescribing classes of persons and information to be supplied to the court and the manner in which information is to be supplied for the purposes of subsections 11 (2) and (3);
(e) prescribing practices and procedures related to the filing and withdrawal of support orders and support deduction orders and to the enforcement, suspension and termination of such orders filed in the Director's office;
(e.1) defining "in compliance" for the purposes of subsection 16 (1.1);
(e.2) prescribing methods of electronic transmission for the purpose of subsection 22 (2.1);
(f) prescribing deductions for the purposes of subsection 23 (5);
(g) prescribing information that shall be supplied under subsection 25 (1);
(g.1) prescribing practices and procedures relating to the filing and withdrawal of alternative payment orders under section 28;
(h) governing the form and posting of security by a payor under section 28 and the realization thereon;

Note: On a day to be named by proclamation of the Lieutenant Governor, section 63 is amended by the Statutes of Ontario, 2005, chapter 16, subsection 36 (3) by adding the following clause:

(h.1) prescribing classes of licences for the purposes of Part V.1;
See: 2005, c. 16, ss. 36 (3), 42 (2).

(i) respecting proof of income for the purposes of sections 35, 40 and 41;

(j) prescribing other information that may be disclosed by the Director to a consumer reporting agency under subsection 47 (1);

Note: On a day to be named by proclamation of the Lieutenant Governor, clause (j) is repealed by the Statutes of Ontario, 2005, chapter 16, subsection 36 (5) and the following substituted:

(j) prescribing, for the purposes of clause 47.2 (e), other information that may be disclosed under section 47 or 47.1;

See: 2005, c. 16, ss. 36 (5), 42 (2).

(k) prescribing,

(i) fees to be charged by the Director for administrative services, including preparing and photocopying documents on request, and

(ii) fees for any steps taken by the Director to enforce a support order in response to the persistent or wilful default by a payor;

(k.1) prescribing fees for the repeated filing of a support order or support deduction order, and specifying what constitutes repeated filing;

(l) prescribing the maximum fees, costs, disbursements, surcharges and other charges, or a method for determining the maximum fees, costs, disbursements, surcharges and other charges, that an assignee under section 4 may charge a payor, including fees, costs, disbursements, surcharges and other charges for services for which the Director is not permitted to charge and including fees, costs, disbursements, surcharges or other charges that are higher than the fees, costs, disbursements, surcharges and other charges that the Director may charge for the same service, prescribing how and when such fees, costs, disbursements, surcharges and other charges may be collected, prescribing the manner in which they may be applied and prescribing the rate of interest to be charged on any of them;

(m) prescribing methods of and rules respecting service, filing and notice for the purposes of this Act, including different methods and rules for different provisions and different methods and rules for service on or notice to the Crown;

(n) providing that a support deduction order is not effective against the Crown unless a statement of particulars in the prescribed form is served with the notice of the order;

(o) defining "health information" for the purposes of subsection 54 (5);

(p) prescribing the manner in which payments received by the Director are to be credited;

(p.1) governing the delivery of payments to recipients, including requiring recipients to provide the Director with the information and authorization required to enable the Director to make direct deposits into the recipients' accounts with financial institutions;

(p.2) setting out recommended standard terms for support orders;

(q)   prescribing anything that is required or authorized by this Act to be prescribed. 1996, c. 31, s. 63; 2005, c. 16, s. 36 (1, 2, 4, 6-8).

Repeated filing

(2) A fee prescribed under clause (1) (k.1) may be charged against both the payor and the recipient, regardless of which one of them files the order. 2005, c. 16, s. 36 (9).

64. Omitted (provides for re-enactment of Part V of this Act). 1996, c. 31, s. 64.

65.-73. Omitted (amends or repeals other Acts). 1996, c. 31, ss. 65-73.

74. Omitted (provides for coming into force of provisions of this Act). 1996, c. 31, s. 74.

75. Omitted (enacts short title of this Act). 1996, c. 31, s. 75.

Note: This form of mediation-arbitration agreement reflects the changes in the *Family Statute Amendment Act, 2005*

IN THE MATTER OF THE *ARBITRATION ACT* S.O. 1991, c. 17 as amended
and
the *FAMILY LAW ACT*, R.S.O. 1990, c.F3, as amended

B E T W E E N:

[HUSBAND]

(herein called "   "),

and

[NAME]

(herein called "   ")

MEDIATION/ARBITRATION AGREEMENT

[Husband] and [Wife] wish to mediate or arbitrate certain issues as set out in this Agreement and have agreed to submit those issues designated in this Agreement and to appoint [NAME] as Arbitrator.

SUBMISSION

1. This document constitutes a submission to arbitrate pursuant to the provisions of the *Arbitration Act*, S.O. 1991, c. 17 and the *Family Law Act*, R.S.O 1990, c.F3 and amendments thereto.

SUBSTANTIVE ISSUES

2. The following issues are submitted for final determination:
    (a) Equalization of net family property;
    (b) Terms of possession or sale of the matrimonial home;
    (c) Ownership and possession of other property;
    (d) Quantum and duration of spousal and child support; and
    (e) Costs of the arbitration.

CONFIDENTIALITY

3. The proceedings and the record thereof shall be private and confidential, subject only to their being produced in proceedings for enforcement, appeal or review.

SUPPORT

4. Issues related to spousal support shall be determined in accordance with the provisions of the *Divorce Act*, R.S.C. 1991 c. D-3.4 (2nd Supp.) and the *Federal Child Support Guidelines*, as may be applicable.

WAIVER OF RIGHTS TO LITIGATE IN COURTS

5. By submitting to arbitration those issues designated in paragraph 3 above, the parties hereby waive any right to further litigate those issues in Court, whether pursuant to the *Family Law Act*, R.S.O. 1990, c. F.3, as amended; the *Divorce Act*, R.S.C. 1991, c. D-3.4 (2nd Supp.), as amended; or any other statute or law, subject to the right of appeal, and rights under section 46 of the *Arbitration Act*.

MEDIATION

6. The parties will first attempt to resolve the issues through mediation, with [NAME] as mediator. On [DATE] at [TIME], the parties and their counsel will meet with the mediator to explore the issues and the process herein. Thereafter the parties may continue in mediation at a date and time to be arranged. If the mediation does not achieve a resolution of the issues, the mediator may declare the mediation ended, and an arbitration will take place as set out below.

PROCEDURAL ISSUES IN RESPECT OF ARBITRATION HEARING

7. Time and Place: The hearing shall take place at [PLACE] at a date and time to be arranged in the event that mediation does not achieve a resolution of the issues.

8. Arbitrator: The Arbitrator shall be [NAME]

9. Procedure on Hearing: The procedure shall be similar to court procedure wherever possible, and in particular:
   (a) all witnesses shall be sworn or affirmed and shall be subject to examination in chief and cross-examination and re-examination;
   (b) all usual rules for the admissibility of evidence in court proceedings will apply as will the *Rules of Civil Procedure* and the *Family Law Rules*.

10. At least seven days before the scheduled date for arbitration, each party shall provide the other party with a Position Statement of no more than ten (10) typewritten (double-spaced) pages setting out his/her position in respect of the above issues, including reference to all relevant documents.

11. The arbitration proceedings shall [not] be recorded by a verbatim reporter.

REPORT OF ARBITRATOR FOLLOWING THE ARBITRATION HEARING

12. Within thirty days after the evidence has been received and submissions on the law have been made the Arbitrator shall deliver an Award in writing on all issues submitted for determination.

AWARD

13. Subject to the right of appeal and rights to apply to set aside the Award under section 46 of the *Arbitration Act*, the Arbitrator's Award shall be final and binding upon the parties and may be incorporated in a consent Order or Judgment, as the case may be, of the Ontario Superior Court of Justice.

ARBITRATOR'S FEES AND DISBURSEMENTS

14. The Arbitrator's fees shall be $ per hour for the hearing, any pre-arbitration conference, interim arbitration, preliminary meetings, mediation, arrangements, preparation for the hearing, preparation of a report and any follow-up, plus disbursements and GST.

15. The parties shall forthwith provide the Arbitrator with a total retainer of $ this retainer to be refreshed from time to time as the Arbitrator shall direct.

COSTS

16. As the issue of costs is submitted to the Arbitrator pursuant to paragraph 2 above, the Arbitrator's discretion regarding costs shall include the power to require one party to pay more than one-half, or all of the Arbitrator's fees and disbursements.

MEDIATION AND ARBITRATION

17. The parties agree that the Arbitrator can mediate all issues in dispute and the participation of the parties and/or their counsel and the Arbitrator in the mediation process shall not disqualify the Arbitrator from arbitrating the issues in dispute; and the parties waive the provisions of s. 54(6) of the *Arbitration Act*.

WAIVER OF ARBITRATOR'S LIABILITY

18. The parties hereby waive any claim or right of action against the Arbitrator arising out of these proceedings.

INDEPENDENT LEGAL ADVICE

19. Each of the parties had received independent advice as to the terms of this arbitration agreement; [Husband] from [LAWYER 1] AND [Wife] from [LAWYER 2].

DATED:

_____

Solicitor for   _____[HUSBAND]_____

_____

Solicitor for   _____[WIFE]_____

_____

Arbitrator